ECONOMICS OF THE PUBLIC

Economics of the Public Sector

D.I. Trotman-Dickenson, PhD, MSc. (Econ.), B. Com.
Professor Emeritus, University of Glamorgan

MACMILLAN

First published 1996 by
MACMILLAN PRESS LTD
Houndmills, Basingstoke, Hampshire RG21 6XS
and London
Companies and representatives
throughout the world

ISBN 0–333–59669–2

A catalogue record for this book is available
from the British Library.

10   9   8   7   6   5   4   3   2
05   04   03   02   01   00   99   98   97

Printed in Malaysia

To
Caroline, Emma, Oliver and Thomas

Contents

PART 6   MANAGEMENT OF THE ECONOMY

List of Tables

List of Figures

Acknowledgements

I would like to thank Mr Stephen Rutt for all his help and suggestions on how to improve this book, for which I am most grateful. Also, I wish to express my thanks to Keith Povey for his editorial work. I am indebted to Sir Aubrey Trotman-Dickenson, Professor R.E. Groves, Professor of Accountancy at University of Wales, Cardiff and to Mr Martin Corteel for reading an early draft of the manuscript and making helpful comments. My thanks are also due to Mrs Janice Shaw of the Information Technology Centre at the University of Glamorgan for all her work in typing the manuscript onto the computer. I very much appreciated her unfailing patience and efficiency.

The author and publishers wish to thank the Controller of HMSO and the Central Statistical office, United Nations Statistical Division, New York; *The Economist* (London); *Euromonitor* (London); Phillips and Drew (United Bank of Switzerland); Policy Studies Institute; Commission of the European Communities; and other copy-right holders for permission to abstract and reproduce some of their statistics.

D.I. TROTMAN-DICKENSON

Foreword

This book on economics of the public sector is concerned with the functions and finance of central government, local authorities and the public sector of industry within the framework of a national economy. The subject is of primary importance to any study of society in which people live.

The theory and practice of public finance presented in this book cover public expenditure, taxation and the national debt. Fiscal policy, with its economic, social and political objectives, is discussed and viewed in relation to monetary policy and prices and incomes policy. International comparisons are made and points are illustrated by examples from the British economy, European Community and other countries.

It is hoped that *Economics of the Public Sector* will serve as a source of information to the general reader, and as a textbook for students in their final year at school and on various courses at institutions of higher education. The bibliography at the end of each chapter is intended to give guidance on further reading. The various publications and books listed deal with topics at different levels and provide a basis for continuation of the study of public finance.

The material in *Economics of the Public Sector* is presented in such a way as to facilitate self-study for part-time students. Exercises at the end of each chapter can be used as a basis for revision.

The subject matter of the book is suitable for use for General Certificate of Secondary Education examinations in Economics as the syllabuses of the examining Boards cover public finance. The book is also appropriate for Business and Technician Education Council (BTEC) and degree courses and also for those leading to qualifications of professional bodies such as the Institute of Public Finance and Accountancy and the Institute of Chartered Administrators.

A large number of tables and diagrams have been provided so as to relate the theory to the real world. Students are advised to examine the economic data and to consider its implications.

Every effort has been made to provide the latest statistics available. In some cases, particularly with the United Nations data, there is a considerable gap between the date of publication and the year to which the figures refer. Nevertheless, even if the data becomes superseded by more recent information, the figures are still of value in indicating magnitudes of money flows and the dimension of economic problems. Some historical background is also helpful in the study of public sector economics. To understand the present and plan for the future, we need to know the past.

Part 1

The Economic Framework

1 Economic Systems and Models

POLITICAL ECONOMY

Economics of the public sector lies in the field of study of political economy. In *An Inquiry into the Nature and Causes of the Wealth of Nations* (1776), which came to be regarded as the first book on economics as a subject, Adam Smith wrote:

> Political economy, considered as a branch of the science of a statesman or legislator, proposes two distinct objects: first to provide a plentiful revenue or subsistence for the people, or more properly to enable them to provide such revenue or subsistence for themselves; and secondly to supply the state ... with revenue sufficient for the public services.

It is largely with the second objective that this book is concerned. Economics of the public sector involves the study of *public finance*, *government's policies* and its role in the *industrial sector* of the economy.

People have the same basic needs for subsistence irrespective of the period, the place, or the political system of the economy in which they live. The differences that arise are in the ways and the extent to which these needs are met.

TYPES OF ECONOMIC SYSTEM

Three types of economic system can be clearly distinguished. They are:

(a) *The market economy.* In theory under a pure market economy system, consumer demand determines the pattern and volume of supply and the market forces – the interaction of demand and supply – determine price. It is assumed that there is no state intervention in the economic life of the country. However in practice governments do intervene and a pure market economy does not exist.

The USA most closely resembles a pure market system. The American economy is, however, subject to considerable state

3

intervention. The government uses its powers to influence prices and incomes; it protects consumers from monopolies and provides an increasing range of public goods and services. There are no nationalised industries as such, but various public bodies engage in economic activity. The term 'capitalist system' has in the past been used to describe a market economy such as that of the United States, but this label has now largely fallen into disuse. It is a misleading term since, under any economic system, capital, in the form of plant and machinery, is needed to produce an output.

(b) *The centrally-planned economy.* This operates on Marxist principles and, under a communist system, the state owns all the means of production and distribution. The government determines what will be produced, and at what price, and for whom.

Again, there is no pure centrally-planned economy. Over the years Marxist theory and communist practice have diverged, and governments increasingly allowed the re-emergence of some private enterprise.

The economic system which most closely resembled a pure centrally planned economy until 1990 was that of the USSR, but even in the period up to that time the impact of market forces on its economy had not been altogether eliminated. This was particularly noticeable in the field of foreign trade, since the USSR bought and sold goods and services on the world markets.

At the time of writing (1995), apart from Cuba and North Korea, examples of countries with centrally-planned economics that approximate to the pure model, would be difficult to find. The government in China, although still advocating Communist ideology in theory, has in practice introduced reforms that have allowed the establishment of a private sector in the economy.

(c) *The mixed economy.* Here the private and public sectors of industry coexist as partners and the government is an important, but not sole, decision-maker on how the economy is run. A mixed economy is a political compromise and an economic half-way house between a market economy and a centrally planned one. It is to this mid-point that both the developed and developing countries have increasingly been gravitating.

| Market economy (e.g. USA) | → | Mixed economy (e.g. countries of the European Union) | ← | Centrally planned economy (e.g. Cuba) |

The relative size of the private and public sectors does, however, vary considerably from country to country. In many of them in recent years, particularly in Europe, the private sector has been expanding but governments are still expected to provide a range of services. In doing so, they have to forecast the demand and need for these services, budget, plan provision and implement policy in an ever-changing environment.

SHIFT FROM MARXIST PRINCIPLES TO MARKET FORCES

It was the interaction of political, social and economic factors that set off the transition from centrally-planned to market economies on a global scale in the 1990s. The weakening power of the USSR had enabled countries that had been annexed to the Soviet bloc to abandon Marxist principles and to revert to a market economy model. Poland was the first of those countries to begin to dismantle the Communist system in the 1980s. The process in Europe accelerated after September 1990 when the Supreme Soviet gave powers to the First Secretary of the Communist Party to introduce measures to establish a market economy in the USSR.

The disintegration of the USSR that ended Communist dominance in Central and Eastern Europe had enabled Poland and Hungary to sign an association agreement in 1991 with the European Community and to apply for a full membership by the turn of the century. The acceptance of these countries will by then depend largely on the speed of their transition to a market-orientated economy. This, according to the Commission of the European Community, requires

> ... transformation of production and distribution systems with an emphasis on private ownership and investment as well as the establishment of the broader regulatory, organisational and commercial infrastructure without which a competitive market economy can neither function properly nor attract investment. This includes the necessary framework of laws, regulations and institutions, a reform of accounting procedures, company laws, banking and insurance.

To facilitate this transition the Community Member States and the USA have provided crucial assistance. The failure of Communism can be attributed to many causes but a major underlying reason was economic failure. Centrally-planned economies failed to deliver the range, quality and quantity of goods and services that people wanted. The state failed to pay workers a level of wages that would have enabled them to achieve the standard of living of their counterparts in other European and industrialised countries (p. 35). 'Man does not live by bread alone' – but man, woman and child certainly cannot live *without* bread.

Collective farms and state factories had little incentive to supply goods and services in response to consumer demand, to cut costs or to increase efficiency. They could not go bankrupt, did not have to compete and were, in general, not subjected to the discipline of market forces.

Events in Russia and widespread disillusionment with Communism over the years also had far-reaching repercussions in the West. Not only did Communist parties in Britain, France and Italy lose support but there was a knock-on effect on Socialism. With the swing to market economies among the electorate, Socialist parties lost parliamentary elections in the UK (the Labour Party) in 1992 and in France in 1993 where socialists held on to less than 20 per cent of parliamentary seats after the biggest swing in voting since the beginning of the century.

The ideology of market-orientated national governments that have been elected in recent years in Europe is likely to have a considerable impact on fiscal policies, privatisation and the size of the public sector in these countries' economies and also on the European Union.

ECONOMIC MODELS

The purpose of economic activity under any system is to satisfy the material needs of that society. People receive incomes, spend, save and invest. They pay taxes and are given state benefits. A model of an economy can show such money flows and the inter-relationships of the various sections.

Different models can be constructed depending on the purpose for which they are required.

THE SECTOR MODEL OF AN ECONOMY

To construct a sector model an economy has to be divided into its constituent sectors and the flow of money into and out of each one recorded separately (p. 8). A payment by one sector is a receipt of another. Thus a tax on consumption will result in a transfer of money from households to the government. The six basic sectors of a mixed economy are:

Household	Business	Central Government	Local Government	Nationalised Industries	External
H	B	C	L	N	E

Private Sector — Public Sector

In national income statistics there are corresponding sectors and a social account is compiled for each one (p. 22). In some of the UK's official publications the labels are slightly different but the sectors are the same.

Thus the household sector is the personal sector, business sector is the companies sector, the nationalised industries sector is the public corporations sector and the external sector is the overseas sector. Central government and local authorities are similarly labelled.

The external (overseas) sector differs from the other sectors in the sense that it is not a producer and consumer of goods and services as such, but is the link between a country and the outside world. Through this link flows money in settlement of international transactions. Payments are made and received for imports and exports. Property income from abroad is transmitted or sent to foreigners and capital transfers are made. These transactions are recorded as entries in the balance of payments account.

The household sector is the largest in terms of the money flow as it consists of the total population of a country. All of its people are consumers and most, at some time of their life, are also producers. Industrial, commercial and financial enterprises that are privately-owned are in the business sector and those that belong to the state are in the nationalised industries sector.

The basic model of a mixed economy can be adjusted for use in a market economy or a centrally-planned economy by removing whichever sector is not appropriate to a particular economic system (Table 1.2).

A sector model can be constructed for the purpose of theoretical economic analysis and for practical application as an aid to governments in the management of their economies. It can, therefore, be used to:

(a) improve understanding of how an economy functions by showing the inter-relationship of its constituent sectors;

Table 1.1   Money flows in a mixed economy

Households	Business	Central Government	Local Government	Nationalised Industries
Receipts:				
earned income wages, salaries	revenue from sales	revenue from taxes	revenue from tax	revenue from sales
unearned income, dividends, rents, interest		charges	charges	
transfer payments, social security benefits	grants subsidies		grants subsidies	grants subsidies
Payments:				
expenditure on goods and services	expenditures on goods and services	expenditure on goods and services	expenditure on goods and services	expenditure on goods and services
taxes	taxes			taxes
social security contribution	social security contribution	social security contribution	social security contribution	social security contribution
		transfer payments		
Savings:	ploughed back profit	budget surplus	budget surplus	ploughed back profit
Investments:	investment	investment	investment	investment

gross domestic fixed capital formation

Table 1.2　Adaptation of the mixed economy model

Type of economic system	Basic Sectors						Deduct
mixed economy	H	B	C	L	N	E	
market economy	H	B	C	L		E	-N
centrally-planned economy	H		C	L	N	E	-B

Note: H is the household, B is the business, C is the central government, L is the local government, N is the nationalised industries and E is the external sector.

(b) trace repercussions on the economy of changes in a government policy or of events such as an oil crisis and the consequent price increases:
(c) forecast changes in the money flow;
(d) plan provision of public goods and services within the limits of available resources;
(e) formulate governments' economic policies;
(f) evaluate the use of different fiscal and monetary measures;
(g) measure the relative importance of the private and public sectors of the economy;
(h) calculate the total output of a country (gross national product, p. 31) and of the resources available.

The value of such models is now widely recognised and they are used in conjunction with others such as the input–output model.

INPUT–OUTPUT MODEL

Like the sector model, an input–output model shows money flows between the constituent parts of an economy, but it also provides a detailed basis for the study of its output in relation to the inputs required to produce goods and services. It is sometimes called the Leontief model after Professor Wassily Leontief (b. 1906) who developed it and subsequently received a Nobel Prize in economics for his contribution to the understanding of the structure of an economy and the knowledge of economics. The input–output table which he constructed was published in a book, *The Structure of the American Economy, 1919–29* (1941). The government of the USA was the first to appreciate the input–output technique as a tool of

Table 1.3   An input–output model (inter-industry transactions)

Sales by	Agriculture, forestry and fishing 1	Mining and quarrying 2	Food, drink and tobacco 3	Other manufac- turing 4	Building and con- tracting 5
			Purchases by		
1. Agriculture, forestry and fishing	—	—	460	28	—
2. Mining and quarrying	5	—	12	196	11
3. Food, drink and tobacco	66	—	—	6	—
4. Other manufacturing	84	73	125	—	340
5. Building and Contracting	15	20	7	70	—
6. Electricity, gas and water	3	6	13	107	3
7. Other production and trade[1]	100	20	150	490	70
8. Other[2]	—	—	—	—	—
9. Imports	60	12	323	798	36
10. Adjustments[5]	—	—	—	19	—
11. Goods and services valued at factor cost	333	131	1090	1714	460
12. Wages and Salaries[6]	249	348	220	2347	572
13. Profits,[4] rent and depreciation	374	41	280	1075	123
14. Net indirect taxes	—	—	—	—	—
15. Total input	956	520	1590	5136	1110

Notes:
1. Transport and Communication, distributive trades and other services.
2. Public administration and defence, public health and educatinal services, owner- ship of dwellings, domestic services to households and services to private non–profit–making bodies.
3. Includes private non–profit–making bodies.

Table 1.3   (*continued*)

| Final Buyers | | | | | | | | |
Electricity, gas and water 6	Other production and trade[1] 7	Other 8	Persons[3] 9	Public Authorities 10	Gross domestic Capital Formation — Fixed 11	Stocks[4] 12	Exports 13	Total Output (£million) 14
—	2	—	405	19	—	32	10	956
107	61	—	85	7	3	-3	35	520
—	9	—	1339	20	—	60	90	1590
60	330	—	1375	335	773	389	1252	5136
3	103	—	260	·85	517	30	—	1110
—	45	—	195	15	36	2	5	430
55	—	—	2379	205	69	—	445	3983
—	—	—	449	987	—	—	—	1436
2	180	—	590	122	35	-20	58	2196
—	—	—	-30	—	-20	—	31	—
227	730	—	7047	1795	1414	490	1926	17357
118	1724	1116	—	—	—	—	—	6649
85	1529	320	—	—	—	—	—	3827
—	—	—	1345	33	52	5	32	1467
430	3983	1436	8392	1828	1466	495	1958	29300

Notes:
4. Includes stock appreciation.
5. Sales by final buyers.
6. Includes employers' insurance contributions and (in column 8) the pay and allowances of the Armed Forces.

Source: *National Income and Expenditure, 1946–51* (London: HMSO, 1952).

economic analysis and its value in planning the use of resources and in predicting bottlenecks in production. The work of Professor Leontief was continued with the support of public funds and later the Department of Labour, in co-operation with the Bureau of Labour Statistics, began to compile and publish official tables for the American economy. The original table was limited in scope and did not show transactions within individual industries – an omission which subsequent tables remedied.

In the UK, Tibor Barna began work on input–output analysis and constructed a table for 1935, but it was not until much later that a government department (the Board of Trade) began to co-operate with the Department of Applied Economics at Cambridge University on input–output analysis. This resulted in a table for 1948 which was the first to be published in the government's National Income and Expenditure Blue Book, 1946–1951 (1952) (Table 1.3). Official input–output tables started in 1954.

However, subsequent tables were not compiled and published annually with the national accounts, but rather appeared at intervals. This reflected the problem of getting reliable data. Statisticians use a variety of sources, industry and household surveys and enquiries, census of production, companies and corporations reports, government's own records on expenditure and taxation, balance of payment accounts and other accounts from national income and expenditure accounts. Nevertheless for some industries information on purchases is scarce and figures in the input–output tables are based on estimates. There is a considerable time lag between the date of publication and the year to which the tables refer.

The original decision was to compile input–output tables at regular intervals and the tables were duly published, approximately every five years up to 1992. The National Accounts 1992 (Blue Book) included an input–output table for 1989, the last of the periodic tables. The Central Statistical Office now intends to publish input–output tables annually from 1993 onwards, to provide better estimates of final demand needed to manage the national economy.

Construction of a Model

An input–output model requires the construction of a matrix table based on the principle of *double entry*. Thus each transaction is shown twice – as a purchase and as a sale or as a receipt and as payment. On one side the table shows current purchases (inputs) of goods and services by each industry from others at home and abroad, including the purchase of factors of production such as services of labour. On the other side, the table shows

Table 1.4   Simplified input–output model for an economy

Receipts (output/ sales by) (£m)	Payments (Input/purchases by) (£m)				
	Agriculture	Services	Manufacturing	Construction	Total
Agriculture	600	50	900	90	1640
Services	150	1600	700	1000	3450
Manufacturing	800	5000	8000	6200	20000
Construction	90	200	7000	100	7390
Total	1640	6850	16600	7390	34480

sales (outputs) by each industry to other industries and to final buyers in the private and public sectors. Sales to them of plant and machinery represent gross domestic capital formation investment. All goods and services sold to foreign buyers are entered as exports.

We can illustrate the principle on which an input–output table is con structed by a simplified example of a hypothetical country's economy, that has only four industries and does not engage in foreign trade, but records transactions within each industry on an inter-industry basis (Table 1.4). In our example, agriculture produces a total output worth £1,640 million of which farmers sell to each other £600 million. These transactions take place within the industry itself and the rest of the output is sold outside it. Sales to service industry, manufacturing and construction industries are, respectively, £50 million, £900 million and £90 million and these figures also show how much each one bought from agriculture, e.g. raw materials. Thus the total sales figure equals the total for purchases. But agriculture also buys goods and services from other industries: £150 million from the services industry, £800 million from manufacturing and £90 million from the construction industries. When all these figures are added together, the total purchases by agriculture will correspond to its sales and the input will equal output. Similarly, output and input of the service industry equal each other and finally the total for all industries will be the same, at £34,480 million. This last figure is higher than the gross national product of a hypothetical country would be, as shown by national income statistics (p. 31), because the input–output table takes into account intermediate transactions.

The Purpose and Use of an Input–Output Model

The purpose of constructing the model is to show what each industry and sector produced, consumed and invested in a particular year, and thus to give a quantitative picture that would provide a basis for the analysis of structural inter-relationships – past, present and future – required for decision-making. We can illustrate how an input–output model can be used to serve the purpose of allocating scarce resources. Suppose a country, Hobiton imports raw materials, one of which is rubber from neighbouring Mordor. Mordor is a poor country and its economic difficulties lead to revolution, as a result of which the supply of rubber to foreign markets is cut off. An input–output table will show the government of Hobiton which of its industries are using rubber imported from Mordor and what is their level of consumption of this particular raw material. On the basis of this information the government can predict the likely consequences for the industries' output of the fall in supply of rubber, anticipate bottlenecks in production as a shortage of the raw material develops, formulate a scheme for rationing stocks in the short term, and search for another source of supply or decide on a policy to secure a substitute raw material in the long run, such as synthetic rubber that could be manufactured in Hobiton.

Businesses and other organisations wanting to use information on inter-industry transactions can, in the UK, access the government's input–output data for the British economy.

Limitation of Input–Output Analysis

Computation of the tables takes time and is costly. An input–output table is likely to be several years out of date when it is published. Furthermore, a single table gives only a static picture and successive tables are needed to analyse changes. These limitations are not, however, as great as they might appear. Structural changes are gradual and it may take a long time before the inter-relationships within an economy alter appreciably. The development and use of computers have made it easier and cheaper to process statistical data and thus to compile input–output tables at more frequent intervals. In the meantime a government can fill in some of the gaps in the information available by using national income statistics, which in most countries are compiled annually.

SUMMARY

1. Three distinct types of economic system can be distinguished in theory: the *pure market* economy (without a public sector of industry); the *centrally-planned* economy (without a private sector of industry); and the *mixed* economy where both sectors operate side by side. In the 1990s, there has been a global shift from centrally planned to market economies. In Europe, after the disintegration of the USSR, Communism ceased to be a political and economic force.
2. Most developed and developing countries have established some form of a mixed economy. However, the size of their public sectors does differ considerably.
3. *Economic models* have been devised to aid the understanding of how economic systems function and to serve as basis for government decision-making.
4. The *sector* model is one of the economic models used by governments. It shows the inter-relationship of the private and public sectors as both are producers and consumers.
5. The sectors are linked by a *flow of money*. Each sector receives income or revenue from which it consumes, saves and invests.
6. Government *transfer payments* (benefits and taxes) appear in the model as expenditure and revenue of the government and as receipts and payments of the private sector.
7. The *input–output* model (Leontief model) shows how resources have been used to produce the final product. Each industry is a buyer of inputs and a seller of outputs.
8. Input–output data can be of help in *forecasting* the demand for and supply of goods, services and business.
9. Input–output analysis is an aid to *economic planning* in the private and public sector.
10. Both the sector model and the input–output model provide the basis for the *formulation* of governments' fiscal and monetary policies.

SUGGESTED FURTHER READING

D. Begg, S. Fisher and R. Dornbusch, *Economics* (London: McGraw-Hill, 1991).
S. Borner (ed.), *The European Community after 1992* (London: Macmillan, 1992).
Commission of the European Communities, *PHARE: Assistance for Economic Restructuring of the Countries of Central and Eastern Europe* (Luxembourg: 1992).

D. Coombes, *Understanding the European Community* (London: Macmillan, 1992).

W. Leontief, *The Structure of American Economy* (New York: M.E. Sharpe, 1976).

A. Nove, *The Soviet Economic System* (London: Routledge, 1987).

A.R. Prest and D.J. Coppock (ed. M.J. Artis), *The UK Economy* (London: Weidenfeld & Nicolson, 1992).

P.A. Samuelson, *Economics* (Maidenhead: McGraw-Hill, 1992) (see for US economy).

United Nations Economic Commission for Europe, *Economic Reforms in the European Centrally-Planned Economies*, Vol. 1 (Geneva: 1989).

EXERCISES

1. Explain why and how the same economic model can be used to study different economic systems.

2. Suggest some of the reasons why the centrally-planned economic system of the former USSR did not produce goods and services and generate incomes that would allow its people to achieve a standard of living comparable to that in the European Community.

3. Explain why, in a market-orientated economy, governments still need to plan and what form such planning takes.

4. In what sense does the overseas sector differ from the other sectors in an economic model and what is the purpose of including it?

5. Consider the value of a sector model as an aid to a government in planning and formulating a policy to control the money flow in a country.

6. Compare and contrast the sector model and input–output model as a tool to facilitate decision-making in the public sector with increasing current consumption by the central government.

7. With the help of the sector model trace the likely effects on a national economy of an expansion of the government's house-building programme. Take, as your starting point, an increase by local authorities in their investment in council houses and follow the repercussions of this on other sectors and the money flow between them.

8. What would be the likely changes in the money flow between the sectors as a result of an increase in taxation?

9. Discuss how an input–output model can provide information that could facilitate the allocation of resources by rationing at a time of emergency, such as war.

10. 'The fact that by the time of its publication an input–output table is already several years out of date, makes it little more than of historical interest.' Give your reasons for agreeing or disagreeing with this assertion.

11. Explain why an analysis of the inter-relationship between the private and public sectors is necessary to the understanding of national economies and how it can be improved by the construction of models.

12. 'An economic model is no more than a toy that takes up time and wastes public money.' Comment on the validity of this statement.

2 National Income

National income is one of the leading economic indicators of the state of an economy and of its resources. It can be defined as 'a measure of the goods and services becoming available to a nation for consumption or adding to wealth'. Thus, a discussion of national income can serve as a useful introduction to a study of the public sector within an economic framework and to public finance in theory and in practice. But national income as an introductory chapter makes demands of a reader. The calculation of national income is a complicated exercise and a brief explanation of how it is done is not easy to follow. It could take several chapters or even a book, to do justice to theories relating to consumption, saving and investment that have a bearing on national income, but here they have to be summarised in a few pages to provide a background to the main themes. Nevertheless, national income has been included in this book because an understanding of the subject is essential in assessing governments' fiscal and monetary policies.

Professionals and students of public finance need to consider public finance expenditure and taxation within an economic framework. As national income is a major indicator of the state of the economy, it is an essential guide to its study.

PURPOSES OF NATIONAL INCOME DATA

National income can be looked at as the sum total of all incomes derived from the economic activity of the residents of a country – that is as factor incomes accruing to factors of production. It can also be looked at as all final expenditure on goods and services or as the total output, after adjustments for overseas transactions and consumption of capital.

Figures can also be expressed in terms of Gross National Product (GNP) or Gross Domestic Product (GDP). The difference in the terminology is explained in the following pages. In the long run it does not matter much whether GNP or GDP is used. In the short run, GDP is considered to be a more reliable indicator as it does not include international flows of money that are notoriously difficult to calculate and may contain large margins of error. Most industrial countries now use GDP. The USA shifted emphasis to it in 1991.

Governments require accurate information on national income for informed decision-making in the administration and management of an economy. The purposes for which they calculate national income figures are numerous. The data may be used to:

(a) Improve understanding of the economy and of the inter-relationship of the sectors.
(b) Provide a basis for an assessment of an economy's performance and the measurement of economic growth. Whether a country is doing well or badly is relative to its past rate of growth and that of other countries. Thus, British economic growth of 2.9 per cent in 1960–70 may appear historically high for the UK but gives little cause for satisfaction when compared with that of the Member States of the European Community and of other industrialised nations. Then, in the 1970s, rates generally fell, but the Japanese rate – at half of what it had been – still looked impressive when compared with the growth of France, Germany, UK or USA over this period. In the 1990s all this changed and the estimated percentage increase in British GDP in 1995 of 2.9 per cent surpasses that of its major competitors. Thus a 2.9 per cent rise in GDP that had been considered an

Table 2.1   Growth of GDP: international comparison

	Average rates of growth								
	France	*Germany*	*UK*	*USA*	*Japan*	*India*	*Pakistan*	*Singapore*	*Hong Kong*
1960–70[*]	5.7	4.4	2.9	4.3	10.5	3.7	5.2	7.9	9.8
1970–80	3.2	2.6	2.0	5.4	4.4	3.3	5.2	8.4	9.2
1980–85	1.8	1.2	2.1	0.6	3.8	5.4	6.3	6.7	5.8
1985–89	3.1	2.9	4.0	1.9	4.5	6.1	6.1	8.3	9.3
1982–92[**]	2.1	2.9	2.3	2.8	4.0				
1992–93	–0.9	–2.1	2.0	2.8	–0.5				

Note: Data from various sources may not be strictly comparable due to differences in concepts and methods used by source organisations.

Source: [*]   1960–70 series, *UN Statistical Yearbook 1979/80* (New York, 1991) except for Japan, Pakistan and Hong Kong; other rates all from *UN National Accounts Statistics 1988–1989* (New York, 1991) except for USA. Information provided by UN Statistical Division (1995).

UN Statistical Yearbook, New York, 1979 (figures for GNP).

[**]   OECD, *National Accounts* (Paris 1994).

indication of poor performance is now an indication of good performance. In economic terms, much is relative (Table 2.1).

(c) Identify factors that contribute to a high rate of economic growth
     and to indicate measures to foster them.

     Analysis of national income data has shown that countries with a
     high rate of fixed capital formation have high rates of growth, while
     countries that invest less have a rate of growth of less than half of
     that of high investors. There are, of course, other contributory
     factors, but it would appear that investment is an important one.

(d) Indicate the timing of corrective fiscal and monetary measures to
     counteract fluctuations in the level of economic activity, that give
     rise to unemployment and inflation.

(e) Present the data necessary for the formulation of fiscal and mon-
     etary policies.

(f) Serve as a basis for forecasting the availability of resources and the
     demand for and supply of goods and services.

(g) Provide a basis for planning.

(h) Measure and compare the standard of living on the basis of national
     income per head of the population.

(i) Calculate national contributions to international bodies such as the
     International Monetary Fund or to determine the level of foreign
     aid as when the richer countries undertook to devote 1 per cent of
     GNP to help the poorer ones.

EARLY ESTIMATES OF NATIONAL INCOME

The pioneering work on the development of national income accounting
was carried out in the UK. William Petty (1623–87) is credited with
making the first national incomes estimate in 1655. He was a professor of
anatomy at Oxford, a physician in Cromwell's army and later a tax admin-
istrator in Ireland. It may well be that this background led him to apply the
techniques of the physical sciences to political economy, using what he
called 'political arithmetic'.

Petty calculated the national income of England by aggregating all expenditure. He assumed that the annual national income equalled expenditure and
left savings out of the account. His estimated expenditure on food, housing,
clothing and other necessities was $4\frac{1}{2}$d. per person, per day. This amounted
to just under £7 per annum for each man, woman and child and, as the population of England was about 6 million, the total expenditure came to approximately £40 million per year and this was also the figure for the national
income. Petty estimated that £15 million of it was income from property and

£25 million was remuneration for labour. Some three hundred years later the national income of the UK exceeded £400,000 million. The next step in the development of national income accounting was Gregory King's estimate in 1692. It laid the foundation on which estimates are based to this day and was a remarkable achievement in many ways (Gregory King, *Natural and Political Observations and Conclusions upon the State and Conditions of England*, 1696). King's contribution to national income accounting was that he:

(a) Introduced savings into the calculation and arrived at the equation

$$Y = C + S$$
(income = consumption + savings)

that will be found in most modern textbooks on economics.
(b) Computed separately data on incomes, expenditure and savings for each occupational and social group. Lords temporal came at the top, then lords spiritual, considerably poorer in material terms, followed in descending order of affluence by merchants, gentlemen, persons in science and the liberal arts, clergymen and farmers.
(c) Calculated distribution of incomes showing annual income per family in each group and also income, expenditure and savings per head (see Table 2.2).
(d) Estimated quantity and value of output from which he deducted costs, such as costs of seeds from the value of crops, and arrived at 'neat product' (what we would now call net value output used in the calculation of national income by the output method).

Table 2.2   Example of income distribution (King's estimate for 1692)

Top Income range				
Annual income (£) per		*Number of families*	*Number of persons per household*	*Description of the Head of the household*
Household	*Person*			
2,800	70	160	40	Lord
44	8	150,000	5	Farmer

Note: Average income per head was £12 – of this 96 per cent was spent on consumption.

(e) Compared national income internationally and for this purpose cal-
     culated the national income of England's two great trading rivals:
     France and Germany. This comparative study is believed to be the
     first of its kind.
(f) Used past data and projected the series, thus anticipating modern
     forecasting practice by some 250 years.

After this remarkable start in the seventeenth century, there was little
progress in national income accounting in the eighteenth century until the
outbreak of the American War of Independence and the Napoleonic wars,
when interest in national income was revived. The data acquired some
propaganda value as an indication of a country's resources and therefore
of its war potential. In the nineteenth century and the early part of the
twentieth century a number of private estimates of national income
appeared and some work, notably by Alfred Marshall (1842–1924), was
done in clarifying the concept underlying the calculations.

First Official Estimates

Although most of the early work on national income was done in the UK,
other countries were first to publish their estimates as official statistics:
Australia (1886), Germany (1929), New Zealand (1931), USA (1934),
Turkey (1935), Yugoslavia (1937) and Switzerland (1939). It was not until
the Second World War that the British national income estimate appeared
in a government publication, *Analysis of the sources of war finance and
estimates of the national income and expenditure* (Cmd. 6261, 1941). It
introduced the concept of a two-sided account of income and expenditure
for the whole of the economy. The 1941 Budget was built around the estimates and national income data has been published annually ever since.
The government recognised its importance to the planning of the war
effort and later of the economy in peacetime.

Social Accounting

The development of a double entry national income accounting led to the
application of the principle to all the sectors of the economy and to the construction of social accounts. For the purpose of *social accounting* or, as it is
sometimes called, *sector accounting*, the total for national income is broken
up by sectors (as shown in Figure 2.1). The income and expenditure of

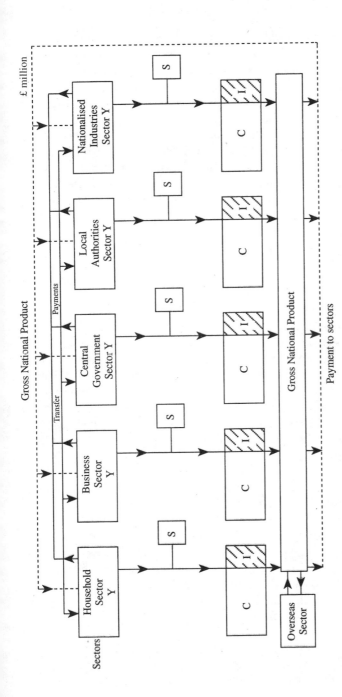

Figure 2.1   Sector model of an economy

Notes:

1. Where: C = Consumption, I = Investment (gross domestic fixed capital formation), S = Savings and Y = Income.

2. Household sector = personal sector, business sector = company sector, nationalised industries sector = public corporations and public enterprises.

each sector is shown separately by a social account. The aggregate of all the social accounts gives the national income and expenditure of a country. The value of social accounting is that it shows the inter-relationship of the sectors, the flow of money between them and the structure of the economy. The development and acceptance of social accounting owes much to the work of Professor James E. Meade (b. 1907), Richard N. Stone (b. 1913), and Lord Kaldor (b. 1908). The National Income and Expenditure White Paper (Cmd. 7099, 1946) was based on the principle of social accounting. It was left to Professor Stone to convince professional opinion of its usefulness and in 1947 he prepared a report for the committee of statistical experts of the United Nations. Today social accounting is an internationally accepted practice in presenting national income.

PROPOSALS FOR REFORMING NATIONAL INCOME ACCOUNTS

'Green' Accounting

Principles and practices of national accounting evolve in response to the needs of societies as they become preoccupied with particular issues. One of these currently is the environment. A number of attempts have been made to compile 'greener' accounts as governments wish to demonstrate their concern for the environment. The European Community has taken the first steps towards developing green accounting. In the Netherlands, the Central Bureau of Statistics has published, in 1993, 'satellite accounts' which show the impact of industry, service and household sectors on:

greenhouse effect, depletion of ozone layer, acidification, eutrophication and waste accumulation.

Dutch statisticians did not value the damage to the environment in monetary terms. Instead they calculated relative contributions of the sectors to environmental problems. This, however, raises the question of attribution. Should, for example, pollution of rivers with nutrients resulting from the application of nitrogen fertilizers that increase acidification, be attributed to the agricultural industry or to the households which consume agricultural products.

Citizens of a rich industrialised country may value highly the beauty of a landscape. In a poor country, where scarce land is needed to feed a hungry population, preservation of picturesque views is likely to have a low priority. Some aspects of improvement or deterioration of environment are not readily quantifiable. Valuation can be subjective and may differ from country to country.

There have been some developments, however. France and Norway have initiated programmes to collect information on the physical stock of their natural resources, that could provide a basis for an adjustment of the conventional measure of GDP. Other members of the European Union have yet (1995) to follow this example. Similarly, the United Nations has considered ways of dealing with green issues in the process of revision of its System of National Accounts (SNA) which sets out the basis for measurement of income and wealth. In its new (1993) handbook UN statisticians suggest how governments could produce satellite accounts that would distinguish between depletion and degradation of the environment as a result of economic activity. Thus, for example, open-cast mining depletes coal reserves and degrades the environment by polluting and scarring of land. Mining creates output and increases GDP but in the conventional national income account no deduction is made for the cost to the environment.

Extraction of minerals reduces natural wealth but, whereas man-made capital such as mining machinery can be replaced and provision is made in the accounts for depreciation during its working life, nature-made capital is not replaceable within a meaningful time-span, if at all. There is still, however, little agreement on the appropriate way to value depletion, as can be seen from a recent publication of the World Bank (Erner Lutz (ed) – full details in further reading at end of chapter).

It is debatable whether national income accounts can meaningfully take into account environmental factors and conform to an internationally accepted practice. However, this does not mean that green issues can be ignored at a national level. There are different ways in which they can be accounted for.

'Housewife' Accounting

In their reforming zeal, politicians not only looked at the environment but also turned their attention to unpaid labour, particularly that of housewives, which until recently had been ignored in so far as national accounting was concerned. In 1993, there were moves to change this. Members of the European Parliament voted overwhelmingly in favour of a report proposing recognition of the value of unpaid labour throughout the European Community. They called on the governments of Member States to include domestic work done at home in the calculation of a country's Gross National Product.

Of course, European MPs were not the first to consider putting a value on housewives. The Bible, written some 2000 years ago, says of a virtuous woman '....her price is far above rubies' (*Proverbs*, XXXI). A more precise market valuation was arrived at in London in 1833 when a wife was sold for 5 shillings (25 pence) which was a large proportion of a working man's wage in the nineteenth century. Such a method of valuation, quite apart from the question of legality of the deal, met with little public support. The *Times* correspondent at the time reported that the sale took place amid '... the hissings and hootings of the populace who showered stones and missiles on the parties'.

These days a commercial valuation of a housewife is done with proper decorum by a life insurance company, Legal and General. They calculated how much it would cost to replace the work of a wife and mother by paid labour, estimating that a housewife on average spends 71 hours per week on domestic chores such as cooking and cleaning. These hours are longer for a mother with young children and lower if she has a part-time job. The going rate for domestic hired help is put at £5.35 per hour. Nannies are more expensive. L & G assesses the commercial value of a wife and mother at £349 per week (£18,150 per year) which exceeds the average wage of a man in the UK.

To include unpaid domestic work by women in the national output of a country would be to open a 'Pandora's box.' First there is the political correctness of such an exercise as if it were in reverse. Men also do jobs around the house, and according to the L & G survey, some 50 per cent of them help with the washing up. If housewives are to be counted what about housemen? To produce comparable statistics for countries with diverse economies, cultures and social habits would severely challenge the most ingenious of statisticians.

Results of such an exercise would produce some startling results. On paper all countries would appear richer but none would, in fact, be better off. Poor countries where people cannot afford to buy goods and services and households have to provide for their own needs, would appear to have gained relatively more than rich countries, where people can afford to pay others to do domestic chores for them. Such payment would represent household expenditure and give rise to earned incomes of the homehelps which, according to the normal practice, would have already been included in gross domestic product. The unrecorded, unpaid housework would therefore account for a smaller proportion of domestic output and have less impact on the national income. In the UK if it were included it would add up to some £100 billion a year equivalent approximately to the total output of the Danish economy. To appreciate what the reforms of national accounting practices would involve it is necessary to look at how national income is defined and calculated.

DEFINITION AND CALCULATION OF NATIONAL INCOME

There are three different ways of defining and calculating national income and the definition is indicative of the chosen method of calculation. Thus, if national income is defined in terms of total factor income, total expenditure or total output of a country, then the *income*, the *expenditure* or the *output* method of calculation can be used. National income is the total monetary value of goods and services produced by a country after a number adjustments have been made, e.g. for international transactions and consumption or capital (see Table 2.3). In economic literature, references may be made in the same context to national income, gross national product and gross domestic product. For example, economic growth may be shown on the basis of any one of these three measures. In interpretation of the data it has to be remembered that the terms are not synonymous and each has a specific meaning – figures calculated on the basis of one definition can be adjusted to fit another (see Table 2.4).

National income can be shown at *factor cost* or at *market prices,* and figures can be calculated (i) at current prices, prevailing in the year in question, and (ii) at constant prices using a base year. This is explained in Appendix 3 at the back of this book. In theory the three methods – of calculating national income – the income method, the expenditure method and the output method–should give the same final figure. In practice the result may differ as Table 2.5 shows. Thus, if the income method of calculation is used the growth of GDP appears greater. The discrepancies can be explained by the fact that these figures are estimates – all methods produce data that is inaccurate. It had been suggested by Prof. D. Morgenstein that a margin of error of 10 to 15 per cent may have to be allowed for in the calculation of the national income (*Fortune*, October 1963).

Income Method

We can now discuss in greater detail how national income is estimated using the income method which, of the three methods, is likely to produce the most reliable result.

Since all incomes generated within a country and earned by it abroad have to be expressed in monetary terms and *aggregated*, it is necessary to

Table 2.3   National Income of the UK

(a) Gross national product by category of expenditure   £ million

---

	1960	1970	1980	1990	1992
At market prices:					
Consumers' expenditure	16 939	31 778	135 738	347 527	382 696
General government final consumption	4 224	8 991	48 424	112 934	132 378
Gross domestic fixed capital formation	4 190	9 470	39 411	106 776	92 892
Value of physical increase in stocks and work in progress	562	421	−2 706	−1 118	−1 992
Total domestic expenditure	25 915	50 660	220 867	566 119	605 974
Exports of goods and services	5 156	11 594	63 158	133 284	139 827
Total final expenditure	31 071	62 254	284 025	699 403	745 801
less Imports of goods and services	−5 549	−11 147	−57 913	−148 285	−149 164
Gross domestic product at market prices	25 522	51 107	226 112	551 118	596 165
Net property income from abroad	233	554	−273	1 630	5 777
Gross national product at market prices	25 755	51 661	225 839	552 748	601 942
Factor cost adjustment:					
Taxes on expenditure	3 378	8 413	36 882	78 298	87 679
Subsidies	493	884	5 308	6 066	6 108
Taxes *less* subsidies	2 885	7 529	31 574	72 232	81 571

Table 2.3 (*continued*)

£ *million*

	1960	1970	1980	1990	1992
At factor cost:					
Consumers' expenditure	14 548	26 093	113 395	295 964	324 428
General government final consumption	4 112	8 351	44 659	106 128	123 496
Gross domestic capital formation	4 482	9 170	33 929	98 130	83 826
Total domestic expenditure	23 142	43 614	191 983	500 222	531 750
Exports of goods and services	5 044	11 111	60 468	126 949	132 480
Total final expenditure	28 186	54 725	252 451	627 171	664 230
less Imports of goods and services	−5 549	−11 147	−57 913	−148 285	−149 164
Gross domestic product at factor cost	22 637	43 578	194 538	478 886	514 594 *x
Net property income from abroad	233	554	−273	1 630	5 777
Gross national product at factor cost	22 870	44 132	194 265	480 516	520 371
less Capital consumption	−2 047	−4 428	−27 223	−61 200	−63 984
National income (i.e. net national product)	20 823	39 704	167 042	419 316	456 387 x

Notes: * Adjusted for statistical discrepancy of 472.
x Compare with figures in table (b).

Table 2.3   (*continued*)

(b) Gross national product by category of income	£ *million* 1992
Factor incomes	
Income from employment	341 009
Income from self-employment	58 060
Gross trading profits of companies	62 574
Gross trading surplus of public corporations	1 813
Gross trading surplus of general government enterprises	89
Rent	48 846
Imputed charge for consumption of non-trading capital	4 207
Total domestic income	516 598
less Stock appreciation	−2 216
Gross domestic product (income-based)	514 382
Residual error	212
Gross domestic product (expenditure-based)	514 594 x
Factor incomes after providing for stock appreciation	
Income from employment	341 009
Income from self-employment	57 980
Gross trading profits of companies	62 469
Gross trading surplus of public corporations	1 782
Gross trading surplus of general government enterprises	89
Rent	46 846
Imputed charge for consumption of non-trading capital	4 207
Gross domestic product (income-based)	514 382
Residual error	212
Gross domestic product (expenditure-based)	514 594
Net property income from abroad	5 777
Gross national product	520 371
less Capital consumption	−63 984
National income (i.e. net national product)	456 387 x

Note: x Compare with figures in table (a).
Source: *National Income and Expenditure* (London: HMSO, 1982); Blue Book *UK National Accounts* (1993).

Table 2.4 National Income definitions

Gross national product at market prices
– (net factor income from abroad)
= gross domestic product at market prices

Gross domestic product at market prices
– (indirect taxes net of subsidies)
= gross domestic product at factor cost

Gross domestic product at factor cost
– (depreciation i.e. provision for consumption of capital)
= net domestic product at factor cost

Net domestic product at factor cost
+ (net property income from abroad)
= national income i.e. net national product at factor cost

add to cash incomes the imputed value of payments in kind, such as managers' cars provided by a company as part of their remuneration, or miners' coal provided free of charge by the employer. The total figure arrived at represents *factor incomes*, that is incomes accruing to factors of production: wages to labour, interest to capital (lenders), rent to land (owners), profit to enterprise (business).

National income figures *exclude*:

(a) Transfer payments, such as social security benefits, even though representing income to the recipients are not included in the calculation. The reason for this is that the benefits are transfers of income

Table 2.5 Discrepancies in National Income data (increase in GDP at constant factor cost)

GDP calculated on the basis of:	Index numbers*		
	Period I	Period III	Increase between I and III
Expenditure data	63.1	107.8	44.7
income data	62.8	108.0	45.2
output data	65.4	107.8	42.4

Note: * Period II (year) = base year = 100.
Table derived from UK national income data.

through taxation from one group, the taxpayers, to another, the recipients, who have not produced an output in return for the payment. To include such transfer payments would be counting the same income twice.

(b) Value of work for which no payment is made is also excluded from the calculation of national income. Thus the value of the work of a housewife to her family is omitted, whereas a wage paid to a housekeeper is included (see p. 25).

Taxing authorities who require individuals and businesses to disclose their incomes, including income in kind for tax assessments are a usual source of data. Tax returns, thus provide detailed information that statisticians can use to calculate national income. Problems in calculation arise because:

(a) Information on incomes may be unreliable if there is widespread tax evasion in a country.

(b) The valuation of payments in kind on a fair and consistent basis raises difficulties.

(c) Transfer incomes have to be identified and excluded.

Expenditure Method

To calculate national income by the expenditure method all expenditure on consumer and capital goods and services is added together. This represents *current consumption* and *fixed capital formation (investment)*. Only final expenditure is taken into account to avoid double counting. Thus, expenditure on the steel used in the production of a car is not shown separately but is included in the price paid for that car.

Data on expenditure basis has to be compatible with that calculated on income and output basis. Therefore adjustments are made:

(a) Expenditure figures are adjusted to take into account international transactions. To total domestic expenditure a figure for the value of exports is added and value of imports is deducted (see Table 2.3). Exported goods are not available for domestic consumption but sales abroad earn income for the country. National income is spent on goods and services produced for the home market and on imports, but the latter do not generate income in the importing country. In addition, we have to take into account *net property income from abroad*.

(b) Adjustment is also made for payments in the form of taxes on consumption and subsidies which represent a transfer of money to and from the government (see Table 2.3).

Information on expenditure can be obtained from censuses of distribution, showing wholesale and retail sales, household expenditure surveys, and tax returns for taxes on consumption.

Problems in calculation can arise because:

(a) Data may be unreliable. It has been found that people tend to underestimate some expenditure, such as that on alcohol and tobacco. If the amount is large, as in the UK (where for some years it was approximately equal to the expenditure on housing), underestimation may considerably affect the total figure for consumption.
(b) Figures may be distorted by inaccurate tax returns.
(c) Adjustments required raise statistical difficulties. The balance of payments figures are known to contain a considerable margin of error.

Output Method

To calculate national income by output method, the value, in money terms, of all goods and services produced in the country is added together. This figure is the gross national product.

Again the basis of calculation has to be compatible for all the methods of calculating national income and adjustments must be made.

(a) Output figures have to be adjusted for imports of raw materials and components that are incorporated in the finished product. Rubber imported from Malaysia for making car tyres in the UK cannot be included in the British national product.
(b) Changes in the volume of stocks during the period for which national income is calculated have to be taken into account. Stocks may change in value because their volume has increased or decreased, but they may also appreciate or depreciate as a result of changes in the price level.
(c) Capital consumption, e.g. depreciation of plant and machinery, has to be deducted from the output figure to arrive at the actual value added in the process of product.
(d) Net property income from abroad is additional to the value of domestic production (using the term 'production' in the widest sense). If we

wish to measure a country's output, this means that income received
from abroad is added and income paid out is subtracted.

Information on output can be obtained from censuses of production,
surveys and tax returns.

Problems in calculation arise because:

(a) As censuses cannot be held frequently, up-to-date comprehensive
    information may be difficult to obtain, while supplementary surveys
    may vary in reliability.
(b) Calculation is complicated by the need to adjust figures for inter-
    national transactions, e.g. the return on British assets abroad.
(c) Valuation of stocks presents problems particularly at a time of rapid
    inflation.
(d) What government allows for depreciation for tax purposes may
    differ substantially from the amount that firms may have to set aside
    to replace their plant and machinery.
(e) Dangers of double counting are considerable.

CHOICE OF METHOD OF CALCULATING NATIONAL INCOME FOR DEVELOPED AND DEVELOPING COUNTRIES

A government's choice of method for calculating national income will be
influenced by the nature of the country's economy and its level of development. Developed countries are likely to use all three methods.
Developing countries with small administrative machinery and limited
statistical resources may have to restrict themselves to one method, e.g.

Methods used for first estimates
India, Pakistan, Nigeria   Output method
Ghana   Output and expenditure

In a predominantly agricultural society based on a largely self-sufficient
family unit, employment of labour and expenditure on goods and services
will be relatively low and below the value of the country's output. The
income method of calculating the national income has the disadvantage
that a high proportion of work done by members of a family for themselves, being unpaid, will not be counted. When payment is made some of
it is likely to be in kind and its value will be difficult to impute. The task
will be made more difficult by lack of reliable tax returns. The expenditure

method also has drawbacks since relatively few of the goods and services consumed are purchased. The output method has the advantage that it reflects more accurately the resources available to the people in the country. With knowledge of the land area under cultivation and range of crops, the yield can be estimated and valued at current. prices. This will give some indication of the gross domestic product and is likely to be more meaningful than if the GDP were calculated on the basis of either the income or the expenditure method. A developing country is unlikely to have much in the way of property income coming from abroad. Its GNP will not, therefore, be very different from its GDP.

INTERNATIONAL COMPARISON OF NATIONAL INCOME

In international comparison of data caution needs to be exercised to avoid misleading conclusions. It is not just a question of converting national incomes to a common currency, e.g. US dollars. The following are some of the important points that have to be kept in mind.

Only national income calculated on the same conceptual basis can be meaningfully compared. Thus national incomes of centrally-planned economies based on the Marxist concept of productive labour cannot be compared with figures for market economies that include, in their national income calculation, all payments to labour, whether it produces physical output or intangible services, such as those of teachers. Comparison of the national income of countries at very different level of economic development can also be misleading (see Table 2.6). The way of life in a

Table 2.6 National Income: international comparison

Per capita national income in US dollars, 1993–94*

Japan	37 561	Singapore	19 092	South Africa	3 002
USA	25 687	Italy	17 600	Brazil	2 585
Germany	23 520	Australia	17 303	Russia	2 100
France	22 670	UK	16 300	Pakistan	446
Sweden	22 660	Spain	12 180	Nigeria	305
Hong Kong	21 500	Argentina	8 700	India	298
Canada	21 318	Saudi Arabia	7 006	Ukraine	105

*estimates.
Source: The Economist, *The World in 1994* (London: Economist Publications, 1993).

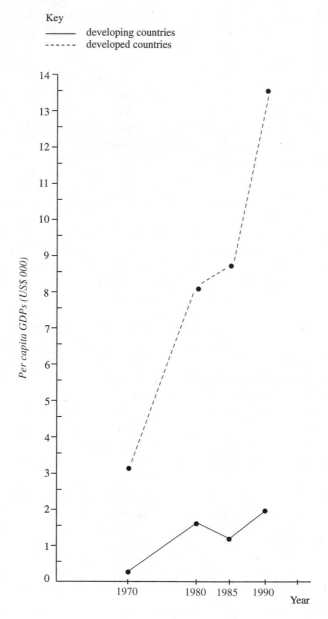

Figure 2.2   GDP of developed and developing countries, 1970–90

Source: *United Nations National Accounts Statistics*, Part II, 1991 (New York: UN, 1993). Copyright UN, reproduced by permission.

developing agricultural society will differ from that in a developed industrial country, where households have to purchase most of the goods and services they require. As a result, the national income will appear much bigger in a developed country, but the higher expenditure will not necessarily mean an equally higher level of consumption. In 1993, the average annual income per person in India was estimated at approximately £200. Nobody could survive on this in the UK, where it would not be enough to buy a cup of coffee every day, but in India 902 million people manage to live, even though their average income, by British standards, is below the subsistence level.

The total national income of a country has to be looked at in relation to its population to be indicative of a standard of living, even when countries are at a comparable level of economic development.

Per capita or per head national income is the total income divided by the number of people and is the *average income* for that country. The accuracy of this figure depends to a large extent on how reliable is the population data. It is not just of demographic interest and economic importance but can also have far-reaching political implications, for example, in federal countries such as Nigeria where political representation of the regions on governing bodies is determined by the size of their population. This in turn affects the relative share in federal revenue. The results of three censuses of population since the country's independence were declared to be unacceptable. It was alleged that the figures were not the result of a head count but rather of negotiation between regional leaders. The 1962 results were considered particularly controversial. The Northern region in 1963 and Southern region in 1973 questioned the returns of the other. Eventually, the 1991 census was conducted with UN observers present. The results, when they were published in 1992, came as a shock. The population of Nigeria was shown to be 88.5 million and not over 100 million as had been assumed. This difference in the population changed the place of Nigeria in the World Bank's ranking of countries. Nigeria ceased to be 13th poorest and moved up because its income per capita of $250 was recalculated at somewhere around $360, yet Nigerians were just as poor the day before as they were the day after.

Comparison of the total national income of, say, India and Iceland, would suggest that India was much the richer of the two, but per capita income shows the opposite (see Table 2.7).

The distribution of income must also be considered in drawing a true comparison. The concept of average income is of little use in economic analysis when national income of a country is very unevenly distributed, with a few very rich people at one end of the scale and a very large

Table 2.7   National Income, GDP and population

	1980*			1990*		
	GDP *(million $US)*	population *(000)*	GDP per capita *($US)*	GDP *(million $US)*	population *(000)*	GDP per capita *($US)*
India	172 723	663 596	251	303 282	843 931	358
Iceland	3 230	228	14 104	6 024	205	23 622
USA	2 688 470	227 658	11 804	5 464 795	248 709	21 861

Note: * or nearest year.
Source: data supplied by UN Statistical Division (current figures in UN National
            Accounts Statistics database). Copyright UN; reproduced by permission.
            See also *UN Statistical Yearbook* (New York, 1994).

Table 2.8   GDP in the UK at constant and current market prices

1990=100	1982	1990	1992
GDP at current market prices	50.6	100	108.2
GDP at 1990 (constant) market prices	77.2	100	97.3

Source: CSO *Blue Book UK National Accounts* (1993).

number of very poor at the other, with a comparatively small number in
the middle. Where a large divergence does not exist, then the per capita
income shown in Table 2.6 is indicative of the affluence or poverty of the
people of a particular country.

Growth in per capita income or total national income can be measured
as a percentage change at an annual rate from the previous years or as an
average rate over a period. An increase in real income (see Appendix 3) is
indicative of economic growth in real terms. When there is inflation an
increase in national income or GDP expressed at current price will appear
greater than when measured at constant prices but people will not be better
off (Table 2.8). In International comparisons changes in price levels in
different countries need to be taken into account (Table 2.9).

Table 2.9   Consumer price index: international comparison

Year	Argentina	Brazil	Chile	France	Germany	Japan	UK	USA
1980	100	100	100	100	100	100	100	100
1990	79,531	142,023	636	184	129	122	189	159
1991	–	723,218	774	190	134	126	200	165

Note: 1980 = 100 – base year.
Source: *UN Statistical Yearbook*, 38th issue (1993). Copyright UN; reproduced by permission.

COMPLEMENTARY INDICATORS

National income figures, being indicators of economic welfare, do not take into account quality of life. The two are, however, to a large extent interdependent. Quality of life can be enhanced by possession of material resources, capital or income. Money cannot buy happiness but it can relieve misery.

To account for quality of life, it has first to be defined and herein lies the problem. There is no one generally accepted definition or a method of measurement. How does one put value on freedom of speech? Is the ease of obtaining a divorce a plus or minus point? Any indicator of the quality of life is bound to be subjective. Decisions have to be made on what to include and how to quantify abstract concepts such as happiness or misery.

The perceived shortcomings of national income as an indicator of a measure of welfare have led to the publication of a number of quality of life indicators (Table 2.10). The following three examples show how these endeavours have produced very different results.

(a) *The Human Development Index,* calculated by the United Nations, has attempted to measure the quality of life in 160 member-states. It is based on a ranking system that takes into account a wide range of factors such as literacy and life expectation, as well as income. In 1992, Japan was at the top of the rankings, having displaced Canada by a small margin, making the two the most desirable countries in the world in which to live. This may come as something of a surprise to a salaried man in Japan who commutes to Tokyo wedged for several hours daily in stifling heat on a commuter train or paying very high rent ($5700 per month in 1992) for a two-bedroom flat in the city, to be nearer to his place of work.

Table 2.10   Complementary indicators of quality of life

Countries with the highest quality of life in descending order

---

Type of Indicator	Human Development Index	Human Suffering Index	New Social Indicator
Compliled by	*United Nations*	*Population Crisis Committee USA*	*Economic Planning Agency Japan*

Rank			
1	Japan	Denmark	Japan
2	Canada	Netherlands/Belgium	USA
3	Norway	Switzerland/Canada	UK
4	Switzerland	Norway/Austria	France
5	Sweden	USA	Germany
8	(USA 8th place)	(Japan jointly with Luxembourg 11th place)	(Sweden 6th place)
	(UK 10th place)	(UK 22nd place)	

A Canadian traversing vast empty spaces in the arctic circle, may also question this assessment of his well being.

(b) *The Human Suffering Index* (1992), compiled by the Population Crises Centre (Washington, USA), ranked 141 countries on the basis of ten indicators of well-being, some more readily quantifiable than others. They were:

> political freedom, civil rights, number of telephones per 1000 of population, secondary school enrolments, access to clean water, daily calorie supply, life expectancy, immunisation, per capita income and the rate of inflation.

The UK came 22nd. This may perhaps puzzle the British who were unlikely to have been aware that they suffered that much more compared with people in the Member States of the European Community and in just about every major industrialised country. Their misery was registered at twice the levels of the Finns. The Japanese were not doing all that well in the happiness stakes. *New Social Indicators* published by the Economic Agency of Japan (1990), would, however, have reassured them. Japan came out at the top. Categories covered by NSI were:

health, economic stability, family life environment, safety, regional and social activities, academic and cultural activities.

Nevertheless the *Japan Times* of April 14,1990 worried, commenting that 'the quality of family life in Japan is generally higher than in other industrial countries, but is showing signs of deterioration'

This comparison of countries' rankings tables on basis of social indicators highlights the problem of measuring and comparing quality of life. In formulating policies to improve welfare, governments are on surer ground relying on national income data as an indication of the standard of living.

Caution in the Analysis of National Income Data

Analysis and interpretation of national income data is difficult for some of the reasons already mentioned. The following are some of the other factors calling for caution to be exercised in drawing conclusions from the figures:

(a) *Revisions*. National income figures are estimates and as such are subject to revision. The margin of error can vary considerably from country to country but corrections tend to be relatively small. At any one time a large and sudden adjustment, as was the case with Italy, can have far-reaching consequences. In 1987 the government's statistical office increased its estimate of Italy's GDP by an additional 18 per cent. The result was that Italian GDP jumped overnight 10 per cent above the British and Italy moved to become the fourth largest market economy in the world after the USA, Japan and West Germany, and just ahead of France.

(b) *Hidden Economy*. One reason why adjustment of national income figures may be needed is the existence of a 'hidden' economy. This term describes a state of affairs where incomes from the sale of goods or services are concealed from the government, largely to evade taxation. Undeclared incomes result in the understatement of the national income of a country and this will give a misleading indication of its economic performance. The size of the 'hidden' economy and the extent to which official statistics need to be adjusted to take account of it, is arrived at on the basis of guesswork because of the very nature of the 'hidden' economy and this impairs the reliability of government national income data.

(c) *Exchange Rates*. The relative size of national incomes and changes over a period may be distorted by conversion from one national currency to another that is used as a common measure, e.g. the US dollar at a given point of time. Under a system of floating rates of exchange, the Deutschmark may be up against the dollar and the French franc one day but the next the exchange rates may move the other way. Thus, the size of the national incomes of the two countries will differ depending on the time of their conversion into dollars. To avoid problems associated with the exchange rates, other bases for comparison have been adopted.

The European Union uses the purchasing power standard (SPA) and the OECD compares on the basis of purchasing power parity (PPP). Both look at how much has to be paid in the different currencies to buy a given amount of the same goods. If in each of two countries one unit of their respective currencies is required, then the purchasing power of the currencies is the same or on par.

(d) *Industrial Structure.* Changes in the industrial structure of a country may result in miscalculation of the rate of growth of its Gross Domestic Product.

   (i) In rich industrialised countries economic growth has largely come from the services sector. In the USA this accounts for about three-quarters of the GDP, but its contribution to the GDP tends to be underestimated. This happens partly because of the problems involved in measuring a unit of output but also because official statistics do not take into account improvements in quality. The consequences of this can be illustrated by an example of a firm providing transport services. It installs a computer system which identifies the shortest routes for drivers for delivery from suppliers to customers. Both benefit from the shorter time that the goods are in transit. The firm also benefits as consumption of petrol and drivers' time are reduced, but output measured in terms of mileage covered is lower. In national accounts, this would be shown as a reduction in GDP even though, as a result of improved efficiency, there was an overall gain.

   (ii) Price-Index Problem. Expansion of fast growing sectors of the economy can also create problems in the measurement of changes in the GDP. Firms in these sectors, such as the computer industry, tend, over a period of time, to reduce the prices of their output so that it becomes relatively cheaper than that of the other sectors. At lower prices, the value of the output would appear to be lower, and the importance of the sector to the national economy smaller. This would be reflected in the weight that statisticians attach to the sectors in calculating figures for the base year of a GDP index. As the industrial structure of the economy changes, governments may need to shift the base year to reflect this. When, in the period between the old and the new base year, fast-growing industries cut their prices, growth of the GDP would appear to be lower and indicate deterioration in the performance of an economy. This may not reflect the fact that, looked at from another point of view, GDP would have improved, contributing to a higher standard of living of the people.

COMPARISON OF THE STANDARD OF LIVING

National income data can be used to measure changes in the standard of living in a country over a period of time and to compare it internationally. The term 'standard of living' can be variously interpreted. If it is defined as the material well-being of the people in a country, then standard of living is synonymous with *economic welfare* and can be measured in terms of goods and services consumed. It is assumed that a higher level of consumption is preferable to a lower level even though, for instance, industrial production may pollute and spoil an environment. In assessing the standard of living in a narrow economic sense we are not concerned with the quality of life, and compare economic welfare only on the basis of national income per head of population.

The standard of living will be influenced by a great variety of factors, and we have to confine ourselves to mentioning the more important ones, which are:

(a) *The size of the per capita national income.* By itself it is insufficient to indicate the standard of living accurately but it does show that if one country has a per capita income over 100 times that of another (Table 2.6) then we can reasonably assume that the standard of living of the people in Japan (US$37,561) and Nigeria (US$307) will differ greatly.

(b) *Economic conditions.* To draw conclusions on the standard of living, knowledge of the different economies is needed. Thus, in a tropical country such as Mali, people do not have to spend money to heat houses and the electricity industry does not need to generate power for this purpose. In a colder country, such as Sweden, heating in winter is essential. As people spend more on electricity, industry produces more and national income goes up – but this does not mean that people in Sweden are necessary better off than people in Mali on that account.

(c) *Inequality in the distribution of incomes.* We also have to keep in mind the distribution of incomes within the countries which are being compared, to which we have already referred (see p. 37).

(d) *The level of taxation and social security benefits.* The standard of living depends on the final disposable income of the people, i.e. earned and investment incomes less tax and social contributions plus state cash benefits. Thus changes in, and the level of, taxation and social security benefits have to be taken into account. An increase in the tax burden in a country, or a higher level of taxation in one as compared with another, unless it is offset by corresponding benefits, will reduce the standard of living.

(e) *Public goods.* Provision of certain goods and services by the state removes the need for people to secure them for themselves out of their disposable incomes. Therefore, the value of the public goods may represent, if the benefits exceed tax liability of individuals, an addition to personal resources. In the UK before the introduction of the National Health Service, individuals had to pay for their medical treatment out of their incomes. The health services are now financed out of taxation. Provision of public goods, however, does not necessarily result in an increase in the standard of living generally.

(f) *Social wage.* This term refers to the value of tangible and intangible benefits provided by the state. It can, therefore, be argued that social wages should be added to earned and investment incomes of the people for the purpose of measuring the standard of living. There is a problem, however, since social wages include payments that are not included in the calculation of the national income.

(g) *Price level.* What an income will buy depends on the price level (Tables 2.9). Thus changes in prices in a country over a period, or difference in price levels in different countries at a given time, have to be taken into account when comparing incomes, unless these are already shown at constant prices. An increase in income as a result of inflation, accompanied by a corresponding rise in price, does not improve economic welfare. The purchasing power of incomes is important, but what is an acceptable standard of provision of goods and services in a particular country has also to be taken into account. At an Ideal Home Exhibition in London in 1991, Intermediate Technology exhibited a two roomed house priced at £100 designed for developing countries and using local materials for construction that were plentiful, cheap and energy-efficient. The house, built of processed and compacted soil blocks, required the energy equivalent of half a tree, where, if it were to be built out of bricks, the equivalent of twenty trees would have had to be used.

These houses are now being introduced in Kenya where the urban population is increasing, rapidly creating severe housing shortages yet more affluent urban dwellers would hardly consider them as ideal homes. In the rich industrialised countries the price of 'little boxes' two-bedroom flats in a central location of a major city is not only sky-high but varies greatly from country to country, as a recently published (1993) comparison by *The Economist* shows. A would-be owner would have to pay (in US$) 1,290,000 in Tokyo; 850,000; in Milan; 360,000 in Paris; 350,000 in London; 180,000 in Madrid; and 175,000 in Sydney. The average property prices as a multiple of average income (annual GDP per worker) was nearly 10 in Tokyo, 8 in Milan, 5 in Paris, 4 in London, 4 in Sydney and 3 in Madrid in 1992. Such a high cost of housing in relation to peoples' incomes depresses their standard of living and a higher income in Tokyo may not provide the comfort that a lower one in Europe might ensure.

(h) *Availability of consumer goods.* An increase in income in real terms may not raise the standard of living if there are not enough consumer goods for people to spend their money on. This may happen when a country (i) launches an industrialisation programme and diverts resources to investment in heavy industries, (ii) exports a large proportion of its output and restricts imports, (iii) produces consumer goods of the type or quality that consumers do not want, as has happened in some centrally-planned economies; (iv) rations goods during a war; (v) experiences a lack of economic stability, leading to the breakdown of a national economic system as in some of the former USSR republics and a consequent disruption of the production and distribution of goods; or (vi) suffers from natural disasters, such as floods in Bangladesh or earthquakes as in Los Angeles with the consequent destruction of farms and factories and impairment of the productive capacity of the area.

(i) *Own produce.* Since national income figures do not include the value of goods and services for which no payment is made, the data underestimates the level of consumption and therefore the standard of living. Payment for entertainment or to watch a football match adds to the country's GDP but participation in the game just for the fun of it does not, though it may be more enjoyable.

In the short run a government can increase the standard of living of one group of people at the expense of another by transfer of income by means of taxation and benefits under a policy for redistribution of income and wealth. In the long run, the only way of increasing the standard of living of everybody is through economic growth that results in a higher national income, which will be discussed further in Chapter 22. But now we have to turn our attention to factors that determine the level of national income.

DETERMINATION OF NATIONAL INCOME AND THE MULTIPLIER

In theory the size of the national income depends on the level of economic activity of a country and the circular flow of money within it. This flow is increased by *injections* of money and reduced by *withdrawals* (leakages) which are:

Injections	*Withdrawals*
(a) government expenditure	taxation
(b) investment	savings
(c) exports	imports

We can express this by an equation:

$$Y = C + G + I + (X - M)$$

Where Y = income, C = consumption spending, G = government expenditure (net), I = investment, X = exports, and M = imports.

To illustrate how injections and withdrawals can affect the flow of money, let us consider international trade. When a country exports goods, foreign buyers pay for them and these payments increase its flow of money. If the country imports goods this will require a withdrawal of money and a transfer of currency abroad.

Consumption

Empirical evidence suggests that a relationship exists between consumption and income. We can thus say that *consumption is a function of income* and express it as $C = f(Y)$. From this we derive the *propensity to consume*. *Marginal propensity to consume* is a measure of the relationship between changes in consumption and changes in income. Thus, if out of each £1 that is added to our income we consume 75p worth and save 25p then our marginal propensity to consume is 3/4 and the marginal propensity to save 1/4.

The factors influencing the propensity to consume

Following the classification of John Maynard Keynes (1883–1946), factors which influence the propensity to consume include the following:

(a) *Objective factors.* The decision to consume and incur expenditure will be influenced by a variety of factors of which the following are some of the important ones: (i) *Price*, when income remains unchanged; (ii) *Taxation*, direct taxes change disposable income and indirect taxes change prices; (iii) *The rate of interest*, the extent to which changes in the rate of interest affect people's decision to spend or save is a controversial point amongst economists. The Keynesian argument is that people save for a specific reason such as the precautionary motive, to provide for an emergency. A change in the rate of interest would not, therefore, make much difference to their decision to save. The view of the economists of the monetary school is that it would, since an increase in the rate of interest makes savings more attractive by providing a higher return on accumulated capital. At the same time the increased cost of credit would discourage borrowing for the purpose of consumption.

(b) *Subjective factors.* Decisions on consumption and expenditure are also influenced by individual characteristics, temperament and preferences of persons and of firms. Some people and firms are prone to thrift; they save or plough back profits, while others are extravagant and go for ostentatious expenditure.

Various theories have been put forward to explain consumer behaviour and since they help us to understand how an economy functions, it may be useful to mention these, however briefly. Some of the better known ones are:

(i) *Permanent income hypothesis.* According to Professor Milton Friedman (b.1912) (winner of the Nobel Prize in Economics), how people will behave will depend on the nature of their income (M. Friedman, *A Theory of the Consumption Function*, Princeton: Princeton University, 1957). He distinguishes between permanent and transitory income. (a) *Permanent income* is that income which a person expects to receive regularly over a period of time.

This may be in the form of a wage or interest on investment. Permanent income gives rise to permanent consumption. Housing can be regarded as a service, therefore, a purchase of a house on mortgage can be looked as consumption of an asset with a life of twenty years. A building society will give a mortgage for house purchase for an amount fixed at, say three times a person's regular income. (b) *Transitory income* is uncertain and irregular. It may be a once-and-for-all payment such as a lump sum royalty to an author, who is then likely to spend it on transitory consumption that need not be repeated, such as a world cruise.

(ii) *The Life Cycle Theory*. Some economists (F. Modigliani, A. Ando, R. Brumberg) who subscribe to the life cycle theory, hold that consumption is influenced by the phases of peoples' lives and that it will change over the period of youth, middle and old age (F. Modigliani and R. Brumberg, 'Utility Analysis and the Consumption Function', in K.K. Kurihara (ed.), *Post Keynesian Economics* (1954), and 'The Life-cycle Hypothesis of Saving', *American Economic Review*, 1963).

(iii) *Demonstration effect theory*. Professor Duesenberry (b. 1918) explained consumption by reference to relative rather than to absolute income, when one person's expenditure is influenced by the life style of a neighbour, a desire to keep with the Joneses (James S. Duesenberry, *Income Savings and the Theory of Consumer Behaviour*, Cambridge, Mass., 1949).

Investment

The way people behave, their propensity to consume and the pattern of consumption have a bearing on investment. New investment (*gross fixed capital formation*) e.g. in plant and machinery, is the other important determinant of national income in addition to consumption.

The *multiplier effect* demonstrates how an increase in investment will generate incomes in excess of the original capital outlay. The theory of the multiplier was developed by Lord Kahn (b. 1905) in the 1930s and came to occupy an important place in Keynesian economics. To illustrate it let us suppose that a government decides to invest £1 million in a new road. Contractors will require additional equipment and will employ more workers. The contractors, suppliers and the workers will be paid for their services. They will receive income of which they will spend some and save the rest. Their consumption will create new demand for goods and services. The suppliers of these will, in turn, be paid. They too, will consume and save some of the additional earnings and the process will continue for a time. The impact of an investment on the economy can be calculated using a formula where K = the multiplier and S = marginal propensity to save, which shows how much of each additional £1 a person will save:

$$K = \frac{1}{\text{Propensity to save}} \quad K\frac{1}{\frac{1}{4}} = 4$$

Let us assume again that out of each addition £1 (100p), the people mentioned above spend 75p and save 25p. Their marginal propensity to consume is 3/4 and marginal propensity to save therefore is 1/4 and the multiplier will be 4. This means an injection of £1 million will increase the flow of money four times.

Empirical evidence suggests that the multiplier for the UK is 2. Generally speaking the higher the propensity to consume the higher will be multiplier but its size may be reduced by such factors as:

(a) *Leakages*, from the money flow e.g. taxation and imports.

(b) *Stocks*, which make it possible to meet increased demand for goods without increasing production. For example, investment in housing will set the multiplier in motion, builders will want to buy bricks, suppliers will employ additional men to make more of them and incomes will be generated. But, if there are large stocks of bricks, there will be no need to expand production to meet the increased demand.

(c) *Unused capacity*, that enables more goods to be produced without additional need for plant, machinery and labour since the existing factors of production are not fully utilised. In our example, a brickworks operating at, say, 60 per cent capacity can meet the new demand for bricks by increasing output to 100 per cent capacity without requiring additional resources.

The Equilibrium Level of National Income

An economy is in equilibrium when it is in balance. Figure 2.3 illustrates this, showing the relationship between onsumption, investment and income. The equilibrium point is where a line drawn at 45 degrees through the origin intersects the line for Consumption plus Investment. At any point to the left

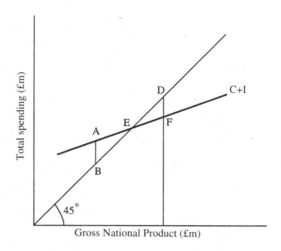

Figure 2.3   The equilibrium level of National Income
Note:
E = Equilibrium point, C = Consumption and I = Investment.

of the equilibrium point expenditure will exceed income, and there will be an inflationary gap, e.g. AB. At any point to the right, income will exceed expenditure and there will be a deflationary gap, e.g. FD.

It is the object of the government's fiscal and monetary policy to counteract inflation and deflation, reduce fluctuations in the level of national income and stabilise the economy.

FLUCTUATIONS IN NATIONAL INCOME

Fluctuations in the level of economic activity that result in changes in national income have been observed to occur in cycles, which create a repeating pattern (Figure 2.4).

A trade cycle (or business cycle) has four phases:

Phase	Characteristics
(1) Boom	High level of economic activity and employment
(2) Recession	Decline in economic activity and employment
(3) Slump	Low level of economic activity, unemployment
(4) Recovery	Increase in the level of economic activity, reduction in unemployment

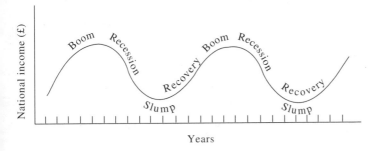

Figure 2.4   Trade cycles

Inflation can occur during any phase of a trade cycle, and may manifest itself during a period of full employment or high unemployment.

There is little doubt that trade cycles exist. The time gap between booms and slumps is subject to debate, but it is on the causes and remedies of the trade cycles that economists disagree most. The duration of the cycles is difficult to measure and the turning point is even more difficult to predict since neither peak nor trough can be accurately pinpointed. There appear to be two types of cycle – the long cycle and the intermediate cycle.

(a) *The Long or Kondratieff Cycle.* The problem in establishing the existence and the duration of long cycles is the lack of reliable statistical data going back sufficiently to reveal the presence or absence of a cyclical pattern. Professor N. Kondratieff, a Russian economist developed an analysis of comparable series for England, France and the USA which showed a remarkable similarity in the pattern of cyclical fluctuations and led him to conclude that there appeared to have been three great fifty year cycles since the 1780s up to the time when his analysis ended in the 1920s. The last great depression reached its lowest point in 1931. Fifty years later the leading industrial countries of the world again plunged into slump.

(b) *Intermediate cycle.* The evidence also suggested the existence of intermediate cycles of 7–9 years duration. (It is tempting to speculate whether the mention in the Bible of the seven lean and seven fat years did not in fact refer to an observed fact of cyclical fluctuations in the level of economic activity in ancient Egypt.) The present-day view among economists is that the length of the intermediate trade cycle is between eight and 10 years.

Not all countries plunge into recession and recover at the same time. Figures 2.5 (a) and (b) show the trends for Britain and Japan. In the early 1990s the economy of the UK ran into trouble ahead of some of the other major industrial countries, but began to improve sooner than, for example, France and Germany.

(a) Phases of the trade cycle in the UK

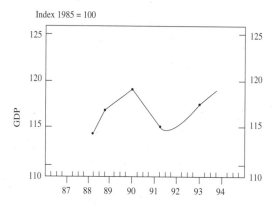

Index 1985 = 100

(b) Phases of the trade cycle in Japan
Source: *Economic Trends*, 490 (London: HMSO, 1994).

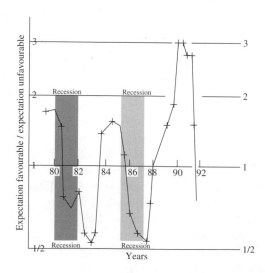

Ratio of manufacturing companies assessing conditions as favourable to the ratio of companies assessing conditions as unfavourable. Figure is based on Bank of Japan data.
Source: CSO figures.

Figure 2.5 (a) and (b)   Trade cycles: UK and Japan

TRADE CYCLE THEORIES

Various theories have been put forward to explain the cycles – some more colourful than others. Professor Stanley Jevons, a famous economist of the nineteenth century, established a correlation between sun spots and trade cycles. This is not as strange as it might seem at first sight, since any effect of sun spots on the weather will obviously affect the level of economic activity in an agricultural society.

Trade cycle theories can be grouped under the following headings: (i) Primarily external or exogenous theories; (ii) Primarily internal or endogenous theories. However, a clear distinction between the two groups is difficult to maintain in practice.

External theories show the trade cycles as a consequence of events, outside the economic system. The sun spot theory is an obvious example, explanations by reference to wars and revolutions are less so. A shot fired at Sarajevo was followed by the First World War, the Boston Tea Party by the American War of Independence, the storming of the Bastille by the French Revolution, but the real causes of wars and revolutions tend to be of an economic nature: the struggle for markets, resentment of taxation without representation, great inequality in the distribution of income and wealth.

Internal theories explain trade cycles by reference to a mechanism within the economic system that gives rise to self-generating cycles of boom, recession, slump and recovery. An example of a pure internal theory is that of the echo waves of replacement. Assume that during a period of boom a stock of machinery and of durable goods with a life-span of ten years has been acquired. Their replacement gives life to a boom. This process repeats itself, giving rise to ten year cycles. An objection to this line of argument is that in real life not all assets have the same life span and will therefore not all be replaced at the same time.

The Acceleration principle shows the effect of a change in income on investment, relating the change in gross national product to changes in capital spending on plant and machinery. If income goes up, more goods and services will be demanded and greater investment will be required to expand productive capacity. If income stops growing, then only the replacement of plant and machinery will be needed. Investment will drop and a recession may develop. The concept of the accelerator was given prominence by J.M. Clark at the beginning of this century and it now occupies an important place in trade cycle theories.

Figure 2.6 highlights some of the external and internal factors that have had a bearing on the level of activity in the European Community.

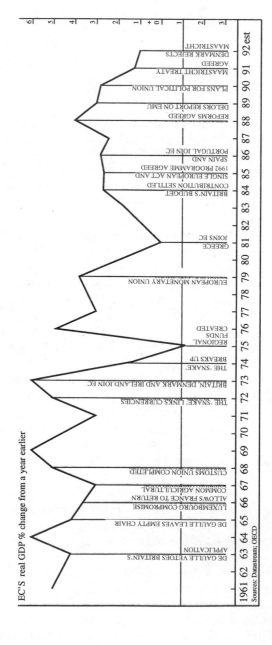

Figure 2.6   Internal and external factors in the European Community affecting trade cycles

Source: *The Economist* (London) (19 December 1992).

MULTIPLE CAUSES

Trade cycles cannot be attributed to a single cause. Most modern economists accept a combination of internal and external theories as an explanation of the trade cycle but differ in emphasis and on the policies needed to counteract the fluctuations. Keynesian economists favour fiscal policy to manage the economy. Professor Milton Friedman's study of the *Monetary History of the United States 1867–1960* (Princeton: Princeton University Press, 1963) showed a relationship between the supply of money, price level and economic activity. This relationship still appears to exist and not only in the USA, with the result that in recent years governments of major countries had been shifting emphasis from fiscal to monetary policy in an attempt to stabilise their economies and to secure economic growth.

FORECASTS

In anticipating turning points of trade cycles and in formulating fiscal and monetary policies governments need information not only on the past but also on the future trends in national income. The problem with forecasts is that they tend to go wrong. Commenting on this, *The Times* (January 1, 1994) pointed out that 'the year just past (1993) was marginally better for forecasters who use stars ... than for those who use statistics to gaze into the future'. *Old Moore's Almanac* has a team of six astrologers. Analogously, the British Treasury has a team of economists known as the 'Seven Wise Men', who come from the City, industry and academia and can forecast from different perspectives.

Table 2.11 shows not only the extent to which their forecasts of changes in the GDP differ from each other's and from the Treasury's own prediction, but also from the actual performance.

It is perhaps not just a question of the difficulties of computation. Anticipation of economic and political developments and government policies worldwide that can affect any one country's GDP is a risky business.

To make it easier forecasters tend to base their predictions on the assumption of no policy changes. But then forecasts in themselves can change peoples' behaviour and policies. Thus, for example, a forecast of a fall in GDP and an ensuing recession may prompt consumers to cut their spending and the government to reduce taxation.

To be more realistic, forecasters can produce forecasts based on alternative assumptions. In Figure 2.7 forecasts for GDP are given on the basis of

Table 2.11   Forecasts of economic variables

	GDP	Retail Prices (Q4)	Exports	Imports	PSBR*
Wise Men from:***		*(% change on year earlier)*			£bn
NIESR[#]	2.1	3.5	5.8	5.6	18.5
Lombard Street Research	2.0	2.0	5.4	5.0	17.0
London Business School	1.9	3.3	5.0	4.5	16.1
Goldman Sachs	2.2	3.5	4.9	5.7	21.0
Liverpool University	−0.1	3.1~	–	–	12.0
CBI	1.7	3.5	4.9	5.0	18.1
Treasury	2.3	4.0	6.0	7.5	28.0**
Outturn[##]	−1.0	3.3	3.3	6.5	37.0

Notes: Forecasts made in Oct./Nov. 1991 for Calendar Year 1992.
  *Public Sector borrowing requirement financial year ending 31 March 1993.
  [#]National Institute of Economic and Social Research.
    **March 1992 forecast [##]Outturn is estimate based on Autumn statement 1992.
  ***One of the wise men does not publish comparable forecasts.
Source: *The Economist* (12 February 1992) and HM Treasury, *Financial Statement and Budget Report 1994–95* (London: HMSO, 1993).

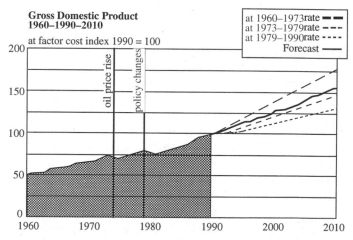

Source: CSO and Cambridge Econometrics

Figure 2.7   Forecasts of growth in the UK to 2010

The projections provide forecasts of likely growth between 1990 and 2010 both for gross domestic product as a whole and for its various component parts.
Source: Northcott, J., *Britain in 2010* (London: Policy Studies Institute, 1991).

different assumptions. It is for decision-makers to make the choice as to which is the most accurate.

Forecasts can be very wide of the mark. Nevertheless, governments and international organisations produce forecasts of national income to aid the formulation of economic, fiscal and monetary policies.

SUMMARY

1. The national income of a country is the aggregate of the income of its citizens. This total equals total expenditure and each in turn equals total output – after adjustments for foreign transactions and government transfer payments and taxation.
2. There are three ways of calculating national income: the income method, the expenditure method and output method.
3. The United Nations, the European Community and individual states have sought ways to reform national income accounting to account for environmental factors and the contribution to the gross domestic product of work done at home. Attempts have also been made to develop satellite accounts (social indicators) to complement national income accounts.
4. National income can be expressed at: (a) current market prices or (b) constant prices (in real terms) – that is those prevailing in the base year with which subsequent years are compared, to avoid distortions due to changes in the value of money (i.e. inflation). Per capita national income is the total national income divided by the number of people in a country. This gives national income per head of the population. Governments use national income data for the purpose of managing of national economies and as a measuring rod for international commitments. For this they need to undertake analysis of past trends and forecasts.
5. International comparison of economic welfare (the standard of living) on the basis of national income is difficult and can lead to misleading conclusions without a thorough knowledge of the economies that are being compared. Average income is not a reliable measure of the standard of living of an average person when incomes are unevenly distributed and there are some very poor and some very rich people in the country.
6. The size of the national income is determined by the level of economic activity. This depends on the proportion of the income that people consume and save.

7. The marginal propensity to consume and the marginal propensity to save are concepts that play an important part in Keynesian economic analysis. The greater the propensity to consume, the bigger will be the multiplier effect. The multiplier formula measures the impact on the money flow of an injection (investment). The multiplier effect of an increase in public expenditure is considered by Keynesian economists as an important factor in increasing the level of economic activity.

8. The expansionary effect will depend on people's behaviour with regard to consumption and savings. Their decisions will be influenced by objective and subjective factors. Explanations have also been put forward on the basis of other hypotheses: permanent income hypothesis, the life cycle theory and the demonstration effect.

9. Fluctuations in the national income are associated with the phase of trade cycles. There are four identifiable phases. Economic activity is at the highest during a boom and at the lowest in a slump.

10. Trade cycles are explained by a variety of theories which are classified as either internal or external theories. There is also a variety of views among economists as to what fiscal and monetary policy is appropriate to counteract cyclical fluctuations.

SUGGESTED FURTHER READING

J. Harvey, *Modern Economics* (London: Macmillan, 1993).

E. Lutz, *Towards Improved Accounting for the Environment* (Washington: World Bank, 1993).

M. Parkin, and D. Kind, *Economics* (Massachusetts: Addison-Wesley Publishing Co., 1993).

P.A. Samuelson, *Economics* (New York: McGraw-Hill, 1992).

Government and Official Publications (annual):

Eurostat, *Basic Statistics of the Community* (Luxembourg).

OECD Economics Outlook.

UK Central Statistical Office, *United Kingdom National Accounts* (London: HMSO).

UN Statistical Yearbook (New York).

UN Yearbook of National Accounts Statistics (New York).

EXERCISES

1. Explain what is meant by the national income and how it differs from the gross national product. Why is the difference of significance?
2. List what you regard as the five most important reasons for calculating the national income of a country and give reasons for your choice.
3. Consider arguments for and against putting of monetary value on damage to the environment, and incorporating the figures in national income estimates.
4. Outline the three methods of calculating national income and consider the problems involved.
5. Which method of calculating national income would you recommend to a government of a developing country if you were its economic adviser?
6. Why are international comparisons of national income data difficult and, if not treated with care, liable to lead to misleading conclusions?
7. Explain why an increase in the national income may not result in an increase in the standard of living of the inhabitants of a country.
8. Consider how changes in economic welfare can be measured and compared over a period time and internationally, and the usefulness of social indicators.
9. Discuss the significance of social accounting as a basis for a government's policies on expenditure and taxation.
10. Consider factors that will influence fluctuations in the level of national income and their consequences.

3 Allocation of Resources and Provision of Public Goods

OPTIMUM ALLOCATION

Resources can be defined in different ways. They can be considered as the available factors of production: labour, land (including mineral wealth and fisheries), capital and enterprise. Resources can be tangible, such as coal, or intangible, such as the skill of an engineer, and some may have to be imported if they do not exist or are not obtainable in sufficient quantity within the country. Resources can also be looked at as the funds available for consumption and investment – from accumulated wealth or from current economic activity – shown by the national income data (as discussed in Chapter 2), while input–output analysis indicates the resources that will be needed to produce different goods and services.

A government's decision on the allocation of resources between the private and public sectors of the economy and the pattern of distribution within them will be influenced by political, social and economic considerations. A government can leave the allocation to the market forces or, if this is considered to be undesirable – as for example at a time of war – it can allocate resources directly by such means as rationing, priority schemes and the provision of funds to specific users.

The *optimum* allocation of resources will maximise the economic welfare of the people of a country and, as a goal of governments policy, this will require: (a) the measurement of costs and benefits that result from the use of resources (however, these are not easily quantifiable – see p. 406); and (b) the establishment of principles of welfare, although no one single principle is generally accepted.

Pareto Optimality

In modern welfare analysis we still use a concept developed by Professor Vilfredo Pareto (1848–1923) and called 'the Pareto improvement'. It applies to a change in economic organisation that results in everyone becoming better off. Pareto optimality is reached when the allocation of resources is at an optimum level, such that no further increase in the economic welfare of one person is possible without a decrease in that of another (detailed in Pareto's *Manual of Political Economy*). The problem of how to quantify and compare welfare, however, now has to be tackled.

UTILITARIAN APPROACH TO ECONOMIC WELFARE

The theory of marginal utility seeks to provide a basis for the measurement of satisfaction (utility) derived from consumption of one additional (marginal) unit of a good or service. According to the theory, a person will maximise their satisfaction by acquiring goods or services up to the point where the ratio of price to the utility of the additional unit will be the same for all items. Thus, in the example (Table 3.1), this will be when the ratio is 2 (50 : 100, 40 : 80, 20 : 40). Assuming that the person has £3, he will buy 2 units of good *X*, 3 units of good *Y* and 4 units of good *Z* (2 units at 50p, 3 units at 40p and 4 units at 20p). This combination will give the highest total utility. In addition, a change in the pattern of expenditure would reduce satisfaction, because if the person were to buy one less unit of *X* – in order to buy, say, one more unit of *Y* – they would experience a net loss in utility. The application of this *equi-marginal utility principle* will result in the optimum allocation of a person's resources. The principle can also be applied to a society – in that case requiring the aggregation of satisfaction of all its members. In practice neither an individual's nor a society's satisfaction can be precisely or objectively measured and consumers of public goods and services may not have to pay a price directly. The principle of maximising utility has, however, found expression in cost–benefit analysis, which attempts to put monetary value on tangible and intangible benefits and costs resulting from the use of resources (see p. 406).

Table 3.1   Equi-marginal returns

Unit	Good X (50p per unit)		Good Y (40p per unit)		Good Z (20p per unit)	
	Marginal utility	ratio	Marginal utility	ratio	Marginal utility	ratio
1	125	$2^1/_2$	110	$2^3/_4$	80	4
2	100	2	90	$2^1/_4$	70	$3^1/_2$
3	90	1 4/5	80	2	60	3
4	80	1 3/5	70	1	40	2

MARKET ALLOCATION OF RESOURCES AND GOVERNMENT INTERVENTION

Market Mechanism

In a market economy the demand for goods and services determines the allocation of the resources required to produce them. The satisfaction that people expect to derive from consumption will be reflected in the value that they put on the goods and services and is expressed by the prices that they are prepared to pay to secure a supply. Suppliers' allocation of resources to production will depend on such factors as the demand for the final product, the price of different inputs and technological considerations.

In a perfect market, resources used in the production of goods and services would be allocated efficiently. In the real world, however, markets are imperfect. Monopolies and various pressure groups may distort the demand for and supply of goods and services. A monopolist may charge an excessive price that consumers cannot afford to pay, or restrict production. Some goods and services that a society needs will not be produced by the private sector as there is no market for them, e.g. national defence, or because they cannot be sold at an economic price.

Government Intervention

Governments influence the allocation of resources in an economy by direct control: e.g. legislation and setting up of public bodies such as the Monopolies Commission in the UK and regulatory authorities in the European Union, or indirectly by taxation and expenditure. They may consider such intervention to be necessary to counteract market imperfections, to secure the supply of public goods at a certain level or to ensure what they regard as fair distribution of resources between private and public sectors.

OPPORTUNITY COST IN THE PUBLIC AND PRIVATE SECTORS

Both the private and public sectors have opportunities to use resources for various purposes, but not all resources are readily transferable from one use to another. The supply of some can be increased in the long run, e.g. capital. Other resources, e.g. land, are in inelastic supply which means that however much demand for them rises and their prices increase, the total supply will remain unchanged. Suppose there is an increase in the demand for council houses, all that can be done in such circumstances is to transfer land from one use, say agriculture, to another use as sites for local authority housing. Thus, the opportunity cost of a resource (land) used for the purpose of housebuilding is its *foregone use for another purpose* such as growing crops. The opportunity cost of resources in the public sector is their foregone use in the private sector. It is not measured in terms of money but in terms of sacrifice of an opportunity to use the resources for one purpose to make them available for another. Opportunity cost requires a choice by the decision-maker.

Social Choice

A society has a choice between producing market goods and public goods.

(a) *Market goods* are those that have a price. This may be a full economic price or a subsidised one. The purchaser of market goods acquires ownership, exclusive use and the right to consume, sell and dispose. Both the private and public sectors supply market goods.

(b) *Public goods*, sometimes referred to as social goods, are those that are provided by the State and can be variously defined. Insofar as there is no direct charge for consumption they are sometimes called 'free goods', but this is a misnomer. All goods and services have to be paid for in one way or another either out of income or temporarily through borrowing. Public goods are paid for out of taxation, but the person who receives the benefit may not be the same person that pays the taxes. In this sense, for some consumers, public goods are free. Pure public goods are collective goods and services that are provided for the people as a group and confer benefits collectively. Such goods are characterised by *non-exclusiveness*. No one person can be debarred from benefitting and nobody can opt out from consumption of a collective good or service such as national defence.

In a discussion of public expenditure, it is useful to extend the definition of public goods to include individual goods and services that are provided by the State for the exclusive consumption and use of a specific person who qualifies for them by fulfilling certain requirements. A child of school age will be provided with a place at a school, a sick person is entitled to a bed under the National Health Service scheme.

Economists also classify certain public goods as *merit goods*. The idea of merit goods is derived from what may be regarded as the paternalistic role of the State. The underlying assumptions are that: it is for the State to decide which goods are meritorious, to advise us on their desirability and in certain circumstances to force us to avail ourselves of them, whatever our views on the subject. Not all of us who qualify for such public goods may need them or want them. Free school meals are usually classified as *merit goods*. Provision of compulsory education is another example. In this case the benefit is not only to the child who is being educated willingly or reluctantly, but also indirectly to the community at large.

Using the wider definition, public goods can be provided on a variety of basis such as:

		Examples of different types of goods or services in the UK
(i)	*Universal entitlement* – everybody in the country can use them.	motorways
(ii)	*Selective entitlement* – only certain persons in specified circumstances are eligible.	university education
(iii)	*Free to all*, irrespective of a person's income.	police protection
(iv)	*Means-tested* – when entitlement to benefit depends on the individual's or household's income.	housing

The basis of provision varies from country to country and can change over a period of time. For example, in some Member States of the European Union there are charges for the use of motorways and in the UK the introduction of a toll system is under consideration.

Means-testing

The provision of certain public goods and services, and of the various State cash benefits, is often subject to a means test. This practice has been widely criticised on the grounds that it is an invasion of privacy, can be humiliating to applicants and may deter some people who are entitled from applying. Governments, irrespective of their political persuasion, have applied the principle and defended it by arguing that when resources are scarce they should be used to provide for those most in need.

'Free Riders'

Individuals or groups of people who can afford, and would be prepared, to contribute towards financing the provision of some public goods, but do not do so, are described as 'free-riders', since they benefit on the basis of collective consumption without a cost to themselves. In a democratic society, people can express their preference for market goods by willingness to pay the price and for public goods by the willingness to pay taxes to finance a particular level of spending by the State. Free-riders avoid paying.

SUMMARY

1. The resources of a country are both tangible and intangible. Some resources have to be imported from abroad.
2. Optimum allocation of resources (Pareto optimality) will maximise economic welfare.
3. Economic welfare cannot be measured precisely.
4. The approach to the allocation of resources on the basis of marginal utility theory is now considered to be of little practical value.
5. The market allocation of resources is determined by the demand for and supply of resources.
6. The imperfections of the market may lead a government to intervene in the allocation of resources.
7. Governments can allocate resources by rationing, by provision of funds for their purchase by others, or by direct expenditure on their own account.
8. In a mixed economy resources will be allocated to both the private and the public sector.
9. The opportunity cost of allocating resources to one sector if their foregone use in another.
10. The public sector provides both market goods (output of nationalised industries) and public goods. Merit goods are a type of public goods. All 'free' goods have to be paid for by somebody. The cost of their provision is financed out of taxation. There are economic and political restraints as to how much a government can provide in the way of public goods.

SUGGESTED FURTHER READING

A. Asimakopulos, *Economic Theory, Welfare and the State* (London: Macmillan, 1990).

C.V. Brown and P.M. Jackson, *Public Sector Economics* (Oxford: Basil Blackwell, 1992).

J. Craven, *Social Choice* (Cambridge: Cambridge University Press, 1991).

Hans van del Doel and Ben van Velthoven, *Democracy and Welfare Economics* (Cambridge: Cambridge University Press, 1993).

F.E. Foldvary, *Public Goods and Private Communities* (Cheltenham: Edward Elgar, 1994).

C. Henry, *Microeconomics for Public Policy* (Oxford: Clarendon University Press for the Centre National de la Recherche Scientifique, 1991).

P.R. Jones and J.G. Cullis, *Public Finance and Public Choice* (New York: McGraw-Hill, 1992).

A. Peacock, *Public Choice Analysis in Historical Perspective* (Cambridge: Cambridge University Press, 1991).

EXERCISES

1. Discuss factors that need to be taken into account in an attempt to achieve the optimum allocation of resources.
2. Is Pareto optimality a meaningful concept? Give reasons for your answer.
3. How can economic welfare be maximised?
4. What useful purposes can be served by drawing a distinction between market goods and public goods?
5. Discuss the arguments for and against the application of a means test to the provision of public goods.
6. In what sense can public goods be regarded as free goods?
7. Consider the basis on which the state should provide for the needs of the people.
8. Discuss the relevance of the marginal utility theory to decisions on the allocation of resources.
9. How can social choice be expressed under different economic systems?
10. Define opportunity cost and explain how it can be measured. Consider why a government may require information on it.

Part 2

Public Finance: Expenditure

4 Public Expenditure

PUBLIC FINANCE

The subject-matter of public finance is: (i) public expenditure on provision of goods, services and state benefits; (ii) government revenue, the chief source of which is taxation; (iii) public borrowing and the national debt. William Ewart Gladstone (1809–98), one of Britain's great Chancellors of the Exchequer, declared that 'expenditure depends on policy'. It also depends on resources, which include tax revenue and the proceeds of borrowing.

Public finance reflects historical events and gives rise to actions that change the course of history. In seventeenth-century England, King Charles I quarrelled with Parliament over revenues to finance his expenditure. The King lost and was beheaded after the country was plunged into a civil war. King Louis XVI of France (1754–1793) met with a similar end. The French Revolution, which resulted in the overthrow of the monarchy, was fuelled by resentment of an unjust system of taxation. King George III lost some of the British colonies, partly because his American subjects objected to taxation without representation in general and to changes in import taxes on tea in particular. The failure of fiscal and monetary policies to contain inflation in Germany, when between July and November 1923 prices rose over 7 million times, brought the collapse of the economy, creating instability and resentment which paved the way for Hitler's rise to power.

From this oversimplified view of history, of causes and effects, a message does, however, emerge. Those who ignore the issues of public finance do so at their peril. In the following chapters we shall pay due attention to public finance in theory and in practice and we will discuss fiscal policy, which embodies the government's decisions on the size, composition and timing of public expenditure and revenue to achieve economic social and political aims.

FUNCTIONS OF THE STATE

Public expenditure arises out of the functions of the state that have evolved to reflect the prevailing political, economic and social views of a society. However simple or complex the form of government, there are some basic functions that are common to all. What has changed over time is the range of the functions and the scale of operations by the state.

The basic need of any community is and has been for defence from external aggression and for internal administration of law and order. Thus, those in authority, whether village elders, feudal lords, monarchs or elected governments become responsible for the protection of the members of the society. This entailed expenditure on the military and judiciary, that had to be financed by assorted levies from which a system of public finance evolved.

Gradually, to these basic functions of the state, others were added that aimed at improving the welfare of the society. As far back as 1776, Adam Smith wrote that the sovereign had the duty of '... erecting and maintaining those public institutions and works which, though of the highest degree advantageous to a great society, could never repay the expense to any individuals such as works for facilitating the commerce of the society and for the promoting the instruction of the people'. This required public expenditure on what we would call today economic and social objectives, though Adam Smith did not believe that the government should provide for the people what they could obtain for themselves. He did, however, allow for the fact that some of the needs could not be met by individuals and that in such circumstances public expenditure was justified.

Functions of present-day governments can be grouped under a variety of headings, a number of them fall into more than one category.

Functions	*Type of expenditure*
Basic or essential functions:	Expenditure on:
defence	military programmes
Administration of law and order	police, law courts
certain basic social services	primary, school education
Optional functions improve economic welfare but are not essential. As society develops they may come to be regarded as essential	various social services
Legal commitment, functions arising out of legislation that requires the government to provide certain goods and services and makes use compulsory	schooling
Contractual obligations, functions arise out of an agreement between	pensions

Functions	*Type of expenditure*
the State and groups of people e.g. National Insurance scheme, when in return for specific contributions the government offers specific benefits	
Membership of international organisations Functions arise out of the membership, e.g. European Community, UN	European Community Budget contributions, aid to developing countries
Policy functions, economic objectives	
(a) achieve economic growth	investment grants to industry
(b) stabilise the economy	public works
(c) improve the standard of living	housing
Policy functions, political and social objectives e.g.	
(a) extension of the public sector	nationalisation
(b) redistribution of income and wealth	benefits for people in lower income range
(c) protection of the environment could also be regard as an economic objective	pollution control

This classification serves a useful purpose in indicating to the government areas in which expenditure programmes can be adjusted. It also helps in understanding the basis on which fiscal policy is formulated.

Compatible Functions

Provision of goods and services under the heading of one function may reinforce a policy under another. Thus expenditure to counteract unemployment has both economic and social objectives.

Conflicting Functions

Not all government aims are compatible. Redistribution of income, in so far as it reduces investment in industry, can conflict with a policy to foster economic growth since an increase in investment is considered to play an important part in it.

In some countries a different tier of government may be responsible for a particular function or it may be shared. Countries with Federal governments such as USA, Germany, India and Nigeria may divide the various functions between: (a) federal government; (b) state government, and (c) local government. Countries with a two-tier government such as the UK divide functions between central government and local authorities. The split and range of functions will be influenced by the political and economic system and the level of economic development.

DEFINITION OF PUBLIC EXPENDITURE

Public expenditure can be defined in different ways as: (i) the expenditure of central and local government; (ii) the combined government expenditure plus disbursements out of the National Insurance (social security) Fund; or (iii) the total government expenditure as in (ii) plus expenditure of the public corporations.

The size of the public expenditure will depend on the definition adopted and will differ accordingly. This can give rise to confusion when comparisons are made over a period of time or internationally. Thus, if public expenditure is defined in terms of what the central government and local authorities spend, it will appear smaller than when expenditure by public corporations is also included.

The basis on which public expenditure once defined is analysed, does not, however, affect the total figure which represents the absorption of resources by the public sector. The analysis can be undertaken on the following basis:

(i) *Spending authority*: central government, local authorities, public corporations.
(ii) *Economic category*: current expenditure account (expenditure on goods, services, transfer payments), capital account (investment).
(iii) *Programme*: defence, agriculture, housing.

The total figure for public expenditure, whichever basis is used, should be the same and represents the absorption of resources by the public sector.

THEORIES OF PUBLIC EXPENDITURE

The Doctrine of Laissez-faire

Some of the philosophers and classical economists of the eighteenth century subscribed to the doctrine of *laissez-faire* which was based on the principle of minimum state intervention in the workings of the economy. 'Governments are always and without exception the greatest spendthrifts of society' because, argued Adam Smith, 'they spend other people's money'. Adam Smith believed that individual people acting in self-interest will promote public good under the guidance of the 'invisible hand'. The supporters of *laissez-faire* therefore maintained that people should be left unhindered to pursue their best interests and in the process they would benefit the society. The implication of this was a low level of public expenditure and taxation but the need for some increase in public expenditure was conceded. Social injustice which was intensified by the Industrial Revolution undermined the belief in the doctrine of state non-intervention.

Individual Choice Theory

Emphasis in theoretical discussion of public finance shifted to the consideration of the basis on which collective decisions in the public sector should be made. Writers, such as Ferrara (1850), advocated individual choice as the basis of social choice and of collective decision making. The problem of this approach to government intervention and public expenditure was the aggregation of individual preferences and of relating them to policies.

The Authoritarian Conception or the Organic Theory

The organic theory avoided this difficulty, since it was based on the assumption that the decisions were made by a ruling group.

Optimum Level of Public Expenditure Theory

Having accepted the need for some public expenditure, economists turned their attention to the question of what was its desirable level. As far back as the turn of the nineteenth century Emil Sax attempted to provide an answer by the application of the marginal utility theory to public finance. The theory is chiefly associated with W. Stanley Jevons (1835–82), who was an English economist, and with Karl Menger, an Austrian. However, Leon Walras in France and Herman Gossen in Germany also formulated it independently. The theory postulates that, as a person's consumption increases, each additional (marginal) unit of a good consumed gives lower satisfaction (utility) than the one before. Thus the consumer experiences diminishing marginal utility.

The concept can also be applied to money. The more money a person has, the less importance he or she will attach to each additional £1. Thus to somebody who has only £10 per week £1 may make all the difference between being able to buy such necessities as food or going hungry. To a person with £100 a week £1 will make little difference. With an income of £1,000 a week having £1 more or less will hardly be noticeable. Nevertheless, a person's economic welfare will be higher, the greater the number of £1 coins they have – even if the marginal increase is less and less.

The theory is based on the relationship between the satisfaction derived from the consumption of goods and services provided by that state, and the sacrifice involved in paying taxes to finance public expenditure. To calculate this a way would have to be found of measuring all individual satisfactions and sacrifices and also of *aggregating* them.

No objective and precise way of doing this has been found and the theory is more of academic interest than of practical value to any Chancellor of the Exchequer in the formulation of fiscal policy. As Professor A.T. Peacock (b. 1922), a leading contemporary authority on public finance, has pointed out, economists are becoming increasingly sceptical of the value of welfare economics for the study of actual economies and of the associated theories of public expenditure.

The marginal utility theory does, however, shed some light on how people behave. We may not go around calculating our diminishing marginal utility of each public good we consume. Nevertheless, all of us are aware that there is some point at which the burden of taxation appears greater than the various state benefits are worth to us. We may not be able to put a figure on that point and it may not be the same for all the people, but we may prefer to go without some public goods and services rather than pay more in taxation to finance the increase in public expenditure.

The *optimum level* of public expenditure can be defined as the point at which the benefit to all individuals from additional expenditure is equal to the additional sacrifice by them involved in paying more tax (see p. 60). There is no agreement, in theory or practice, on the optimum size of public expenditure. What will be regarded as a desirable level will be influenced by political, social and economic considerations. It will vary from society to society, and change over time.

A discussion of the optimum level of public expenditure does, however, have more relevance to a government's decision when it has a choice whether to spend or not. At a time of war or economic crisis it may have no option but to increase public expenditure.

The ability of a government to spend in a democratic society depends in the long run on the following factors:

(i) national resources (national income),
(ii) the level of taxation required to finance spending,
(iii) the acceptability of the public expenditure programmes to the electorate.

The Ballot Box Theory

In a democratic society people have the opportunity to decide how much they wish to provide for themselves and how much they want the state to provide for them. Their individual preferences can be expressed by putting a vote in the ballot box at the next election for a political party whose manifesto most closely reflects their views. It is the majority vote, which is the aggregate of individual preferences, that gives the government the mandate to carry out its policies. The problem however is that at a general election people vote on a number of issues and for a manifesto 'package' containing various proposals. Consequently, the electors have no opportunity to express their view on a particular issue or measure. Not all of the proposals in a manifesto may be equally acceptable to them. Examples of instances where a choice was possible are few. The following is a case in point.

A referendum in California gave the state's residents an opportunity to vote on one specific point – the level of taxation to finance local public expenditure. Proposition 13 proposing to cut taxes and halt the growth of public expenditure was put before them, and they overwhelmingly voted for it in 1978. This was followed in 1979 by a proposition to put a ceiling on public expenditure. The result of the second referendum was three to one in favour of the proposal. But, in 1980, a third attempt to cut income tax was rejected. Californians had decided this would have required a reduction in public expenditure to below an acceptable level.

In the UK, resort to referenda is rare. In between elections, various pressure groups such as the Confederation of British Industry can seek to influence government's expenditure programmes by persuasion, protest or the use of the power to strike by the trade unions.

The Positive Theory of Government Expenditure

This theory has been advanced by present-day writers such as A. Downs, J.M. Buchanan (winner of the Nobel Prize for Economics in 1986) and G. Tullock. It could perhaps be described as the 'clinging to power' theory, since it is based on the assumption that in a democratic society governments seek to maximise their life span, while voters seek to maximise the benefits they receive from the government. An increase in public expenditure is popular with voters – if they do not have to pay the taxes to finance it.

OBSERVATIONS ON THE GROWTH OF PUBLIC EXPENDITURE

Wagner's Law

Adolf Wagner (a German economist in the nineteenth century) analysed trends in the growth of public expenditure and in the size of the public sector in major countries of the world. His observations led to what is now called *Wagner's Law* or the *Law of Rising Public Expenditure*. (He preferred to call it an observation.) It postulates that (a) the extension of the functions of the state leads to an increase in public expenditure on administration and regulation of the economy; (b) an increase in national income of a country will bring about a growth in public expenditure on such programmes as education, health and welfare; and (c) the rise in public expenditure will be more than proportional to the increase in the national income and will thus result in a relative expansion of the public sector. The cause and effect can therefore be stated as follows: social progress leads to increased state activity, this is turn gives rise to greater public expenditure which results in a bigger public sector. Wagner's Law demonstrated a tendency but not the inevitability of continuous growth of public expenditure.

Displacement Effect

Growth of public expenditure during a war is, however, inevitable. Analysis of the time pattern of public expenditure by Professor A.T. Peacock and J. Wiseman has established the Displacement Effect. They found that public expenditure increases during a war or a period of social crisis. When the war ends or the crisis is resolved, public expenditure falls, but not to the original level at the start of the emergency, with the result that growth in public expenditure occurs in stages.

TRENDS IN PUBLIC EXPENDITURE: CURRENT AND CONSTANT PRICES

The trends in public expenditure can appear very different depending on the definition of public expenditure used and the prices at which it is expressed. Prices can be as follows:

(i) *Current prices*. They are those that prevail at the time under consideration and represent the actual amount that has to be paid for goods and services.

(ii) *Constant prices*. They are the prices that were current at a specified period (e.g. a certain year, a day or the date of a price survey) which is then used as the base for comparison with other periods (see Appendix 3, p. 475). In this way changes in consumption in volume terms (actual quantities of goods and services) can be shown and changes in the figures indicate real improvement or deterioration. The effect of changes in the value of money is removed so that the expenditure figures are not calculated in terms of inflationary prices. Expenditure at constant prices (or survey prices) does not, however, show what will have to be paid or had been paid in years other than the base year. What is shown is what public expenditure on the goods and services would have been if the purchasing power of money had remained constant. Government expenditure programmes such as the British Government's Expenditure Plans had been shown at 'survey figures'. When payments were eventually made the amounts tended to exceed planned totals that had been calculated at constant prices. Since 1982, expenditure plans have been expressed in terms of the cash needed to pay for them.

Choice of the base year for comparison can also make a great deal of difference to the appearance of a trend. The need is to select a year that is as normal as possible, that is one in which nothing very exceptional has happened. War years or years of economic crisis such as: 1914–1918 (the First World War); 1939–45 (the Second World War); 1932 (the worst year of the Great Depression) or 1973 (the Oil Crisis), should be avoided as they distort the trend by selecting one of the more abnormal years for comparison. It is possible to give a distorted impression when using the same figures. In the study of a trend of public expenditure it is therefore preferable to look at data for as many years as possible.

Problems in using 'constant prices' and in choosing a base year can make governments' control of expenditure more difficult.

Caution in the Interpretation of Data

Figures for government expenditure on various programmes as an indication of the level of provision of goods and services should also be treated with caution. Particularly when international comparisons are made,

Table 4.1   Public expenditure on health

Health expenditure on health per head (US dollars)		Hospital, length of stay days (average)	
UK	909	UK	18.6
Sweden	1 421	Sweden	22.7

Note: Date relate to 1990, the latest figures available.
Source: 'European Marketing Data and Statistics', *Euromonitor* (London, 1994).

a great deal of additional information is required before meaningful conclusions can be drawn.

We can illustrate this point by reference to expenditure on health services and on defence.

The figures in Table 4.1 could be taken to imply that people in the UK are worse off than the Swedes in so far as the health services are concerned. But whether that is the case or not cannot be ascertained before answering such questions as:

(a) Are people in the UK healthier? If they are, then they would not need to spend as much on medical care.
(b) Is lower spending the result of greater efficiency in provision of services or evidence of less provision?
(c) Do lower figures for expenditure reflect lower prices in the UK?
(d) Do British doctors prefer to treat people at home rather than in hospital?
(e) Do British people rely more on private medical health service for which they are prepared to pay? Private medicine might reduce the demand for a national health service.

The use of percentages to show the level of public expenditure, e.g. on defence, also presents difficulties and may give a misleading indication of the extent of provision of goods and services (see Table 4.2).

Germany could buy twelve times as much in armaments as Denmark for approximately the same percentage of gross national product. The UK devotes a higher percentage of her GNP to defence but, because Germany is a richer country (her GNP per capita is higher than that of the UK), a lower percentage will be needed to buy the same number of tanks or guns.

Table 4.2 Public expenditure on defence

	Expenditure on defence as percentage of GDP	US$ million
Germany*	1.7	31 030
Demark	1.8	2 590
Finland	1.8	1 980
Italy	3.6	43 790
Belgium	3.8	7 660
Hungary	3.8	1 160
UK	8.1	84 810

Notes: Figures represent the latest available data (1993–4). For the UK this
figure is higher than the British government's own figures.
*Figure for what was West Germany.
Source: 'European Marketing Data and Statistics', *Euromonitor* (London, 1994).

EMPIRICAL EVIDENCE ON THE INTERNATIONAL GROWTH OF PUBLIC EXPENDITURE

The growth of public expenditure observed by Wagner in the nineteenth century has continued in the twentieth century (see p. 82). A study of public expenditure by the Organisation for Economic Co-operation and Development (1978) has shown that, over a period of twenty years, public expenditure in all the major countries grew at a faster rate than the national product, with the result that the public sector of the economies expanded. In the mid-1950s, public expenditure was on average less than 30 per cent of the countries' GNP; by the mid-1970s it was over 40 per cent for many and 50 per cent for some. On the basis of the definition used for the comparative study, the figure for the UK was 45 per cent.

Pattern of Growth

No typical pattern of growth in public expenditure emerges from the analysis. In some of those countries that had a particularly sharp increase this was the result of above average expenditure on welfare – in others, the impetus came from education.

Dispersion

There also did not appear to be a tendency for countries with low expenditure on some of the social welfare programmes and for countries with high expenditure to converge to some common norm. On the contrary, the dispersion not only continued – it also increased.

Trend

Faced with a rising trend in public expenditure governments in Europe sought to retrench and reduce the public sector's share of GNP. In the 1980s some governments, for a time, succeeded in achieving this objective, but in the 1990s the upward trend has resumed.

REASONS FOR THE GROWTH OF PUBLIC EXPENDITURE

Various factors – political, social and economic – have contributed to the growth of public expenditure and the growth of the public sector. The following are some of the major factors:

(a) *The abandonment of the* laissez-faire *doctrine.* As the climate of public opinion changed new theories began to emerge and old ones were abandoned; among the latter was the doctrine of *laissez-faire*. The self-correcting mechanism of an economic system that the classical economists believed in appeared to have failed. Unemployment, which to them was a theoretical impossibility, not only proved possible, but became a major international problem. During the Great Depression of the 1930s over 20 per cent of the insured population of the UK was unemployed. The theory of governmental non-intervention could no longer command support. There was a pressure of public opinion on governments to provide relief for the unemployed and to create jobs. In order to do so, public expenditure was increased.

(b) *The advent of Keynesian economics.* One book, *The General Theory of Employment, Interest and Money* (1936), by John Maynard (later Lord) Keynes, had a profound and pervasive influence on economists and on governments for many generations. His arguments that the government not only could but should use public expenditure as a tool of economic policy to manage a national economy so as to counteract unemployment, found ready acceptance in a world that had not yet recovered from the Great Depression. The Keynesian prescription was to inject money into the economic system. If the people were not spending, then it was up to a government to do so.

This required an expansive fiscal policy, in which a government would deliberately aim at a Budget deficit by spending more money than it raised in taxation. To cover the difference (deficit) the government would borrow. The 'Multiplier' effect (see p. 48) of public expenditure would counteract unemployment. Such fiscal policy was attractive to the governments and popular with the public. By increasing public expenditure, a government was seen to be doing something about unemployment whilst the public were getting something (additional state benefits) for nothing, as it appeared, since there was no increase in taxation. Government therefore had an incentive to increase public expenditure and they did. What is more the policy appeared to work, unemployment began to fall. But to what extent the increase in economic activity can be attributed to governments' conversion to Keynesian economics, and to what extent it was the result of rearmament on which major countries embarked at the time when the General Theory was published, is debatable. Increased expenditure on defence was a response to the threat of war. As such it was a political measure but it did inject money into the economy and therefore had economic consequences.

(c) *Wars and social crises*, such as severe and prolonged unemployment had resulted in the growth of public expenditure. The effect of such events on the British government spending have been analysed by Professors A.T. Peacock and J. Wiseman. The results demonstrated the 'displacement effect' (see p. 78).

(d) *Increase in the range of economic activities by the state.* Emergence of political philosophies, social attitudes and economic theories that advocated extension of the activities of the states prepared the way for goverments to expand public expenditure.

(e) *Psychological conditioning* of the general public, during a period of war and social crisis, to a greater government intervention and higher levels of expenditure and taxation made it easier for governments in subsequent periods to retain and to expand their activities.

(f) *Post-war reconstruction* of countries' economies involved governments in planning, allocation of resources and in financing some of the projects.

(g) *Economic development*, according to some economists, has considerable impact on the level of public expenditure. Before a developing country can industrialise, it has to invest in transport, water and power supplies, sanitation, education and other basic social projects to reach a 'take-off' point. In this early stage of development a high proportion of total investment will have to be made by the government, since the projects do not offer any, or foreseeable, return to investors. Once the country has reached a more advanced stage of economic and social development, private investment expands alongside public investment but, because of the imperfections of the market, government intervention grows and with it public expenditure.

Analysis of statistical data (OECD, *Public Expenditure Trends*) does not provide evidence to link the level of public expenditure to stages of a country's industrial development. Under the famous model of Professor Rostow, four stages of development can be identified: agricultural, take-off period, industrial maturity and the age of high consumption (W.W. Rostow, *Politics and Stages of Growth* New York and Cambridge: Cambridge University Press, 1960).

(h) *Growth of national income* is related to the level of government economic activity. Some economists, Wagner among them, had argued that an increase in national income results in an increase in public expenditure on economic welfare. The richer a country the more resources, in theory, are available to the government. The OECD international data does not establish, however, a direct relationship between the size of national income and the level of public expenditure.

(i) *Increased public expectation.* It can, however, be argued that, although it cannot be statistically proved, an indirect relationship exists between the growth of national income and public expectation of an improved standard of living, and hence public expenditure. Governments are likely to be under pressure to increase provision of public goods and services so as to increase the standard of living in general and of the poorest members of society in particular.

(j) *Extension of the franchise.* The increased expectation of a higher standard of living has manifested itself through the 'Ballot Box' in a vote for higher public expenditure. The extension of the franchise had given the right to vote at elections to people who had previously been excluded from a choice of a political party to govern them and from influencing the policies that they wished the government to pursue.

In the UK those still excluded are: peers, insane, felons, foreigners and children. From 1430 to 1832, voting rights were restricted to holders of property of specified value. In 1928 adult women got the vote and in 1968 the voting age was reduced to 18, thus enabling students to vote. Under a progressive system of taxation it is those in the lower income groups who stand most to gain from the extension of provision of goods and services by the public sector. They have least to lose from increases in taxation required to finance higher expenditure since they may not be liable to any direct taxes. The gradual extension of the franchise has put pressure on governments to respond to the electorate's demands.

The extension of the franchise in Europe did not follow a uniform pattern and come simultaneously. For example, women in Liechtenstein only voted for the first time in 1986. It can be argued that votes for women have resulted in votes for higher public expenditure. It has been suggested that as women are more directly involved in their children's education and safeguarding the health of the family, they are likely to demand improvements in state provision of social services, through the ballot box.

(k) *The establishment of the welfare state.* This has created a base for the long term growth of public expenditure (see p. 92).

(l) *Socialism.* Socialist parties, committed by their ideology to the extension of the public sector, won general elections and formed governments after the Second World War in a number of countries, including the UK. Implementation of the policies set out in the election manifestos furthered the development of mixed economies and contributed to the growth of public expenditure.

(m) *Nationalisation.* The state takeover of private enterprises has increased public expenditure in two ways, firstly by a government paying compensation to former owners and secondly by subsidising loss-making nationalised industries.

(n) *New technology and science.* Some new technological developments in such fields as atomic energy, aerospace and computers, are so costly that in some countries they can only be financed by the state or with substantial aid from government funds. Scientific advances have enabled doctors to prolong life and reduce suffering, but in some cases at an enormous cost to governments' health programmes by creating ever-increasing demands.

(o) *Creation of supranational organisations.* The United Nations, NATO, European Community and other multinational organisations that are responsible for the provision of public goods and services on an international basis, have to be financed out of funds subscribed by member states, thereby adding to their public expenditure.

(p) *Foreign aid.* Acceptance by the richer industrialised countries of their responsibility to help the poorer developing countries has channelled some of the increased public expenditure of the donors into foreign aid programmes.

(q) *Increased complexity of national economies.* As economies develop they become more complex and the interests of various groups within a society come into conflict. This has led to the proliferation of public bodies whose costs, arising out of their co-ordinating, regulatory, administrative or judiciary functions, are borne by governments.

(r) *Inflation.* A general increase in prices has been an international phenomenon during the 1970s–1980s. Inflation increased the cost of all the activities of the public sector and was thus a major factor in growth in money terms of public expenditure in many countries.

(s) *Demographic changes.* Since public expenditure is intended to benefit the people of a country, it could therefore be expected that an increase in total population would result in higher public expenditure. But other demographic trends such as changes in the structure of the population (age and sex) and its geographical distribution also have to be taken into account. The overall effect of the various trends on public expenditure may be such that they cancel each other out, thus the extent to which the growth of population has led to growth of public expenditure depends on the specific conditions in different countries.

RESTRAINTS TO THE GROWTH OF PUBLIC EXPENDITURE

Some of the factors in the growth of public expenditure that we have discussed are of a temporary nature, others contribute to structural changes that result in an increasing financial commitment by governments on a permanent basis, but the ability to spend is not unlimited. The following are the four main restraints:

(a) *Resources.* In the long run, public expenditure cannot exceed the resources of a country.

(b) *Taxable capacity.* This imposes a ceiling on the government's revenue from taxation (see p. 243) and thereby on an increase in public expenditure that is financed out of it.

(c) *Limit to borrowing.* For a time public expenditure can outstrip revenue either as a matter of necessity or of fiscal policy, and the deficit can be financed out of loans. But there is a limit to how much money lenders at home and abroad will be prepared to make available to any government.

(d) *Public opinion.* The final major restraint is the growth of public opinion. The level of public expenditure in a democratic society will depend on the size of the public sector that people want and are willing to pay for through taxation.

CONSEQUENCES OF THE GROWTH OF PUBLIC EXPENDITURE

Political, social and economic consequences are interrelated. They cannot therefore be easily isolated and compartmentalised. Some are, however, more identifiable than others and are listed below:

(a) A political consequence of the growth of public expenditure is the increased size of the public sector and hence of the power of the state.

(b) A social consequence of the extension of the welfare system is to allay the fear of deprivation that is consequent to unemployment, sickness and old age. The need for people to provide for themselves is reduced.

(c) Development of a welfare mentality is likely to increase people's dependence on government support and to lead to the creation of what politicians and social commentators call the 'underclass' in a society. Its members caught in the poverty trap may lack the means, ability, resourcefulness and incentive to break out.

(d) An economic consequence is an increase in taxation or borrowing or both, to finance rising expenditure.

(e) A disincentive effect on work and enterprise (see p. 152) may result from an increase in taxation required to finance provision of public goods and services but economists disagree on this.

(f) National debt will increase as a result of borrowing and this will affect the rates of interest and supply of capital to industry.

(g) The rate of economic growth may be adversely affected by the transfer of resources from use in manufacturing in the private sector to the public sector for provision of social services.

(h) The productive capacity and export potential of an economy may be reduced. Public goods and services, such as social security benefits, are not exportable and do not earn foreign currency.

(i) The balance of payments will suffer if exports are reduced and when interest payments on the money that the government had borrowed abroad, or repayment of capital, become due.

(j) The prosperity of a country may, however, be increased if public expenditure is on projects that further economic development. If this happens then the balance of payments may improve.

(k) The standard of living of the people in general and of some groups in particular can be increased by the provision of public goods and services.

(l) Inflation resulting from the injection of public spending into the income flow of a country adversely affects not only the standard of living but the whole economy

(m) Stabilisation of the economy may result from the use of public expenditure to counteract inflation and deflation.

(n) The level of employment may rise, but if the effect of increased public spending is inflationary, employment will be likely to fall.

(o) A more egalitarian society can be achieved by narrowing the difference in the level of consumption among its members by means of state benefits financed out of progressive taxation.

(p) Increased efficiency in provision of public goods and services as governments put greater emphasis on value for money in an attempt to curb growing public expenditure.

This list of favourable and adverse effects that may follow an increase in public expenditure is by no means conclusive. Whether its consequences will be beneficial or not will depend on the existing level of expenditure, the purpose for which the additional money is used, the way that the expenditure is financed and the specific circumstances of a particular country.

SUMMARY

1. Public expenditure can be defined in different ways. The widest definition includes expenditure by: the central government, local authorities and nationalised industries.

2. The need for public expenditure arises out of the functions of the state.

3. Certain functions are basic to any society. As a society develops, the range of functions widens.

4. Optimum level of public expenditure is at a point at which benefits from additional expenditure are equal to the additional sacrifice of paying taxes to finance it.

5. Theories of public expenditure seek to determine the desirable level of public expenditure. These have included: marginal utility theory, the ballot box theory and the positive theory of government expenditure.

6. Interpretation of the trends in public expenditure over time and international comparisons require care since there are statistical problems and problems of definition.

7. Wagner's law and the Displacement Effect (Peacock and Wiseman) are two important observations on the growth of public expenditure.

8. Reasons for the growth of public expenditure are economic, social and political. Its growth is an international phenomenon.

9. Restraints to the growth of public expenditure are: the availability of resources, the taxable capacity of a country; and the limits to borrowing and public opinion.

10. Consequences of the growth of public expenditure can, like the reasons for it be grouped under the headings: economic, social, political. The growth has resulted in: the expansion of the public sector; a rise in its absorption of resources; increased provision of goods and services, higher taxation and greater power of the state. Some of these consequences are desirable – others are not. The judgement as to whether the balance is a desirable one at any particular time is a controversial issue among economists, political parties and the general public at large.

SUGGESTED FURTHER READING

D. Begg, S. Fischer and R. Dornbusch, *Economics* (London: McGraw-Hill, 1994).

C.V. Brown and P.M. Jackson, *Public Sector Economics* (Oxford: Basil Blackwell, 1991).

N. Gemmell (ed.), *The Growth of the Public Sector* (Cheltenham: Edward Elgar, 1992).

R.A. Musgrave and P.B. Musgrave, *Public Finance in Theory and Practice* (New York: McGraw-Hill, 1989).

OECD Observer, *The Rise in Public Expenditure* (OECD: Paris, 1978).

A. Peacock and J. Wiseman, *The Growth of Public Expenditure in the UK* (London: George Allen & Unwin, 1967).

A. Peacock, *Public Choice Analysis in Historical Perspective* (Cambridge: Cambridge University Press, 1992).

C.T. Sandford, *The Economics of Public Finance* (Oxford: Pergamon Press, 1992).

EXERCISES

1. How would you account for the present-day revival of a modified form of the doctrine of *laissez-faire*?
2. What is meant by the optimum level of public expenditure in theory? Can the concept be meaningfully applied in practice?
3. Discuss the reasons for and the consequences of the growth of public expenditure.
4. Consider the validity of the observation that has given rise to Wagner's Law.
5. Define the 'Displacement Effect' and discuss its significance for an economy.
6. Explain in what way extension of franchise can affect the level of public expenditure.
7. Which type of expenditure is the easiest for a government to vary, if it wants to?
8. Consider the effectiveness of the restraints on an increase in public spending.
9. When trends in the public expenditure of different countries are compared, what considerations need to be taken into account to indicate changes in economic welfare?
10. Explain what is meant by expenditure in 'real terms' and how it can be calculated.

5 Public Expenditure in Practice: The British Experience

PHASES IN THE GROWTH OF PUBLIC EXPENDITURE

There are identifiable and distinct phases in the growth of public expenditure, which can be traced from the late 1780s when the government's budget, in its modern form, was first introduced. The landmarks are associated with political, social and economic events such as the following:

(a) *Development of administration in the eighteenth and nineteenth centuries.* In the late eighteenth century and for the greater part of the nineteenth century public expenditure was largely of an administrative and judicial nature and increased as a result of development of the apparatus of the state.

(b) *The First and Second World Wars during the twentieth century.* Wars had been a major contributory factor to the growth of public expenditure in the UK. The cost of financing the Napoleonic wars led to the imposition for the first time of income tax but it was the two World Wars that pushed public expenditure to unprecedented levels, as the figures in Table 5.1 illustrate.

The war periods, although temporary phases, resulted in a long-term increase in public expenditure. Approximately 28 per cent of the first and 50 per cent of the Second War was financed out of

Table 5.1 Public expenditure during the two World Wars

Public expenditure (£m) (1914–1918)	First World War (1939–1945)	Second World War
In the last year before the war	305	1 587
At the end of the war	2 427	5 779

Source: D.I. Hewell, 'British Public Debt in the Two World Wars,' *Public Finance*, vol. 8, no. 2 (1953).

loans. This increased the national debt and interest payments on the money that had been borrowed became a sizeable proportion of post-war public expenditure. The national debt itself had not been repaid.

(c) *Establishment of the Welfare State in the 1940s.* Various measures to provide some basic social services had been introduced on a piecemeal basis during the eighteenth and nineteenth centuries by successive governments, but it was the establishment of the Welfare State in the 1940s that led to the creation of a comprehensive system of provision of public goods and services from 'the cradle to the grave'. This created structural changes in the British economy that resulted in an expansion of the public sector and set public expenditure on an upward trend. In the UK, as in other major countries, expenditure on education, health and income maintenance accounts for a major share of public expenditure.

(d) *Nationalisation in the 1940s and 1950s.* The major stages early in nationalisation of industry were in the late 1940s and 1950s when the Labour government brought basic industries into public ownership. To pay compensation the government increased the national debt. There was also need for further borrowing for new investment, for grants and subsidies to help with the operating costs and to reduce large deficits of the public corporations (see p. 365). By 1980, the British Steel Corporation alone was losing money (at the rate of over £10 million a week).

(e) *Inflation in the 1970s and 1980s.* Prices had been rising for several decades but it was not until the 1970s that the phase of high inflation began. In the UK the rate of price increase was higher than that of most of the other leading industrialised countries. Inflation was triggered off by the oil crisis of 1973 when, within a matter of months, the price of oil was quadrupled. It continued to rise for the rest of that decade. There were also sharp increases in prices of commodities that the UK had to import. At home, increases in earnings also added to inflation. In 1975 they rose by over 26 per cent, and the average for the 1970s was 16 per cent compared with some 6 per cent during the 1960s.

As the public sector is labour-intensive, inflation had a particularly severe effect on the cost of public administration and the provision of public goods and services. High rates of interest increased the cost of public borrowing. Rising unemployment increased the claims for state benefits and these were paid at increasing rates. Within ten years, public expenditure increased nearly five-fold (see Figure 5.2).

DEVELOPMENT OF SOCIAL SERVICES

The provision of social services such as education, care of the sick and the destitute is not an innovation of the Welfare State. These social services have been provided in some form or another for hundreds of years. What was new was the acceptance by the State of the responsibility to provide social services as of right. Before they were largely provided as a charity by religious orders, feudal lords, merchants, craft guilds, philanthropists and later, to some extent, by local authorities and central government. Nearly all the major services that the State now provides were pioneered by voluntary organisations. For two hundred years, from the seventeenth century, the social services were mainly financed out of private contributions.

EDUCATION

Various religious orders, such as the Benedictines, gave education to poor children. The State first spent money on education in England when in 1833 it allocated £22,000 to two voluntary bodies: the National Society (Anglican) and the British and Foreign Society. Between them, since the early part of the nineteenth century, they had been building and running schools. The *Education Act (1870)* marked the beginning of active state participation in education. The Act provided for the setting-up of schools in areas where voluntary societies had not established them. By the 1880s, local authorities were empowered to provide elementary and, if they wished, secondary education and to finance it out of rates. In 1899, the Board of Education was set up to supervise the provision of education. By this time, government had made elementary schooling compulsory and available to all children free of charge. The *1944 Education Act* made secondary schooling compulsory up to the age of 15, and this was subsequently raised to 16.

Today, university education is also free and those students whose parents' income is below a specified level, receive mandatory grants from the state supplemented by a loan system introduced by the government. In recent years there has been a shift in support from grants to loans, whereby students borrow money to finance themselves.

HEALTH SERVICES

The decline of feudalism and the later dissolution of the monasteries undermined the voluntary system of caring for the sick that had developed over the centuries. The State was forced to step in to supplement the charitable works and to provide some sort of a health service to the community. The *Poor Law Act of 1601* placed responsibility for the sick and the destitute on the local authorities and provided for the cost to be financed out of rates. This marked the beginning of the acceptance of the principle that care of the sick was a function of the State. But such provisions as had been made were limited and restricted to the poor. The impetus in the eighteenth century to an improvement of economic and social welfare owed less to changes in political philosophy than to the work of philanthropists.

Between 1720 and 1750, eleven of the great voluntary hospitals were established in London and 46 elsewhere in Britain, but these voluntary efforts were insufficient to deal with the increased health problems that followed the industrialisation and urban development of the nineteenth century. Inadequate sanitation contributed to the spread of infectious diseases and to epidemics. This caused increasing concern among clergymen, doctors, lawyers and other reformers who sought to improve conditions, particularly of the working population. Prominent among the reformers was Sir Edwin Chadwick (1801–90). His efforts to bring about sanitary improvements led to the passing of the *Public Health Act,* (1848). It was the first national measure and a landmark in the development of social services. This legislation set up a comprehensive public health system with minimum prescribed standards of service. It was subject to unified control and a Board of Health was appointed. The *Public Health Act* (1875) provided for consolidation and development of the system and served as the basis for subsequent legislation on public health.

Admission to Poor Law hospitals after 1875 became free to patients suffering from smallpox or fever. The principle of free treatment of hospital patients was further extended under the Poor Law Act (1889). Managers of metropolitan asylums were permitted to admit any person who was not a pauper and was reasonably believed to be suffering from fever or smallpox or diphtheria and to 'recover the amount of their expenses from the said person or from any person liable by law to maintain him'. Provision was also made for the care of the dangerously insane. Those who were sane and not infectious were left to look after themselves.

By the beginning of the twentieth century, provision of health services had improved but the majority of the people still had to pay for medical care. The *National Health Insurance Act* (1912) established a scheme to cover wage earners with less than £160 per year. In return for their, and their employers', contributions to approved societies the wage earners became entitled to the medical services of general practitioners. Patients who were not members of contributory schemes were admitted to hospitals on the basis of a means test. Those with incomes above a certain level were admitted to private wards and charged according to their income. Some of the revenue thus raised was used for the medical care of the poor, who were admitted to general wards free of charge. The beginning of universal free health service started in 1917 with free treatment of patients with venereal disease. Infirmaries that had been set up under the Poor Law legislation were, after 1929, transformed into general hospitals run by local authorities. The provisions of the *National Health Service Act* (1946), which came into effect in 1948, established the National Health Service. It offered free medical and dental care and medication, but as demand grew and expensive new treatments became available prescription charges and payments for some services e.g. dental care, were introduced. The National Health Service was subsequently reorganised in the 1980s and 1990s (see p. 105).

RELIEF OF THE POOR

Poverty has been associated with sickness, old age and unemployment. This link is reflected by the fact that, up to July 1988, the relief of the poor was administered by the Department of Health and Social Security. Subsequently, it was split into two separate departments.

The underlying assumption of poor relief by the state for over three hundred years has been that it was the duty of the members of a family to support each other as far as possible so that they would not become a burden on the community. Not all families could – or were willing to – undertake this duty. Destitute vagrants were viewed as a danger to the society. The *Poor Law Act (1536)* placed on the parishes the responsibility of relieving the 'impotent poor' and of putting vagrants to work. Funds for this were to be obtained from charitable contributions and clergy were to exhort their flocks to charity. This pious hope was again expressed in the *Poor Law Act (1552)*, which stated that parishioners were to be 'gently exhorted and admonished' to provide according to their means. They must have proved unresponsive and contributions were made compulsory. The *Poor Law Act (1601)* was of major importance in the history of poor relief. It established the fundamental principle of compulsory assessment for the relief of the poor on owners of houses and land. Local authorities became responsible for the care of the poor. They provided workhouses and outdoor relief.

Poor relief in aid of wages, during the famine of the 1790s when prices increased sharply, was linked to the rising cost of food and the family size of the recipients and continued to be so related for some forty years. This form of indexation was well ahead of its time and helped to provide assistance to the poor outside the workhouses where conditions were appalling. They were run in such a way as to deter the poor from seeking public assistance.

The abuses of the Poor Law led to the setting up of a Royal Commission and resulted in the *Poor Law Amendment Act (1834)*. Its two important provisions were: (a) the establishment of a central supervisory body which became the Local Government Board and later the Ministry of Health, to control local authorities responsible for poor relief; and (b) the prohibition of relief to able-bodied paupers and their families except in workhouses. The stigma of poverty persisted and there were no appreciable changes in public assistance to the poor until the twentieth century.

The Liberal government (1906–1916) distinguished the aged from the other poor for the purpose of providing relief and introduced, under the *Old Age Pensions Act (1908)*, a non-contributory pension scheme. It applied to those aged over 70 and with an annual income of less than £32.10s. In 1910 the Ministry of Labour opened its first Labour Exchange to help the unemployed find work. The *National Insurance Act (1911)* introduced an important change in provision of assistance. Payments to the unemployed and the sick who had contributed to the fund were made as of right and ceased to be regarded by the state as charity. However, there still remained many poor who were not eligible for these benefits. The *Local Government Act (1929)* placed the responsibility for the administration of public assistance on county councils and boroughs. A comprehensive and compulsory national insurance scheme to cover the aged, the sick and the unemployed was finally established in 1948. As claims and payments increased, most of the cost had to be financed out of general tax revenue.

ESTABLISHMENT OF THE WELFARE STATE

Over the period from the beginning of the provision by the government of some basic services to the establishment of the Welfare State over three hundred years later, the following are the important changes that took place:

(a) Gradual shift from private charity to public assistance provided and administered by local authorities;

(b) Transfer of responsibility for some social services from local authorities to the central government;
(c) Emergence of contributory schemes to provide financial assistance in times of need;
(d) Abandonment of the distinction between 'deserving' and 'undeserving' poor for the purpose of granting relief;
(e) Development of the welfare principle and provision of assistance to all in need irrespective of the cause.

These changes were the result of the interplay of social pressures, political expediency and changes in economic conditions.

The UK had pioneered the establishment of the Welfare State. The development of public services over the years provided the base and public opinion the stimulus to its creation. The advocacy of the Welfare State can be traced back to 1790 and the publication of *The Rights of Man*. In this book, Thomas Paine (1737–1809) argued in favour of collective responsibility and the provision of benefits as of right and not as charity. He advocated compulsory education for all, family allowances and old age pensions, with graduated income tax to finance them. Clearly, Paine was ahead of his time. He was branded as a revolutionary and fled to France, but the seeds of the Welfare State had been sown and they germinated some 130 years later.

The blueprint of the Welfare State was the 'Report on Social Insurance and Allied Services' (Cmnd. 6404), 1942. The committee sat under the chairmanship of Lord Beveridge (1879–1963) who was, during his distinguished career, a Liberal member of Parliament and Director of the London School of Economics and Political Science.

The Beveridge Report

Lord Beveridge had been concerned with what he called the great social evils of 'want, disease, squalor, ignorance and idleness' arising out of lack of employment. The report put forward proposals to overcome them by provision of: (i) free medical services; (ii) unemployment insurance for all; (iii) retirement pensions; (iv) child allowances; (v) maternity and funeral benefits. This was summarised in the phrase 'from the cradle to the grave' State care.

The Beveridge Report was a most remarkable document, not only for its vision but also in its consequences. The major proposals were implemented one by one: *the Family Allowances Act (1945), National Health Service Act (1946), National Insurance Act (1946),* and the

Table 5.2 Total UK public expenditure by programme, general government expenditure, £billion

	Estimated outturn	New plans/projections			Changes from previous plans/projections[1]		
	1993–94	1994–95	1995–96	1996–97	1993–94	1994–95	1995–96
Central government expenditure							
Social security[1]	61.0	62.0	65.3	67.8	1.5	0.9	0.9
Health	29.3	30.8	32.1	33.0	0.2	0.4	0.5
Defence	23.4	23.5	22.7	22.8	−0.1	−0.3	−0.5
Education	6.5	7.6	8.6	9.0	–	0.6	1.1
Scotland Wales and N. Ireland	17.9	18.9	19.6	20.1	0.2	0.5	0.7
Other departments	32.0	30.1	31.6	31.7	1.7	−1.8	−0.1
Total	**170.1**	**172.9**	**179.9**	**184.4**	**3.4**	**0.4**	**2.6**
Local authority expenditure	70.2	71.7	73.7	75.6	0.9	−0.5	−0.6
Financing requirements of nationalised industries	4.7	3.2	2.4	1.9	−0.4	–	−0.4
Adjustment	−0.3				−0.3		
Reserve		3.5	7.0	10.5	−4.0	−3.5	−3.0

National Assistance Act (1948) marked the final demise of the Poor Law. Under the new scheme, everybody in need became entitled to National Assistance out of central government funds. The various provisions of the Acts became effective from 1948. The Welfare State had come into existence. The conditions for it were propitious. The war had just ended and the public was looking forward to a better way of life. They did not wish to return to the discredited social and economic policies of the Depression years. A Labour government had won the general election and was committed to the expansion of the public sector. The economy was buoyant. Thus the plans of a Liberal were put into operation by a Labour government and the provisions were extended by the succeeding Conservative government. Public expenditure was set on an upward trend (Table 5.2 and Figures 5.1 and 5.2).

Table 5.2 (*continued*)

	Estimated outturn	New plans/ projections			Changes from previous plans/projections[1]		
	1993–94	1994–95	1995–96	1996–97	1993–94	1994–95	1995–96
New control total	244.7	251.3	263.0	272.3	–0.4	3.6	–1.5
– real terms[2]	237.0	234.0	236.1	238.5	–1.4	–4.1	2.3
– real growth[3]	2.0	–1.3	0.9	1.0			
Cyclical social security	14.0	14.8	15.5	16.2	–1.1	–1.3	–1.4
Central government debt interest	19.4	22.5	24.5	25.6	–	–0.8	–1.3
Accounting adjustments	8.0	8.8	10.1	11.0	0.4	–	0.6
GGE excluding privatisation							
proceeds	286.1	297.3	313.1	325.2	–1.1	–5.7	–3.6
– real terms[2]	277.0	276.9	281.0	284.7	–2.3	–6.2	–4.3
– real growth[3]	2.9	–0.1	1.5	1.3			
– per cent of GDP	45	43³/₄	43¹/₄	42¹/₂			

Notes:
1. Excluding cyclical social security.
2. Using GDP deflator 1992–93 = 100.
3. Per cent.
Source: HM Treasury, *Financial Statement and Budget Report, 1994–95* (London: HMSO,1993).

As the Welfare State grew, so did concern about its aims, consequences and costs (Figure 5.3). Economic conditions began to change and with them public opinion and political pressures shifted. The country was committed to a Welfare State but it was no longer clear what was meant by welfare. Sir Maurice Kendall in the 1975 Beveridge Memorial Lecture pointed out that 'Our current social aims are either not defined at all or are so loosely defined as to be non-operational. We have a Welfare State but we do not know how to measure welfare. We are deploying scarce resources in many different fields without any clear idea of the relative importance of the competitive demands made on them.'

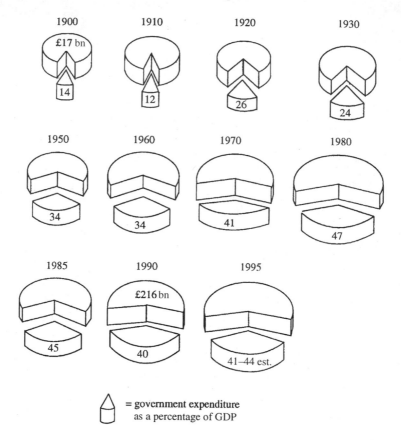

<figure>*Figure* 5.1   Growth of government expenditure in the UK</figure>

Source: A.T. Peacock and J. Wiseman, 'The growth of public expenditure in the UK, 1967: Government's Expenditure Plans', HM Treasury, *Economic Briefing*, no. 5 (1993).

It is not just the ranking of priorities that matters. What is also important is the size of the cake, how much it costs, who pays for it through taxation and what are the consequences. The different aspects of a government's fiscal policy all have to be considered simultaneously.

The Civil Service, however, could not provide the House of Commons Committee on Social Services with information on the combined effect of government's decision on benefits, charges, taxation, incentives and the 'poverty trap' and argued that no answer to this was possible (Third Report from Social Services Committee, Session 1979–80, HMSO, 1980).

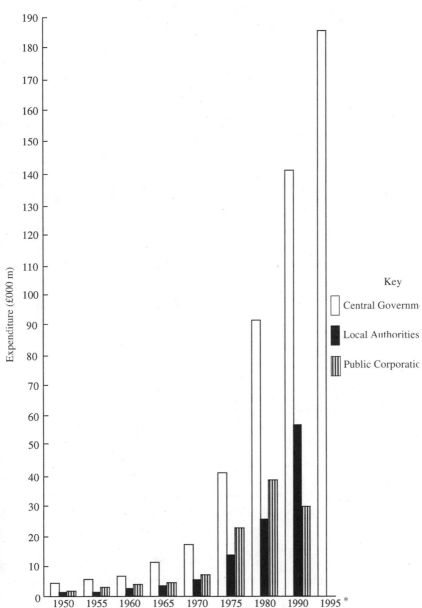

Figure 5.2   Growth of the public sector in the UK

* forecast.

Source: CSO *Blue Books, UK National Accounts*, annually and Government Expenditure White Papers.

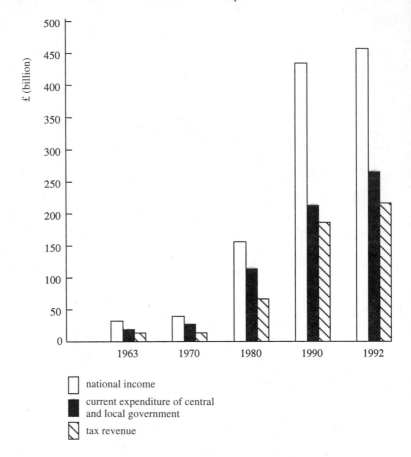

Figure 5.3   National income, public expenditure and tax revenue in the UK
Note:
* Including local government tax (Rates/Community Charge/Council Tax).
Source: CSO, Blue Books, *UK National Accounts*, annually (1993).

Without knowledge of such facts, it is very difficult for a Welfare State to function effectively.

It is not just in the UK but also in other countries of Europe that the effectiveness and efficiency of the welfare state was questioned. The European Commission called for a review of welfare policies in the Community and political and economic commentators increasingly focused on the crisis in welfare.

'FROM WELFARE STATE TO WELFARE SOCIETY'

Thus wrote the Secretary-General of the OECD (*OECD Observer*, No. 107). The welfare system that had evolved over the years was no longer sustainable, and one country after another began to modify its provisions. The original intentions were gradually to provide basic and selective assistance to those most in need. The concept of a Welfare State based on comprehensive and universal provision of services by the public sector came later. It was perceived as a great step towards a better way of life for the people and gained widespread support. Countries in Europe followed the British example and set up their own versions of the Welfare State. Initially, economic growth in Europe created resources and generated tax revenues out of which more public services could be provided to all. This, along with public acceptance of an increased role of the government in the life of the country, facilitated the expansion of the Welfare State. Then, economic conditions, political ideologies and social attitudes changed. A variety of factors contributed to the plight of the Welfare State. The following are only some of them:

(i) Economic growth in Europe slowed down and recession spread in the late 1980s and early 1990s.

(ii) Tax revenues failed to keep pace with public expenditure.

(iii) High unemployment increased claims for unemployment benefit payments and reduced proceeds of taxes on earnings at the same time.

(iv) Competition for funding by social security, education, health and other government programmes intensified.

(v) The 'Peace Dividend' that was expected to follow the end of the Cold War and the split up of the Soviet Union did not, in the UK release resources. Defence spending instead of going down between 1991 and 1994 went up, by which time the United Nations and NATO were involved in the fighting in the Balkans. British government's attempts to contain military expenditure by cutting down on armed forces and armaments contributed to unemployment and income support claims.

(vi) Inflation in the meantime, by increasing costs of state benefits, public goods and services, reduced the scope for improvements in provisions in real terms

(vii) Public expectation of improvement in the standard of living was unabated and fostered by political parties.

(viii) People were less willing to believe that the state was giving them 'free' public goods and services, and were becoming increasingly aware that they themselves were paying for them through taxation.

(ix) Unwillingness of the public to pay more in taxes, as demonstrated through the 'ballot box', forced political parties to rethink their welfare policies.

(x) Re-emergence of market economics ideology and decline in support for socialism in countries in Europe resulted in a shift from state monopolies in the provision of a wide range of goods and services to competition and privatisation (see p. 376).

The pattern of public expenditure in the UK has began, gradually, to reflect these changes. In some areas instead of being the sole provider of goods and services, the government became more of a facilitator, regulator, setter and enforcer of standards and evaluator of performance of suppliers. The transformation of the Welfare State has begun.

The Welfare society that some governments are now advocating is one of greater self-reliance, targeting of state benefits at those most in need in place of universal entitlement, competition, increased efficiency in the public sector, value for money and cost cutting so that such resources that are available could be used more effectively, tax increases avoided and budget deficits contained. These objectives are now much less contentious political policy issues, but the means of achieving them remain controversial.

CHANGES IN ADMINISTRATIVE STRUCTURES: MANAGEMENT AND PROVISION OF PUBLIC SERVICES

In the 1980s and early 1990s the British government policy aimed to give people a choice of suppliers, and a greater say and involvement in the provision of public services. This required re-organisation of administrative structures and management changes. The outcome was: (a) the setting up of Executive Agencies; (b) provisions for contracting-out of work by public bodies; (c) scheme for opting out of schools from local government control; and (d) granting of Trust Status to hospitals in the National Health Service and giving choice to doctors who wish to become budget-holding General Practitioners.

Executive Agencies

In the process of decentralisation, large government departments were split up into Executive Agencies following the publication in 1988 of

'Management in Government: The Next Steps' (The Sir Robin Ibbs Report). Within three years there were 51 Agencies. The first one was the Vehicle Inspectorate, the largest was the Social Security Benefits Agency, employing some 66,000 people and the smallest, the National Weights and Measures Laboratory with a staff of 40. Government's objectives in setting up of the Agencies were to make managers more accountable for the units, more business-like and, where possible, to bring market pressures to bear on delivery of services. Recipients of state benefits were designated as customers and, where it was feasible, given a choice of suppliers of a service. The extent to which the Agencies were exposed to internal market and external competition varied considerably, depending on the nature of the service that they provided. Some were already run on business-like lines. Her Majesty's Stationery Office (HMSO) publishes, prints and supplies office material, selling its output to government departments, local authorities, other public bodies and the general public. Some of its products face competition from other suppliers and are subject to market forces.

Contracting Out

Central and local government does, however, continue to be responsible for, and spends large amounts of money on provision of a wide range of services, but some of the work can now be subcontracted to private sector businesses (see p. 323).

Opting Out

Traditionally local government has been responsible for expenditure on schools but the *Education Reform Act (1986)* introduced a provision for school governing bodies to opt out of local authorities' control. Such schools receive funding directly from the Treasury and manage their own budgets. Thus, governors, parents and representatives of local communities have a direct involvement in the provision of education.

Trusts and Budget Holding

Health is one of the biggest of government's expenditure programmes and one that is not easily containable. Since the inception of the National Health Service, costs have risen sharply and public expectation of benefits has increased. Clinical decision making and financing were separate. Thus, treatments were prescribed by doctors without reference to the expense involved. The financial burden went on increasing but public satisfaction did not. Government embarked on a series of improvements, and began to introduce a variety of measures to improve performance. Competition between hospitals within the service and with the private sector was a major feature. NHS hospitals were enabled to apply for a trust status that would allow them to manage their finance and attract patients and funding that went with them. According to the OECD 1994 Review of the UK economy, reforms of the NHS have produced 'increasingly encouraging results' and make the service 'a remarkably cost-effective institution, providing health care at lower cost than in comparable countries'. In the UK some of these reforms had come under criticism and debate on their merits continues.

In the primary care service doctors who opted for 'budget holding' could shop around on behalf of their patients and buy hospital services for them. Here it is only possible to highlight a number of points to illustrate how the Welfare State has, over the years, been modified. Political parties' commitment to welfare, if not to the Welfare State, continues.

THE CITIZEN'S CHARTER

The Charter presented to the Parliament in 1991 (Cmnd. 1599, HMSO) reinforced the central principle of the British government's policy that 'essential services – such as education and health – must be available to all, irrespective of means', and set out new proposals to improve the provision of public services generally. But the Charter goes further than that. It aims to give greater power to the citizens and recognition that citizenship not only confers right and benefits but also creates responsibilities. The document amplifies this. 'All public services are paid for by individual citizens, either directly or through their taxes. They are entitled to expect high quality services, responsive to their needs, provided efficiently at a reasonable cost.' Public services must give value for money within a tax bill the nation can afford. The citizen is perceived as a 'customer' whose interests are best served by the provision of choice, information on standards to be expected, competition between providers of services and assessment of their performance.

The scope of the Citizen's Charter is wide. It applies to all public services provided by government departments, agencies, local authorities, National Health Service, nationalised industries and key utilities in the private sector.

A spate of charters followed, each reflecting the particular nature of the service provided and catering for customers who fall into three categories: recipients of benefits, purchasers of services and financiers of provisions, i.e. the taxpayer. There was a Parent's Charter and a Patient's

Charter. For example, the Charter of the Social Security Benefits Agency provides information on the benefits available to the customers, publishes targets and programmes to improve services, procedures for handling of customer enquiries and complaints. There are 'customer service managers' to respond to them. Some Charters go even further. The British Rail Passenger's Charter allows for compensation to be paid in some cases when services are not up the required standard. By contrast, the Taxpayer's Charter of the Revenue Departments – Customs and Excise and the Inland Revenue – is more about the obligations of the 'customers'. Whether taxpayers regard themselves as customers is perhaps debatable. They have no choice in paying taxes and cannot take their custom elsewhere, short of emigrating. Under the Charter the taxing authorities, however, .are to make their tax demands more comprehensible, to make payment easier and complaints procedures more effective. The Charters have been followed by performance indicators. The value of some of them such as school or hospital league tables has been questioned by teachers and health services professionals because the ranking system is based on a limited numbers of factors that are more readily quantifiable.

The British government sees the Citizen's Charter as '... the most comprehensive programme ever to raise quality, increase choice, secure better value and extend accountability ... it will set a pattern, not only for Britain but for other countries to follow' (Cm. 1599). Having pioneered the Welfare State, the UK is leading the field in the transformation to a Welfare Society.

Trends in Europe

The size and pattern of public expenditure in the UK cannot be viewed in isolation from developments in the rest of the European Community. Its aim is to achieve a comparable provision of public goods and services by the Member States. This will be discussed in Chapter 16.

SUMMARY

1. Introduction of the government budget in its modern form in the 1780s provides a starting point for a study of the growth of public expenditure in the UK.
2. Major contributory factors to the growth have been: wars, social crises, nationalisation of industries, the establishment of the welfare state and inflation.

3. Social services were first provided by religious bodies and feudal landowners, later by voluntary associations and philanthropists. Gradually the responsibility was taken over by local authorities and the central government

4. The Poor Law Act (1601) introduced compulsory assessment on houses and land to enable local authorities to provide relief for the poor. This marked the beginning of a policy of raising tax revenue to finance social services.

5. Education became free and compulsory, the destitute sick were admitted to hospitals free of charge and the old into workhouses. Appalling conditions in many of these institutions led to demands for reform.

6. The next stage heralded a period of change in public opinion. Social services ceased to be regarded as a charity and came to provided as of right. Responsibility for provision and the cost of financing social services shifted to a large extent from local authorities to the central government and was met out of tax revenue.

7. The Beveridge Report provided the blueprint for the Welfare State. It came into existence in the late 1940s to provide for people from 'the cradle to the grave'. The range and cost of the welfare provisions increased rapidly and this brought on the demands for reassessment of government's expenditure policies.

8. A shift from Welfare State to Welfare Society has been stressed in the 1990s. This resulted in changes in the administrative structures in the public sector and exposure of providers of public services to market forces in the UK and other countries in Europe.

9. The Citizen's Charter, published by the British government, and setting out proposals for raising standards and improvements in the provision of public services within an affordable budget, spelt out the rights and responsibilities of citizens on the one hand and the obligations of public bodies on the other.

10. The trend in public expenditure in the UK cannot be viewed in isolation. Convergence of welfare policies within the European Community will affect national budgets of Member States.

SUGGESTED FURTHER READING

J. Bates, *Managing Value for Money in the Public Sector* (London: Chapman & Hall, 1993).

Beveridge Report, *The Report on Social Insurance and Allied Services*, Cmnd. 6404 (London: HMSO, 1942).

Citizen's Charter, *Raising the Standard*, Cmnd. 1599 (London: HMSO, 1991).

Individual Charters 1991–1994 include: *The Charter for Social Security Benefits Agency, Taxpayer's Charter, Patient's Charter, Parent's Charter* and *The Charter for Higher Education.*

A.W. Dilnot, J.A. Kay and C.M. Morris, *The Reform of Social Security* (London: Institute for Fiscal Studies, 1985).

D. Fraser, *The Evolution of the British Welfare State* (London: Macmillan, 1973).

A.T. Peacock and J. Wiseman, *The Growth of Public Expenditure in the United Kingdom* (London: George Allen Unwin, 1967).

A.T. Peacock, *Public Choice Analysis in Historical Perspective* (Cambridge: Cambridge University Press, 1992).

D. Wilson, *The State and Social Welfare* (Harlow: Longmans, 1991).

EXERCISES

1. What factors have led to the establishment of a Welfare State in the UK?

2. 'State provision of goods and services to all, from the cradle to the grave is neither necessary nor desirable'. Comment on the validity of this statement.

3. Suggest the reasons for the gradual shift in responsibility for provision of social services from the local authorities to the central government.

4. Consider the consequences of the principle that social services should be provided as of right.

5. Discuss the significance of the Beveridge Report in relation to the provision of the social services in the UK.

6. Is the Citizen's Charter a great step forward in raising standards in the public sector, ensuring that public expenditure programmes give value for money, or a gimmick?

7. Is it a fair comment to say 'we have a Welfare State but we do not know how to measure welfare'. Give reasons for your answer.

8. A shift from the Welfare State to Welfare Society appears to be an international phenomenon. Suggest reasons for this and the most likely consequences.

9. Economic welfare depends not only on the level but also on the pattern of public expenditure. Comment on this statement and illustrate your points by reference to the British experience, or that of another country in the European Community.

10. The European Community's policy is to harmonise the provision of public services in the Member States. Suggest what problems this is likely to create and how they could be overcome.

    (To do this exercise you will also need to read Chapter 16.)

Part 3

Public Finance: Taxation

6 The Theory of Taxation and the Tax System

THE NEED FOR REVENUE

A government needs funds to provide goods and services. The methods of financing public expenditure have changed over time but there is no escape from the fact that in the end somebody has to foot the bill.

EARLY TAXES

In Ancient Greece the cost of public activities was directly financed by the rich members of the community. A person was assigned a liturgy which was a public office or duty. It was a compulsory obligation and an honour. The holder of a liturgy was responsible not only for defraying the cost but also for organising the activity. There was no assessment for a specified payment. The assignment involved a specific task and it was up to the person to decide how much to spend. It was quite common to boast at public assemblies in Athens that one spent more than was needed. The liturgies, which originated in the financing of religious festivals, sports and theatrical entertainments, were later extended to the provision of ships, maintenance of roads, supply of corn for the army and billeting of soldiers.

Roman emperors followed the Hellenic practice and increased the range of the liturgies. Holders of the various offices, for which there was competition, were expected to make donations and these in time became regular obligations. As the burden of the benefactions grew, the appeal of the honours associated with them diminished. The increased power of the state and the extension of its activities required regular and increasing revenue. This was obtained by compulsory levies from which a system of taxation developed.

One of the early forms of taxation on which the Greek city-states and the Roman republic relied were harbour taxes. These were a lucrative source of revenue because of the volume of foreign trade. Business ventures have always been risky. The wish to look into the future and the demand for forecasts is not a modern phenomenon, though the methods of prophesying have changed. Where there is a demand a tax is sure to follow. In antiquity it was the Oracle at Delphi that provided prophesies to the Greeks, and to the Romans when they acquired Delphi in 191 BC. Whoever wished to consult the Oracle had to pay a tax, the 'teleno', one of the earliest taxes on a service. By the time the Roman empire was established the bulk of the tax revenue came from land.

At the peak of its power the Byzantine Empire had a sophisticated system of taxation. It had been developed by a financial genius, John the Cappadocian (sixth century AD), the imperial treasurer to Emperor Justinian. Taxation was based on property. Taxes were paid per capita according to the wealth owned. Duties were collected at the ports of the empire and taxes were levied on food, meat, corn oil, horses and carriages. It was said that defaulting taxpayers left the treasury naked or dead. The vast revenue was required to wage wars, build magnificent churches and palaces and to provide for the administration of a great empire.

Ibn Khaldun, the great historian who lived in Tunisia in the fourteenth century, in his introduction to the history of the world observed,

> When cultural enterprises grow the number of individual imposts and assessments mounts. In consequence, the tax revenue which is the sum total of the individual assessments increases. The people of the dynasty then acquire qualities of character related to cleverness. Their customs and needs become more varied because of the prosperity and luxury in which they have become immersed. As a result imposts and assessments upon the subjects, agricultural labourers, farmers and other taxpayers increases. Thus state treasuries are forced to seek an ever-wider basis for taxation until a time comes when virtually nobody and nothing is exempt.

This was the stage that Britain reached in the nineteenth century according to William Cobbett (1763–1835), the politician and reformer, who wrote in 1829:

> If we ride in a chaise, or coach, or on a horse, if we keep a dog, if we have a window to see through, a servant to assist us, a large part of the cost is tax. We can have no title to property, no right to occupation; we can neither lend nor borrow, nor pay nor receive money; nor can we ask for law or justice without paying tax; and when the breath is out of our bodies, the government demands a strict account of our bequests, and takes from our children or others a large part of what we leave behind.

Until well into the twentieth century, the main purpose of taxation was to raise revenue. There were, however, exceptions. Peter the Great (1672–1725), in an attempt to westernise the Russians, imposed taxes on beards. These were favoured in St. Petersburg but were out of fashion at the royal courts of Europe. As a cultural measure, the tax was a failure.

THEORIES OF TAXATION

There had been little interest among philosophers and statesmen in the theories of taxation until the eighteenth century. Taxes were seen as a matter of expediency. David Ricardo (1772–1823), in his book *Principles of Political Economy and Taxation*, defined taxation as 'a proportion of the produce of the land and labour of a country, placed at the disposal of the government and always ultimately paid either from capital or from the revenue of the country'.

The Economic Surplus Theory

Some theories of taxation offered less scope for practical application than others. One that aroused interest but gained little support was the economic surplus theory as applied to taxation by J.A. Hobson (1857–1940), who defined it as an excess over what was 'physically and morally necessary to secure continued use of the factor of production whose owner received it'. Suppose an owner of land is prepared to lease it for £500 per year. If he is offered £600 then he receives £100 surplus that can be taxed away. The problem is to establish the minimum amount required by different individuals or businesses and to determine morally acceptable levels.

The two main theories of taxation are the benefit theory of taxation and the ability to pay theory. Their origins go back some several hundred years. Over time, they have become modified and elaborated upon but the basic concepts underlying them have remained the same.

The Benefit Theory of Taxation

This theory is based on the assumption that all should contribute to the cost of the state in relation to the benefits they derive from the state. It could thus be argued that if one person owns property worth twice as much as somebody else, then their contribution to the state for protection should be twice as big. Taxes are therefore regarded on the basis of this theory, as payment for value received and as a reflection of the demand for public services.

The critics of this theory have argued that, firstly, it requires measurement of what is immeasurable – the value, for example, to an individual of defence of the country from foreign aggression – and secondly, it is incompatible with social justice since those most in need of state benefits, such as the aged, the sick or unemployed, would be least able to contribute through payment of taxes.

Revival of the benefit theory

In recent years the theory has regained some support. It can be argued that, in the long run, the majority of people in a democratic society will not be prepared to tolerate a fiscal system from which they do not benefit. Willingness to pay specific taxes for specific benefits is therefore indicative of the society's preference, on the basis of which decisions on public expenditure can be made.

Application of the benefit theory

A system of taxation based on the benefit theory would be unacceptable and inoperative in a modern society, but the theory has been applied in some cases, when particular taxes have been earmarked for specific purposes. Two examples are illustrative: (a) *Gasoline taxes in the USA.* Drivers of motor vehicles and consumers of goods transported by road benefit from highways built and maintained by the government. Motor vehicles require gasoline. A tax on gasoline is therefore a tax on those who use roads directly or indirectly. In the USA, proceeds of gasoline tax are earmarked for the Highway Trust Fund and are used to finance the cost of the Federal Highway Network. Thus gasoline tax is levied on the basis of the benefit theory of taxation. (b) *National Insurance Contributions in the UK.* These are a compulsory payment to the government and can therefore be regarded as a tax. The proceeds go into the National Insurance Fund and are used to provide benefits for those who qualify on the basis of contributions (taxes) paid.

Earmarking of proceeds of different taxes for specific purposes is not a widespread practice, as it has a number of disadvantages. These are the main ones:

(a) Earmarking reduces the flexibility of the fiscal system.

(b) The yield of tax and the expenditure required for a particular purpose may not coincide. Thus one fund may accumulate a deficit while another has a surplus but the deficits and surpluses cannot be offset against each other.

(c) Resources are not likely to be allocated in the most efficient way.

However, arguments in favour of earmarking have persuaded some governments to adopt the practice, as for example in the case of revenue from oil (see p. 184).

Ability To Pay Theory of Taxation

This theory is based on the proposition that, on grounds of equity and expediency, people should contribute to the finance of the state according to their means. Whereas income is indicative of a person's ability to pay taxes, ownership of property may not be, unless the asset yields a return or can be realised. A house that is let produces rent which can be taxed, but an owner-occupied house yields no income on which income tax can be assessed and there is no ability to pay a capital tax on it until the property can be sold. Thus the theory postulates that assessment for tax has to take into account individual circumstances.

Tax threshold

A person is deemed to have no ability to pay tax unless their income is above the subsistence level. As far back as the 1780s, Jeremy Bentham (1748–1832), an influential writer on law and political economy, argued in favour of exempting from tax those with small incomes, and for a tax threshold that would leave '... a certain minimum of income sufficient to provide the number of persons ordinarily supported from a single income, with requisites of life and health, and with protection against habitual bodily suffering, but not with indulgence' (*Introduction to the Principles of Morals and Legislation*, 1789).

The tax threshold is now a feature of income tax in all major countries but the level of income at which liability to the tax begins differs among them, depending on the amount of revenue required, the nature of the tax system and what is regarded as the acceptable minimum standards of living (see Table 12.3).

EQUALITY OF SACRIFICE, RATES OF TAXATION

Discussion of the meaning of equality is perhaps more a subject matter of philosophy than of public finance, but since some of the early writers on economics were philosophers, it is not surprising that the concept of equality has come to occupy an important place in economic literature. Equality can mean different things to different people. What is generally agreed on, is that the payment of taxes involves sacrifice. An equitable system of public finance to Adam Smith was one under which people contributed fairly to the upkeep of the state and, in turn, were fairly treated by it. John Stuart Mill (1806–73), one of the leading exponents of economic doctrines in the nineteenth century, commented:

> As a government ought to make no distinction of persons or classes on the strength of their claim on it, whatever sacrifices it requires from them should be made to bear as nearly as possible with the same pressure upon all, which it must be observed, is the mode by which least sacrifice is occasioned on the whole ... Equality of taxation, therefore, as a maxim of politics, means equality of sacrifice. (*Principles of Political Economy*, 1848).

This involves two principles of taxation: (a) revenue should be raised with the least aggregate sacrifice; and (b) all taxpayers should make equal sacrifice in paying taxes.

Professor A.C. Pigou (1877–1959), a prominent welfare economist, picked up this theme later on when he wrote:

> In practice ... tax arrangements that conform to the principle of least sacrifice always and necessarily conform to the principles of equal sacrifice among similar and similarly situated persons.

This led him to conclude that:

> ...for academic persons there may be a more complex and esoteric doctrine, for politicians and men of affairs we may assert that the least aggregate sacrifice is the one ultimate principle of taxation. (*Public Finance*)

But for Chancellors of Exchequer this still leaves unsolved the problem of measuring individual sacrifices and aggregating them. Valuation of sacrifice is inevitably subjective. The sacrifice that a person feels that they are making will depend on their psychological make-up and on individual material circumstances. These may be as follows:

(a) *Similar circumstances.* If we take two people with the same income, the same number of dependants and financial commitments, but where one is thrifty by nature and attaches more importance to material possessions, whereas the other is extravagant and relatively indifferent to material comforts, then payments of the same amount in taxes would involve a greater personal sacrifice for the former than for the latter.

(b) *Different circumstances.* When people's incomes and obligations differ, equality of sacrifice becomes even more difficult to calculate. It could be argued that on grounds of equity all should pay the same percentage of their income or wealth in taxation. Alternatively, it could be argued that the rate of tax should be higher the bigger the income or wealth-holding. The latter argument is based on the diminishing marginal utility theory (see p. 75) and the assumption that the more money one has, the less value one attaches to it. Consequently to equate sacrifice taxes would have to be levied at different rates depending on the amount of money owned.

Much of the discussion of equity is of a theoretical nature. For practical purposes of taxation, governments make the following broad assumptions: (i) people in similar circumstances are similar in other respects; (ii) the value of additional income to a recipient decreases as his or her income increases.

There is, therefore, a need to distinguish between horizontal equity and vertical equity and tax measures should be designed in such a way as to take both into account.

Horizontal equity requires the same treatment for tax purposes of people in the same economic circumstances. Receipt of identical income is not taken as an indication of identical economic circumstances. One person may have a family to support out of the income, while another has no dependents. They may or may not have financial commitments such as mortgage payments on a house.

Possession of assets with the same monetary value may again, not be an indication of the same economic circumstances. If the asset is used in business, e.g. machinery, it wears out and at the end of, say, a ten year period and may have only scrap value. However, if the asset is a postage stamp collection, then instead of losing value over time it is likely to appreciate, but yields no income. Allowances therefore have to be made in tax assessment to provide for horizontal equity. Certain amounts are deducted as allowances from income received to arrive at a taxable income. Allowances may take the form of dependants' allowances, relief on interest payment on a mortgage, or 'wear and tear' allowance on certain assets which is deductible from the return they yield.

Vertical equity is concerned with the equality of sacrifice of taxpayers in different circumstances and with their equitable treatment for tax purposes. The object here is not only to raise revenue in a fair way but also to achieve a more egalitarian society by narrowing the differences in the distribution of income and wealth (see p. 459). For this purpose governments levy progressive rates of taxation.

RATES OF TAXATION

Depending on how equity is interpreted and on the purpose of taxation, taxes can be imposed on the basis of different rates which are:

  (i) Uniform flat rates;
 (ii) Proportional;
(iii) Regressive;
(iv) Progressive.

Uniform Flat Rates

A tax levied at a flat rate is a fixed sum payable:

(a) *Per person irrespective of their income.* In the UK National Insurance Contributions were levied at a flat rate on all persons in a given category. Thus all adult males in employment paid the same amount and there were separate flat rates for all women employees and for juveniles. The contributions are now a proportional tax and there are few examples left of direct taxation on a flat rate basis.

(b) *Per article purchased.* The tax is charged as a fixed amount per unit, e.g. a bottle of whisky or a metric amount of tobacco, irrespective of its price.

(c) *Per capital asset.* A fixed uniform tax may be levied on all land as so much per each acre or per each house. In England there was a window tax between 1696 and 1851. A flat rate of two shillings

(10 pence) was charged per house, and on top of that a levy determined by the number of windows was imposed. Now capital taxes are assessed by reference to the value of the property.

Proportional Taxation

Proportional rates of taxation can be levied on income, capital and expenditure. The tax is fixed as a certain percentage of the income or the price or value of an item. Thus if the income is £100 per week and the price or value of an asset is £100, a tax of ten per cent means a tax payment of £10 in each case. If the income is £200 and the price £200 a ten per cent tax means that £20 will have to be paid, so that the bigger the income or the value of an asset the bigger the tax payment. Examples of proportional taxation in the UK in 1994–5 were:

(a) *On income* – the corporation tax, at the rate of 33 per cent of companies' taxable profits.
(b) *On capital* – capital gains tax, at the rate of 20, 25, 40 per cent on a realised gain resulting from an increase in the value of an asset.

Classification of a percentage tax on expenditure, however, presents a problem. A tax of 10 per cent on the value of an article can be said to be proportional but since the actual amount that has to be paid in taxation is determined by the price and not by a consumer's income, taxes on consumption are generally regarded as regressive.

Regressive Taxation

Taxes that are unrelated to the taxpayer's ability to pay are regressive. They may be regressive in a number of ways as the following examples show:

(a) *Taxes on expenditure*, whether specific or proportional are regressive, because a levy of £10 or ten per cent of the value of an article will represent a greater burden by absorbing a bigger share of a small income than of a bigger one. Thus, for a person earning £100 per week, a tax of £10 will be 10 per cent of their income, but for somebody earning £200 the same amount of tax would account for 5 per cent.
(b) *Taxes on income or capital* will be regressive if higher rates of tax are levied on the poorer than on the richer taxpayers, or if the wealthier people are exempt altogether.

Most governments tax consumption and therefore impose regressive taxation in some form or another. The use of customs and excise duties to raise revenues is widespread. In the UK and in the other countries of the European Union there is also value added tax (VAT). In the United States there are sales taxes. Direct taxes at regressive rates are generally regarded as unacceptable since they clearly appear to be incompatible with the principle of equitable taxation.

Progressive Taxation

A tax is progressive if it is graduated in such a way that the rate of tax rises more sharply than the increase in income or capital (see p. 143).

In a discussion of progressive taxation we have to distinguish between the average rate of tax and the marginal rate of tax. The average rate of tax is calculated by expressing the total amount of tax payable as a percentage of the total taxable income. Suppose a person starts paying tax at the rate of 30 per cent on their first slice of taxable income, 40 per cent on the second, then 45 per cent and 50 per cent on the last increment. This person has a total taxable income of £22,250 and pays £8,500 in tax. The average rate of tax is 38.2 per cent. The marginal rate of tax is the rate a person pays on successive increments of income or wealth. In our example the top marginal rate of tax is 50 per cent. For a tax to be progressive, the marginal rate of tax has to be higher than the average rate. The effects of progressive taxation on the economy will be discussed later on (see pp.145, 158).

Differentiated Rates of Tax

Rates of tax may vary not only according to the level of income, size of a wealth holding, or the price of an article purchased, but they may also be differentiated according to the nature or origin of what is taxed.

The following are examples of differentiated rates that are now, or have been at one time or another, levied in the UK.

(a) *Tax on consumption.* Purchase tax was levied at higher rates on luxuries, rising to a maximum of 100 per cent on the 'most luxurious' goods, and at lower rates on necessities that were not exempt from taxation.

(b) *Tax on income.* Income tax was imposed at a lower rate on earned income and an additional surcharge was imposed on unearned income.

(c) *Tax on profits.* A lower rate of tax was imposed on profits that were ploughed back into the business and a higher rate on profits that were distributed to shareholders.

(d) *Tax on capital.* Capital transfer tax was assessed at a lower rate on transfers of capital in lifetime than on death (see p. 223).

(e) *Taxes on inheritance.* The bequest of capital to a spouse is not taxed, but all other transfers are. In some countries the rate of tax on inherited wealth is differentiated according to the relationship of the beneficiary to the donor, so that direct descendants pay a lower rate than distant relatives. This practice is not applied in the UK nor has the proposal that transfer of capital accumulated by the tax-payer should be taxed at lower rates than inherited wealth.

Differentiation is usually introduced to achieve a specific policy objective such as to make taxes on consumption less regressive, to achieve more equal distribution of income or wealth, to encourage business savings and investments, or to preserve family businesses.

PRINCIPLES OF TAXATION

The principles of taxation which were formulated by Adam Smith and set out in his *Wealth of Nations* – known as the famous four canons of taxation – are still held to be valid some two hundred years later. These principles or maxims postulate that:

(a) 'The subjects of every state ought to contribute to the support of the government, as nearly as possible in proportion to their respective abilities.' To Adam Smith a proportional tax was an equitable tax, but he was well ahead of his time in suggesting that it was not 'unreasonable for the rich to contribute to public revenue not only in proportion to their income but something more than that proportion'. Adam Smith thus foreshadowed progressive taxation.

(b) 'The tax which each individual is bound to pay ought to be certain and not arbitrary. The time of payment, the manner of payment, the quantity to be paid, ought to be clear and plain to the contributor, and to every other person.' Efforts to devise such a tax met with limited success but British income tax goes some way to meet these requirements.

(c) 'Every tax ought to be levied at the time or in the manner, in which it is most convenient for the contributor to pay it.' To a taxpayer no time is convenient for tax payment but the pay-as-you-earn (PAYE) income tax scheme (see p. 141) is perhaps less inconvenient than most other ways of paying tax.

(d) 'Every tax ought to be so contrived as both to take out and to keep out of the pockets of the people as little as possible over and above what it brings into the public treasury of the state'. Unless the cost of tax administration and tax compliance is kept down, the burden of taxation increases without benefiting the Exchequer.

Since the doctrine of *laissez-faire* (see p. 74) prevailed in his day, Adam Smith was not concerned with the use of taxes for the purpose of managing a national economy though this has now become an accepted function of the state. The following new principles of taxation need to be added to the canons of Adam Smith.

(a) Taxes should be flexible so that they can be adjusted to changing conditions in order to counteract fluctuations in the level of economic activity.

(b) Taxes should be devised in such a way as to minimise the disincentive effects to work and enterprise, which adversely affect economic growth.

(c) Taxes should be internationally compatible to avoid double taxation of people working abroad and in multinational companies.

(d) Taxes should be adaptable so that they can be used, if so desired, to achieve greater vertical equality by redistribution of income and wealth.

Tax provisions modelled on these principles, however commendable in themselves, are not necessarily compatible with each other. Flexibility is a desirable characteristic but it raises the problem of stability in the tax system. Frequent changes in the rates of a tax, exemptions and allowances tend to create confusion which would go against the principles of certainty and of administrative efficiency aimed at keeping down the cost of collection and of tax compliance. A high marginal rate of income tax might be regarded as desirable because of its redistributive effect, but it could have adverse effects on incentives. The principle of equity between taxpayers and the principle of simplicity are not of a compatible nature. As the Royal Commission of Income Tax (1920) pointed out:

....a tax that aimed at providing legislative provisions for every case, so that no hardship of any sort should be possible, would be so intricate

and detailed, so full of exceptions and provisos, that it would be
unintelligible to the ordinary taxpayer and would render the machine
ineffective (i.e. the machinery of taxation for raising revenue).

In discussing the desirable characteristics of taxation, the Meade
Committee on the 'Structure and Reform of Direct Taxation' (1978)
concluded that, '... where those characteristics conflict, it is essential function of the political process to determine how much weight to give to each
of them'.

A TAX SYSTEM

A tax system that consists of a variety of taxes cannot comply with all the
requirements of the principles of taxation. It has to be based on a
compromise. Different taxes have their own particular advantages and
disadvantages, but these tend to be shared by taxes that fall into the same
category. A tax system of a developed economy consists of three types of
taxes which are:

Taxes on income (direct taxation)	income tax, tax on profits (corporation tax in the UK) compulsory social security contributions
Taxes on consumption (indirect taxation)	value added tax, customs and excise duties
Taxes on capital	inheritance tax, capital gains tax, wealth tax, stamp duties

Direct and Indirect Taxation

The distinction between direct and indirect taxes lies in the difference in
relationship between the taxing authority and the taxpayer. *Direct taxes
are taxes on income.* The taxing authority assesses the liability directly on
each taxpayer, whether a person or a business, according to their specific
circumstances. They then pay the tax directly to the authority. Indirect
taxes are taxes on consumption. Liability to the tax is determined by the
taxpayers themselves, since it depends on what and how much they buy.
They may however have little scope to vary their consumption of essential
goods and services for which that are no substitutes. In some cases there

may be a choice. For example when a tax on domestic fuel is increased householders may reduce consumption by increasing efficiency in energy use by such means as loft insulation. The assessment in the first instance may be on the manufacturer or distributor but the tax is finally paid by the consumer. The method of tax payment is, however, indirect, since it is the supplier who hands the money over to the taxing authority.

Opinion differs on the classification of capital taxes. It can be argued that they are a direct form of taxation since capital taxes can be assessed directly on an estate (see p. 217). In theoretical discussion and for practical purposes the common practice now is to treat capital taxes as being in a category of their own.

A Chancellor of the Exchequer has to rely on both direct and indirect taxation to manage an economy and to raise the bulk of public revenue. William Gladstone, when he was the chancellor, said in his budget speech of 15 April 1861:

> I have always thought it idle for a person holding the position of Finance Minister to trouble himself with what to him is necessarily an abstract question, namely the question between direct and indirect taxation each considered upon its own merits... I can never think of direct and indirect taxation except as I should think of two attractive sisters... both having the same parentage... for parents of both I believe to be necessity and invention... differing as only sisters may differ... when there is some variety of manner, the one being more free and open and the other somewhat shy and retiring and insinuating. I have always thought it not only allowable but even an act of policy to pay my respects to both.

Successive Chancellors have continued to pay their attentions to both, though some have found one to be distinctively more attractive than the other.

MERITS AND DEMERITS OF DIRECT AND INDIRECT TAXATION

Direct taxation has a number of advantages not only from the point of view of a government but also from that of a taxpayer faced with an alternative way of paying taxes. Merits of direct taxation can be listed as follows:

(a) *Equity*. Fairness is an important aspect of taxation. Direct taxes are more equitable than indirect taxes since the sacrifice involved in tax payment is related to the ability to pay and a system can be devised to provide for horizontal equity by means of allowances, and for vertical equity by means of progressive rates of tax.

(b) *Certainty.* Direct taxes are certain in the sense that the taxpayers are individually identifiable and the rates of tax, allowance and the time of payment are predetermined and known to them.

(c) *Convenience.* A direct tax can be regarded as 'convenient' if it is levied on pay-as-you-earn basis, since the tax payment coincides with the receipt of an income.

(d) *Known incidence.* The incidence of the tax cannot be shifted by the person on whom the tax is assessed (for discussion of *incidence* see p. 245). The taxing authorities can, therefore, establish on whom the tax burden falls and take it into account to provide for an equitable treatment of taxpayers and to estimate consequences of direct taxation.

(e) *Avoidance of distortion in allocation of income.* Direct taxes reduce income but leave the decision on how to allocate the after-tax income, i.e. the disposable income, to the taxpayer. Thus the proportions of income saved and spent on consumption, and the pattern of expenditure, are not distorted by taxation.

(f) *Flexibility.* Direct taxes are flexible in that the rates and allowances can be adjusted to increase or decrease disposable incomes depending upon whether the government is pursuing a fiscal policy to expand or contract the economy.

(g) *Built-in stabiliser.* The stabilising effect results from the response of direct taxation to changes in economic conditions. Since the taxes are related to income, an increase in income increases tax liability and reduces the expansionary effect. A decrease in income reduces tax liability and reduces the deflationary effect. If a person's income falls below the taxable level, the taxpayer may become entitled to a tax refund, increasing his disposable income. This reduces the deflationary effect of a recession and of a rise in unemployment.

Conversely the *demerits* of direct taxation include the following:

(a) *Complexity.* Successive Chancellors of the Exchequer have introduced allowances and exemptions to provide for horizontal and vertical equity, so that direct taxation has become full of anomalies and is so complex that it no longer complies with the simplicity principle of taxation.

(b) *Increasing cost of compliance.* As taxes have become more complex the cost of compliance to the taxpayers has increased. Tax returns are more time consuming, requiring an increasing level of expert tax knowledge and expensive professional advice (see pp. 222, 256).

(c) *Tax evasion.* The more complex the taxes are, the greater is the scope for tax evasion. The higher the level of taxation, the greater is the temptation for taxpayers to take advantage of any loopholes. If they succumb and succeed in reducing the tax liabilities by defaulting on payment then the burden of taxes on other taxpayers will increase – assuming that a government has to raise a given amount of revenue in taxation.

(d) *Disincentive effects.* Direct taxes are regarded by many as a disincentive to work and enterprise since effort that is rewarded with an increase in pay results in an increased tax liability (see p. 152).

(e) *Taxpayer resistance.* Direct taxes have a psychological effect. Taxpayers are more conscious of direct than of indirect taxation. They can legally reduce their liability only by reducing their income. Direct taxes are not optional in the way that indirect taxes are, and the resentment of paying them is therefore likely to be greater. The resistance to direct taxes can manifest itself in a variety of ways: a growth of the 'hidden' economy (see p. 257); a preference for leisure over work; or a vote at the next election against a government that had become unpopular by levying direct taxes.

Indirect taxes, like taxes on income, have their advantages and disadvantages from the point of view of the government, taxpayers and the economy. The *merits* of indirect taxation are:

(a) *Universality.* Assuming that if the proposition is accepted that all should contribute to some extent to the support of the state, on the grounds that all benefit from its existence, then indirect taxation is the only practical way of raising revenue from those with small incomes. The desirability of such a policy is, however, questionable because of its effect on the welfare of the poor.

(b) *Limited scope for evasion.* A consumer has little scope for evading indirect taxes on consumption since they are included in the price of goods and services.

(c) *Psychological palliative.* Indirect taxes are psychologically less painful to pay since the satisfaction compensates to some extent for the sacrifice of paying the tax. What is more, with indirect taxes, consumers may be hardly aware of paying them, if taxes such as customs and excise duties are not shown separately from the suppliers' price.

(d) *Optional nature.* To some extent indirect taxes are optional. In theory a person may decide not to pay them by refraining from the purchase of any of the taxed goods and services. In practice it is possible to vary the tax liability only to some extent by changing the level of consumption.

(e) *Flexibility.* Government can adjust the rates and ranges of indirect taxation to further an expansionary or a contractionary fiscal policy. An increase in indirect taxes penalises consumption and encourages saving. A decrease encourages expenditure and has the opposite effect on saving. A government can also use indirect taxation to change the pattern of consumption to achieve social and environmental objectives. An increase in a tax on cigarettes is likely is reduce smoking and improve peoples' health. A decrease in tax on unleaded petrol reduces pollution of the environment.

(f) *Simplicity.* Taxes on goods and services are easier for the consumer to understand than direct taxes are for those who are taxed on their incomes.

(g) *Low cost of compliance.* Payment of indirect taxes does not involve ordinary people in tax returns, but they may not escape compliance costs altogether, since some of the cost to suppliers of goods and services, of making tax returns for VAT, customs and excise duties may be passed on to them in higher prices.

(h) *No disincentive to work.* Indirect taxes do not discourage work as they are not related to the level of earnings, and may even encourage it. An increase in indirect taxes increases prices, so that to maintain the same standard of living as before, consumers would have to earn more, unless they are able and willing to run down their savings.

(i) *Political appeal.* For some of the reasons listed, taxpayers' resentment of indirect taxation is likely to be weaker than of direct taxation. Indirect taxes, therefore, appear attractive to and are levied by governments irrespective of their political persuasion.

The *demerits* of indirect taxation are a controversial topic. They refer to:

(a) *Regressive nature.* Indirect taxes are regressive. Since they are not related to the ability to pay, the sacrifice involved is not equitably distributed.

(b) *Distortion of consumer preferences.* Indirect taxes distort consumer preferences for consumption and savings depending on the rate at which they are taxed. Only if all goods and services are taxed uniformly is the effect of the taxes on the pattern of consumption neutral.

(c) *Distortion of the pattern of production.* Distortion of consumer demand will also affect the pattern of production. A government can discriminate by means of indirect taxes in favour of home-produced goods and imports. Protection through taxation depending on whose point of view it is looked at, can be regarded as a disadvantage or as an advantage. But, in the long run, it is not likely to be in a country's interest if it incites retaliation. Member States of the European Union and of GATT (now the World Trade Organisation) have sought to remove tax impediments to international trade.

(d) *Inflationary effect.* Indirect taxes, by increasing prices, may add to inflationary pressure in the absence of an incomes policy. Employees faced with a rising cost of living are likely to press for pay increases which push costs up. This, in turn, leads to further price increases and new demands for pay rises and cost-push inflation sets in. Some economists,however, regard indirect taxes as anti-inflationary in so far as they discourage consumption.

All the disadvantages of direct and indirect taxation are intensified at higher levels of taxation. To minimise the adverse effects of any one tax and to benefit from what are the 'desirable' effects of the others, governments tend to rely on a tax system that comprises a wide range of tax measures.

PATTERN OF TAXATION

The nature of the pattern of taxation will depend on such factors as: (i) the administrative structure – taxes may be levied by central government only or by both the central government and local government; (ii) the level of economic development of the country; (iii) the amount of the revenue required; (iv) the political party in power – different governments have their own ideological preferences; (v) policy objectives; and (vi) what the people are prepared to accept.

Table 6.1   Patterns of taxation: international comparison

Taxes and social security contributions by category as a
percentage of gross national product at factor cost, 1991

	Direct taxes		Indirect taxes	Taxes on Capital	Social Security contributions
	Households	Corporations			
Austria	12.0	2.2	16.2	–	12.5
Belgium	14.0	2.8	12.2	0.3	16.0
Denmark	–	–	18.1	0.3	1.6
Finland	18.1	2.1	15.6	0.2	12.1
France	6.9	2.5	14.8	0.6	19.4
Germany	10.3	1.7	13.0	0.1	16.0
Greece	4.4	1.7	19.0	0.5	11.1
Irish Republic	–	18.7	0.2	–	
Italy	11.7	3.0	12.1	0.1	13.3
Japan	8.3	5.4	7.7	0.6	9.1
Luxembourg	–	–	13.1	0.1	–
Netherlands	13.3	3.6	12.8	0.2	17.8
Norway	13.6	4.4	17.3	0.1	12.5
Spain	–	–	10.7	0.4	–
Sweden	19.5	0.9	18.5	0.1	15.7
Switzerland	12.2	1.4	6.0	0.7	9.6
UK	10.7	3.2	14.3	0.2	6.4
USA	10.4	2.2	8.4	0.3	7.7

Source: *Economic Trends*, 484 (London: HMSO, February 1994).

In developed countries, a pattern of taxation has evolved that comprises a variety of direct and indirect taxes and taxes on capital (see Table 6.1). When there are two tiers of government, each with the right to tax, a particular tax may be imposed by one taxing authority only, e.g. in the UK inheritance tax is levied by the central government. Alternatively, as in Sweden, a tax may be duplicated so that each tier of government levies a corresponding tax. This may be on personal income or consumption, for example.

Central government taxes	*Corresponding local government taxes*
National income tax	Local income tax
Value added tax on goods and services	Sales tax

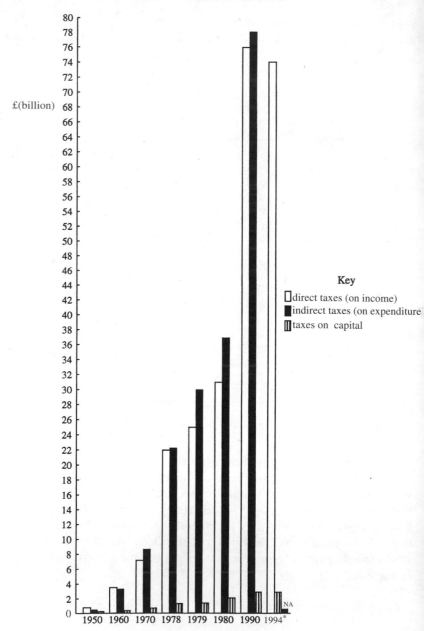

Figure 6.1   Direct taxes, indirect taxes and taxes on capital in the UK

Note: * forecast.

NA not available.

Source: Inland Revenue Board, *Inland Revenue Statistics* (1993) and CSO Blue Book, *UK National Accounts* (1993).

In the European Community the differences in the patterns of taxation in the Member States have important implications for its policy to harmonise taxes. This is an objective of the Community. Harmonisation of indirect taxation was made imperative as a result of the Single European Act which came into force in 1987 and provided for the creation after 1992 of a free internal market within the Community and for abolition of tax frontiers. To allow for a free flow of goods and services, the Value Added Tax and Customs and Excise duties of the Member States had to be brought into line. In the past some, more than others, had relied for revenue on indirect taxation and rates of tax have differed considerably (Tables 6.1, 9.3).

The harmonisation process, starting with indirect taxation, is likely to affect the following aspects within each Member State: (a) the relative importance of indirect and direct taxation as a source of revenue; (b) the equity of the tax system depending on the emphasis that is placed on indirect taxes, which being of a regressive nature, are less fair; and (c) the pattern of taxation as further measures are taken to harmonise taxes on incomes, profits and capital.

The future pattern of taxation of the European Community will be moulded not only by fiscal requirements and economic and social policies relating to the Community as a whole, but also by political measures advocated by some governments seeking to establish a federal Europe (see Chapter 16).

In a developing country, a government may have little choice but to rely on indirect taxation, the most practical form being customs duties. Imported goods, apart from those smuggled in, enter a country at a limited number of places where records can be kept and dues collected. A general sales tax has a limited base in an economy where households are, to a large extent, self-sufficient and where there are few established channels of retail distribution. Income tax and tax on profits have an even more restricted scope. A low level of income and of profits means that a large proportion of wage earners and of businesses have to be exempt. Submission of tax returns is difficult when illiteracy is high and collection of revenues is expensive without a well-established administrative machinery.

Capital taxes are hardly practical if, as in an agricultural society, the bulk of the wealth is invested in agricultural holdings that have to support a whole family. Tax payments would require the sale of some of the property that could well impair functioning of the productive unit. Without a ready market, valuation and disposal of the assets creates problems. Even if some form of capital taxation were possible, because of its very nature it could not provide a regular and stable flow of revenue that a government requires to finance its activities. Thus, in the short run, the equity of the tax system may have to be sacrificed in the name of expediency.

The equity, effectiveness and efficiency of any tax system has to be assessed by reference not only to the pattern of taxation but also to the pattern of public expenditure and the level of both.

REVENUE MAXIMISATION AND 'LAFFER CURVE' ANALYSIS

The point at which revenue from taxation is maximised can be shown on the Laffer Curve, named after Professor Arthur Laffer. For the purpose of the analysis two assumptions are made: (i) tax revenue is zero when tax rates are zero; and (ii) tax revenue is zero when tax rates are 100 per cent because people have no incentive to earn income and businesses to produce goods and services. A curve is drawn between the two extremes, measuring changes in tax revenue that result from changes in the tax rate. The rate required to maximise revenue may be different for different countries.

In Figure 6.2 revenue will be maximised at point *B*, when the tax rate is 50 per cent of the country's national income. At points *A* and *C* revenue is zero. The curve shows that as the tax rates rise, tax revenue increases up to point *B*. This may be explained by the incentive effect of taxation (see p. 148). As taxpayers' disposable incomes are reduced by taxes they may seek to increase their earnings to compensate for the tax payment. The additional earnings attract additional tax so that the total revenue rises. The *disincentive effect of taxation* (see p. 152) will not reduce tax revenue so long as the percentage increase in tax rate is greater than the percentage drop in income.

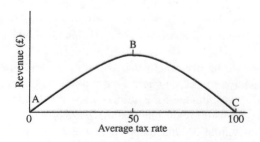

Figure 6.2   An example of Laffer Curve analysis

Suppose taxpayers decide that because the tax rate had gone up they will work less overtime. Their taxable earnings consequently drop from £200,000 to £190,000 as is illustrated by the following example:

A tax at a rate of 40 % on £200,000 produced tax revenue of £80,000.
A tax at a rate of 50 % on £190,000 produced tax revenue of £95,000.

An increase in tax of 10 per cent and a drop in earnings of 5 per cent resulted in an increase in tax revenue of £15,000. Figure 6.2 shows that when the tax rate exceeds 50 per cent tax revenue falls. The percentage drop in incomes will be greater than the percentage increase in the tax rate. The disincentive effect in this case reduces the tax yield.

SUMMARY

1. The history of taxation goes back to the ancient world. The early taxes were mainly levied on buildings and land; imports were subject to duties and port dues were charged. Their purpose was to raise revenue to finance the activities of the state.
2. The two main theories of taxation are the benefit theory and the 'ability to pay' theory. The underlying assumption of the former is that all who benefit from the activities of the state should contribute to their finance. The latter theory postulates that contributions should be related to the means of an individual.
3. Equity in taxation can be considered from the point of view of horizontal equity and of vertical equity.
4. In order to achieve horizontal equity people in the same circumstances should be treated in the same way for tax purposes.
5. In order to achieve vertical equity people in different circumstances should be treated differently with the richer paying more than those who are less well off; in this way the burden of sacrifice can be equalised.
6. Taxes can be: (i) progressive, when the rate of tax rises more steeply as income increases, (ii) proportional, when the rate of tax is the same percentage irrespective of the level of income; or (iii) regressive when the burden of tax is greater on smaller than on higher incomes.
7. Principles of taxation lay down the requirements for a 'good' tax. To the canons of taxation formulated by Adam Smith, new principles have been added since taxes are now used to regulate the economy and not only to raise revenue.

8. The tax system of a modern state comprises: direct taxes (on income), indirect taxes (on consumption); and taxes on capital.

9. Two of the important advantages of direct taxes are that they can be related to the ability to pay and that they can be levied at progressive rates. Their possible disincentive effect to work is one of their greatest disadvantages. Indirect taxes are regressive but are nevertheless a necessary source of revenue for most governments.

10. What the pattern of taxation of any one country will be depends not only on what is desirable but on what is practical, and this will be influenced by the country's stage of economic development and the level of revenue it requires. When countries form an association such as the European Community it becomes necessary to harmonise taxes in the Member States. As a consequence, a uniform pattern of taxation will emerge.

SUGGESTED FURTHER READING

C.V. Brown and J.P. Jackson, *Public Sector Economics* (Oxford: Basil Blackwell, 1992).

G.C. Hockley, *Fiscal Policy* (London: Routledge, 1992).

S. James and Nobes, G., *The Economics of Taxation* (London: Prentice-Hall, 1992).

J.E. Meade, *The Meade Report on the Structure and Reform of Direct Taxation* (London: George Allen & Unwin for the Institute of Fiscal Studies, 1978).

R. Musgrave and P. Musgrave, *Public Finance in Theory and Practice*, (New York: McGraw-Hill, 1989).

C.T. Sandford, *The Economics of Public Finance* (Oxford: Pergamon Press, 1992).

M. Wilkinson, *Taxation* (London: Macmillan, 1992).

G. Winkler (ed.), *Tax Harmonisation in Europe* (London: Macmillan, 1992).

EXERCISES

1. What is meant by the benefit theory of taxation? What are the problems of putting it into practice?
2. Discuss the validity of the main assumptions of the ability-to-pay theory of taxation.
3. Distinguish between horizontal and vertical equity and explain their relevance to tax policies.
4. Progressive taxation has both desirable and undesirable features. Comment on this statement.
5. What are the main disadvantages of indirect taxation from the point of view of the taxpayer?
6. Explain why, in the raising of state revenue, equity and expediency may require the levying of different forms of taxation.
7. Consider the argument that taxes on income are fairer than taxes on expenditure.
8. Suggest reasons why taxes on consumption are by their very nature regressive.
9. Principles of taxation are a product of their time and reflect current political, social and economic thought. Comment on this statement.
10. Explain why a tax system that is workable in a developed country may not be suitable for a developing one.

7 Taxes on Income

We have looked at taxation in general. Now we shall consider individual taxes and illustrate the investigation with examples from the UK (see Figure 7.1).

Income Tax is a tax on the income of a person and is therefore a personal tax. It is also a direct tax on the taxpayer. For the purpose of taxation a distinction may be drawn between two types of income, which are: (i) *earned incomes* – wages, salaries, professional fees, benefits in kind; (ii) *unearned income* – rent, interest, dividends.

The description 'unearned' may, however, be misleading in so far as a return on investment may be the result of considerable effort and enterprise on the part of an individual. An alternative term to 'unearned' income which is in use is 'investment income'. It clearly indicates that the income is obtained from money that had been invested. However, it does not make it explicit that interest on money which is lent is also treated for tax purposes as investment income, although loans are not an investment. In the discussion of income tax a number of other terms are also used and it may, therefore, be useful to provide a list of them with a short explanation at the beginning. They are:

Tax base – the income of a person.

Tax unit – the person liable for the tax payment.

Tax return – a statement by a recipient of income and the basis for assessment to tax.

Tax threshold – the point on an income scale at which liability to tax begins.

Tax assessment – the determination of tax liability. In the UK this is done by the Inland Revenue. Some countries, the USA among them, operate a self-assessment system, whereby the taxpayer establishes the amount of income tax due and the treasury carries out checks.

Tax rate – a specific proportion of a unit of taxable income that a taxing authority collects in revenue. The rate can be expressed as a percentage, e.g. 50 per cent of a taxable £1, or as a given amount, e.g. 50 pence per £. Different rates may be applied depending on the size of income or its origin. The Chancellor of the Exchequer proposes the tax rates and Parliament approves them.

Table 7.1   Standard rates of income tax in the UK, 1900–95

Year	Standard/basic rate (pence per taxable pound)	Year	Standard/basic rate (pence per taxable pound)
1900	5.0	1955	42.5
1910	6.0	1960	39.0
1920	30.0	1965	41.0
1930	22.5	1970	41.0
1935	22.5	1975	35.0
1940	42.5	1980	30.0
1945	50.0	1990	25.0
1950	45.0	1995	25.0
1955	42.5		

Standard rate of tax, or basic rate as it is sometimes called – is a flat rate levied on incomes between the tax threshold and the point designed as a higher income level, at which higher rates apply (see Table 7.1).

Graduation – the operation of tax allowances and reliefs, and rising bands of taxable income (see Table 7.2).

Differentiation – the distinction between earned and investment income (see Table 7.2).

THE ORIGIN OF INCOME TAX IN THE UK

Income tax originated in wartime. It was first imposed in 1799 by William Pitt (1759–1806) as a temporary war measure. It was a graduated tax on incomes between £60 and £200 a year, with top rate of 10 per cent on incomes above £200. The thresholds were such that manual workers with average earnings were exempt. Income tax did not become a permanent feature of the British tax system until half a century later.

The following dates are major landmarks in the history of income tax in Britain:

1799–1802   Income tax was imposed for the duration of the war between Britain and France and was repealed after the Treaty of Amiens.

1803–15   Income tax was re-introduced for the duration of hostilities as the two countries were at war again.

1842	Sir Robert Peel imposed income tax to raise revenue in peacetime. It was to be a temporary measure for three years but the period was later extended.
1853	William Gladstone again extended the tax for another seven years with a promise of repeal, but as the Crimean War broke out the need for revenue increased and the tax was continued.
1860	Free trade policy led to the repeal of tariffs and forced Gladstone to shift emphasis from indirect to direct taxation. He renewed the provision for the continuation of income tax. This was no longer accompanied by a promise of a subsequent repeal. Thus in 1860 income tax ceased to be regarded as a temporary measure. Soon after this, it became the most important single source of government revenue.

COMPLIANCE OF INCOME TAX WITH THE PRINCIPLES OF TAXATION

Of all the different taxes, income tax comes nearest to complying with the principles of taxation; as regards certainty, convenience and equity (see p. 123).

Certainty of Income Tax

Income tax is certain, as taxpayers are not in doubt that a liability to tax will arise if the income received exceeds a given exemption level. Deductible allowances and rates of tax are set out in the Finance Acts. The period over which income tax is charged, i.e. the fiscal year, is fixed at twelve months. The time of tax collection is made known – weekly on wages, monthly on salaries and at specified times on various other forms of income.

Convenience of Income Tax

The payment of income tax has been made convenient for those in employment by the deduction of tax at source. The employer, on behalf of the Inland Revenue, deducts income tax from the earnings of his employees and pays them a wage or salary net of tax, hence the name of the 'pay-as-you-earn' (PAYE) system. The principle of deduction at source dates back to the Income Tax Act of 1803 but it was not until the Finance Act (No.2) (1940) that the first provisions were made for universal deduction of tax from earnings.

PAYE

The *pay-as-you-earn scheme (PAYE)* was announced in a White Paper, 'A new system of the taxation of weekly wage earners' (Cmnd. 6469, 1943), and came into operation in April 1944. Under the scheme, the Inland Revenue allocates to each employee a code number which is determined by reference to the personal allowances to which a person is entitled. These allowances reduce the tax liability. The code tells the employer how much of each employee's pay is tax-free. The employer can then calculate from tax-tables what is the amount of tax payable on any given level of income, and then deduct the tax. A change in personal circumstances of the taxpayer results in a change of the code number and the tax liability is adjusted accordingly, so that if a person becomes unemployed they may become entitled to a tax repayment. It is this cumulative feature of the PAYE scheme that distinguishes it from the other schemes of deduction at source under which any over deduction is not rectified until the end of the year.

The *advantages* of PAYE are:

(a) The advantage to the taxpayer is that the tax is paid at a time when income is received. Thus, there is the ability to pay and any changes in that ability are taken into account.

(b) The advantage to the Inland Revenue is that PAYE shifts to the employers much of the work involved in the calculation of tax liability and in the collection of the tax.

(c) The scope for tax avoidance by employees on their wages and salaries is removed.

The *disadvantages* of PAYE are:

(a) A disadvantage of the scheme to employers is the cost of calculation that falls on them. The Inland Revenue does not reimburse them for the expense of acting as if it were its tax collecting agent.

(b) The scheme results in what amounts to an employment tax payable by employers and may therefore adversely affect demand for labour. Since no such employment tax officially exists on the statute books, it is not taken into account in estimating the tax burden.

(c) Deduction at source is considered a disadvantage by some politicians who are concerned with the growth of public expenditure. In their view, deduction of income tax by employers before payment of wages and salaries, reduced the employees' awareness of tax burden that results from the growth of public expenditure. This makes it easier for a government to increase its spending and for the illusion to be created that public goods and services are free and no one has to pay for them.

Fluctuating incomes

The PAYE scheme does not apply to earnings such as artists' fees or authors' royalties that are irregular and may vary greatly from year to year. Tax liability is assessed on the previous year's earnings. This could mean that in one successful year, as fees or royalties shot up, they would be liable to high rates of tax, whereas in an unsuccessful year earnings could be below the tax exemption limit. Provisions for the spreading of earnings over a period have been introduced by the *Income Tax Act* (1952) and *Finance Act* (1953) to allow for equitable treatment of fluctuating incomes.

Equity of Income Tax

Income tax that is related to the ability to pay can be regarded as an equitable form of taxation and compatible with both the principles of horizontal and vertical equity.

Horizontal equity

Horizontal equity is a principle of equity that people in similar circumstances should be treated in a similar way. When incomes are the same but circumstances differ – as when one person is married and another single – incomes are brought to a common denominator by allowances, such as a married couple's allowance. It will still be granted in the tax year 1995–96 as the following example shows. It is however the government's intention to phase out the married couple's allowance. Both working spouses are now entitled to a personal allowance.

Personal allowances can be grouped under distinct headings and relate to: (i) type of household – single person, married couple, one parent family; (ii) special circumstances and disabilities, e.g. age (tax allowance for the elderly) and blindness (blind person's allowance); and (iii) financial

Example for tax year 1995–96 for married couples

	Both earning one child		non working spouse, children
	Husband	Wife	
Gross annual income	£12,000	8,000	£15,000
Personal allowance	3,525	3,525	3,525
Taxable income	8,475	4,475	11,475
Married couple allowance relief	258	0	258
Tax thereon	1,959	959	2,709
National insurance contributions	955	555	1,255
Child benefit		540	980
Net income	9,344	7,028	12,274

commitments, e.g. tax relief for interest paid on specified loans such as a loan from a building society for house purchase.

Vertical equity

The provision to achieve vertical equity may take several forms, such as: (i) the exemption of low incomes from income tax; (ii) graduation and progressive rates of taxation; and (iii) surcharges on higher incomes and on investment incomes.

The exemption of low incomes from taxation dates back to the introduction of income tax. People with an annual income of less than £60 were exempt from the tax. This meant that they were below the tax threshold. There is now no one standard threshold for income tax. The level at which a person starts paying it depends on the allowances to which they are entitled.

Gradation and progressive rate

When first introduced, income tax was a proportional tax levied at a fixed percentage of income, but since this resulted in a bigger payment the bigger the income, public opinion accepted proportional tax as equitable. Later, as the view on the equity of sacrifice began to change, unearned and higher incomes were taxed more heavily.

Differentiation

A distinction for tax purposes between earned and unearned income was first drawn in 1907 when a lower rate of tax was levied on the former. Subsequently, unearned incomes were subjected to an investment income surcharge in addition to income tax (see p. 145). Differentiation is a controversial issue. A case for it can be made on the following grounds:

(a) Earned income is more 'precarious', since ability to earn depends on a variety of uncontrollable factors such as health, and diminishes with old age. The Royal Commission on Profits and Income (Cmnd. 9105, 1954) attached weight to the argument that investment income is more stable. It has to be remembered that it was reporting at the close of a period when the *Bank Rate* had been maintained for nearly twenty years at a fixed rate of 2 per cent and other interest rates had remained correspondingly stable. Since then they have fluctuated sharply with the *Minimum Lending Rate* rising to a peak of 17 per cent before it was discontinued in 1981. Consequently, investment income in the form of interest has fluctuated also, and so too have dividends. Thus not only was the level of income uncertain; occasionally income disappeared altogether, as the number of companies going bankrupt increased.

(b) Lower rates of tax on earned income give greater incentive to effort. But since income tax can hardly be regarded as an incentive, this point should perhaps be restated and the phrase 'lower disincentive' substituted. There is considerable disagreement among economists on the subject of taxation and disincentives (see p. 152).

(c) Investment income confers psychological benefits in that it creates a feeling of security. This is a subjective assessment because a wage or salary may be more secure than dividend or interest.

(d) Differentiation equalises sacrifice. In the view of the Royal Commission '... it is based on the idea that, if a given amount is to be raised by taxation, the burden of the sum is more fairly distributed if £1 of earned income is treated as not being the taxable equivalent of £1 of investment income'.

(e) Redistribution of income and wealth can be increased by an investment income surcharge.

Whether one accepts all or some of the arguments in favour of differentiation, it is still necessary to take into account the disadvantages of such a surcharge.

A higher rate of tax on investment favours consumer expenditure as against saving and investment and can therefore contribute to inflationary pressure. If investment is discouraged by the higher rate than this can be

expected to have an adverse effect on economic growth – in which investment plays an important part. A government needs to consider the
economic, social and political implications of differentiation and to
balance the advantages against the disadvantages. It was the pre-First
World War Liberal government which introduced differentiation in favour
of earned income but successive Liberal, Conservative and Labour administrations have continued with the practice. It was eventually abolished by
Conservatives in 1984.

Progressive Taxation

Super tax was a first step towards progressive taxation. It was introduced
in 1909 and was levied, in addition to the standard rate of 1 shilling, at the

Table 7.2   Progressive tax on income

Labour government		Conservative government			
Last budget 1978		*First Budget 1979*		*Budget 1994–95*	
Taxable income bands (£)	*Rate of tax 1978–79 (%)*	*Taxable income bands (£)*	*Rate of tax 1979–80 (%)*	*Taxable income bands (£)*	*Rate of tax 1982–83 (%)*
Earned Income					
1–750	25	1–750	25	1–3,000	20
751–8,000	33*	751–10,000	30*	3,001–23,700	25*
8,001–9,000	40	10,001–12,000	40		
9,001–10,000	45	12,001–15,000	45		
10,001–11,000	50	15,001–20,000	50		
11,001–12,500	55	20,001–25,000	55		
12,501–14,000	60				
14,001–16,000	65				
16,001–18,500	70				
18,501–24,000	75				
over 24,000	83	over 25,000	60	over 23,700	40
Investment Income Surcharge					
1–1,700	nil	0–5,000	nil	nil	
1,701–2,250	10	over 5,000	15		
over 2,250	15				

Notes:
* standard rate of tax.
  Combined maximum marginal rate of tax was 98 per cent in 1978.
  Top rate for 1995 is 40 per cent.

flat rate of 5 pence per £1 (£1 = 240 pence) on incomes over £5,000, imposing a combined rate of just under 6 per cent. (Seventy years later the top rate of combined tax on earned and investment income reached 98 per cent.) But it was the *Finance Act (1920)* that established a system of graduated income tax. In the Budget of 1927–28 super tax was renamed surtax. It was levied on higher incomes at a rate ranging from 1 shilling per £1 (5 per cent) on the first £500, to 7 shillings and sixpence (38 per cent) on incomes above £2,000.

Unified personal taxation

Income tax and surtax were replaced in 1975, as a result of a major change in the structure of personal taxation, by a unified, graduated personal tax. Advantages claimed by the government for the unified system were: (i) simpler tax, (ii) smoother graduation; and (iii) lower cost of collection since simplification of income tax and abolition of surtax were expected to result in administrative economies. The two features of taxation that were retained were differentiation between earned and investment incomes and steeply progressive rates of taxation applicable to both.

The principle of a progressive rate of income tax is now firmly established, but there is no one correct or desirable scheme of progression. What progression a government will regard as desirable will be influenced by its political ideology. What will be practical will depend on the economic consequences of the progressiveness of the rates. What will be acceptable will be influenced by public opinion.

During the period from 1909 to 1978 there was a gradual increase in the progressiveness of income tax. At the same time the combined burden of direct and indirect taxation and of capital taxes rose from 6 per cent of the national income to approximately 33 per cent. The higher level of direct taxation intensified the effects of its progressiveness on the economy. The 1979 Budget of the Conservative government reversed this trend, reducing progressiveness and giving some relief to investment incomes, subsequently differentiation between earned and unearned incomes was discontinued for tax purposes and Investment Income Surcharge was abolished in 1984. This can be seen by comparing the last Budget of Labour government with the first one of the new Conservative administration (see Table 7.2). It should be noted that the raising of tax thresholds is not in itself indicative of the lessening severity of taxation but in a time of inflation may merely be a reflection of the diminishing value of the pound.

The stated objective of the Conservative government was to reduce direct taxation and to shift some of the burden to indirect taxation. This, it

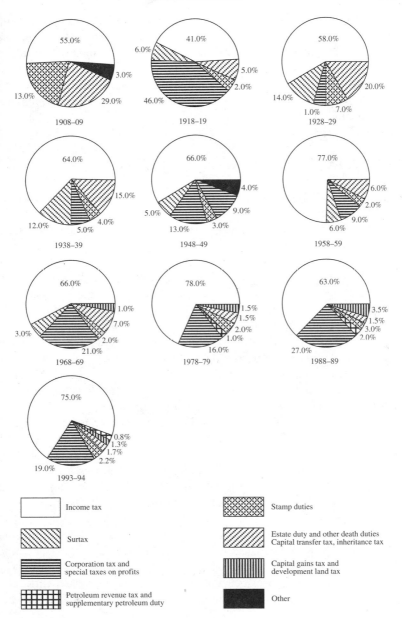

Figure 7.1   Revenue from direct taxation

Source: Board of Inland Revenue, *Inland Revenue Statistics*, annually up to 1994.

was argued, would make consumption relatively less attractive to saving, and at the same time provide incentive to work and to invest. The reduction in the progressiveness of the income tax was, to some extent, made possible by changes in the evaluation of its economic consequences and in public attitude. The view that income tax is a disincentive to work and that a surcharge on investment income is a disincentive to savings and investment has been gaining ground.

INCOME TAX AND INCENTIVES IN THEORY

Economists have been divided on the disincentive effect of direct taxation. They have been able to show that theoretically an increase in income tax can be an incentive to work, and also that it can be a disincentive. Thus there are two identifiable effects:

(a) *The income effect.* An increase in income tax reduces the taxpayers' disposable income. They are unable to shift the tax burden since the effective incidence of the tax is on them (for discussions of tax incidence see p. 245). Consequently they become poorer, but their financial commitments, such as hire purchase of furniture or mortgage payments remain the same. To meet them the taxpayers can either cut down their consumption of other goods and services and reduce their standard of living or work harder and take on overtime to earn more to compensate for the increased income tax. But as, under a progressive system of taxation, their pre-tax income increases so will, after a time, the marginal rate of tax, and they will keep a smaller and smaller fraction of each additional £1 earned. Until the progressiveness was reduced in 1979, the amount retained when the combined top rate of tax was applied was 2 pence out of every £. If people continue to work harder when the tax goes up then that increase produces an income effect. Thus the tax rise acts as an incentive to effort.

(b) *The substitution effect.* If people decide that the additional income earned after the payment of tax is not worth the effort then they substitute leisure for work in their order of preferences. Thus an increase in tax results in a substitution effect and creates a disincentive to work, and conversely a decrease in tax could therefore be expected to increase the incentive.

The substitution effect is an indication of the inefficiency and waste that may arise for the following reasons:

(a) A person may decide to reduce their hours of employment so as to have time to do odd jobs around the house themselves, instead of paying somebody, e.g. to redecorate a room. From the point of view of the national economy this would be a waste of manpower resources. The theory of division of labour postulates that everybody should concentrate on that which they do best. Thus, if the houseowner is a surgeon it would be better if he/she devoted his/her time to operating and employed a decorator to paint. If the surgeon had paid tax at the top rate of tax on earned incomes in 1979, which left him/her with 17 pence out of each additional £1 he/she earned, he/she would have to earn an extra £294 to pay a decorator's bill of £50.

(b) Workers opting for leisure and taking an unofficial day off may impair the efficiency of a whole production unit.

(c) High-fliers may refuse promotion because they are unwilling to sacrifice their leisure for financial rewards that after tax appear unattractive. This may adversely affect the whole organisation for which they work.

There can also be another kind of substitution effect. Instead of substituting leisure for work, a skilled person may substitute a relatively low after tax income in their home country for a higher income abroad, where it would be less steeply taxed. The growth of multinational companies has increased the mobility of labour. Since emigration tends to deprive a country of its more highly trained and enterprising manpower, the national economy is likely to suffer as a result.

INCOME TAX AND INCENTIVES IN PRACTICE

Taxpayers' ability to respond to changes in income tax by working a greater or lesser amount, depends on the nature of their work. In some jobs, effort and output can be identified, measured and paid for according to a person's performance. The size of the pay packet and thereby the liability to income tax can thus be determined by an individual's decision to work or not to work but for some people this is not possible. The following examples illustrate this point.

(a) Manual workers, paid on piece rates, earning bonuses related to output or working overtime can adjust their effort. For example, among coalminers the practice of taking unofficial days off was well established and was known as 'laiking'. In 1977–78 absenteeism was 17.6 per cent of all shifts, 17.1 per cent in 1978–79 and 14.8 per cent in 1979–80. A typical story was that when a miner asked by his pit manager why he only worked four shifts a week, explained that he could not manage on three.

(b) Manual workers paid on a time basis cannot vary their earnings. In some industries, such as the chemical industry, where the various processes take time, output does not depend on the speed with which an individual operator works. There may, however, be the opportunity to work overtime, paid at higher rates, and thereby to augment earnings.

(c) Services and salaried workers are much less likely to have this opportunity to vary their earnings as earnings and effort are not directly related, but by working harder they may indirectly raise their pay by being rewarded by promotion.

(d) The self-employed, members of professions and tradesmen, such as architects and plumbers working on their own account, have the greatest scope to determine how much work they will undertake and therefore how much they will earn.

SUPPLY OF LABOUR AND TAXATION

In so far as income tax affects incentives to work it will also affect the supply of labour. It can be looked at in two ways: (i) the total number of people who are willing to work; and (ii) the number of hours that people are willing to work. Thus supply of labour may be:

1st week   10 workers working   40 hours a week = 400 hours per week
2nd week   8 workers working   50 hours a week = 400 hours per week
                              (including 10 hours overtime)

In both weeks, the total number of hours worked is the same. Thus the supply of labour can be said to be unchanged if it is measured in terms of units of time, but if it measured by the number of workers employed, then the supply has decreased by 20 per cent from 10 to 8 workers. Statements on the change in the supply of labour need to be analysed carefully as they can have different meanings.

Elasticity of Supply

If the supply of labour – defined either in terms of the number of people or the number of hours worked – changes in response to a change in the price of labour (wages) then supply is said to be *elastic* (in economic jargon) or responsive (in plain words). If the supply of labour does not decrease as a result of an increase in the tax which reduces the take-home pay, then it is *inelastic*, that is, unresponsive.

Figure 7.2(a) shows an *elastic* supply of labour. Suppose there are eight people prepared to work part-time for a take-home pay of £600 a month after tax. When income tax is reduced so that pay goes up to £700 a month, ten people are willing to work.

Figure 7.2(b) shows an *inelastic* supply of labour. If there are eight people willing to work for £600 a month and when, after a tax reduction, the take-home pay goes up to £700 a month and there are still only eight people, then the supply is inelastic. If the tax is increased so that the pay falls to £500 but the number of people remains as before, the supply is

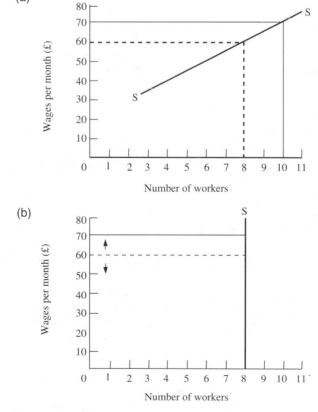

Figure 7.2   Supply of labour

said to be perfectly inelastic over this range.
The elasticity of supply is measured by the following formula:

$$E \; = \; \frac{\% \text{ change in the quantity supplied}}{\% \text{ change in price}} \quad \text{i.e.} \quad \frac{20\%}{10\%} \; = 2$$

Where E stand for elasticity, *quantity supplied* refers to the number of workers who offer themselves in the labour market and the *price* is the price of labour, that is wages.

Suppose that the number of workers who wish to work increases by 20 per cent when the wage offered increases by 10 per cent. On the basis of our formula, the elasticity of supply is 2. This means that the supply of labour is responsive to a change in price.

Supply is elastic	If E is greater than one
Supply has unit elasticity	If E is one, i.e. supply and price change in the same proportion
Supply is inelastic	If E is less than one
Supply is perfectly inelastic	If E is zero, that is when supply does not respond to a change in price, as in Figure 7.2(b).

The majority of people have to work for their living. Consequently changes in income tax are not likely to have an appreciable effect on the supply of labour as measured in terms of the number of people. A reduction in income tax may, however, attract some married women or retired people into the labour market, and increase the supply. Low tax thresholds and high rates of tax on the one hand, coupled with high social security benefits to the unemployed on the other, will make it less attractive for them to seek employment. If this happens, the combined effect will be to decrease the supply of labour.

EMPIRICAL EVIDENCE ON TAX DISINCENTIVES AND THE SUPPLY OF LABOUR

Evidence on tax disincentives comes from official sources and unofficial sources, i.e. private research.

Official Sources

Over the last fifty years a number of Royal Commissions have enquired into the various aspects of taxation. The following are the major reports in which the disincentive effects of taxes on work, enterprise and saving have been discussed:

(a) The *Royal Commission on National Debt and Taxation* (Cmnd. 2800, 1927) believed that for employees on fixed salaries the effect of income tax on the incentive to work was 'largely neutral'. So far as the professional man was concerned '...we find it very difficult to believe on purely financial grounds, that income tax will be a potent factor in making him less ready work or to sacrifice his leisure'. The Commission wrote:

> Over the whole field of income we conclude that the income tax borne by employees and professional men had had no important effect on their work and enterprise. It does not deter them from effort in such a way as to affect materially their income, that is to say their potential standard of living and saving.

(b) The *Royal Commission on the Taxation of Profits and Income* (Cmnd. 9105, 1954). The two commissions differed in one important respect. The 1927 report claimed that for an employee, 'the operation of the tax in diminishing his present income is the thing that he realises most clearly'. Whereas the 1954 report took the opposite view, 'very few of them [workers], it seems, have sufficient knowledge of the way that they are affected by the tax to be able to take that factor accurately into account in deciding upon behaviour at work.' Thus the psychological effect of taxation that the first Commission conceded in theory was ruled out by the later one. Otherwise it largely reiterated the earlier findings, stating that the tax had no effect on effort or absenteeism and that the deterrent effects on efficiency of production had not been substantiated.

Both Commissions based their conclusions on evidence submitted to them, but the second one in an attempt to appraise the effects of taxation on incentives, relied mainly on a Social Survey by the Government Sociology Research Unit.

(c) The *Royal Commission on the Distribution of Income and Wealth,* 1st Report (Cmnd. 6171, 1975), 8th and last report (Cmnd. 7679, 1979). The new evidence from industry in the private and public sector submitted to the Commission left little doubt as to the widespread belief in the adverse effects of income tax in general and of the steepness of its progression in particular. Representatives of companies and of public corporations argued that the decrease in pay differentials after tax had serious economic consequences which were: (i) The absence of acceptable differentials made it difficult for management to offer incentives and to reward skill and effort. British Rail pointed out, 'As social scientists have shown, money is by no means the only factor that counts, but it is very important nevertheless'. (ii) Staff had become demoralised. (iii) It had become more difficult to recruit staff of high quality. (iv) Promotions were refused. A representative from a multinational company argued that such motivating factors as status and job satisfaction were of transitory nature and did not survive long after promotion.

Many of those who appeared before the Commission appeared to share the view of an oil company spokesman that,

> The present tax structure makes it impossible to reward adequately the executive directors and management on whose inventiveness, initiative, judgement and skill enterprises, whether great or small, depend to produce employment opportunities and the wealth from which most public, social, as well as private expenditure, must come. (Selective Evidence submitted to the Royal Commission for Report No.3 Cmnd. 6383, 1976)

These published views are at variance with the Commission's conclusions which appear to be based on six studies listed in its report. Four of them relate to the UK and two to the USA. None of them are recent and none are extensive. The earliest mentioned study dates back to 1946–47 and the latest to 1971. The rest had been carried out in the 1950s. The samples ranged in size from just under two hundred people to just over 2,000 but the number of respondents was smaller. The Commission concluded that '...none of the studies (including a single study covering higher incomes in the UK) gives support to the proposition that high levels of taxation have a significant effect on work effort'.

Unofficial Sources

Findings of a number of studies which were the result of private academic research have been published in journals in the UK and USA. In an attempt to find out what was the effect of taxation on incentives and the supply of labour economists use: (i) the *survey method*, in which information was obtained from answers to questionnaires by a number of people selected for the purpose of the study; and (ii) *the econometric method*, requiring construction of mathematical models. The following are very brief summaries of studies selected to show the affect of taxation on different types of workers and the different methods of approach to the subject:

(a) *Self-employed.* A survey of self-employed members of a profession was carried out by G.F. Break in 1956 ('Income Tax and Incentives to Work: An Empirical Study', *American Economic Review*, September 1957). His sample covered 306 self-employed accountants and solicitors in England. The study was repeated by D.B. Fields and W.T. Stanbury in 1968 ('Income Taxes and Incentives to Work: Some Additional Empirical Evidence', *American Economic Review*, June 1971). The results are shown in Table 7.3.

It is interesting to note that the standard rate of tax was 42.5 pence in 1956 and 41.0 pence in 1968.

These two investigations were relatively major studies in terms

Table 7.3   Income tax and the incentive to work

	Number of persons giving the answer as a percentage of the total	
	1956 (%)	*1968 (%)*
Respondents claimed that:		
Tax had a disincentive effect	13	11
Tax had an incentive effect	10	19
Tax had no effect	77	70
Total in the sample (%)	100	100
Number	306	285

Source: G.F. Break, *American Economic Review* (1957).
D.B. Fields and W.T. Stanbury, *American Economic Review* (1971).

of numbers. One survey covering as few as seven respondents is to be found in literature on the subject of tax effects. However, general-isations, even on the basis of 306 answers, are insufficient evidence on which to establish definitely the effects of taxation on work effort.

(b) *Executives*. A survey of 100 executives in 1967 by Professor C.T. Sandford (*The Economics of the Public Sector*, 1978) showed that the 63 who answered the questionnaire believed that the tax had a disincentive effect.

(c) *Manual workers*. A survey of 2010 weekly-paid workers in Britain was carried out to find out the effect of tax on overtime (C.V. Brown and E. Levin, 'The Effects of Income Taxation on Overtime', *Economic Journal*, December 1974). Investigators tabulated answers by 1,348 men and considered 1,248 claims to be 'highly plausible'. These are given here in Table 7.4 and show a considerable difference in the effect of tax on single men and on married men with children.

The question that respondents were asked was whether the tax made them work 'more overtime', 'less overtime', 'does not apply/neither'. But since no government can abolish taxation, the choice for a Chancellor is between an increase or decrease in taxes. The effect on incentives will, therefore, depend on changes in taxation rather than on the existence of a tax.

An earlier study by S.E. Rolfe and G. Furnes ('The Impact of Changes in Tax Rates and Methods of Collection on Effort', *Review of Economics and Statistics*, 1957) did investigate the effect of tax

Table 7.4   Effect of tax on overtime

Highly plausible *Claims in the sample*	*less*	*Overtime worked* *(percentage of claims)* *no change*	*more*	*Total*
All men (number 1,248)	7	79	14	100
single men	8	84	8	100
married men with children	6	77	17	100

Source: C.V. Brown and E. Levin. 'The Effects of Income Taxation on Overtime', *Economic Journal* (December 1974).
   See also C.V. Brown and P.M. Jackson, *Public Sector Economics* (Oxford: Basil Blackwell, 1992).

reductions in 1946 and 1947, and found that the result was an increase in the supply of labour.

More recent work by M. Beenstock ('Does the UK Labour Market Work?', *Economic Outlook*, July 1979) predicted that a reduction in the standard rate of tax from 33 per cent to 30 per cent would initially increase the supply of labour by approximately 0.6 per cent. Beenstock and others, at the London Business School, applied the 'Laffer Curve' analysis to the British economy and demonstrated that a 5 per cent reduction in tax revenue from the then current rate of 40 per cent of gross domestic product would increase the supply of labour by about 15 per cent. This would lead to economic growth, whereas an increase in taxation would produce a disincentive effect (M. Beenstock and A. Gosling, 'Taxation, Incentives and Government Revenue in the UK', mimeo, London Business School and M. Beenstock, 'Taxation and Incentives in the UK', *Lloyds Bank Review*, October 1979).

Similarly, more recent studies by P. Minford and P. Ashton suggest that higher rate cuts would lead to a substantial increase in work incentives (*Fiscal Studies*, vol. 9, No. 2 1988 and *Liverpool Quarterly Economic Bulletin*, 1988), but C.V. Brown sees little evidence to support this view (*Fiscal Studies*, vol. 9. No. 4, 1988). On the basis of their research S. James and C. Nobes have concluded that small incentive and disincentive effects largely cancel each other out, though tax changes appear to have a greater effect on the work effort of women than on that of men (*The Economics of Taxation*, 1992).

These examples selected from work done in a period of over fifty years illustrate the point that there is no straightforward, agreed answer to what is the effect of direct taxation on incentives. The answer depends on various factors, such as: (i) on whom the tax is levied; (ii) at what rates taxpayers pay it; (iii) the degree of progressiveness of the tax system; and (iv) the scope to vary the amount of work a person does. From the point of view of supply of labour what is important is not only whether, and to what extent, a reduction in tax on earnings will increase it, but whether there is demand for labour. More people may have the incentive to look for jobs but there may be no work for them if there is no economic growth. Since investment plays an important part in the whole question, we have to consider the effects of taxation on investment.

EFFECT OF PROGRESSIVE INCOME TAX ON THE LEVEL OF
PERSONAL SAVINGS AND THE PATTERN OF INVESTMENT

Progressive income tax has a two-fold initial effect that will be intensified
the higher the level of taxation and the steeper the progression. The tax
will reduce the disposable incomes of all taxpayers, but it will reduce
higher incomes more than proportionately. It is people with higher
incomes who have a greater propensity to save – they tend to save a bigger
proportion of their income than people with lower incomes. The latter
have a greater propensity to consume since they may have to spend their
entire income on the bare necessities of life. It can therefore be expected
that progressive income tax would reduce personal savings and
investment. But again there is no simple answer as to what in fact
happens.

The ability to save depends on the level of income. However, the willingness to save is also influenced by psychological factors. A person
whose income is reduced by taxation may decide: (i) to maintain the same
standard of living and decrease savings; (ii) to reduce consumption but
keep the level of savings intact; or (iii) to cut both. What a taxpayer will
do will depend on their personal characteristics, the reasons they have for
savings and the way in which they save.

Reasons for Saving

People may save simply because they have some income left over or for a
more specific reason such as: (i) to provide for greater security for
themselves and their dependants; (ii) for emergencies; (iii) to acquire an
asset that is too expensive to buy out of current income, e.g. a house;
(iv) to satisfy a desire to become a person of substance; (v) to secure an
investment income on the accumulated capital; or (vi) to invest in the hope
of making a capital gain.

Forms of Savings

The form that savings take varies depending to some extent on whether the
savings are planned or residual. A person may plan to save a certain
proportion of their income or a fixed amount at regular intervals. If they
enter into an agreement with a financial institution to do so, their savings
are contractual and may take the form of insurance premiums or a life
policy or mortgage repayments to a building society. The rate of saving is
fixed for some years ahead. A person whose income is reduced by an

increase in taxation cannot cut down on this form of saving without incurring a penalty and would therefore have to reduce consumption or earn more. Residual saving, which is the balance between income and expenditure, tends to fluctuate and is more likely to take the form of a deposit, e.g. with a bank.

The Level of Savings

This is influenced by personal, monetary and fiscal considerations. Individual circumstances and reasons for saving are important facts that determine how much people save, but savings can be encouraged or discouraged by a government's policy on interest rates and taxation. Thus, in so far as high interest rates increase a return on capital, they make saving more attractive. The imposition of an income tax surcharge on investment income reduces the return and can adversely affect the incentive to save. But low rates of interest may result in people saving more if they want to reach a certain level of investment income and, in their case, a removal of the surcharge would reduce the need to save. An increase in taxation will reduce the ability to save, other things remaining the same, but a reduction in taxes need not necessarily increase the level of savings – for example, the increased income may be swallowed up by inflation. We can thus see that the level of savings cannot be explained by reference to any one factor. Nevertheless, the effect of income tax on savings cannot be ignored.

The pattern of savings and investment are both distorted by progressive income tax in several ways, such as:

(a) *Tax concessions.* By reducing the tax burden on a discriminatory basis, the government can make some assets a more attractive form of investment and channel savings accordingly. Thus, tax relief on payment of interest on certain types of loans to acquire specified assets, e.g. a house or an insurance cover, can influence a person's decision on whether to borrow or to save and also the choice of investments.

(b) *Tax exemptions.* By exempting from tax income derived from certain forms of investments, e.g. National Savings Certificates, a government can increase the appeal to investors of its own stocks and thereby affect demand for the shares of companies.

(c) *Progressive rate of tax.* Redistribution of income and consequently of wealth from richer to poorer people means that there are fewer people who can save a lot and more people who can save a little.

Those with relatively small incomes tend to opt for 'safe' investment and channel their savings either into government securities or into banks, building societies and insurance companies. Such savings become institutionalised. Financial institutions are restricted in the use of money that is entrusted to them and are obliged to invest some of the funds with the government and the rest in relatively safe assets. As a result of this and the fact that progressive taxation reduces the number of individuals who can save and invest on a large scale and take risks, the supply of risk capital to industry, particularly to small firms and those venturing into new and unproven fields, is likely to diminish.

(d) *Investment Income Surcharge.* This distorts the pattern of investment by making it more attractive for taxpayers to put their savings into assets that yield no income but are likely to increase in value.

EMPIRICAL EVIDENCE ON EFFECTS OF TAXATION ON SAVINGS AND INVESTMENT

(a) The *Royal Commission on National Debt and Taxation* (Cmnd. 2800, 1927) investigated the effects of taxation on savings and investment and concluded that, 'The savings of the income tax-paying class have therefore suffered: the effect has been most severe in the larger incomes liable to high effective rates of tax.' The report went on to point out that in consequence the supply of capital to industry had been reduced but that wider causes than taxation had also influenced this reduction.

(b) The *Royal Commission on Taxation of Profits and Income* (Cmnd. 9474, 1955) returned to the subject. Its belief was that, 'A complex of reasons, moral, social and economic, supports the view that a man ought to save from consumption some part of his income during most parts of his life...' The Commission concerned itself with tax allowances to encourage savings rather than with the search for evidence on what effect income tax had on them.

(c) The *Royal Commission on the Distribution of Income and Wealth* (Eight Reports) (1st Report, Cmnd. 6171, 1975, last report, Cmnd. 7679, 1979). The Commission neither in its report on lower incomes nor in its report on higher incomes concerned itself to any appreciable extent with how people in the two groups were affected by income tax, in respect to their ability and willingness to save. This lack of interest is surprising, since the extent to which people save, or are deterred from saving by taxation, must have a bearing on the distribution of wealth. The study of the effects of income tax on savings and investment has been a relatively little explored field of non-governmental academic research.

INFLATION AND INDEXATION FOR INCOME TAX PURPOSES

Inflation can distort a system of income tax, undermine the principle of equity on which it was developed and set the tax in conflict with the overall objectives of the government's fiscal policy. We can illustrate the effects of inflation on income tax by the following examples:

(a) *Tax thresholds.* Unless they are revised in step with inflation, people who were formerly considered too poor to pay income tax become liable. Suppose in Year 1 the tax threshold is set at £2,000 for a person and inflation runs at an annual rate of 20 per cent; in Year 2 the same threshold is equivalent in terms of purchasing power to £1,600.

(b) *Tax allowances.* Inflation also reduces tax allowances' value to taxpayers as money depreciates. This has the effect of increasing the tax burden on different taxpayers in an arbitrary manner, depending on the rate of inflation, and not according to any scheme devised to spread the burden fairly.

(c) *'Fiscal drag'.* Increase in incomes due to inflation pushes taxpayers, under a progressive tax system, into higher income bands to which higher rates of taxation apply and results in bigger tax payments. This is known as 'fiscal drag'. It was the twofold effect of: (i) increasing the tax burden on taxpayers whose income in real terms may have remained unchanged or might even have fallen; and (ii) increasing the revenue of the state in a way and to an extent that was not budgeted for.

A government can attempt to counteract the effect of inflation on exemption/threshold limits, on tax allowances and tax bands in two ways: (i) it can adjust them at frequent intervals; or (ii) it can introduce *indexation*.

Indexation

Indexation means the linking of the tax threshold, income tax bands and of allowances to the *retail price index* (RPI), which reflects changes in the price level. An *increase* in the retail price index results in a corresponding rise of the tax threshold and allowances, and keeps them at the same level in real terms at a time of inflation. Such a provision does not preclude the government from increasing or decreasing them as a matter of policy.

The advantages of indexation

From the point of view of the taxpayers the advantage is that indexation protects their standard of living from erosion by taxation, the burden of which is intensified by inflation. From the point of view of a government, indexation enables it to spread the burden of taxation and to give benefits on the basis of criteria that are regarded as desirable rather than to leave both to be determined by inflation.

The need for indexation has been recognised by governments but they have been slow to act. Indexation is more likely to appeal to them in theory, on the grounds of equity, than in practice, on the grounds of expediency. Without indexation, inflation, through the fiscal drag, increases tax revenue and the government is spared the odium of having to raise tax rates by as much as it would otherwise have to do to finance higher public expenditure.

The disadvantages of indexation

For a government, indexation has a number of disadvantages: (i) the danger that inflation may become 'established' as a result of a process of legitimising it by putting provisions to deal with it on the statute book; (ii) the demand for the indexation of state benefits as well as index-linking of taxes; (iii) unpopularity, if index-linked benefits are reduced when inflation falls; and (iv) the creation of a budget deficit, when expenditure rises and revenue falls, as a result of indexation at a time of rising prices. The government is then faced with the problem of closing the gap and has either to raise tax rates or cut expenditure programmes unless it is willing and able to borrow – but that itself is likely to add to inflation and make matters worse.

The introduction of indexation

In spite of the problems involved, the advantages of indexation appear to outweigh its disadvantages and several countries have introduced some form of indexation. These have included Netherlands in 1972, Canada in 1974 and Australia in 1976. In the UK, indexation dates back to 1977 when, during a parliamentary debate on the Labour government's Budget proposals, an amendment (the 'Rooker–Wise' amendment) to the Finance Bill was forced through to provide for indexation of personal allowances. The Conservative Government in the 1980 Budget introduced a system of indexation that provided, in addition to index-linking of personal allowances, for adjustment in personal taxation. Provisions were made for taking into account changes in the retail price index and adjusting the basic tax rate band, the bands for higher rates and the investment income surcharge threshold. For this purpose the RPI at December in the year preceding the year of assessment is to be compared with that for the previous December. If the price level has changed then corresponding adjustments are made for tax liability. In some years (e.g. 1994/1995), personal allowances were not raised in line with inflation by the Chancellor in his budget because of the fiscal constraints.

RECENT INNOVATIONS

Governments innovate and introduce tax reforms in response to social, economic and political developments. Embodiment in legislation of the principle of equality between sexes and the increase in the number of women in employment led to a reform of personal taxation to allow for privacy and independence for husbands and wives in tax matters. This brought to an end a practice dating back to the early nineteenth century, whereby taxing authorities regarded income of wives as belonging to their husbands. The *Finance Act (1988)* provided for the independent tax treatment of wives and for setting-off of any interest and dividends that they may receive from their savings and investments, against their own personal tax allowance. The government's objective of promoting savings and wider share ownership was furthered by measures introduced in the 1990 Budget. Under the new Tax Exempt Special Savings Accounts (TESSA) scheme individuals could receive interest free of tax. Also, under Personal Equity Plans (PEPs), dividend payments and capital gains on the investment were not subjected to taxation. The 1993 Budget brought in the

Enterprise Investment Scheme to encourage investment in unquoted securities by exempting gains in these securities from Capital Gains Tax and providing tax relief on losses. It also gave tax concessions on profit-related pay in order to give employees a greater financial interest in the businesses for which they work. In line with its political philosophy of shifting some responsibilities from the state to the people, the government also introduced Gifts Aid schemes to promote charitable giving by providing tax relief on donation, thus, to some extent, replacing public finance by private philanthropy.

NEGATIVE INCOME TAX (NIT)

Negative Income Tax (NIT) is a scheme for linking tax payments to social security benefits. Proposals for a negative income tax have arisen largely out of dissatisfaction with the system of taxation and state benefits. They have become complex, anomalous and at times operate at cross-purposes. This was intensified when, as in the UK, one government department is responsible for taxation and another for payment of benefits. Cases have arisen of people being assessed for income tax while at the same time being officially designated as living below the poverty line and entitled to social security benefits. Those caught in the 'poverty trap' are faced with the problem that, if they seek to increase their earnings, they will increase their tax liability, and disqualify themselves from some of the state benefits. Thus, ironically, they could be worse off than before.

This is not solely a British phenomenon. Other countries have similar problems. Discussion of negative income tax has become international and, in the early 1970s, governments of major industrial countries began to study schemes of negative income tax. The UK was one of the first countries to introduce NIT on a limited scale. However, NIT can operate in different forms. The following example shows how it would work.

Outline of a Scheme

Under a hypothetical NIT scheme each person is given credits appropriate to their personal circumstances. Each credit is for a flat amount and can be traded in for tax payment. Suppose a credit for each child is £4. Then a person with two children will receive £8 and, together with other credits, his total entitlement comes to £16 a week. If it so happens that his tax liability on earned income is also £16 then the credits are used to offset it and no tax payment is necessary.

Total tax credits	Income tax liability	Tax payment
£16	£16	Nil
£16	£20	£4
£16	£10	£6 (credit retained)

If credits exceed tax liability, then the difference is handed over to a person as a cash payment.

The *advantages* of NIT are as follows:

(i) *Administrative convenience.* The scheme facilitates co-ordination between tax payments and social security benefits and can be administered by one department.

(ii) *Administrative economies.* There is scope for a reduction in cost of administration, as the whole scheme can be operated on a PAYE basis.

(iii) *Simplicity.* NIT simplifies the welfare system. Means-testing of benefits can be abolished, since differences in incomes and in circumstances are already taken into account in tax assessment.

(iv) *Wider coverage.* People who are reluctant to apply for means-tested benefits to which they are entitled are allocated credits automatically under the scheme.

(v) *Provisions of relief.* A decrease in income tax rates and increase in allowances does not help the poor who do not pay the tax, NIT does help them since those who are entitled to credits can cash them, whether they pay income tax or not.

These are the arguments in favour of NIT. A government has to decide before introducing such a scheme, whether the advantages outweigh the disadvantages. We will therefore need to consider both.

The *disadvantages* of NIT include the following:

(i) *Burden on employers.* NIT results in more unpaid work by employers on behalf of the government, insofar as the scheme is operated on the PAYE basis. This is equivalent to an increase in the cost of labour or to a labour tax levied on employers.

(ii) *Threats to employment.* Employers, in view of (i), may seek to substitute machinery for labour. As a result, demand for labour could fall and unemployment increase.

(iii) *Difference in the level of support.* Determination of the monetary value of each credit presents some difficulties. If credits were fixed at a level adequate to support income of the poorest, this would mean payment of correspondingly large amounts to those who did not need the help. As recovery of the money via taxation might be difficult, the scheme could be costly and people with very low incomes would have to be excluded from the scheme and some separate social security system would have to be operated for those in the lowest income groups.

(iv) *The problem of self-employed.* The scheme is not suitable for the self-employed and some system of personal allowance for income tax purposes would have to be retained for them.

The British NIT

In the early 1970s the Conservative Government undertook preparatory work for the introduction of NIT and published a Green Paper, 'Proposals for a Tax Credit System' (Cmnd. 5116, 1972). It outlined a scheme which, when fully operative, would have applied to 90 per cent of the adult population and their dependents. It was proposed to include all persons in employment and earning above the threshold for entry into the scheme, and also recipients of National Insurance benefits. A suggested threshold was at a level corresponding to 25 per cent of the average male industrial wage. Persons with incomes below the threshold and the self-employed were to be excluded. It was not the government's intention to replace the social security system, but rather to retain it in a modified form for those outside the NIT scheme.

The Select Committee of the House of Commons reported on the scheme (The Report and Evidence of the Select Committee on Tax Credits, 1973). The Conservative Government, however, lost the General Election in 1974 before it could implement NIT. The Labour Government that followed made the first step towards implementing the scheme on a modified and limited basis in 1978–79 by gradually replacing child tax allowances with cash benefits that were payable to mothers. As a result of this decision, the advantage of NIT, whereby tax and benefit payments are linked on a PAYE basis, was lost.

SUMMARY

1. Income tax is levied on the earnings and investment incomes of individual persons.
2. In the UK income tax was first introduced in 1799 as a temporary war measure and it did not become a permanent tax until 1860.
3. Income tax complies with the principles of taxation more closely than other taxes.

4. The PAYE scheme allows for deduction of the tax at source. This makes payment more convenient and evasion more difficult.
5. Horizontal equity is provided for by means of personal allowances and vertical equity by progressive rates of income tax.
6. An increase in income tax may create an income effect when people seek to earn more to compensate for higher tax, or a substitution effect when they opt for leisure instead of work.
7. Evidence on the disincentive effect of income tax comes from official sources and private research but is inconclusive.
8. The effect of high and progressive rates of income tax is to reduce the ability to save. However, the willingness to save depends on a variety of factors of which income tax is only one.
9. Inflation has distorted the system of income tax, undermined its equity, created a 'fiscal drag' and led to demands for indexation of tax thresholds and allowances.
10. Negative income tax is a system of taxation that operates on the basis of tax credits than can be used either to off-set tax liability or to be cashed in. NIT has been introduced in the UK on a limited scale.

SUGGESTED FURTHER READING

M. Beenstock, 'Taxation and Incentives in the UK', *Lloyds Bank Review*, October 1979.
Board of Inland Revenue, *Inland Revenue Statistics* (London: HMSO, annually).
C.V. Brown and P.M. Jackson, *Public Sector Economics* (Oxford: Basil Blackwell, 1992).
C.V. Brown, 'Will the 1988 Income Tax Cuts Either Increase Work Incentives or Raise More Revenue?', *Fiscal Studies*, Vol. 9, No. 4, 1988.
A. Dilnot and M. Kell, 'Top-Rate Tax Cuts and Inventiveness: Some Empirical Evidence', *Fiscal Studies*, Vol. 9, No. 4, 1988.
G.C. Hockley, *Fiscal Policy* (London: Routledge, 1992).
S. James and G. Nobes, *The Economics of Taxation* (London: Prentice-Hall, 1992).
J.A. Kay and M.A. King, *The British Tax System* (Oxford: Oxford University Press, 1990).
OECD, *Negative Income Tax* (Paris: OECD, 1974).
P. Minford, 'Outlook After the Budget', *Fiscal Studies*, Vol. 9, No. 2, 1988.
P. Minford and P. Ashton, 'The Poverty Trap and the Laffer Curve: What Does the GHS Tell Us?' (Liverpool: Liverpool University, 1988, mimeo).
Royal Commission on Debt and Taxation, Cmnd. 2800 (London: HMSO, 1927).
Royal Commission on the Distribution of Income and Wealth, Cmnd. 6171 (London: 1975; First report, Cmnd. 7679, 1979).
C.T. Sandford, *The Economics of Public Finance* (Oxford: Pergamon Press, 1993).
M. Wilkinson, *Taxation* (London: Macmillan, 1992).

EXERCISES

1. Consider the extent to which income tax complies with the principles of taxation.
2. Consider the arguments for and against drawing a distinction between earned income and investment income and treating them differently for the purpose of income tax.
3. Explain the difference between the income effect and the substitution effect of a decrease in income tax and the likely consequences of both for an economy.
4. Make a case for and against a steeply progressive tax on personal income.
5. Discuss the measures that can be taken to provide for horizontal equity of income tax.
6. Outline a negative income tax scheme and suggest reasons for introducing it into the British tax system.
7. An increase in income tax will adversely affect the incentive to work and will reduce the supply of labour. A cut in the tax rate will have the opposite effect. Comment on the validity of these statements.
8. Consider the advantages and disadvantages of indexation for income tax purposes.
9. Discuss the likely effects of a change in income tax on the level of savings and the pattern of investment.
10. Define 'fiscal drag' and discuss the distorting effect of inflation on direct taxation.

8 Taxes on Profits

EARLY TAXES ON INCOMES OF BUSINESSES

Most countries tax business profits but they do so in a variety of ways and at different rates. Taxation of profits, like income tax, was first introduced in the UK as a war measure and then became a permanent feature of the tax system. The earliest legislation relating to a limitation of profits was the *Munitions of War Act (1915)*. It contained provisions for a new distinct tax on profits that was to be additional to income tax on businesses. The tax was imposed partly to raise revenue but mainly for psychological reasons. The outbreak of the First World War created a great demand for armaments. Munitions manufacturers made large profits. It was widely felt that it was morally wrong that some got rich because of the war, whilst thousands died in the trenches. The Munitions Levy was imposed to tax profits of establishments making munitions. It was followed in the same year by the Excess Profits Duty that extended taxation of profits to other manufacturers for the duration of the War. By 1937, rearmament had started and a tax on profits was reintroduced in the form of National Defence Contribution that subsequently became the Profits Tax. It continued to be levied until 1965 when it was replaced by Corporation Tax.

DEFINITION OF PROFIT AND BUSINESS

All the different forms of taxation of profits distinguish profits as a distinct source of income resulting from business activity. The Finance Act (1915), in setting out the provisions for the first tax on profits, referred to 'trades and businesses' that were to be taxed. But a search through that and subsequent acts for a definition of either of the two terms would have proved unrewarding. The Income Tax Act (1918), threw some light on the matter, though it could hardly be regarded as enlightening. It stated that for tax purposes, 'trade includes any trade, manufacture or concern in the nature of trade', leaving the 'nature of trade' for accountants and lawyers to interpret as best they could.

Courts have shown even more caution in their definition. It was held that: 'A business is almost anything which is an occupation as

169

distinguished from pleasure' (*Rolls* v. *Miller*, 1883 R 2413, Chancery Division, vol. XXVII, 1884). The present tax on profits, the Corporation Tax, is levied on companies and public corporations.

A *company* is defined as a legal entity existing in its own right. It can sue and be sued in a court of law. A company does not have to be dissolved if one of the owners dies or sells out. The owners are the share-holders. They are the people who for a payment of a certain amount of money have acquired a share in the company's assets and are entitled to a share of the profits. A person ceases to be a member of a company by disposing of their shares to somebody else who replaces them as a shareholder.

A *public corporation* is a state enterprise intended to operate on a commercial basis. It sells its output to the general public. The State owns the assets of a public corporation.

Profit is the net income of a business from its trading activities. It can be expressed in terms of money as so many pounds, or as a percentage of assets (capital) employed in the business, e.g. a profit of £100,000 represents a return of 10 per cent on £1 million of capital.

COMPUTATION OF PROFITS

Profits are difficult to compute and here we can only outline a method of calculation. A company or a public corporation receives revenue from the sale of its products or services. The revenue depends on the volume of trade and the price charged. Production also involves costs. They can be classified as:

(a) *Prime (or variable) costs*, e.g. labour and materials; such costs vary with the level of production.
(b) *Overhead (or fixed) costs*, e.g. rent, administrative expenses – such costs remain the same in the short run, whatever the level of output. Rent has to be paid for premises whether a company is producing 10,000 units of output or nothing, as may happen when its labour force is on strike.

Costs are aggregated and deducted from revenue. If the difference is: (i) negative (the costs are greater than the revenue), the company makes a loss and is not liable to corporation tax, (ii) positive (revenue is greater than costs), the company makes a profit from which capital allowances are deducted to arrive at a taxable profit.

Capital allowances, which provide a relief from taxation of profits, are related to investment in machinery and industrial and agricultural buildings. An *initial allowance* enables a company to deduct a proportion of its capital expenditure on specified assets, from profits in one year. A *writing-down allowance* makes it possible to set off the cost of an asset against profits over the number of years. The size of a capital allowance will depend on the type of capital expenditure and on the location of the firm. Firms in Development Areas may be given more generous allowances in order to encourage investment (see p. 443).

The need for allowances arises because capital assets wear out – suffer from depreciation – in the process of production. Suppose a piece of machinery has a working life of ten years, at the end of which it becomes scrap. A company will therefore have to put aside each year some of its profits to replace the machine, otherwise at the end of the period the company will have no machine and no internally accumulated funds to buy a new one.

Thus the calculation of taxable profit is as follows:

number of goods sold × price   = revenue
Revenue – cost of production   = profit
Profit – capital allowances   = taxable profit

Inflation and Depreciation Provisions

The money that a company allocates annually for depreciation, so as to create a fund that would be equal to the original price of the machine – that is, its *historical cost* – will only be sufficient to purchase a new one if prices remain stable. If there is inflation, the replacement cost may be much higher than the historical cost. A company that provided £10 per year for depreciation after ten years would have accumulated £100, which was equivalent to the historical cost of the original machine. If, however, prices had risen so that an identical new machine now costs £200, the company would not have enough in reserve for replacement and would have to raise additional funds by issue of shares or by borrowing. The problem for industry has been that the Inland Revenue, for tax purposes, allows depreciation on a historical and not on a replacement basis. As a result, profits appear higher than they really are and Corporation Tax is assessed on these 'higher' profits.

Table 8.1   Effect of inflation on small firms

Capital employed in business (£)	Profit (£)		Rate of return (%)		Rate of corporation tax on profit (%)
	taxable	real	taxable	real	
Year 1 600,000	60,000	60,000	10	10	40 (small business rate)
Year II 600,000	75,000	60,000	12½	10	52 (standard rate)

ILLUSORY PROFITS, INFLATION AND TAXATION

Professor G. Lawson of the Manchester Business School has produced evidence to show that the real tax burden on industry has been in excess of what the rate of taxation on profits would indicate. According to Professor Lawson, the effective rate of tax on the UK companies has averaged 71 per cent over the period 1954–75 and in three years it actually exceeded 100 per cent, whereas the higher rate officially fixed for the corporation tax up to 1980 never went beyond 52 per cent.

It was high inflation in the 1970s and 1980s which created an illusory increase in profits but a real increase in the tax burden on industry. Firms that had previously been exempt from taxation were caught in the tax net. Small companies that had been assessed for a tax at a lower rate of corporation tax (40 per cent for 1980–81) saw their profits rise above the level at which a higher rate of tax applied even though in real terms their earnings might have declined.

Let us take as an example a hypothetical firm and assume a 25 per cent rate of inflation. The firm's profits increase at the same rate as inflation so that in real terms its earnings stay the same, but its tax liability does not. Profits below £70,000 are taxed at a lower rate, and this ceiling for small firms remains unchanged (see Table 8.1).

In the UK, the exemption level and the point at which the higher rate of tax applies has been raised from time to time but not in step with the rate of inflation. The combined effect of inflation and of the system of taxation has been to reduce drastically the profitability of British industry. Its ability to plough back profits and to increase capital formation has been adversely effected.

By the mid-1990s this had changed. The rate of inflation came down to around 3 per cent corporation tax standard rate was reduced to 33 per cent and the small companies rate to 25 per cent (Table 8.2).

Table 8.2   Taxation of profits

Year	Profit Tax (per cent)		Income tax standard rate (per cent)
	undistributed profits	distributed profits	
1947	5.0	12.0	45.0
1951	10.0	50.0	47.5
1956	3.0	30.0	42.5
1958	10.0	10.0	42.5
1965	15.0	15.0	38.5

	Corporation Tax (per cent)		
Year	1966	1982	1995
standard rate	40*	52	33
small companies rate	–	40	25

Note:
* No concession to small companies.

PROFITS TAX: DIFFERENTIATED RATE ON DISTRIBUTED AND UNDISTRIBUTED PROFITS

To encourage the ploughing back of profits, profits tax can be charged at different rates – a lower rate on undistributed profits (i.e. those ploughed back into the business) and a higher rate on profits distributed to the shareholders in the form of dividends.

Arguments *for* a differential rate of tax have been put forward on the following grounds:

(i) *Incentive to invest.* A lower rate on undistributed profits encourages business to plough back their profits and thus increases investment in plant and machinery and other productive assets.

(ii) *Anti-inflationary measure.* Higher rates on distributed profits discourage payment of higher dividends. This keeps shareholders' incomes and consumption down and provides a check to inflation.

(iii) *Easier borrowing.* At a time when the government is following a cheap money policy and keeping interest rates low (as it did in the

UK from 1932 until the early 1950s), government bonds, which offer a small return to investors, appear unattractive compared with shares on which higher dividends are paid. A higher rate of tax on distributed profits, by discouraging this, makes it easier for the government to borrow.

Arguments *against* differential profits rates are:

(i) *Uncertainty*. Retention of profits is not the same thing as ploughing them back into plant and machinery. A company may use retained funds in other ways than to increase its productive capacity.

(ii) *Inefficiency*. Retention of profits may distort the pattern of investment and need not be in the national interest. A company may use the ploughed-back profits inefficiently whereas, if the profits were distributed, the shareholders would have an opportunity to put their money to a more productive use. There is no reason to assume that shareholders would necessarily spend their dividends on current consumption. If the market mechanism is allowed to operate, funds are more likely to be invested in response to demand for them.

(iii) *Incompatibility with social policy*. Ploughed-back profits are likely to increase the capital value of the shares of a company. If such capital gains are tax-free or taxed lightly, then as some critics of the differential system of taxation believe, the inequality in the distribution of wealth will be increased.

In the UK, profits tax was charged from 1947 to 1958 at differential rates shown in Table 8.2. Subsequently, a uniform rate of profits tax was imposed in addition to income tax that companies paid at the standard rate.

The *Royal Commission on the Taxation of Profits and Income* (Cmnd. 9474, 1955) advised against differentiated rates of tax on profit. It is of interest to note that, since they were abolished, companies have financed a smaller proportion of their investment out of retained profits. The self-financing ratio fell from approximately 80 per cent to 70 per cent between the early and late 1950s and has fluctuated in the region of 50 to 60 per cent since.

CORPORATION TAX: THE NEW SYSTEM OF COMPUTATION

The *Finance Act (1965)* replaced the profits tax with the corporation tax and imposed a single rate of tax. However, since companies were also responsible for the deduction of income tax from the dividends that they paid out, distributed profits were still more heavily taxed.

A *new system of computation*, introduced by the *Finance Act (1972)*, set out provisions, the effects of which were:

(a) Companies were relieved of the responsibility of deducting income tax at source from dividends.

(b) Companies were required, on payment of dividends, to pay Corporation Tax in advance, calculated by reference to the amount of profits distributed and the tax liability on dividends.

(c) The shareholders received a tax credit equivalent to the advance tax payment on their dividends. They could then use the credits to offset against their income tax liability (at a specified rate of tax) and if there was no such liabilty then the credit could be cashed.

(d) The companies, at the end of their accounting period, had the liability to the Corporation Tax on their taxable income reduced by the amount paid in advance.

(e) A single rate of tax was imposed on their taxable profits.

Small Companies Rate of Tax

Having abolished one system of differential taxation of profits, the government introduced another in 1972. Its purpose was to discriminate in favour of small companies, originally defined as those with income not exceeding £15,000. This was gradually raised to £300,000 as inflation increased. The *Finance Act* provided for a lower rate of tax to be levied on income of small companies. The tax rate currently stands at 25 per cent, as compared with 33 per cent for other companies (1994–95 rates). The reason for the discrimination was the government's desire to foster small businesses and appreciation of the fact that they, more than the other sectors of industry, have to rely on self-finance out of retained profits to provide for their investment.

THE EFFECTS OF PROFITS TAXES

A tax on profits such as the corporation tax has widespread direct and indirect effects on businesses which include the following.

(a) Corporation Tax reduces companies' ability to invest out of their own resources and forces them to rely on the money market for funds. This may lead to changes in ownership and capital structure of a company.

(b) A high rate of tax may reduce the willingness to innovate, launch new products, adopt improved methods of production or introduce new technology. Such ventures are risky. If they succeed a large share of the reward will be claimed by the government in taxation.

(c) Waste and inefficiency may result. Since the cost of production is a deductible expense for the purpose of taxation, managements have less incentive to keep costs down.

(d) Insofar as Corporation Tax reduces the return to the shareholders, the incentive for them to invest in industry decreases. Since investment is an important factor in economic growth, Corporation Tax not only affects the companies but also the performance of the whole economy.

The advantage of Corporation Tax to a government is that it is a lucrative source of revenue (see Figure 7.1). Furthermore, there is relatively little opposition to this form of direct taxation from those people who do not have to pay it.

Whereas Corporation Tax is a permanent feature of direct taxation in the UK, Excess profits taxes are not. They tend to be short-lived, crisis measures. There is no excess profits tax at present. However, once a government finds a new tax base, successive administrations of whatever political persuasion, tend to revive it. For this reason, in an outline of the structure of taxation, a mention of a tax on excess profits may be helpful.

TAXATION OF EXCESS PROFITS

Excess profit taxes differ from other forms of taxation in that they are levied on income that is regarded as *abnormal*. To assess a tax on excess profit, a definition of *normal* profit is required. This raises the problem of establishing a set of tax principles relating to a normal and abnormal tax base. Excess profits can be defined as those that exceed a certain level of earnings set by the government as the norm.

There are two different ways of *measuring* excess profits:

(a) *Standard profit base.* A government determines a period of, say, three years, and this becomes the standard period. The average profit a firm earns during that time is then taken as the standard profit and earnings above this level are regarded as abnormal and subject to an excess profits tax.

(b) *Percentage standard base.* Government fixes a certain rate of return on assets employed in the business as the standard rate of profit. Any firm that earns more is taxed on the excess.

Whichever method is used, excess profit taxes in theory and in practice fall short of the principles of a 'good' tax (see p. 123). They fail to distinguish between the increase in profits that result from: (i) hard work and enterprise; (ii) inflation, which creates illusory improvements; and (iii) exploitation of particular circumstances, such as a rise in the demand for munitions during a war. Thus, for tax purposes, increased profitability of industry which is in the public interest, is treated in the same way as increases in profits which are not so attributable. The yield of excess profits taxes is also difficult to predict. Governments in the past have imposed them primarily to achieve psychological, social and political objectives, rather than to raise revenue.

In the UK, taxes on excess profits have been emergency measures associated with war (Table 8.3). The *Excess Profits Levy,* introduced in 1952 as a peacetime tax, was a failure and was repealed after one year It had been imposed at a time of increased international tension, and under the threat of another world war. The Chancellor of the Exchequer justified the tax on the grounds that, '...at a time like this, sacrifices should be borne equally, and we are not prepared to see excessive profits being made as a result of injection of rearmament into the economy' (*Hansard*, vol. 1497, 11 March, 1952). The excessive profits did not appear to materialise; the tax was unpopular, and no government made an attempt to revive it. In

Table 8.3   Taxation of excess profits

Year	Excess profits duty rate of tax (% of excess profit)	Year	Excess profits tax rate of tax (% of excess profit)	Year	Excess profits levy rate of tax (% of excess profit)
1915–16	60	1939–40	60	1952–53	15
1917–18[1]	80	1940–45[2]	100		
1919	40	1946	60		
1920	60				
1921	40				

Notes: 1. First World War.
2. Second World War.

recent years, some pressure groups have campaigned for the reintroduction of an excess profits tax on political and ideological grounds.

Selective Excess Profits Tax

A new type of selective excess profits tax was introduced in the UK by the Conservative government in 1981. It took the form of a special tax on banking profits and applied to some fifty banks. The tax rate was fixed at 2½ per cent of the tax base which was defined as the average of non-interest bearing sterling bank deposits on three selected days in the last quarter of 1980.

The tax was selective in that it fell on banks only and not on commercial and industrial companies as well. It was intended to be a tax on excess profits since the 'higher' profits in 1980 were deemed to be above the normal level for the banks' profits in recent years and above the level earned by industrial and commercial companies. The tax was retrospective as it was not in existence at the time that the profits were earned.

Criticism of the tax

There is little to be said in favour of any selective, retrospective tax on higher profits except that it provides revenue. Such a tax can be criticised on many counts, including the following:

(i) *It is a dangerous practice to equate 'higher' with 'excessive' profits.* There are many reasons why profits may increase. There may be a greater demand for the output of a business. It may have become more competitive. Its efficiency may have improved. An additional tax on higher profits is likely to be a disincentive to effort and enterprise.

(ii) A tax on increased profits that does not allow for inflation *taxes illusory profits.*

(iii) A *retrospective tax* is generally considered to be *unfair*, since the taxpayer who is not forewarned of an additional tax liability, is not in a position to make provisions to meet it.

(iv) A tax on higher profits that is assessed on the basis of one year, is particularly unsuitable for businesses with *fluctuating profits*. If the profits of clearing banks was considered on the basis of a six-year cycle then, over the period 1974–79, their rate of return was 2.7 per cent as compared with 3.4 per cent for non-North Sea oil industrial and commercial companies. There was therefore no justification for the tax on this basis.

The idea of a selective tax was resurrected by the Labour Party in 1993 when a proposal for a future tax on the excess profits of utilities came under consideration, prompted by the large profits that water, electricity and gas companies were making after privatisation. The arguments listed above against a selective excess profits tax could also be applied to its imposition on utilities.

TAX ON PROFITS FROM NORTH SEA OIL

The new tax on profits, the petroleum revenue tax, is unique in the British fiscal system, in the sense that, when it was first introduced, it did not impose an *additional* tax burden on anyone. Until recently, North Sea oil as a source of revenue did not exist. It did not belong to any individual or enterprise. The deposits of oil were a 'gift of nature' and they were a gift to the state.

Full-scale exploration of the North Sea for hydrocarbons began in 1964. The search concentrated on areas off the coast of East Anglia and Yorkshire. Three years later the first gas came ashore. In 1970 the Forties field was discovered. It was the first important oilfield to be found in the British sector of the North Sea (Figure 8.1). By 1975 there were 12 British oilfields of commercial value: the first supply of oil was piped ashore and the petroleum revenue tax (PRT) was introduced.

Government revenue from the North Sea is made up of:

(a) *Corporation Tax*. Profits of the oil companies and the public sector of industry arising out of their North Sea operations are subject to the corporation tax.

(b) *Petroleum Revenue Tax*. This tax is levied on profits arising from the extraction of oil and gas under licence in the UK and its continental shelf. Proceeds from each field are taxed separately so as to prevent companies from deferring tax on profits from exploitation of one field and offsetting the tax liability as a development cost on another field.

(c) *Royalties*. Oil companies that have acquired licences from the government to operate in the North Sea have to pay royalties calculated on the basis of the value of the oil at the wellhead.

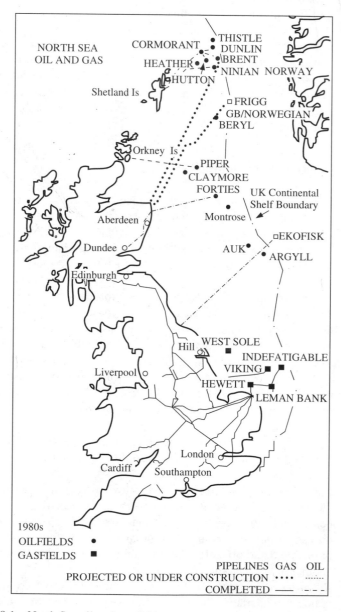

Figure 8.1   North Sea oil and gas fields

Calculation of Petroleum Revenue Tax

Liability to PRT is calculated on the basis of receipts from sales of oil after deduction of: (i) the cost of exploration; (ii) the cost of bringing the oil ashore; (iii) operating costs; (iv) capital allowances; and (v) licences and royalties (Figure 8.2). There are also two types of relief available:

(a) *Non-discretionary relief.* After the various deductions have been taken into account, liability to PRT is reduced by an oil allowance for each field.

(b) *Discretionary relief.* The Secretary of State for Energy has the power, if the Treasury consents, to refund royalties partly or wholly to the licensees. The purpose of this is to encourage companies to explore, develop and to produce oil from fields that would otherwise not be commercially viable. The refunds do not give rise to

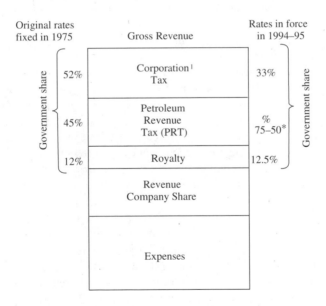

Figure 8.2   Tax revenue from North Sea oil

Note
1. Corporation tax is chargeable on net revenue after deduction of PRT and royalty.
*PRT was reduced from 75% to 50% from 1 July 1993.
Previous rates: 1975–78 45%, 1979 60%, 1980–82 70%, 1983–93 75%.

additional liability to Corporation Tax. PRT and royalties are deductible from the Corporation Tax.

Problems of Estimating Future Yield

The government revenue from oil fields fluctuates, reflecting changes in the volatile oil market. The price of oil is determined by a variety of economic and political factors at national and international level. These include: embargoes, boycotts and wars. The cartel which co-ordinates oil production, the Organisation of Petroleum Exporting Countries (OPEC) has not achieved price stability. In 1970 the price per barrel of oil was nearly US$4, by 1981–82 it shot up to about US$40 and by the beginning of 1994 plunged to around US$10. This affected revenue from PRT. First receipts amounted to £83 million in 1978–79, rising to £7,177 million in 1985 and falling to around £1,000 million in the early 1990s. Nevertheless this represented a sizable contribution to the Exchequer and corresponded roughly to the total government expenditure on the National Heritage programme.

To maintain or increase revenue from oil fields at a time of falling prices a government may try to increase production to compensate for lower price, or withhold supplies to create a shortage and thereby push prices up. It would be difficult for any one government through its activities to affect the world oil market even if the country is not a member of OPEC and bound by its rules.

Future tax yield from the North Sea is difficult to predict. It will be influenced by events some of which cannot be foreseen, or the timing of which is uncertain. The government's revenue from North Sea oil will depend on a variety of factors, some of which are within and some of which are beyond its control, e.g:

(a) *Size of the reserves.* These are not fully known and are subject to revisions as new fields are discovered.
(b) *Volume of production.* This will be influenced by a government's own conservation and taxation policies, world demand for oil and sales by other producing countries.
(c) *International oil prices.* Oil prices are subject to international agreements. The higher the price fixed by the Organisation of Petroleum Exporting Countries (OPEC), the higher will be the producers' revenue for a given volume of sales of oil, and therefore the yield from oil taxation. In recent years, prices have been determined not only on the basis of demand and supply, but also by political considerations.

(d) *Costs of exploration, development and production.* An increase in costs, unless prices rise correspondingly, will decrease profits from oil and consequently revenue from taxation levied on them.

Indirect revenue

A distinction needs to be drawn between direct and indirect revenue that governments derive from oil. Royalties, PRT and the corporation tax on oil companies are a direct form of revenue. Indirect revenue depends on the spin-off effects from the operations of the oil industry. It creates new employment in areas such as parts of Scotland where there had been few employment opportunities before. The additional incomes that were generated from spin-offs – such as in the service industries – are subject to income tax and, when spent, to taxes on consumption. Profits of businesses that have developed to serve the oil industry are subject to Corporation Tax. The overall effect is to increase total government revenue.

Budget Implications

Dependence on, and fluctuations in, government's income from the oil industry can create problems. The size of the problem is to some extent determined by the relative importance of that income for the Budget. In the American state of Alaska, for example, revenue from oil financed some 98 per cent of the State Budget in 1994. In the UK, PRT represented, in recent years, between 2–3 per cent of Inland Revenue Receipts (Figure 7.1). Furthermore, in Alaska there are vast reserves of oil. North Sea British oilfields are expected to run dry in a relatively short time. Such considerations are of importance for governments' budget policies and the finance of long-term projects.

THE USE OF GOVERNMENT REVENUE FROM NORTH SEA OIL

A government can use its oil revenue for different purposes, the object of which may be to: (i) reduce taxation generally or the burden of a particular tax, such as income tax; (ii) increase its level of expenditure on current account, for example, to provide more social services, and on capital account to invest in schools, hospitals and other social assets; (iii) foster projects to improve the productivity of existing industries and develop new industries to expand the basis for the country's economic growth when the oil runs out.

Proposals for an Oil Revenue Fund

Since the government revenue from oil is in the nature of a windfall, it has
been suggested that the money should be paid into a separate account to be
used for specific projects which the government might not otherwise have
been able to afford without raising taxation. Supporters of the fund have
argued that it would reduce the danger of the money being frittered away
on excessive consumption with nothing to show for the expenditure in the
long run. The accounts of the fund would show how much was paid in and
what it was spent on. As a result of this accountability would be improved.

The British government rejected the idea of an oil revenue fund since it
would have reduced the flexibility of the fiscal system. It was left to
successive Chancellors of the Exchequer to decide on how the oil revenue
was to be used within the context of the annual budget. By contrast, the
State of Alaska has established a permanent fund. Its reserves can be used
to offset fluctuations in oil revenue. It was this revenue that enabled
Alaska to abolish state income tax in 1980 and to give each resident an
annual cheque for US$900. In the UK arguments for such a national
dividend found little favour.

General Benefit from Oil

British self-sufficiency and the ability to export oil will not, by itself, solve
the balance-of-payments problem, but it will reduce the pressure on the
government to adopt restrictive fiscal and monetary policies to counteract
deficits. The stop–go policies of the past (alternating between putting a
brake on or accelerating economic activities) had disruptive effects on the
national economy.

SOCIAL SECURITY CONTRIBUTIONS AS A FORM OF TAXATION

The term social security is an American import dating back to the days of
the New Deal in the United States, but has since come into international
use. In the UK, the contributions were originally referred to as National
Insurance Contributions.

Principles of the Contributions

The National Insurance Scheme, when it came into operation in the UK in
1948 (see p. 97), was intended to run on an actuarial basis and to be self-

financing. The money came from the government's own contributions and from compulsory contributions by employees, employers and the self-employed, and was paid into the National Insurance Fund. Benefits were paid out of this fund. Entitlement to a full benefit depended on the period over which the beneficiary had contributed, but there was a time limit to unemployment and sickness benefits. Since payment of the contributions was compulsory, they could be regarded as a form of tax on the following:

(a) *Employees*. For employees the contributions were a direct tax on their earned incomes, which with income tax was deducted at source by employers.

(b) *Employers*. The contributions made by employers on the behalf of their employees could be regarded as a payroll tax, that is a tax on labour. The larger the number of employees on the payroll, the greater was the total amount that had to be paid in employers' contributions. They also had the additional cost of collecting their employees' own contributions on behalf of the government. This resembles the operation of the PAYE system of income tax (see p. 141).

(c) *Self-employed*. Their contributions were an addition to their liability to a tax on profits.

The Nature of the 'Tax'

The nature of the contributions has changed from a regressive to a proportional tax. Originally the contributions were at a flat rate and were not related to the income earned. This imposed a relatively heavier tax burden on those with smaller earnings, and consequently the contributions did not comply with the principle of vertical equity (see p. 143).

A system of *earnings-related* contributions was introduced by the Social Security Act (1973) and became operative in 1975. The contributions were fixed as a given percentage of a person's income. If the income increased the proportion paid in contributions remained unchanged but the total amount payable went up. Thus, at a rate of 5.5 per cent, a person who earned £50 per week paid £2.75 and a person who earned £100 per week paid £5.50.

The employees' rate, i.e. the primary rate, was fixed at 5.5 per cent of their earnings and the employers' contribution, i.e. the secondary rate, was 8.5 per cent of each employee's earnings. For the self-employed, the rate was 8 per cent of their annual profit or gain. There was an exemption limit and a ceiling to the contributions. Both have been raised since the

introduction of the earnings-related system. For 1995 the lower limit is
£57 and the upper limit is £430. The rates are now 10 per cent for employees, 10.2 per cent for employers and 7.3 per cent for self employed.

Reasons for Change

The change from a flat rate to earnings-related contributions was intended
to make the system more equitable but there was also another reason. The
National Insurance Fund needed more money, as the claims on it
increased. Various factors contributed to this, such as:

   (a) An increase in the number of births in the 1950s gave rise to a demand
       for maternity benefits payable under the National Insurance Scheme.
   (b) Longer expectation of life meant that the number of pensioners
       rose. There were twice as many of them when the new basis for
       contributions was introduced as when the national insurance started.
       Entitlement to pensions therefore increased.
   (c) Unemployment went up and so did the number of unemployed
       claiming unemployment benefits.
   (d) Inflation accelerated and the level of benefits was increased as the
       cost of living went up. To pay for the increased cost of the benefits,
       contributions had to be raised, but an increase in the flat rate would
       have placed an unacceptable burden on smaller earnings. Earnings-
       related contributions enabled the authorities to raise more revenue
       and to adhere to the 'ability to pay' principle of taxation.

THE SURCHARGE – DEPARTURE FROM THE PRINCIPLES OF
INSURANCE

A surcharge on the employer's contributions to raise general tax revenue
marks a departure from the contractual principle on which the National
Insurance scheme was based, whereby contributions established the right
to benefits. The surcharge, without corresponding benefits, is regarded by
many employers as a tax on employment.

   The surcharge came in a roundabout way, as a result of a pact between
the Labour Government and the Liberal Party. The Government had
difficulty in getting the House of Commons to approve the Budget proposals in 1976 and eventually got the Finance Act through on the second
reading with a majority of 2. This required the support of the Liberals.

The Chancellor of the Exchequer had to make concessions on income tax to satisfy them. This left him with the problem of how to make good the increase in revenue he had been forced to forego. The surcharge on the employer's contributions was his answer.

Arguments in *favour* of the surcharge are:

(i) The liability to the surcharge is easy to calculate since employer's contributions are known.
(ii) The cost of collection is low, as the surcharge is simply added to the contributions which have to be paid.
(iii) The surcharge does not have the disincentive effect on work that a corresponding amount raised in income tax might have.
(iv) The surcharge is less unpopular than other taxes with the voters since most of them do not pay it. Companies have to pay it, but they do not have votes at general elections.

The Chancellor of the Exchequer argued that the surcharge need not reduce profits and lead to unemployment since it can be passed on to consumers in higher prices.

Objections to the surcharge have nevertheless been raised on the following grounds:

(i) A business may or may not be able to pass the surcharge on to consumers, depending on the price elasticity of demand for its products. If it succeeds, the effect will be similar to an increase in tax on consumption, as a result of which the price to the consumers of goods and services rises (see p. 247).
(ii) The surcharge will, therefore, have the characteristics of a regressive tax.
(iii) If a business cannot shift the tax to the consumers it will have to pay the tax. Since the liability is related to the number of employees, it can be reduced by a cut in the labour force. This is likely to intensify the unemployment problem.
(iv) It involves the use of the National Insurance Scheme for a purpose for which it was not intended and provides a disguise for the imposition of an additional tax burden. The surcharge as a payroll tax does not readily fit into the British tax system – but once a tax reaches a statute book it seldom leaves it. The surcharge is an exception. It was discontinued as opposition from industry mounted and employment was imperilled.

CORPORATE TAXATION IN EUROPE

Taxation of businesses in any one country in Europe has now become a matter of common interest within the Community. At present, businesses in Member States follow a variety of accounting practices, calculate their profits and tax liabilities in different ways and benefit from different tax allowances and concessions from their national taxing authorities.

The extent to which governments rely on corporate taxation for revenue also differs considerably (Tables 8.4 and 8.5). Proceeds reflect national tax structures, rates of taxation and the level of economic activity within countries and at the international level. However, during a world recession, not all countries experience a fall in production and profits at the same time and to the same extent. Some recover sooner than others. Thus, for example the UK came earlier out of the recession at the beginning of the 1990s than the other members of the European Union.

As an increasing number of firms operates on a Europe-wide basis this

Table 8.4 Corporate taxation in Europe

Direct taxes paid by corporations as a percentage of total taxes and social security contributions

Year	1981	1982	1983	1984	1985	1986	1987	1988	1989	1990	1991
Belgium	5.4	6.2	5.9	6.2	6.5	6.6	6.6	6.9	6.7	6.5	6.1
France	5.8	5.9	5.2	5.5	5.6	6.2	6.4	6.6	6.9	6.6	5.6
Germany	4.2	4.3	4.6	4.9	5.4	5.2	4.5	4.8	4.9	4.4	4.1
Greece	3.7	4.0	3.0	3.4	3.3	4.2	4.5	3.9	4.3	5.1	4.7
Italy	4.8	5.3	5.6	5.7	6.4	7.0	8.3	6.3	8.3	8.1	7.4
Netherlands	6.8	6.6	6.0	5.6	6.8	7.3	8.1	7.7	7.6	7.9	7.6
Spain	6.5	6.7	6.7	6.7	1.2	2.0	3.5	2.9	5.4	5.2	–
UK	9.1	10.1	10.7	11.7	12.6	10.6	10.6	10.8	12.3	11.0	8.9
Sweden	2.1	2.7	3.5	3.6	3.1	3.3	4.7	4.7	4.9	3.6	1.7
USA	9.2	7.1	8.1	9.0	8.5	8.9	9.7	9.9	9.3	8.6	7.6
Japan	17.5	17.2	17.1	18.0	19.0	18.6	18.7	19.6	21.4	18.6	17.4

Note:
Data for Denmark, Irish Republic, Luxembourg and Portugal were unavailable.

Source: *Economic Trends*, 484 (London: HMSO, 1994).

Table 8.5   Rates of Corporation Tax in the European Community, 1992

	Rate (per cent)
Belgium	39 standard
Denmark	38[1]
Germany	50
Greece	46[2]
Spain	35
France	34
Ireland	40
Italy	36
Luxembourg	20
Netherlands	35 higher rate 40
Portugal	36[3]
UK	33 small companies 25

Notes:
[1] Income Tax.
[2] Tax on income of legal persons.
[3] Corporate Income Tax.
Taxes on profits in the Community are variously named: Corporation Tax, Income Tax on legal persons, Corporate Income Tax.
Source: Commission of the European Communities (1994).

can lead to problems of double taxation, and tax distortions affecting mergers, subsidiaries and decisions on location. To achieve the greater social and economic cohesion envisaged in the Single European Act that came into force in 1987, corporate taxation will need to be brought more into line. However, the European Commission's proposal (1975) for a directive to harmonise systems of company taxation within the Community has been withdrawn and the emphasis had been shifted from 'systematic recourse to harmonisation' to alignment of national tax policies and co-operation that is more in accordance with the new accepted *principle of subsidiarity*.

After many years of discussion, in 1990 the Council of the European Community reached a milestone in tax matters relating to internal markets and came to an agreement on proposals for three major directives for co-operation between firms. These proposals, put forward some twenty years earlier, are concerned with:

> (i) (1969) Common system of taxation applicable to parent companies and subsidiaries from different Member States.

(ii) (1969) Common system of taxation applicable to mergers, divisions and contribution of assets involving companies from different Member States.

(iii) (1977) Arbitration procedure. The object of this is to eliminate double taxation that occurs when an adjustment made in an enterprise's profits by the tax authority in one Member State is not accompanied by a corresponding adjustment of an associated enterprise in another Member State. Guidelines on company taxation have been submitted to the European Parliament and Council by the Commission in 1990, with the aim of removing tax obstacles to firms' cross-frontier activities by 1993 and thereby furthering the European Communities' long-term objective to achieve greater economic integration in Europe.

UNITARY TAX

This is not a European tax but affects European companies and those of other countries that have established a presence in certain states in the USA, notably in California. These states had introduced Unitary tax even though the US Federal Government was opposed to this innovation that gave rise to international protest. It is a tax on foreign-owned companies that belong to multinational groups and carry on business in certain areas in the USA. Unitary tax is levied on a proportion of the multinationals' total worldwide income and is not limited to earnings of member companies within the tax jurisdiction of a particular state in the USA. The tax base is 'the ratios of the groups' property, payroll and sales in the state to the groups' worldwide property, payroll and sales, and does not necessarily bear any relation to the income actually arising in that state'. Arguments against the Unitary tax are that it:

(a) Distorts international trade and investment
(b) Contravenes the internationally accepted principle of allocating profits of multinational companies between the countries in which they operate
(c) Infringes agreements and may lead to double taxation
(d) Has high compliance costs because of the taxing authorities' requirement that accounts be compiled in accordance with US accounting methods and figures be given in US dollars.

For these reasons the tax had been opposed by the Member States of the European Community, particularly by the UK, France, Germany, as well as by a number of other major industrialised countries with interests in the USA.

The British government and industry have been in the forefront in leading opposition to the Unitary tax and campaigning for its abolition. All the political parties in the government gave their support to a retaliatory clause in the *Finance Act (1985)*, to enable the government to take action against US companies operating in the UK by withholding tax credits available under double taxation relief agreement, if California and a number of the other states in the USA persisted with the levy of Unitary tax. In 1988, under pressure from the federal government, California agreed to allow foreign companies to opt out of the Unitary system under certain conditions. Fees and costs of opting out were high and only one in four of the companies did so. Eventually in 1993 California abolished Unitary taxation (with effect from 1994) and adopted the principle of taxing subsidiaries 'as if at arm's length from the parent company'. This conforms to the internationally agreed practice.

With encouragement from the European Community and a number of other OECD countries, Barclays Bank sought a refund of its payments of the Unitary tax claiming double taxation and infringement of the federal government's right to regulate international trade. The case went to the Supreme Court of the U.S. In court Barclays was supported by the British, German and Japanese governments. In 1994 the judges voted seven to two against ruling Unitary tax unconstitutional.

SUMMARY

1. Profit taxes are a form of direct taxation. They are levied on incomes of businesses. The tax currently levied in the UK is the corporation tax. It is assessed on companies

2. Computation of tax liability requires calculation of revenue and costs of production. Capital allowances are a deduction. The Inland Revenue allows depreciation on the basis of the historic cost of capital assets – this makes it difficult for businesses to replace them when prices are rising. Inflation creates illusory profits which are nevertheless taxable.

3. A profits tax can be levied at different rates on distributed and undistributed profits in order to encourage or discourage the ploughing-back of profits into the business. Distribution of profits is likely to increase shareholders expenditure on consumption.

4. Corporation tax is levied at a single rate on incomes of companies irrespective of whether profits are distributed or not. A lower rate of tax applies to small businesses. Capital allowances are intended to encourage investment in plant and machinery.

5. The effect of a tax on profits is to reduce companies' ability to save and to finance investment out of retained profits. Taxation may also reduce incentives to innovate and to increase efficiency.

6. At various times in the UK excess profits taxes have been imposed as emergency measures and introduced into taxation of business a new concept of normal earnings as opposed to excessive profits.

7. The discovery of North Sea oil has provided government with an expanding and potentially large source of revenue and resulted in a new tax, the Petroleum Revenue Tax, levied on oil companies. Proposals for earmarking the proceeds have found little support. Instead of being paid into an oil revenue fund, they are used to finance public expenditure in general.

8. Social security contributions can be regarded as a form of taxation. For businesses, they are equivalent to a payroll tax. Proceeds of social security contributions by employers and employees go into the National Insurance Fund and are used to finance benefits payable under the scheme. A surcharge on National Insurance Contributions by employers, that successive governments have imposed, represented a departure from the insurance principle on which social security contributions were based when the National Insurance Scheme was introduced. Such a tax falls on profits unless a business can pass it on to consumers in higher prices. Opposition to the surcharge led to its abolition.

9. Corporate taxation within the European Community still varies considerably, but the Commission has brought in a number of proposals for directives to further alignment of taxes and co-operation between firms in tax matters. The long-term objective is to achieve a common system of taxation.

10. Unitary tax introduced by California and a number of other states in the USA had far-reaching implications for multinationals, British firms and those of other countries with interests in the USA. The Finance Act (1985), passed by the British Parliament, provided for retaliatory action unless the matter of Unitary taxation was satisfactorily resolved.

SUGGESTED FURTHER READING

C.V. Brown and P.M. Jackson, *Public Sector Economics* (Oxford: Basil Blackwell, 1992).

M.P. Devereaux and C.N. Morris, *North Sea Taxation* (London: Institute of Fiscal Studies, 1983).

H.J. Easson, *Taxation in the European Community* (London: Athlone Press, 1993).

European Commission, *Report of Independent Experts on Company Taxation* (Luxembourg, 1992) and *Proposals for Directives* (1969 and 1977).

HM Treasury, 'The Problem of Unitary Tax', *Economic Progress Report*, no. 179 (London: HM Treasury, 1985).

HM Treasury, 'Government Revenue for the North Sea', *Economic Progress Report*, no. 183 (London, HM Treasury, 1986) and Budget Statements, annually.

HM Treasury, *Financial Statements* (annually).

G.C. Hockley, *Fiscal Policy* (London: Routledge, 1992).

S. James and C. Nobes, *The Economics of Taxation* (London: Prentice-Hall 1992).

J.A. Kay and M.A. King, *The British Tax System* (Oxford: Oxford University Press, 1990).

R.A. Musgrave and P.B. Musgrave, *Public Finance in Theory and Practice* (New York: McGraw-Hill, 1989).

C.T. Sandford, *The Economics of Public Finance* (Oxford: Pergamon Press, 1992).

M. Wilkinson, *Taxation* (London: Macmillan, 1992).

EXERCISES

1. Consider a case for a separate tax on incomes of businesses from that on incomes of individual persons.
2. Explain the meaning of illusory profits and the consequences of taxing them.
3. Consider the desirability of different rates of tax on distributed and undistributed profits.
4. Would you expect a tax on profits to have disincentive effects? Give reasons for your answer.
5. Some pressure groups have argued for the re-introduction of an excess profits tax. Consider a case for or against implementation of such a proposal.
6. Discuss the forms that public revenue from North Sea oil takes and some of the problems in taxing it.
7. Suggest how the government revenue from North Sea oil could be used to achieve the maximum benefit and examine a case for earmarking of the proceeds.
8. Social security contributions are a payroll tax and as such adversely affect employment. Consider the validity of this statement.
9. Harmonisation of corporate taxation is inevitable if greater economic integration is to be achieved within the European Community, and businesses are to benefit from the internal market. Give your reasons for agreeing or disagreeing with this view.
10. Explain why Unitary tax is likely to be detrimental in the long run to a country that imposes it.

9 Taxes on Consumption

TYPES OF TAXES

An indirect tax is a tax on consumption. Dr. Samuel Johnson, the eighteenth century lexicographer, defined it as 'a hateful tax levied on commodities'. It is now also levied in many countries on services. In Chapter 6, the relative merits and demerits of indirect taxation in general were discussed and now the various taxes on consumption will be considered in detail. They fall into four main categories, which are: (i) customs and excise taxes; (ii) licences; (iii) purchase or sales taxes; and (iv) value added taxes. Taxes in the first two categories tend to be levied on selected goods. The other taxes tend to be in the nature of a general tax on consumption.

Customs are taxes levied on internationally-traded goods. In the past, both exports and imports were subject to customs duties, but now they are confined to imports. Depending on the reason for which they are imposed customs duties, are regarded as:

(a) *Revenue duties*, if the primary object is to raise revenue.
(b) *Protective duties*, if they are used to protect home industries from foreign competition in home markets by making imported goods more expensive (see p. 202).
(c) *Preferential duties*, if they are intended to favour particular countries so as to encourage trade between them or to create special relationships, as has been the case for example between members of the British Commonwealth or the European Economic Community and certain territories associated in the past with other members of the European Community. Different rates of duty are then charged depending on the area of origin of the imports.

Excise taxes are revenue duties on home-produced goods that are imposed to match customs duties on imported goods (see p. 205).

Licences are taxes that are paid for the privilege of using or owning certain assets, or if a person or business wishes to provide certain services (see p. 207).

Purchase or sales taxes are taxes that are imposed on a wide range of goods when a transaction takes place. They became common in Europe in the 1920s and in the USA in the 1930s. A purchase tax was introduced in the UK in 1940.

Value added taxes are levied on both goods and services and are general turnover taxes on consumption. They are imposed throughout the European Union. Some member countries apply a standard rate to all goods and services taxed, while others have applied lower rates for certain essential goods and higher rates on luxuries. The intention of the European Union is to harmonise VAT in all Member States.

CHOICE OF GOODS TO BE TAXED

The nature of the taxes on consumption and the purpose for which they are imposed influences the choice of goods that are taxed. A general tax on consumption covers a wide range of goods and services but it is unlikely that everything will be taxed. Some items of consumption are exempt for social reasons because they are regarded as necessities. The distinction between necessities and luxuries is, however, arbitrary and subjective.

Necessities may be defined as goods and services that are consumed by most people regularly, are required to maintain an acceptable standard of living and unavailability of which would result in hardship. Food is essential and is therefore a necessity, but some forms of it such as caviare or oysters may be regarded as luxuries.

Luxuries are goods and services that improve the standard of living but are not essential. They may be beyond the means of some people or may be regarded by consumers as a treat that they can afford occasionally.

What is looked upon as a necessity or a luxury will vary from country to country and will change over time. Thus supply of electricity for domestic use may be regarded as an essential service in an affluent society but a luxury in a poor country. In the UK a television set was something of a luxury that relatively few people could afford in the 1950s. By the 1990s some 98 per cent of households had one. Tea cost £10 for 1lb when it was first introduced into England in about 1650 – at a time when the average annual wage was about £12. Now (1994) an average adult worker earns £16,580 and the price of 1lb of tea is about £2.60.

A government may choose goods and services for selective taxation for the following reasons: (i) they are mainly imported and pose a threat to home industry; (ii) they are widely consumed and the demand for them is inelastic – that is consumers do not appreciably curtail their purchases when, as a result of the tax, the price of the goods or services goes up (see p. 247). Such items of consumption tend to be a lucrative source of revenue. They are also likely to be necessities.

Tobacco and alcohol are the two items that governments favour for selective taxation, on the grounds that: (i) the demand for tobacco and alcohol is inelastic. Statistics show that over the years prices of both have increased but consumption has continued at a high level; (ii) tobacco and alcohol can be classified as luxuries. People do not have to smoke or drink spirits but many do; (iii) consumption of either one can be damaging to health. A tax on both can therefore be justified as a preventative measure that is beneficial to society. The fewer people develop lung cancer as a result of smoking and the fewer alcoholics there are, the less strain is put on the National Health Service; and (iv) tobacco and alcohol provide a lucrative source of revenue. People appear to take little notice of price increases or health warnings. If they did, and stopped smoking and drinking, they would create a financial crisis by depriving the government of a major tax base for indirect taxation.

Oil is also widely taxed. A case for a selective tax on hydrocarbon oils – light oils (motor and aviation spirit), heavy oils (mainly diesel) and fuel oils – is somewhat different. It is true that oils provide a wide tax base and that the demand for some is inelastic, but the imposition of a tax on oil generally can also be advocated on the grounds that it can help to conserve a natural resource or reduce oil imports by discouraging consumption.

Problems involved in taxing oil are that it enters into the production of just about everything, either directly as a raw material, or indirectly as a source of energy. A tax on oil therefore increases costs of manufacture

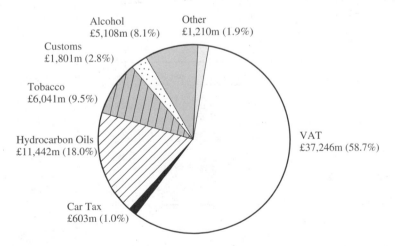

Figure 9.1 Taxes on consumption
Source: Customs and Excise Board, *Annual Report* (1993).

and of transport. A consequent rise in prices is likely to be inflationary, though opinion on this is divided. There is also the difficulty that oil can be regarded both as a necessity and as a luxury, depending on who uses it and for what purpose. Thus, for a salesman, petrol for his car may be essential if he has no other means of reaching his customers – but if he uses the car to go on a holiday, consumption of petrol is a luxury. For the purpose of a selective tax on oil it may be impossible in practice to distinguish between the different use of petrol and to tax accordingly.

TAX RATES

Revenue from indirect taxation depends not only on the choice of goods and services for taxation, but also on the rates of tax. Table 9.1 shows the rates in the UK.

An *ad valorem* rate of tax is a percentage rate on the value of a good or service offered for sale. Thus, if a supplier is prepared to sell an article for

Table 9.1   Rates of indirect taxation

(a) Value Added Tax

Rate of tax (per cent)	Year					
	1973	1974	1975	1976–78	1979–91	1991–95
standard rate	10	8	8	8	15	$17\frac{1}{2}$
higher rate		25	25	$12\frac{1}{2}$	15	$17\frac{1}{2}$

(b) Duties

	1900–1	1909–10	1920–21	1930–31	1940–41	1950–51	1960–61	1970–71	1980–81	1980–82	1990–91	199:
Duty on beer per pint[1] (£)	0.001	0.001	0.017	0.014	0.016	0.038	0.031	0.051	0.091	0.126	0.345	0.
Duty on spirits per proof gallon (£)	0.55	0.74	3.63	3.63	4.88	10.54	10.54	18.85	30.70	13.60	17.35	19.
Duty on tobacco per lb[2] (£)	0.15	0.19	0.41	0.44	0.98	2.91	3.22	5.04	13.20	30.96	33.65	76.2
Duty on petrol per gallon[3] (£)	–	0.001	–	0.014	0.04	0.075	0.125	0.225	0.455	0.138	–	–

Notes: [1] 1981–82 per litre of alcohol.
　　　　[2] 1981–82 per kilo of tobacco.
　　　　[3] 1981–82 per litre of petrol.
　　　　Duty on spirits and tobacco rounded off to the nearest penny.

Source: London and Cambridge Economic Services: *The British Economy*, and Board of Customs and Excise, *Annual Reports*.

£50 and the tax is fixed at 10 per cent, the amount due in tax will be £5 and the price paid by the consumer will be £55. With the same rate of tax, if the value of the article is £100, the tax will amount to £10 and the price will increase to £110. VAT is an *ad valorem* tax.

A *specific* rate of tax is expressed as a fixed amount per unit and is related to the quantity and not the value of what is bought, e.g. tax per gallon of petrol, pint of beer or 1lb of tobacco (see p. 198). In the UK, the duty on a bottle of whisky was £4.08 in 1981 when the retail price ranged from £6.30–£8.30 (*Board of Customs and Excise Report*, 1982). By 1993 the price had risen to £11.24, duty to £5.55 and with VAT total tax amounted to 64.3 per cent of what the consumer paid. For taxes on a packet of 20 King Size cigarettes, see Table 9.2.

Single and discriminatory rates of tax on consumption may be levied (see Table 9.1). A general sales or turnover tax, that is charged at a single uniform rate and is applied to all the goods and services, has the advantage of administrative simplicity. A discriminatory tax, with a lower rate on more essential goods and a higher rate on luxuries, has been advocated for various reasons:

(a) Such a distinction helps to reduce the regressiveness of a tax on consumption, assuming that buyers of luxury goods will have higher incomes than those who buy only essential things. If this assumption is accepted then it can be argued that the tax is in a way related to the ability to pay. In practice it is not likely to be so because of the difficulty of distinguishing between what is essential and what is a luxury good or service.

(b) Discriminatory rates enable a government to discourage consumption of certain goods or to create a protective tariff.

(c) An all-round increase in the rate of a general tax to meet the need for more revenue might impose considerable hardship on households with small incomes. They would be less affected by increases in the rate of tax on non-essential goods only.

Table 9.2   Taxes on consumption

Taxes on a packet of 20 King Size Cigarettes (pence)

	Specific duty	*Ad valorem duty*	*VAT*	*Total tax*	*Price*
1981	38.1	20.0	12.4	70.5	95
1993	97.5	47.4	35.3	180.2	237

Source: *Board of Customs and Excise Report* (1982 and 1993).

The arguments against discriminatory rates are that they distort the pattern of consumption and production and adversely affect industries producing goods and services on which higher rates of tax are levied.

The Level of Tax Rates and the Yield

At what level a government will fix the tax rates will be influenced by the amount of revenue required and the purpose for which the tax is imposed. High rates of tax on consumption do not necessarily produce a high yield. If the demand for goods and services taxed is elastic, people are likely to react by cutting down their consumption and this will reduce the tax revenue. A lower rate of tax may produce a higher tax yield. There was a striking example of this in England when, in the eighteenth century, the average duty on tea was reduced from a rate of 119 per cent to $12\frac{1}{2}$ per cent and the tax revenue substantially increased. With a much lower level of duty smuggling became an unprofitable business. Tax avoidance was hardly worth the effort and tea drinkers became law abiding citizens and paid the duty. It is difficult to think of a present-day example of a comparable tax reduction that resulted in an equally dramatic and direct increase in revenue.

A tax rate that will maximise tax revenue may not, however, be the rate that will be required to achieve a particular purpose. If the purpose is to discourage imports of certain goods then a high rate would have to be imposed. But if, as a result of this, imports ceased, revenue from the tax would cease. A low rate of tax might bring in a large revenue but it would be ineffective as a measure to protect the home industry. Thus, there may be a conflict between revenue and policy objectives. The effect of indirect taxation on the consumers of goods and services is difficult to estimate. It will depend on the range of goods to be taxed, the rate of tax and the incidence of the taxes, which will be discussed later (see p. 245).

NEGATIVE INDIRECT TAXATION – SUBSIDIES

Subsidies can be regarded as negative taxes on consumption. Whereas taxes on goods and services increase their price, the purpose of subsidies is to reduce prices or to prevent increases which producers might otherwise have to make, as their costs go up. Subsidies that are paid to producers of certain goods and services may also help consumers, but this is a debatable point.

Different pressure groups seek subsidies for different purposes:

(a) *Households* stand to gain. Certain essential goods and services are subsidised to keep the cost of living down and to benefit households with small incomes who would otherwise be unable to maintain their level of consumption (as had been the case with the bread subsidy in the UK). However, subsidies do not discriminate between buyers of the same good. A person will pay the same subsidised price for bread irrespective of their income. Subsidising is not the most effective way of helping the poor. It is wasteful, as at the same time it benefits those who are not in need of help.

(b) *Industries and firms*, both in the private and public sector, press for subsidies that would enable them to sell in home and foreign markets at competitive prices, to maintain their level of output and employment (e.g. the shipbuilding industry). It is, however, important to consider why whole industries or individual firms have difficulties in selling their output. This may be because they produce goods and services for which demand is disappearing and will not revive. Subsidisation would then only prolong an inevitable decline and may not be in the overall national interest of a country. Some producers are uncompetitive because they are inefficient and have low productivity; a subsidy by itself will not solve their problems. Uncompetitiveness at home may be due to the fact that foreign governments subsidise their countries' exports. A subsidy to domestic producers in such circumstances can be regarded as a retaliatory measure but a cut-price war is a two-edged sword.

(c) *Infant industries*, it has been argued, need subsidies to establish themselves in the early stages of their existence. The danger is that they will never grow up – industrial Peter Pans.

(d) *Strategic industries* may also be helped for non-economic reasons.

Some subsidies are needed and can be beneficial in the short-run in certain circumstances. In the long run, subsidisation is likely to be costly and, in all probability, counterproductive to the healthy functioning of an economy. The validity of such an assertion, however, is difficult to establish by reference to statistics, since what the situation would have been without subsidies is subject to speculation.

INDIRECT TAXATION IN THE UK

Taxes on consumption in the UK are: (i) customs duties; (ii) excise duties; (iii) value added tax; and (iv) licences and other miscellaneous taxes. Stamp duties can be regarded as a tax on expenditure or as a tax on capital. They will be discussed in Chapter 10.

Customs Duties: Use as Protective Measures

The word customs came to be applied in England to certain forms of revenue. It was the result of an argument concerning the prerogative of the Crown to impose duties on certain imports – owing to a long-standing custom. Customs duties were levied in England before the Norman conquest, and some of the provisions of the Magna Carta (1215) were concerned with their regulation and prevention of abuse and of excessive taxation. The statute of 1275 is believed to be the earliest legislation that authorised the Crown to levy customs duties. They were originally regarded as a charge for the maintenance of ports and protection from pirates. Subsequently they became a lucrative source of revenue. As the number of customs duties proliferated and the rates of duty increased, merchants protested at the burden. A committee of the House of Commons considered this problem and prepared the first Book of Rates in 1642. The practice of offering for sale the right to levy customs was stopped in 1671 when a Board of Commissioners was appointed to deal with customs. The duties were consolidated in 1787 and the revenue from them was paid into a single fund which became known as the Consolidated Fund. Money was made available from it for general state expenditure. This ended the previous practice of allocating revenue from each duty for a specific purpose.

The policy that was subsequently pursued had the following objectives: (i) to simplify customs duties; (ii) to reduce the cost of collection by reducing the number of goods taxed; and (iii) to strengthen home industries by abolishing customs duties on imported raw materials. Up to 1842 there had been 1150 articles liable to customs duties – by 1908 this had been reduced to 15. Customs duties on exports were gradually abolished. The last one, on the export of coal, came to an end in 1845. Since then only imports have been subject to customs.

Free trade period

Britain adhered to its free trade policy from 1860 to 1915. Impediments to international trade such as protective duties were removed and only a small number of customs was retained for revenue purposes. By 1872, all foreign goods entering the country were free from import duties except for ten commodities: cocoa, coffee, currants, figs, raisins, tea, tobacco, wine, spirits and sugar. Apart from the last two, there were no home industries that supplied any of these goods.

Return to protection

Protectionist policies were reintroduced during the First World War and customs were again levied as protective duties:

(a) The *McKenna* duties were *ad valorem* taxes and were first imposed in 1915. Imports from the Commonwealth countries were charged at-two-thirds of the full rate.

(b) The *key industries* duties followed in 1921 as a measure to protect a number of home industries considered to be of national and strategic importance. The rate of duty on imports ranged from 33 per cent to 50 per cent. Goods imported from the Commonwealth countries were allowed free entry.

(c) A *general protective tariff* was established by the *Import Duties Act (1932)*. By this time the Great Depression was at its worst, and unemployment was high and widespread. The new duty was an *ad valorem* tax of 10 per cent on goods that were not alrcady taxed and were not on the free list. All imports from the Commonwealth were exempt from the protective tariff. Imports from other areas were, at the discretion of the Import Duties Advisory Committee, subject to additional protective duties ranging from 15 per cent to 30 per cent on luxury goods.

(d) *Ottawa Preference* (Ottawa Agreement Act, 1933) further strengthened the trading position of the Commonwealth countries. Such goods as were produced outside the Commonwealth and could compete with those of the Commonwealth producers became subject to duties. In return for the concessions, the UK obtained preferential treatment for her exports to the Commonwealth.

Trend Away from Tariffs – GATT and the European Community

After the Second World War governments took steps to liberalise trade again. Arguments pointing out the advantages of free trade that had not been influential for years were now listened to by governments. There was approval for the application of the principle of division of labour with countries specialising in producing that at which they were best and exporting their output unhindered by tariffs. The case for protecting home industries was weakened by the strong world market for goods and services.

An international treaty, the General Agreement on Tariffs and Trade (GATT), to which the UK and some seventy other countries are signatories, came into operation in 1948. This led to a series of conferences, the result of which was that the member countries either froze or reduced their import tariffs.The European Common Market (EEC) and the European Free Trade Area (EFTA) were both set up in 1959, the former under the Treaty of Rome of 1957 and the latter as a result of the Stockholm Convention (1959). Their aims, organisation and rules differed but both were basically free trade areas. Countries in the two associations committed themselves to reducing and eventually abolishing tariffs among their members. Initially the UK only joined EFTA, partly because this made easier the preservation of preferential trade links with the Commonwealth countries. Later, as trade with the Commonwealth relatively declined, and that with Europe increased, the UK left EFTA and in 1973 joined the EEC (see p. 332). Under the Treaty of Accession, the UK undertook to adjust her protective duties over a transitional period so as to: (i) abolish protective import duties against members of the EEC; (ii) align import duty rates of the UK tariffs with the common customs tariff of the Community; (iii) terminate preferential rates of duty on import from the Commonwealth Preference Area; and (iv) abide by preferential agreements between the EEC and other countries.

Freeports

To further facilitate international trade by easing the burden of customs duties, Member States of the European Common Market established freeports on their territories. The UK was the last one to do so in 1984. (There were at that time some 400 throughout the world.) The sites chosen for the British freeports were: England: Birmingham, Liverpool, Southampton; Wales: Cardiff; Scotland: Prestwick; Northern Ireland: Belfast. With the exception of Southampton all the other locations were in areas in need of more jobs, thereby the government linked the freeports scheme to its regional development policy. But this, to some extent, was incidental.

The purpose of the freeports was to enable firms that located there to import goods from outside the Common Market, assemble them into finished products and re-export them to buyers outside the EEC (as it then was) free of all taxes and customs duties.

Liberalisation of the world trade in general, and in the European Community, reduced the attractiveness of the freeports and the importance of customs duties as a source of revenue for governments and as a tool of economic policies. The Single European Act of the European Community has far-reaching effects on indirect taxation (see p. 339).

Excise Duties

Excise Duties were first introduced in 1643 to complement customs duties. The system of levying tax in the form of customs, if the goods are imported and imposing excise duties on similar goods, if they are produced at home, presents the problem of choosing which goods to tax. Those that are generally regarded as suitable for the joint purpose are tobacco and alcoholic drinks. They are the main source of revenue from selective taxes on consumption.

Purchase Tax

The government first imposed purchase tax on a wide range of goods in 1940, as a war measure, but continued to levy it for the next thirty-three years. Its purpose originally was to: (i) raise revenue; (ii) reduce consumption of luxuries; and (iii) counteract inflation. The view at the time was that indirect taxation discouraged consumption and kept price rises down (see p. 418). Some essential goods were exempt; the rest were grouped into categories to which different rates of tax applied. The less necessary a good was considered to be, the higher was the rate of tax. It reached a maximum of 100 per cent on the most 'luxurious' of luxuries. The tax officials, presumably male, classified cosmetics at the maximum rate. Purchase tax was collected at the wholesale stage of distribution. It continued to be levied after the war as a general sales tax until British entry into the Common Market, when it was replaced by the Value Added Tax to conform with the system of taxation within the Community.

Value Added Tax (VAT)

The imposition of value added tax in 1973 marked a departure from the principle of graduated rates of taxation. It was levied at a single standard rate of 10 per cent of the value of supplies. Both goods and services became liable to VAT, unless they were exempt or zero-rated. Exemptions were granted to postal services, education and health services, all forms of insurance, finance, land, betting and gaming. (The last two being already subject to excise duty.)

Zero-rated goods and services were technically taxable but the rate of tax on them was nil. Included in this category were exports of goods and exports of most services, necessities such as food, drugs and medicines supplied on prescription, the output of nationalised industries: (coal, gas and electricity), passenger transport and a small number of other miscellaneous goods and services.

The single rate of tax was abandoned in 1974 when, following the oil crisis of the previous year, a 25 per cent rate of VAT on petrol was imposed to conserve resources. A higher rate was also applied in 1975 on goods designated as less essential, such as: (i) those used for recreation, boats and caravans, (ii) luxury goods (see Table 9.1). Their classification as non-essentials aroused controversy. In 1979 VAT returned to a single rate of 15 per cent. In the early 1990's it was increased to a standard rate $17\frac{1}{2}$ per cent and resulted in a substantial shift from direct to indirect taxation.

Regulatory provision

A Chancellor of the Exchequer can propose in his Budget to change rates of VAT and those of any other tax, but in the case of VAT the Treasury was empowered, for the purpose of management of the economy, to alter the VAT rate of tax by decreasing or increasing it by up to one-fifth.

Operation and collection of VAT

All suppliers are liable to VAT except those who produce goods and services that are exempt, or zero-rated, or whose turnover is below a specified level (set at £46,000 for 1994–95). Everybody with taxable output has to register as a taxable person and to account for VAT. Producers who are taxable persons, whenever they buy raw materials or any other goods and services to which VAT applies, are charged by their suppliers – labelled the input tax. When they themselves sell their output they in turn charge VAT to those who buy from them. VAT then becomes an output tax.

At the end of the taxable period, a taxable person adds together all the input taxes paid by him/her and all the output taxes he/she has charged others. Then: (i) if the total for output taxes exceeds the total for input taxes, the difference is paid to the Customs and Excise Department, (ii) if the total for input taxes exceeds that for output taxes, then the supplier is entitled to a tax refund by the Customs and Excise Board, as the following example shows.

Supplier on his purchases pays VAT (input tax) e.g.	£40,000	£60,000
Supplier on his sales charges VAT (output tax)	£60,000	£40,000
balance	£20,000	£20,000
tax	liability	refund

The way that the system operates is that VAT is passed on at each stage in the process of production and distribution until it reaches the final consumer on whom the tax burden then falls and it rests there.

Licences

Consumers are also subject to indirect taxes in the form of licences that are required for: (i) use of an asset, e.g. television set; (ii) ownership of an asset e.g. a gun; (iii) provision of a service, e.g. gaming facilities. Such licences are issued for a fixed period of time and have to be renewed annually or at more frequent intervals.

Proceeds from the issue of licences go to the central government and to local authorities. The main source of revenue in this category are the television licences and motor vehicle licences. An owner of a television set has to acquire an annual licence from the TV Licensing Authority to watch television programmes. All motor vehicles in use on the road have to be licensed. Licences are issued by the Driver and Vehicle Licensing Agency and the proceeds go to the Exchequer. Local authorities retain money from some licences, such as market-stall licences. Proceeds from gun licences go into the Police Fund. Neither market stalls nor guns are a lucrative source of revenue, in contrast to gaming licences and betting duties. Gaming at casinos is taxed by requiring the person who makes the premises available for play, to obtain a licence. Its cost depends on the rateable value of the premises and on the number of tables provided for gaming. Betting duty is paid by bookmakers or totalisator (tote) operators and covers both on and off course betting and is a percentage tax on the stake money; so too is bingo duty.

Thus a person living in the UK cannot avoid liability to indirect taxation in one form or another. They can only vary total amounts of tax paid by reducing their consumption, but any consequent savings (above the exemption limit) will then be subject to capital taxes during their life and on transfer on death (see Chapter 10). A person can, however, have their body disposed of without VAT being charged by the undertaker. This is one of the few exempt services at present.

ENERGY AND ENVIRONMENTAL TAX MEASURES

The general public has become increasingly concerned about the effects of energy consumption on the environment. The damage from the burning of fossil fuels and the danger from nuclear energy have led pressure groups in many parts of the world to demand government action. In the European Community, the European Parliament recommended that environmental considerations should be taken into account in formulating fiscal policies. The British government approached the problem on two fronts: (a) through public expenditure programmes to promote energy efficiency in homes, industry and transport and initiatives to improve energy conservation in public buildings such as schools; and (b) through tax measures to discourage energy consumption by increasing the price of fuels. This could be expected to make consumers more efficient energy users, bring the level of consumption down, reduce pollution and the rate of depletion of natural resources in finite supply. Thus the government could be seen to respond to environmentalists' demands and at the same time raise more revenue. Over the years, industry and individuals have absorbed increased taxes on motor vehicles petrol and diesel oil.

When one buys a new car or a motor cycle there is a Car Tax (introduced in 1973) which is levied as a percentage rate on wholesale price. To take a vehicle on the road one has to pay for a licence and to run it there is the cost of tax on petrol and oil plus VAT. In an environmentally-friendly gesture in the 1987 Budget, the Chancellor of the Exchequer differentiated between unleaded and leaded petrol and taxed the latter at a higher rate.

However, when the government proposed to extend VAT to domestic fuels there was a widespread protest. In his 1993 Budget speech the Chancellor of the Exchequer justified this by saying 'It will also help to meet Britain's commitment to aim to return carbon dioxide emissions to their 1990 levels by the end of this decade', whilst the additional tax would not affect the job-creating sectors of the economy.

To compensate people on low incomes, social security and pensions, the government announced benefit increases. For most people, it was to be a question of improving the use of energy, conserving, (e.g. through roof insulation), cutting down on consumption or paying more. This the people were unwilling to do whatever the benefits to the environment might be. They protested through the ballot box at the first opportunity which was the local government elections in 1994. These were disastrous for the government. The tax on domestic fuel was widely regarded as a contributory factor, and the government abandoned its intention to levy VAT at the rate of 17.5 per cent on it.

The British government is not alone in using taxation to further environmental objectives. For example, Denmark imposes an *environment tax*. The problem with a tax on domestic fuel is that it is individuals who pay it directly and, unlike businesses, they have a vote, elect governments and bring them down. However, with the expansion of the European Community into European Union, increased coverage in tax matters of the Commission's directives and greater alignment of taxation by Member States, national governments' powers to tax as they wish, will be curtailed.

IMPACT OF DEVELOPMENTS IN THE EUROPEAN COMMUNITY ON INDIRECT TAXATION

The Treaty of Rome (1957) which established the Common Market in Europe had, initially, a limited impact on the tax structure of the Member States. As the focus was on the removal of impediments to the free movement of goods, the harmonisation of indirect taxation was not seen as an immediate priority. The Single European Act, which came into force thirty years later, had much wider implications for the whole system of taxation. The process of harmonisation of indirect taxes has been slow for a variety of reasons: (a) the extent to which governments of Member States rely on indirect taxation has differed in the past and still does (Table 9.3). (b) Although Value Added Tax is now the main indirect tax in the Community, it is levied at different rates. For example, the UK has one standard rate and zero rates on certain goods, whilst Portugal has a zero rate and three other rates – the highest of 30 per cent being levied on such luxuries as perfume. Spain's rates range between 6 per cent and 28 per cent – the highest imposed on items like jewellery. France also differentiates between goods and taxes luxuries at 22 per cent. The Netherlands has a 6 per cent rate for necessities and a 17.5 per cent standard rate.

Value Added Tax

This was established in the Common Market by the VAT Directive (1967) as a general multi-stage, non-cumulative turnover tax. Countries such as the UK that joined later were under obligation to incorporate VAT into their tax system on accession. The VAT Directive (1977) introduced a uniform VAT base for assessment purposes in the Member States, but the rates to be levied by them were not laid down, with the result that they continued to vary. Under the current VAT directive, national governments are required to apply a standard rate of at least 15 per cent until 1996 and

Table 9.3   Indirect taxes as a percentage of total taxes and social security
contributions: international comparison

Country	Years										
	1981	1982	1983	1984	1985	1986	1987	1988	1989	1990	1991
Belgium	27.6	27.1	27.4	26.1	25.5	25.1	25.9	26.2	27.3	97.1	27.0
Denmark	40.6	39.7	38.4	38.0	37.4	38.7	37.7	36.9	36.1	36.3	35.9
France	36.2	36.1	35.5	35.4	35.6	35.3	35.2	35.4	34.7	34.4	33.4
Germany	31.2	30.5	31.2	31.3	30.3	30.0	29.8	30.0	30.4	31.6	31.7
Greece	48.7	47.4	48.7	47.8	48.3	51.1	52.0	51.0	50.6	52.6	51.8
Italy	28.4	27.5	28.2	28.8	27.7	28.1	28.6	29.7	29.2	29.3	30.1
Nether- lands	26.2	25.5	25.2	26.7	27.1	27.6	27.7	27.4	27.4	27.7	26.7
Spain	27.1	28.8	29.2	30.1	38.1	36.4	34.0	34.3	32.2	31.8	*
Portugal*											
UK	43.6	42.8	41.9	41.6	40.9	42.7	43.2	42.9	41.6	37.4	39.4
Finland	39.9	40.2	40.1	40.3	39.2	39.0	41.4	41.0	41.9	39.9	38.9
Norway	34.7	35.1	36.0	36.1	36.5	40.5	39.0	37.6	36.6	35.9	36.9
Sweden	28.4	28.5	30.1	31.4	32.9	32.5	30.8	30.1	29.6	30.8	33.8
USA	28.3	28.6	29.6	29.5	29.0	28.7	27.8	27.5	27.2	27.7	29.2
Japan	28.2	27.8	26.8	27.4	27.5	26.5	27.2	27.5	26.4	26.2	24.8

Note:
*Not available.

Source: *Economic Trends*, 484 (London: HMSO, 1994).

before 1995 the Council of Ministers must decide on the minimum rate to
apply across the European Union. Harmonisation of VAT is still some
way off.

Customs Duties

As the Single European Act came into force and tax frontiers were
abolished within the Community, the largest impact was on customs
duties. Although they are still imposed on goods coming from outside the
Community the relative importance of customs duties in the tax structure
is on the decline.

Excise Duties

The abolition of customs duties in an internal market affected excise
duties which are now considered as consumption taxes on certain products. The major excise duties in the Community are on: tobacco, alcoholic
beverages and mineral oils. Their imposition is justified on the grounds

that consumption of these items may be harmful to health and environ-ment. With the object of alignment of taxation in the case of tobacco prod-ucts the Commission calculated rates of tax on the basis of arithmetical mean for the Community. The same principle was applied for distilled alcoholic beverages, but was considered unsuitable for fermented bever-ages. Instead, they are to be taxed equally per litre when the beverages are in competition with each other.

Traditionally, in the UK and Denmark, high duties have been levied on spirits and tobacco, whereas in the Mediterranean countries – Greece, Italy, Portugal and Spain – these products have attracted relatively low taxation.

In 1972 the Commission proposed that a number of 'minor excise duties' should be abolished that were peculiar to a particular country and collection costs were disproportionate to the tax yield.

Nevertheless, a variety of minor taxes continue to be levied in the Community. For example Denmark has a Hunting Licence, Germany imposes Hunting and Fishing Tax and taxes dogs, as does Italy. The Netherlands imposes a Tax on Waste and Denmark an Environment Tax on disposable tableware.

The system and level of indirect taxation in the Member States of the European Community has come to reflect not only the governments' need for revenue, but also social and cultural differences. Harmonisation of taxes on consumption requires not only greater economic but also social cohesion.

SUMMARY

1. Taxes on consumption are indirect taxes of a regressive nature.
2. Consumption taxes are: customs and excise duties, licences, purchase or sale taxes and value added taxes.
3. The rate of tax may be *ad valorem* or specific.
4. The distinction between necessities and luxuries for tax purposes raises problems. It tends to be arbitrary and the classification changes over time. Necessities are usually either exempt or taxed at a lower rate.
5. Taxation of consumption may be universal, when all goods and ser-vices are taxed, or selective when only some are subject to tax.
6. Customs and excise duties are selective taxes. Customs can be levied on imports and exports, but in the UK only the former are now taxed.
7. The purpose of the customs and excise duties may be raise revenue or to discourage consumption. Customs can also be used to reduce

imports of certain goods, both irrespective of the country of origin or from specified areas, to help the balance of payments or to protect home industries.

8. Establishment of free trade areas and international agreements have led to the gradual dismantling of tariff barriers.

9. Value added tax is levied to raise revenue and to exercise control over the economy. In the UK, VAT is the most important single source of indirect tax revenue.

10. Subsidies can be regarded as a form of negative taxation. They can be used jointly with taxes to manage the economy. The incidence of indirect taxes is discussed in Chapter 12 and diagrams show the effect of taxes and subsidies on price.

SUGGESTED FURTHER READING

C.V. Brown and P.M. Jackson, *Public Sector Economics* (Oxford: Basil Blackwell, 1992).

Commission of the European Communities, *Taxes* (Brussels) series.

Commission of the European Communities, *VAT Directives 1967, 1977 Proposals*.

Customs and Excise Board, *Annual Reports* (London).

H.J. Easson, *Taxation in the European Community* (London: Athlone Press, 1993).

G.C. Hockley, *Fiscal Policy* (London: Routledge, 1992).

S. James and C. Nobes, *The Economics of Taxation* (London: Prentice-Hall, 1992).

J.A. Kay and M.A. King, *The British Tax System* (Oxford: Oxford University Press, 1990).

R.A. Musgrave and P.B. Musgrave, *Public Finance in Theory and Practice* (New York: McGraw-Hill, 1989).

C.T. Sandford, *The Economics of Public Finance* (Oxford: Pergamon Press, 1992).

M. Wilkinson, *Taxation* (London: Macmillan, 1992).

G. Winkler (ed.), *Tax Harmonisation in Europe* (London: Macmillan, 1992).

EXERCISES

1. Explain why *ad valorem* taxes on consumption are regressive.
2. Suggest why harmonisation of indirect taxation within the European Community poses many problems.
3. Discuss the arguments in favour of and against a tariff policy by a country.
4. How would you account for the trend away from customs duties?
5. Consider the problems involved in defining 'necessities' and luxuries for the purpose of taxation.
6. Suggest the criteria for the choice of goods for selective taxation.
7. Can indirect taxes be made progressive? Illustrate your answers by reference to the British tax system.
8. In what way do licences differ from other forms of taxation?
9. Consider the merits and demerits of a value added tax.
10. Explain how the burden of a specific tax is reduced by inflation.

10 Taxes on Capital

DEFINITION OF CAPITAL

To consider taxation of capital it is first necessary to define capital. For tax purposes it means *all forms of marketable wealth*. Thus, in literature on public finance, in government reports and in legislation, capital and wealth are often used as synonymous terms. Wealth, as Figure 10.1 shows, can take a variety of forms all of which have been, or are, subject to capital

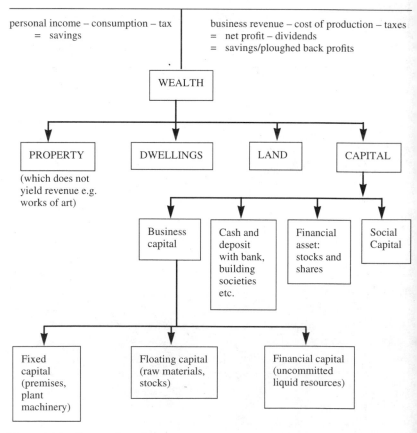

Figure 10.1   Forms of wealth

taxes, with the exception of social capital which represents investment by the state. Its citizens own social capital collectively and cannot dispose of it individually. Wealth can be a *free gift of nature*, such as land or mineral deposits. It can arise from the accumulation of savings that results from foregone consumption. Wealth can be increased by acquisition of *assets* that gain in value and by its own use for productive purposes that result in creation of new wealth. Owners of wealth derive income from it in the form of: rent from land, interest from loans and dividends from investments. This is classified as *unearned income*. Capital taxes are one of the oldest forms of taxation. They were originally levied on land and dwellings. It was an easily identifiable and immovable tax base that made tax evasion difficult and provided a wide coverage in agricultural economies. Gradually, as they developed, the range of assets that were subject to taxation was extended until there were few things that were not taxed.

TYPES OF TAXES ON CAPITAL

There are now several different types of taxes on capital as the following classification shows:

Capital Transfer Tax	Capital Gains Tax	Wealth Tax
(i) Tax on legacies*	(i) Tax on short-term gains	(i) Annual tax
(ii) Tax on gifts in a lifetime	(ii) Tax on both short term and long term gains on assets of:	(ii) 'once and for all' tax
(iii) Tax on (i) and (ii)	(a) individuals	
	(b) businesses	
*Inheritance tax.		

The nature of these taxes will be first considered in general terms and then their features will be discussed in greater detail with reference to the British system of taxation and capital taxes in the European Union.

A recent survey of the major European countries and other members of the Organisation for Economic Co-operation and Development showed that nearly 80 per cent have a tax on transfer of capital, 80 per cent on capital gains and 40 per cent have an annual wealth tax. But it is not only the developed countries such as Germany, France, Netherlands and those of Scandinavia that have introduced wealth taxes. They are also found in India and Pakistan.

REVENUE AND POLICY ASPECTS OF TAXATION OF CAPITAL

Governments levy taxes on capital to raise revenue and for social and political reasons:

(a) *Revenue aspect.* Originally the only purpose of capital taxes was to raise revenue. This is no longer so and the revenue aspect has become relatively unimportant. Taxes on capital accounted for less than 5 per cent of total tax revenue in the twenty or so countries that were members of the OECD in the 1970s. Since then there has been a downward trend. In the UK capital taxes yielded 4 per cent of the tax revenue in 1969, 2 per cent in 1980 and less than 1 per cent by the 1990s. This was in line with yields in the other Member States of the European Community (see Table 10.1).

(b) *Policy aspect.* Capital taxes are now mainly seen as an instrument of fiscal policy to achieve a more egalitarian society. The policy aspect will be discussed more fully in Chapter 23.

Arguments in favour of capital taxation are based on moral, ethical and political concepts. Equality is difficult to define. The definition has to be

Table 10.1   Capital taxes as a source of revenue in the European Community

Taxes on capital in member states as a percentage of their total tax revenue and social security contributions

	1981	1985	1991
Belgium	0.8	0.6	0.7
Denmark	0.4	0.5	0.5
France	0.8	0.6	1.5
Germany	0.2	0.2	0.2
Greece	1.4	1.0	1.2
Italy	0.2	0.2	0.1
Netherlands	0.5	0.4	0.5
UK	0.5	0.7	0.6
Finland	0.2	0.3	0.5
Norway	0.1	0.1	0.1
Sweden	0.2	0.3	0.2
USA	1.0	0.8	0.9
Japan	0.8	1.2	1.8

Source: *Economic Trends*, 484 (London: HMSO, 1994).

based on subjective value judgements, and the term can be interpreted differently. For practical purposes, governments equate a policy to achieve equality with one to reduce inequality by some unspecified amounts. The argument that big inequalities in the ownership of wealth are socially unacceptable is widely accepted.

Arguments against taxes on capital are mainly on economic and practical grounds. In a complex economic system such taxes are difficult and expensive to assess and to collect. Taxpayer compliance is low and the unpopularity of the taxes is high. At a time of inflation the taxes are likely to become unfair. In so far as they discourage savings, capital taxes will reduce the supply of capital to industry. Their adverse economic consequences cannot be ignored, even though they cannot be accurately measured and may not be a primary concern.

CAPITAL TRANSFER TAX/INHERITANCE TAX

Taxation of capital is now a firmly established feature of the tax system of major countries. As the name implies it is a tax on the transfer of capital. The tax is in the nature of a death duty when the transfer is the result of a legacy, and is treated as a gift tax when the capital is transferred during the donor's lifetime. Capital transfer taxes are levied on the basis of two principles:

(a) *The estate principle.* The tax is assessed on the estate out of which the legacy or gift had been made and the tax liability is determined by reference to the size of the estate. Taxes imposed on this principle are sometimes called estate taxes or duties.

(b) *The inheritance principle.* The tax is assessed on the recipients of a legacy or gift and the liability may be determined either by size of the capital transfer or the relationship of the beneficiary to the donor, or by taking both considerations into account.

Arguments put forward in favour of the estate principle are that a tax imposed on this basis is both easier and cheaper to administer – requiring only one valuation. It also yields a bigger revenue, since the estate is taxed as a whole and therefore at a higher rate than would have been applicable had the estate been split.

Arguments in favour of the inheritance principle are that its application results in a fairer tax that takes into account the recipient's circumstances and achieves a greater degree of distribution of wealth by providing an incentive to split the estates. By making more numerous but smaller transfers, the tax burden can be reduced.

The Rate of Tax

A tax imposed on either principle may be levied at different rates, such as:

(a) *Progressive, proportional or regressive rates.* A progressive rate increases more steeply, the larger the transfer of capital. A proportional rate means that the same percentage of the value of an estate, legacy or gift is taken in taxation whatever its size. A regressive rate applies when a small transfer of capital is more heavily taxed than a larger one. Most major countries levy capital transfer taxes at progressive rates – though not all have equally steep progression.

(b) *Discriminatory rates.* The rates of tax may depend on the nature of the capital transfer. In the UK an estate is more heavily taxed on death than in the lifetime of the donor. Thus the tax discriminates between legacies and gifts. The rate may also depend on the relationship of the beneficiary to the donor. In many countries, in contrast to the UK, capital transfers to direct descendants are subject to lower rates of tax than transfers to more distant relatives. The rates usually rise the more remote the relationship and the highest rate is paid by unrelated beneficiaries. Thus, depending on the amount of capital transferred, the rates of taxes range, for example, in France from 5 per cent for descendants up to 60 per cent for an unrelated beneficiary or distant relative, and in Germany from 3 per cent for descendants to up to 70 per cent for an unrelated beneficiary or distant relative (see Table 10.2). In the UK the top rate is 40 per cent irrespective of the relationship, except in the case of a spouse. (Transfer of capital between spouses is not taxed.)

(c) *Reduced rates.* Some countries have applied the principle of tax relief on productive assets and have introduced lower rates of tax on certain forms of capital. This concession was made as a result of lobbying by farmers and owners of small businesses, in whose case sale of some of the assets to meet capital transfer tax liabilities, could impair or destroy the economic viability of the whole enterprise. In many countries, including the UK, land is less heavily taxed than other forms of wealth.

Table 10.2   Rates of taxes on capital in Europe

		Percentage Rate of Tax
	Wealth Tax	*Succession, Inheritance/Gift Tax*
Belgium		3–80*
Denmark	1.2	1.2–90*
Germany	0.5[1]	3–70*
Spain	0.2–2.5	7.65–34*
Ireland		20–40*
Italy		3–33*
Netherlands	8	27–68*
Portugal		4–50*
UK		40

Notes: * Lower rates of tax on related persons, top rate on unrelated beneficiaries.
[1]Rate for natural persons, rate for legal persons is 0.6.
Source: Commission of the European Communities (Brussels, 1993).

The various reliefs and exemptions allowed for capital taxes provide such a variety of loopholes that comparison of the tax burden internationally, to a large extent, is a theoretical exercise. The tax liability that the legislators intended and the money that the taxing authorities succeed in extracting, is likely to differ substantially.

CAPITAL GAINS TAX

This is a less comprehensive and more recent tax in most countries than a capital transfer tax in the form of death duties. A capital gains tax is imposed on the increase in value of marketable assets between the date of their acquisition or some fixed date and the time of disposal, when the tax becomes payable.

The purpose of the tax is to: (i) complement the capital transfer tax in furthering a policy to achieve a more equal ownership of wealth; (ii) discourage speculation, the object of which is to increase wealth, by buying assets when prices fall and selling when they rise; and (iii) close a loophole that made tax avoidance possible. Suppose there is no capital gains tax. A person has capital of £100,000 which increases in value during a year by 10 per cent. A sale of 9.1 per cent of the property at the end of the year will leave the original £100,000 intact and will provide £10,000 in cash which can be used as income during the year, but escapes income tax, since for tax purposes this money is a capital gain.

A capital gains tax may be imposed on short-term gains only, when an asset is sold or disposed of with a certain specific short period, such as six months or one year. Alternatively, both short-term and long-term gains may be taxed. In either form the tax may apply to: (i) private property; (ii) business property; or (iii) to both. In most countries certain assets are exempt, e.g. houses that are the principal residence of the taxpayer. Small gains for practical reasons are not usually taxed but the exemption level varies from country to country. When the value of an asset drops so that instead of a capital gain, a loss is incurred on disposal, then the normal practice is to allow it to be offset against other gains during the period or future gains. Rates of tax can, in theory, be progressive, proportional or regressive. In practice they are proportional in many of the countries that tax capital gains. A major problem in the levying of a capital gains tax is that of valuation which we shall discuss later on (see p. 221). At a time of inflation, a capital gains tax ceases to be a tax on capital gains and becomes rather a tax on wealth, reducing it below its original value in real terms unless gains are indexed to take account of changes in the price level.

WEALTH TAX

This is a tax on the ownership of wealth as distinct from a tax on its transfer or on capital gains. Wealth taxes are levied in some countries such as Denmark, Germany, Netherlands, Norway and Sweden, in addition to other taxes on capital, but a wealth tax may be imposed as the sole tax on capital.

It can be in the form of an annual tax or of a 'once and for all' tax, such as the wealth tax imposed in Poland in 1975. In practice, 'once and for all' taxes are liable to become recurrent ones. The nature of wealth taxes also differs depending on the way that a government intends that the tax liability be met. There can be:

(a) An *additive* wealth tax. It is one that can only be paid by a sale of some assets.
(b) A *substitutive* wealth tax. It is fixed at such a level that a taxpayer has a choice of paying it out of capital or out of annual income.

VALUATION AND PROBLEMS OF INDEXATION

The more comprehensive a tax on capital the greater the problem of valuing the assets is likely to become. The following methods are used depending on circumstances:

(1) *Open market valuation.* For tax purposes the value of an asset that has been bought or sold is its market price. The value of assets held by a person can be readily ascertained if they are of the type that is regularly traded, e.g. stocks and shares. A Stock Exchange quotation gives their price daily and is a market valuation that is acceptable to the Inland Revenue. It is more difficult to determine the value of property that: (i) has been inherited or bought long ago and for which no records of purchase exist; (ii) is not offered for sale; or (iii) is rare. The opportunity therefore to establish the value of an asset by comparison with what has been paid for a similar one is limited.

(2) *Expert valuation* may be required in some cases and this can be expensive. To value a work of art, experts have to recognise and attribute it correctly and estimate the demand in an open market were it to be offered for sale. The fewer the works of a great master that there are in existence, the higher is the value that is likely to be put on each. But it does not follow that if one of them were to be offered for sale, a price corresponding to its estimated value would be paid. Taxation over the years has reduced the number of private-collectors in the UK who can afford to pay high prices. Institutions and museums that have replaced them as patrons of art have seen their budgets reduced by inflation and cuts in public expenditure. Foreign buyers may have the money, but may be deterred from bidding for works of art for which an export licence might be refused if they are national treasures.

We can illustrate the valuation problem by the following cases:

(a) *An unrecognised work of art.* An antique dealer bought a marble bust at an auction by one of the leading auction houses in London for £85 and then sold it to a customer for £240 in January 1980. Some weeks later, the buyer recalled seeing a picture of a similar bust in an art book. Experts at the Victoria and Albert Museum identified it as the bust of Pope Gregory XV by the great baroque sculptor Bernini (1598–1680). One estimate puts its value at £500,000 but when sold its price was only about 20 per cent of that.

(b) *Underestimated demand.* A work of a minor Flemish master, Van Osten, was valued by experts at an auction house in London at £5,000–£8,000. However, when it was auctioned in 1980 it fetched £27,300.

A nineteenth-century calculator, the only one of its kind not already in museum collections, was estimated by a leading London auction house in 1993 to fetch £15,000–£20,000 at a forthcoming sale. It was sold for £7.7 million to a dealer bidding on behalf of a mystery buyer who, according to speculations in the press, was either an American or German computer multimillionaire who wanted the calculator as a souvenir.

(c) *Valuation by taxpayers*. Self-assessment for tax on the basis of one's own valuation may be accepted by the taxing authorities for small holdings of property that fall below the exemption limit. But self-assessment requires knowledge of property values in general and the ability to recognise attribute and value particular objects in one's possession.

What may appear as rubbish to one person may be precious to another. For example, a collection of Victorian pot lids fetched £26,590 in 1993 at Sotheby's in London, even though they have no artistic merit and serve no useful purpose. The pots themselves had been thrown away over the years as junk. There is consequently danger of unintentional or deliberate undervaluation.

In the three cases, (a), (b) and (c), tax liability to a wealth or a capital tax would have been very different depending on the time and the method by which the tax liability was established.

EFFECT OF INFLATION ON THE VALUE OF ASSETS

A recorded increase in the value of assets may be real or illusory in a time of inflation. Thus an owner of an asset which has doubled in value will not be better off than before if the general price level has also doubled. Nevertheless, there appears to be a gain of 100 per cent which may be taxable. An inflationary increase in values will increase the burden of taxation when assets, which before were exempt from taxation, now become subject to it, and under a progressive system attract higher rates of tax on higher value (see Table 10.3). In Chapter 12, there is a discussion of the burden of taxation and indexation that relates changes in the value of assets to changes in the price level, as measured by the Retail Price Index.

COMPLIANCE OF CAPITAL TAXES WITH THE PRINCIPLES OF TAXATION

Although the purpose of capital taxes is to achieve a greater degree of equality they lack some of the characteristics of an equitable, efficient and effective system of taxation, as the following points illustrate:

Table 10.3   Taxes on the transfer of capital in the UK

Net capital Value of estate not exceeding (£)	Estate Duty 1894	1913	1938	1947	1974	Capital Transfer Tax 1980–81 in life	on death	Inheritance Tax 1987–8	1994–95
20,000	4.0	5.0	8.0	10.0	25.0	nil	nil	nil	nil
50,000	4.5	7.0	14.0	22.0	44.0	nil	nil	nil	nil
75,000						20.0	40.0		
100,000	5.5	8.0	19.0	30.0	55.0	22.5	45.0	30	nil
250,000	6.5	22.0	26.0	45.0	70.0	50.0	60.0	50	40
maximum rate[1]	8.0	15.0	50.0	75.0	75.0	75.0	75.0	60	40

Percentage of rate of duty or tax

Notes: To facilitate comparison over the period not all charge bands are shown.
[1]1969–72 top rate of duty was 85 per cent with a ceiling of 80 per cent of total assets.

(a) *Horizontal equity.* This principle requires equal tax treatment of estates of equal size. With the capital transfer tax this does not happen. (i) Estates of the same size may, over a period, pay different amounts in tax depending on the frequency of transfer. Thus an estate held by a grandfather for twenty years and transferred on his death to a grandson will be subject to an inheritance tax once. An estate of the same size bequeathed by the testator to a beneficiary who then transfers it to his son who also dies within the same twenty year period, will be subject to the capital transfer three times and incur greater tax liability. (ii) Estates which are in fact of the same value may be assessed for different amounts of tax if one consists of readily saleable assets for which there is an open market valuation, such as stocks and shares, whereas the other estate consists of rare works of art which had been undervalued or over-valued by experts. The costs involved in valuation of the two estates for tax purposes because of the nature of the assets will also differ.

(b) *Vertical equity.* A capital transfer tax or a wealth tax levied on a progressive principle is intended to impose a tax burden that increases with the size of the estate but, because of the problems of valuation, the burden that is imposed may not be that which was intended. Bigger estates with diverse holdings of assets may require professional evaluation which is more likely to reflect the true value of the property than the self-assessment of smaller estates accepted by the taxing authority. If the small estates are undervalued then they may, as a result of this, be exempt or taxed at lower rates than would have applied if the valuation had been more accurate. The principle of vertical equity will therefore be undermined.

(c) *Certainty of capital taxes.* Capital taxes do not comply with the principle that taxes should be certain, because inheritance tax, capital gains tax or wealth tax cannot be. Liability will depend on such unpredictable factors as the date of death, the change in demand for particular assets, and the rate of inflation, as well as on the type of property held and the accuracy of the valuation.

(d) *Simplicity.* Legislation to close various loopholes by means of which the ingenious or the unscrupulous could legally avoid or illegally evade capital taxes has made them complex and contrary to the principle of simple and easily understood taxation.

(e) *Cost of compliance.* The complexity of capital taxes results in high compliance costs that increase the tax burden beyond the intended level and on a basis that is not uniform, thus discriminating unfairly between taxpayers.

(f) *Ability to pay.* Ownership of property does not necessarily imply an ability to pay capital taxes. If the property is a farm, or a small family business, it may be impossible to sell part of it to pay capital transfer taxes and retain the rest as a going concern. The ability to pay a capital gains tax depends on making a capital gain. At a time of inflation there may be no real gain, but there may still be a tax liability on the inflated value of an asset sold.

(g) *Convenience to pay.* Capital taxes, such as inheritance tax or a wealth tax, are more inconvenient for the taxpayers than other forms of taxation. Assets may have to be sold to pay capital taxes at a time when there is temporarily little demand for a particular type of property or prices are depressed because of an economic recession. In such a case the taxpayer will suffer a double loss of capital, once through taxation and secondly through having to sell in a depressed market. Since all types of property will not be equally depressed, taxpayers will not be affected by the taxes equally.

(h) *Cost of collection.* Capital taxes are expensive for the taxing authority to assess and to collect since they require valuation and inspection. The right of entry to search a taxpayer's residence, such as exists in the UK, tends to cause resentment.

(i) *Flexibility.* Capital taxes are of little use in the management of the economy. They are a small source of revenue. The flow cannot be turned on and off at the will of the Exchequer. People do not necessarily die and pay a death duty at a convenient time when more tax revenue is needed.

(j) *Suitability as an instrument for distribution of income and wealth.* Capital taxes are certainly suitable for use to redistribute both but their effectiveness in achieving appreciably greater equality has been questioned in recent years.

TREND AWAY FROM TAXES ON CAPITAL

Capital taxes score few marks for compliance with the principles of a good tax system (see p. 123) and they yield relatively little revenue. Their main justification is that they are instrumental in redistribution of wealth and income, but the objective of greater equality can also be achieved by progressive income tax and government expenditure programmes.

The *Royal Commission on National Debt and Taxation* (Cmnd. 2899, 1927) gave the view that capital taxes have, 'almost every defect that a tax can possess'. In the 1970s countries increasingly turned away from taxation of capital. In the Republic of Ireland a wealth tax that had been enacted in 1975 was repealed in 1978. In France, the National Assembly approved a capital gains tax in 1976 and postponed it in 1977. In the USA the Congress cut all capital taxes. Australia and Canada abolished federal taxes on transfer of capital. In the UK the Labour Government proposed a wealth tax in 1974 but did not impose it before losing the general election in 1979. In the early 1980s there was some evidence of a return to taxation of capital when the new Socialist government came into office in France. Wealth tax was introduced in 1982 and scrapped in 1986. With the move away from Socialism in Europe in the 1990s redistribution of wealth ceased to be a major policy issue. In many countries now taxes on capital are a small source of revenue (Table 10.1).

TAXATION OF CAPITAL IN THE UK

The central government levies capital transfer tax and capital gains tax. Local authorities impose council tax which in some countries is called property tax, since it is imposed on buildings (see p. 320).

Early Taxes on Capital

There were seven different death duties on the statute book by 1694. The major taxes on transfer of capital – legacy duty and succession duty – continued until 1949 and estate duty until it was replaced by capital transfer tax in 1975. Legacy duty applied to all moveable property of a person dying domiciled in Britain, whilst succession duty applied to immovable property as well. The rate of tax depended on the relationship of the beneficiary to the deceased: a spouse and lineal issue paid 1 per cent on their share of the estate, sisters and brothers 5 per cent and all others 10 per cent. The inheritance principle of taxation was later abandoned in the UK.

Estate duty was criticised as being an optional tax in so far as it could have been avoided by transfer of property to a beneficiary seven years before the death of the testator. Inland Revenue statistics, however suggest that relatively few people made full use of this provision. It may be that the majority of people were either optimistic about their expectation of life or pessimistic about their heirs' willingness to maintain them once the property was handed over. For most taxpayers the tax could hardly be described as optional.

Capital transfer tax (CTT), which replaced estate duty, introduced an important change in the taxation of capital. CTT was levied on the transfer of capital on death but also on lifetime transfers. It was, in fact, a tax on bequests and on gifts (see Table 10.3).

Donors could make as many tax free gifts as they liked provided that they did not exceed the specified limit. Gifts to any one individual were limited but there was an allowance for additional gifts on marriage of the donor's children. Any transfers above the exemption limit were subject to a progressive rate of tax. The object of these provisions was not only to reduce, but also to disperse wealth. This was reinforced by differentiated rates of tax. At what rate the tax was paid depended on the size of the capital transfer and whether it was made on death or during the lifetime.

Over time, inflation has eroded the value of exemptions but, until the *Finance Act (1982)*, successive governments have been reluctant to introduce indexation of thresholds and instead had sought to reduce the burden of taxation on small estates by raising the exemption limit (see Table 10.4). Exemption was given in 1976 to husbands and wives. Property transferred to a spouse ceased to be liable to CTT. However this was more in the

Table 10.4   Exemptions to taxes on the transfer of capital

Year	Exemptions (£)	Year	Exemptions (£)
1946–54	2 000	1972–77	15 000
1954–62	3 000	1977–80	25 000
1962–63	4 000	1980–81	50 000
1963–69	5 000	1986–87	90 000
1969–71	10 000	1994–95	150 000
1971–72	12 500		

Notes: 1975 – Estate duty replaced by CTT.
1986 – CTT replaced by Inheritance Tax.

Table 10.5   Estates passing on death

Number of estates in Britain of £1 million and over at the time of transfer

1911–14 (average)	1920–23 (average)	1924–25	1971–72	1974–75	1978–79	1989–90
9	12	13	15	28	66	614

Source: Board of Inland Revenue, *Inland Revenue Statistics* (annually).

nature of postponement of the tax, since the property would then be taxed on his or her death or when they made a gift to somebody else.

Relief was also available on certain types of property such as woodlands, agricultural property and some business assets, to mitigate hardship arising out of the levy of CTT. The relief was given by reducing the value of the property by a certain percentage for the purpose of the tax.

The high rates of tax and small concessions have not, however, eliminated large estates altogether, though their number must have been reduced below what it otherwise would have been (see Table 10.5). It has to be remembered that, compared with £1 million in 1900, £1 million in 1980 would be worth only about £40,000 in terms of purchasing power and approximately £20,000 in 1990–91.

The Shortcomings of CTT

Limited effectiveness in redistributing wealth, high costs of compliance and collection; change of government and shift in public attitude to equality led to replacement of the tax.

Inheritance tax was introduced by the Conservative government in 1986 and applied to transfers of capital on death after March 17, 1987. The designation is a misnomer. The tax is not levied on inheritance but on estates of the donors. Furthermore, it is imposed in their lifetime on some gifts. Those made seven years before the death of the donor are tax-free (as was the case under the old death duties). For other gifts donated in between there is a tapering relief.

Charge bands were cut from 15 in 1975 to 14 in 1981 to 6 in 1987 and there was a corresponding reduction in rates of tax until, by 1994–95, only one standard rate of 40 per cent applied on estates above £150,000.

The objectives of the new version of tax on transfer of capital were to: (a) reduce the disincentive to save and invest for one's dependants and other future beneficiaries; (b) help owners of businesses by provision of business property relief; (c) provide incentives to maintain heritage property by tax concessions to owners; and (d) simplify the tax to reduce compliance and collection cost.

Capital gains tax on short-term capital was first introduced in 1962 by the Conservative Government to discourage speculation and to put an end to the practice of using capital gains as income and thereby avoiding the payment of income tax. Gains on assets that were held for less than twelve months became liable to capital gains tax. It was extended by the Labour Government in 1965 to include long term gains as well. The present tax is a comprehensive one on all capital gains above the exemption limit on assets held by individuals and businesses.

Liability was calculated by the comparison of the value of an asset on disposal with its value in 1965 or on a subsequent date of acquisition. The difference was then subject to tax. Capital gains made by companies were and are taxed at the appropriate rate of Corporation Tax, those made by individuals were subject to capital gains tax levied at a fixed percentage rate (30 per cent in 1981–82). Now (1994–95) individuals pay tax on capital gains as if these gains formed the top slice of their income. Thus the basic rate of income tax of 25 per cent, the higher rate of 40 per cent or the reduced rate of 20 per cent may apply. The exemption limit has been raised from time to time but, until the introduction of indexation of capital gains, capital gains tax was in fact an unofficial wealth tax. The *Finance Act (1982)* provided a relief for future inflation element to capital gains. Under the new provision, taxpayers were permitted to reduce their capital gains by an 'indexation allowance', applied to the base cost of the asset. After March 1982 inflation could be taken into account, using the new basis.

Wealth tax, as distinct from a tax on transfer of capital and from a tax on capital gains, was proposed by the Labour Government in 1974. An annual wealth tax was to have been levied at a level that could not have been paid out of income and would have required the sale of assets every year by people whose property exceeded the exemption limit. The figure considered was £50,000–£100,000. The tax would have been harsher than wealth taxes in some of the other countries that imposed them, since the British version would have included owner-occupied houses in the computation of wealth, which elsewhere were generally excluded. The proposals, however, did not get beyond a consultative Green Paper, 'Wealth Tax' (Cmnd. 5704, HMSO, 1974). The Chancellor of the Exchequer estimated that only 1 per cent of the adult population would be affected by the introduction of the tax. It was not intended principally as a measure to raise revenue but rather to intensify the process of redistribution of wealth.

STAMP DUTIES

The purpose of the stamp duties had been and still is to raise revenue. They date back to 1694 and now yield revenue exceeding that of capital transfer tax or capital gains tax. Stamp duties can be regarded as capital taxes since they are chargeable on certain kinds of commercial and legal documents relating to capital transactions. Such documents have to be stamped if they are to be admitted as evidence in a court of law. Affixation of a stamp denotes payment of the duty. It can be a fixed duty that is not related to the value of the property, or an *ad valorem* duty which depends on the monetary value of the assets to which the documents relate. It is the responsibility of the individuals involved in the transaction to ensure that the documents are correctly stamped. Failure to do so results in penalties. The advantages of stamp duties are that they are simple to understand and easy to collect. Their disadvantage is that, as they apply only to certain assets, stamp duties are a discriminatory tax and have no rationale to support their collection.

CAPITAL TAXATION IN THE EUROPEAN COMMUNITY

Directives of the Commission of the European Community on direct and indirect taxation, insofar as they affect people's incomes and consumption, will have an impact on savings and accumulation of capital. The establishment of the European financial area in 1990 focused attention on the problems of taxation of savings. The 1988 Directive required the Commission to present proposals to deal with them. The Commission's objectives were to 'eliminate or reduce risk of distortions, tax evasions and tax avoidance linked to the diversity of national systems of taxation of savings'.

Alignment of taxation of capital by the Member States presents difficulties because of: (1) differences in ideology – some governments are socialist others are not, and the commitment to redistribution of wealth differs; (2) national taxes on capital are not based on the same principles of taxation; (3) these taxes take various forms and in some countries several are levied; (4) exemptions and tax reliefs are not uniform; and (5) rates of taxation differ.

The underlying principle of succession and inheritance taxes in most of the Member States, but not in the UK, is that of differentiation between beneficiaries who are and those who are not related to the donor. The latter pay the top rates. Generally speaking, the more distant the relationship the

Table 10.6   Example of Succession Duty in Belgium

Beneficiary	Rate of duty
Heirs	3–30
Brothers or Sisters	20–65
Uncle, Aunts nephews, nieces	25–70
All others	30–80

Source: Commision of the European Communities (Brussels, 1993).

higher the rate of tax. This can be illustrated by examining the succession duty in Belgium (Table 10.6).

The estate principle applies in the UK where the inheritance tax is assessed on the estate and not on individual shares or legatees.

The principle of progressive capital taxation is also adhered to by most governments. In the UK it is no longer applied. The majority of Member States impose tax rates that are determined not only by who the beneficiaries are but also by the size of the inheritance. However, tax bands and rates of tax vary considerably (Table 10.2).

Wealth taxes are imposed by relatively few national governments, but those that are levied differ. The Dutch wealth tax is on net wealth and is charged at 8 per cent. In Germany it is on total assets and a distinction is drawn between natural and legal persons, paying 0.5 and 0.6 respectively. In Denmark, tax liability depends on taxable capacity at the end of the income year and is assessed at 1.25 per cent, whereas in Spain wealth tax is progressive from 0.2 per cent to 2.5 per cent.

Capital gains taxes in the European Union are imposed by Member States in addition to succession/inheritance and gift taxes, and in some cases the wealth tax. National taxes on capital gains differ in respect of exemptions, rates of tax and indexation that takes into account increase in value of assets due to inflation.

The common feature of capital taxation in the member states is its low yield, amounting on average to less than 1 per cent of the governments' total revenues (Table 10.1). This may appear surprising since some of the top rates of taxes are high and generally more than one capital tax is levied. Whether the relative unimportance of capital taxation as a source of revenue is due to: generous exemptions, ingenious avoidance schemes or widespread evasion, is subject to speculation. There is little doubt, however, that any measure to bring capital taxes in the Union into alignment is fraught with difficulties. In the long run, it may be unavoidable. With the free movement of capital and freedom for businesses to locate and for individuals to reside, work and die in the state of their choice, the continuation of disproportionate taxes on capital would be against the Union objective of greater social and economic cohesion.

SUMMARY

1. Taxes on capital are capital transfer tax, capital gains tax and wealth tax. The first two only are levied in the UK.
2. Such rates are imposed primarily for the purpose of redistributing wealth rather than to raise revenue. Capital taxes are not suitable for management of a national economy.
3. A capital transfer tax can be imposed on either the estate or on the inheritance principle. It is payable on the transfer of capital during a lifetime or on death. British inheritance tax is assessed on estates and is levied at a standard rate.
4. A capital gains tax is levied on capital gains that are made on the disposal of assets. It can be a tax on short-term gains or on all capital gains irrespective of how long an asset had been held. Gains above an exemption limit are usually subject to a flat percentage rate of tax.
5. A wealth tax can be a 'once and for all' or an annual tax. It is levied on either an additive or a substitutive basis. Several countries have imposed a wealth tax in addition to the other taxes on capital.
6. All capital taxes require a valuation of assets. The choice of method – open market valuation, expert valuation or self-assessment – depends on the type of asset and the size of the estate.
7. Inflation increases the burden of all capital taxes unless exemption levels and tax bands are index-linked.
8. Capital taxes comply with few requirements of a 'good tax system'.
9. Stamp duties can be regarded as a tax on capital since they are payable on capital transactions.
10. A recent trend in leading industrial countries has been away from taxation of capital but a variety of taxes continues to be levied. In the European Community, they are imposed on different principles and at different rates thus making the alignment of Member States' taxes difficult.

SUGGESTED FURTHER READING

C.V. Brown and P.M. Jackson, *Public Sector Economics* (Oxford: Basil Blackwell, 1992).

Budget Speeches (UK), *Hansard* (London) annually.

Commission of the European Communities, *Taxes* (Brussels: European Commission, 1993).

H.J. Easson, *Taxation in the European Community* (London: Athlone Press 1993).

HM Treasury (UK), *Financial Statements* (annually).

G.C. Hockley, *Fiscal Policy* (London: Routledge, 1992).

Inland Revenue, *Inland Revenue Statistics* (London: HMSO, 1993).

S. James and C. Nobes, *The Economics of Taxation* (London: Prentice-Hall, 1992).

J.A. Kay and M.A. King, *The British Tax System* (Oxford: Oxford University Press, 1992).

R.A. Musgrave and P.B. Musgrave, *Public Finance in Theory and Practice* (New York: McGraw-Hill, 1989).

C.T. Sandford, *The Economics of Public Finance* (Oxford: Pergamon Press, 1992).

M. Wilkinson, *Taxation* (London: Macmillan, 1992).

G. Winkler (ed.), *Tax Harmonisation in Europe* (London: Macmillan, 1992).

EXERCISES

1. Define the estate principle and the inheritance principle. Which do you regard as preferable for a capital transfer tax? Give your reasons.
2. Consider how the difficulties in valuation of assets affect the equity of a tax on capital.
3. Discuss the arguments for and against a lower rate of tax on transfer of capital to the donors' descendants.
4. Explain how inflation transforms a capital gains tax into a tax on wealth.
5. To what extent do capital taxes comply with the principles of a 'good tax system'?
6. Explain the meaning of indexation and its relevance to taxes on capital.
7. Distinguish between an additive wealth tax and a substitutive wealth tax and consider the significance of the distinctions.
8. What justification is there for taxing capital transfers in life-time at a lower rate than transfers on death?
9. Consider reasons for and consequences of taxation of capital on a progressive basis.
10. What do you consider to be the major problems in harmonisation of taxes on capital in the European Community?

11 Reform of the Tax System, Expenditure Tax and the Meade Report; The European Dimension

NEED FOR REFORM

The British tax system has become complicated, cumbersome and costly. Some of the factors that have contributed to this are: (i) *Ad hoc* modifications have undermined any coherent philosophy that the tax system may have had. (ii) Attempts to close tax loopholes and to make taxes more equitable by means of exemptions and allowances have created inconsistencies and anomalies. (iii) Inflation has intensified these anomalies. (iv) Interaction of the various taxes of income, consumption and capital has resulted in distortions of the labour and capital markets.

The need to reassess and overhaul the system prompted the Institute of Fiscal Studies to set up a committee under the chairmanship of Professor J.E. Meade (the Nobel Prize winner) to undertake a review of the tax structure of the UK. The *Meade Report on The Structure and Reform of Direct Taxation* was published in 1978. It was the first major study since that of the Royal Commission on the Taxation of Profits and Income in 1955. The Meade Committee was concerned not only with the reform of the existing system. It also considered an alternative one, based on an expenditure tax.

IDEA OF AN EXPENDITURE TAX

The idea of an expenditure tax is not new. Lord Kaldor suggested it to the Royal Commission but it was not included in its terms of reference. He published his views on the subject in a book, *An Expenditure Tax* (1955), and advised a number of developing countries on the adaptation of the idea. Sri Lanka and India introduced an expenditure tax but it was subsequently withdrawn in India in 1966. The Meade Report revived interest in expenditure tax and in its possible application to the UK. If introduced, an expenditure tax would replace the present system of taxation. There would be no need for taxes on income and capital.

Under a system of expenditure tax, personal taxation is based on consumption. The underlying assumption is that consumption is the appropriation of resources to satisfy personal wants. Saving out of income results in a release of resources into a productive pool, whereas spending absorbs them. People who consume more of the nation's resources are therefore taxed more for the privilege than those who abstain. It would, however, be impractical and undesirable to tax all consumption and some level of exemption would be necessary.

OUTLINE OF A UNIVERSAL EXPENDITURE TAX

Various forms of an expenditure tax can be devised – a universal expenditure tax is one possible version. For the purpose of such a tax goods are classified into registered and unregistered goods and services. Expenditure on the latter category is disregarded so far as tax liability is concerned. Liability is determined on the basis of the purchase and disposal of registered goods and services only. Savings and investment are exempt from tax.

To calculate the tax liability, a person needs to establish their: (i) incomings – income to which are added capital receipts such as proceeds from sale of assets, gifts and bequests; (ii) outgoings – expenditure on registered and unregistered goods and services to which are added any gifts and bequests made; (iii) savings, and (iv) investments.

Incomes – (savings + investment) – expenditure on unregistered goods = Tax base

Thus the tax base is the expenditure on registered goods and services. Table 11.1 shows the tax liability of people with different levels of consumption and savings.

A two-tier expenditure tax is a variation on a universal expenditure tax. Instead of the same percentage rate being imposed, expenditure up to a certain level can be taxed at a basic rate, and the rest at a higher rate. An expenditure tax can be made progressive by increasing the rate of tax, as expenditure rises.

Self-assessment

The Meade Committee considered the introduction of self-assessment as a necessary first step to a changeover to the expenditure tax system since, for administrative reasons, it would be impractical to operate it otherwise.

Table 11.1   An example of expenditure tax

	Person X (£)	Person Y (£)	Person Z (£)
Income	5,000	5,000	5,000
Bequest received		1,000	
Gift received	500		
Capital receipts, proceeds from Sale of an asset, dissaving			1,600
Total incomings	5,500	6,000	6,600
Savings	−500		
Investment		−1,000	
Expenditure on unregistered goods and services	−2,000	−2,400	−3,000
Total exempt outgoings	−2,500	−3,400	−3,000
Expenditure on registered goods and services	2,800	2,600	3,600
Gift made	200		
Total taxable outgoings	3,000	2,600	3,600
Tax when the rate of tax is 50 per cent	1,500	1,300	1,800

Note:
In calculation of the tax liability of X, Y and Z it was necessary to make (i) an expenditure tax adjustment, to take into account capital transfer and non-consumption outgoings; (ii) an income adjustment to allow for dissaving that increases consumption and for saving that reduces it.

PROBLEMS OF INTRODUCING THE NEW SYSTEM

Replacement of the existing system of taxation by one based on expenditure tax would give rise to short-term problems that would resolve themselves when the period of transition ended and to long-term problems that would continue indefinitely.

(a) *Transitional problems* are: (i) *Self-assessment*. This requirement, with which taxpayers are unfamiliar, would initially create difficulties in complying with the tax. (ii) *Unfairness.* Some inequities during the change over to the new tax base could not be avoided, as in the case of people who had saved out of taxed income in the past, to provide for expenditure in the future, e.g. by means of contributory pensions schemes. (iii) *Market distortion.* Capital markets would be disturbed as the relative attractiveness of different assets would be affected by their designation as registered or unregistered assets.

(b) *Long-term problems* would arise out of the tax relations with other countries that did not change over to the expenditure tax and would relate to: (i) *British citizens resident abroad.* It would be necessary to retain income tax to tax UK citizens living abroad on incomes that were not liable to British expenditure tax. (ii) *Immigration.* Immigrants would be deterred from coming to the UK as spending out of wealth accumulated abroad would render them liable to the British expenditure tax. This would have the effect of double taxation, since their incomes out of which they had saved would have been taxed in the home country. However, at a time when the government is following a policy to restrict immigration, the number of people affected would be limited. (iii) *Emigration.* Those who had accumulated savings in the UK, out of untaxed income, would have an incentive to emigrate and to spend their wealth abroad. There are, however, many factors that influence a person's decision to leave their own country and tax is only one of them. Besides, entry to a foreign country is not free to all who might wish to settle there. (iv) *Double tax relief.* Arrangements to avoid taxation of individuals twice over would become more complex.

ADVANTAGES OF AN EXPENDITURE TAX

The supporters of expenditure tax claim that the system would have the following desirable characteristics:

(a) *Simplicity.* The use of one tax base instead of a number, as is the present practice, would simplify the tax system.
(b) *Superfluity of other taxes.* Introduction of the expenditure tax would make it possible to abolish income tax, corporation tax, VAT, capital transfer tax and capital gains tax. There would be no need for them because as soon as income or revenue was spent or capital was transferred, they would be subject to the expenditure tax.

(c) *Removal of disincentive to work.* Under expenditure tax earnings would not be taxed, therefore it would not create a disincentive to work and enterprise.

(d) *Incentive to save and invest.* Since both savings and investment would be allowed as a deduction in the calculation of tax liability, the expenditure tax would provide, through exemption, an incentive to save and to invest.

(e) *Redistribution.* Advocates of the expenditure tax argue that it would be more effective in achieving an egalitarian society than other taxes. This argument is based on the assumption that an egalitarian society is one where people have a similar standard of living and that it depends on expenditure. Large incomes and large holdings of wealth do not give rise to a high standard of living unless they are spent. An expenditure tax, by imposing a heavier burden on big spenders, would equalise the standard of living.

There will be much support among the advocates of an expenditure tax for the view that Sir William Petty expressed some three hundred years ago: 'A man is actually and truly rich according to what he eateth, drinketh, weareth, or enjoyeth; others are but potentially or imaginatively rich, who, though they may have power over much, make little use of it.'

MODIFICATION OF TAXATION

Support for any complete overhaul of the system of taxation, whether at the international or national level, has been somewhat restrained. Government initiatives have been to modify particular taxes rather than to reform the entire system.

In the UK, no government action followed the publication of the Meade Report and its recommendations. The British revenue structure continues to be based on central government taxation, local government tax and National Insurance Contributions. Some taxes have been modified and a new one added but the changes do not amount to a reform of the tax system.

The 'Reform of Personal Taxation' Green Paper (1968) set out government views on taxation of married couples and in 1990 they were given independence in matters of taxation. Whether the Treasury was converted by feminist pressure groups or acted out of prudence, income tax and capital gains tax were amended to allow husband and wife to be assessed and held liable separately.

The 'Reform of Taxation of Profits' Green Paper (1982) considered corporation tax but no major changes followed.

Capital taxation also remained basically unaltered. Capital Transfer Tax was renamed the Inheritance Tax, but this was hardly more than a change in nomenclature.

Indirect taxation, however, has been modified to a greater extent than direct taxation. A new tax on the *consumption of energy* was introduced in the 1993 autumn budget, reflecting the government's response to the environmental lobby and the need for additional revenue. The two objectives coincided neatly making it more difficult for taxpayers to oppose the tax on energy which was presented as a measure to protect the environment. Existing taxes on goods and services were amended to take into account the requirements of taxation policies in the European Community. Central government taxes, apart from changes in the tax thresholds, allowances and rates of tax, remained very much as before.

Local government taxation was an area that was targeted for reform, attracted most attention and protest and led to a taxpayers' revolt. Rates were replaced with the Community Charge (the 'Poll Tax') which was in turn superseded by the Council Tax which reverted to the principle of property as the tax base. Thus the initiated reform ended up as a modification of local government taxation (see Chapter 15).

National Insurance Contributions continue to perpetuate the myth of being a payment for insurance cover for such contingencies as unemployment or sickness. Since the benefits paid out far exceed contributions made, and are financed to a large extent by general taxation, calls for reform of the system have grown. However, the contributions have not been abolished, incorporated into income tax or replaced by a social security tax on the lines of a model in other countries in Europe.

THE EUROPEAN DIMENSION

Reform of a whole tax system is likely to be a painful and prolonged process. This goes some way to account for national government's reluctance to initiate it. Reforms may, however, be thrust by the Commission upon Member States as the European Community presses ahead with policies for the harmonisation of taxes that would, eventually, create a unified system of taxation. Progress towards this objective will depend on the convergence of national economies, governments' ability to achieve consensus on political issues and their determination to deal with the cherished principle of national sovereignty in matters of taxation.

The Commission's move towards harmonisation of company taxation was halted when the proposed directive was withdrawn in 1975. Instead, emphasis was placed on co-ordination. Greater success was achieved in harmonising indirect taxation (see p. 133 and Chapter 16).

The difficulty is that, under the Single European Act, changes in taxes require a unanimous vote of the Member States. 'This goes some way towards explaining why the decision making process as it affects tax matters remains slow and cumbersome' (quote from EC document on taxation, 1992). Alignment of taxes is likely to become even more complicated as the European Community expands into a European Union. In March 1994, Sweden, Finland and Austria agreed terms for entry planned for 1995 but people in Norway, voting in a referendum, decided against membership. By the turn of the century Poland, Hungary and the Czech Republic – all three of whom already have an associated EC status, are likely to join the Union. These countries have only recently ceased to be centrally-planned economies, under which system there was little need for taxation since the State was the producer, employer, paymaster and supplier of goods and services. In such circumstances, it would, as it were, have been paying taxes to itself on profits and a price rise could have been considered to be an increase in indirect taxation.

If the European Union is to achieve a unified system of taxation, then a fundamental reform of direct, indirect and capital taxation in the Member States will be required.

SUMMARY

1. Reform of the British tax system has been advocated because it has become complicated and distorted by *ad hoc* measures.
2. The expenditure tax system has been proposed to replace taxes on income, profits and capital.
3. Under the new system the basis of personal taxation would increasingly be consumption.
4. An underlying assumption of an expenditure tax is that the standard of living depends on consumption and that this reflects inequality in the welfare of individuals.
5. Those who consume more of the nation's resources would therefore be more heavily taxed.
6. For the purpose of the tax goods are divided into registered and unregistered categories; only the former are taxed.

7. Expenditure tax does not have a disincentive effect on work and enterprise since income is not taxed.
8. Saving and investment are encouraged since both are exempt.
9. Advantages claimed for the expenditure tax are: its simplicity; the absence of adverse economic effects – characteristic of other forms of taxation; and its greater effectiveness in the redistribution of income and wealth.

   Few countries have tried an expenditure tax and some of those that did try, subsequently abandoned it. A tax system based on expenditure appears difficult to operate in practice and creates problems unless other countries also change to such a tax.
10. Economic and political developments in the European Community have been followed by measures to reform tax systems in the Member States. Progress at international and national level has been slow.

SUGGESTED FURTHER READING

S. James and C. Nobes, *The Economics of Taxation* (London: Prentice-Hall, 1992).
J.A. Kay and M.A. King, *The British Tax System* (Oxford: Oxford University Press, 1990).
J.E. Meade, *The Structure and Reform of Direct Taxation (Report)* (London: George Allen & Unwin for The Institute for Fiscal Studies, 1978).
J.A. Pechman (ed.), *What Should be Taxed, Income or Expenditure?* (Washington, DC: Brookings Institute, 1980).

EXERCISES

1. Consider the validity of the arguments put forward for the need to reform the British tax system.
2. Do you consider an expenditure tax to be preferable to the present systems of taxation? Give reasons for your preference.
3. Explain the difference between registered and unregistered goods and suggest a basis for classification under the two headings.
4. What would be the advantage of a two-tier expenditure tax?
5. Suggest reasons why the proposals of the Meade Report have not been implemented by either political party when in office.
6. Reform of a tax system requires more than modification of existing taxes. Comment on this statement.
7. Why greater convergence of national economies in Europe has to lead in the long run to harmonisation of taxation of the Member States?
8. Suggest reasons why in the European Community priority was given and greater emphasis put on co-ordination of indirect taxation than on direct taxation.
9. Explain how the establishment of an internal free market in the European Community has necessitated tax reforms.
10. Reform of a tax system in one country cannot be undertaken in isolation from developments abroad. Give your reasons for agreeing or disagreeing with this statement.

12 Taxable Capacity, Incidence of Taxation and the Tax Burden

TAXABLE CAPACITY DEFINED

Taxable capacity is the ability of individuals and businesses to pay taxes. It is not the ability of taxing authorities to raise revenue. The taxable capacity of a country can, therefore, be defined as *the proportion of the national income that is above the 'subsistence' level*, which is the minimum required to sustain its population and to maintain the productive capacity of an economy intact. If a state were to provide for all the needs of its citizens then, in theory, it could tax away their entire incomes and taxable capacity would be 100 per cent. In market economies, including-mixed economies, the majority of people provide for most of their needs out of incomes they receive; a government can therefore take away in taxation only a certain percentage of their resources.

MEASUREMENT OF TAXABLE CAPACITY

The first problem in assessing taxable capacity is to determine the subsistence level. There is no uniform standard that is applicable to all countries, or one that is acceptable in the same country at different times. Even the amount of food that people need to survive varies, depending on the area in which they live, the work they do, their sex and age. Thus a male adult worker doing heavy manual work in a cold climate requires high calorific consumption; a female office worker in a tropical country does not. But food is not all that people need and their other requirements are even more difficult to compare.

To measure taxable capacity it is also necessary to calculate the national income of a country and to deduct from it the amount required to provide an *acceptable* standard of living for its people. The difference is the taxable capacity – that is the amount that a government can appropriate. Since there is little agreement on what is an acceptable standard of living, there is inevitably disagreement over what is the taxable capacity of a country. It cannot be measured accurately and it is determined arbitrarily,

243

as a certain percentage of national income that can be absorbed in taxation without producing harmful effects on the economy.

A French economist, Leroy-Beaulieu, writing at the beginning of the nineteenth century, described the level of taxation as: (i) *moderate* when revenue from all taxes was 5–6 per cent of national income; (ii) *heavy* when it was 10–12 per cent; (iii) *exorbitant* above that range. In his opinion, taxation at the top level would have very serious consequences for the economic growth of the country and the liberty of its citizens.

These views on the effects of high level of taxation were shared by a British economist, Colin Clark, who estimated a limit to a taxable capacity at 25 per cent of the national income ('Public finance and the value of money', *Economic Journal*, December 1945). He believed that taxation beyond this level would set in motion economic, political and psychological forces that would, within a lag of two to three years, result in a general increase in costs and prices and undermine the fabric of the society. Lord Keynes accepted the figure of 25 per cent as the 'maximum tolerable proportion of taxation', and one that was 'exceedingly near the truth'. Thus, the 25 per cent taxable capacity figure has had the endorsement of one of the world's greatest economists.

The UK and some other major countries exceeded this limit some seventy years ago (see Table 12.1). It can, therefore, be argued that a figure for taxable capacity cannot apply indefinitely and needs to be revised as conditions change. But it may be true that it is as valid today as it was formerly, and that the present economic difficulties are the price that countries are paying for exceeding the taxable capacity and for imposing too great a tax burden.

TAX BURDEN OF A COUNTRY

The tax burden is the amount that is *actually* paid in taxation, whereas taxable capacity indicates what can be paid. The tax burden may be below,

Table 12.1   Tax level: international comparison

Tax revenue as a percentage of national income

	France	*Germany*	*UK*	*United States*
1900–1	15	8	10	8
1924–25	20	29	25	11

Source: V. Tanzi, J.B. Bracewell-Milnes and D.R. Myddelton, *Taxation* (London: Institute of Economic Affairs, 1970).

equal to, or above the taxable capacity. There are two ways of looking at the tax burden: from the point of view of individual taxpayers or of the economy as a whole. We can express the total tax revenue plus social security contributions as a percentage of national income or gross national product of a country and this gives us a measure of its tax burden. Alternatively, we can show the tax burden on the basis of a tax liability of individuals and businesses.

TAXPAYERS' BURDEN

The factors that determine the burden for taxpayers are: (i) the total amount raised in taxation; (ii) the nature of the tax system; (iii) the incidence of taxation – a tax system consists of a variety of taxes, some of which can be shifted from one taxpayer to another; (iv) tax avoidance and evasion; and (v) taxing authorities' efficiency in collecting revenue.

INCIDENCE OF TAXATION

Formal and Effective Incidence

Incidence is indicative of where the tax burden falls. In the discussion of incidence we have to distinguish between *formal* and *effective* incidence or, using an alternative set of labels, between *legal* and *economic* incidence.

Formal or legal incidence can be regarded as the starting point in the process of tax shifting. It shows on whom a particular tax is imposed in the first instance. If a tax on consumption is imposed on manufacturers or distributors, the formal or legal incidence is on them, though they may eventually be able to shift the tax on to consumers.

Effective or economic incidence is the final resting place of a tax and shows on whom the burden falls and who in the end pays the tax.

Incidence of Direct Taxes

Income tax is assessed on the recipient of an income, on whom the formal incidence falls. Liability to such a tax cannot be shifted to anybody else, therefore formal incidence will be the same as effective incidence. The person who receives income pays the tax and bears the burden, which depends on the size of the income, exemptions, allowances and the rate of tax.

Corporation Tax is assessed on companies and the formal incidence is therefore on them. The effective incidence of a tax on profits has been the subject of some controversy among economists. Some have argued that the burden can be shifted on to consumers by increasing prices to take account of the tax. Others have argued that the tax does not enter into the price. The *Royal Commission on the National Debt and Taxation* (Cmnd. 2800. 1927) accepted the latter argument put before them and, to a large extent,this view still prevails.

In economic theory, it is assumed that a firm will seek to maximise profits and will sell its output at the most profitable price. It would not, therefore, be to its advantage to change the price to allow for the tax. In practice, since a tax on profits is a direct tax on the income of a company, and is not a deductible expense, if a company were to attempt to compensate for the tax by raising the price of its output and to increase its income, this would increase its tax liability. As companies cannot avoid paying the tax its effective incidence, like the formal incidence, will be on them.

National Insurance Contributions, which in effect are a form of a social security tax, are assessed on both individuals as employees and on the self-employed who had not contracted out. For employees, the contributions are a direct tax that they cannot shift. Thus, formal and effective incidence is the same. For employers, the contributions are a tax on employment. Therefore, they can reduce their liability by cutting down their labour force or employing part-time workers who, in terms of the contributions, are cheaper. In the private sector, employers and self-employed may, in theory, shift the cost of the contributions to consumers in higher prices or absorb the cost, thereby reducing profits. What they will do in practice will depend to a large extent on the price elasticity of demand for their goods and services.

Incidence of Taxes on Capital

The incidence of taxes on capital will depend on the type of the capital tax levied. A capital gains tax is assessed on the person who makes the capital gain. Its size is determined by the market price. A mark-up to compensate for the tax cannot therefore be added to it. The payment of the tax is the responsibility of the person who has been assessed. Since the tax cannot be shifted, formal and effective incidence are the same.

The incidence of an inheritance tax is uncertain. The testator might have cut down on expenditure in order to save more to compensate for the tax on capital transfer, or might have ignored a tax that does not become payable until death. The burden of the tax can, therefore, be said to fall either on the predecessor in his or her lifetime, or on successors.

Incidence of Taxes on Consumption

This incidence will also depend on the type of tax in question. Value Added Tax is intended to fall on final consumers. The burden of some of the other taxes on consumption may be: (i) borne entirely by a supplier; (ii) shared between the supplier and the buyer; or (iii) shifted wholly to the buyer. How incidence falls will depend on the price elasticity of demand and the price elasticity of supply, that is the response of demand and supply to a change in price. In Figure 12.1 (a), (b), (c) *DD* is the demand curve, which shows how many goods will be demanded at each price and

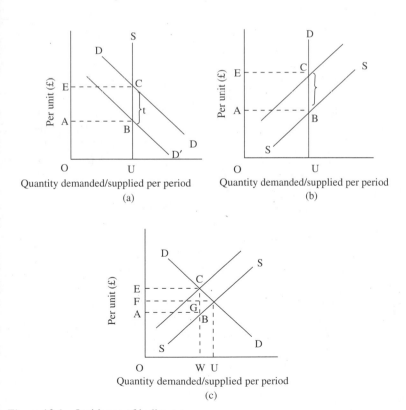

Figure 12.1   Incidence of indirect taxes

SS is the supply curve showing how much will be supplied at each price. The point at which *DD* and *SS* intersect is the equilibrium point which shows the price at which a good is bought and sold. (The curves can be straight lines.)

In Figure 12.1 (a) the supply is perfectly inelastic – the supplier will supply the same quantity of goods whatever the price and will absorb the tax. This can be thought of as a lowering of the demand curve from *DD* to *D'D'*. The price to consumers before tax was *OE* and the quantity sold *OU*.

After tax both remain unchanged. The price that the supplier receives drops from *OE* to *OA* and his receipts fall by the amount indicated by the area *ABCE*. This represents the government's tax revenue. The entire tax burden falls on the supplier.

In Figure 12.1 (b) the demand is perfectly inelastic – the good may be a necessity and consumers have to buy it whatever the change in price. The supplier can shift the whole of the tax on to them. This can be thought of as raising the supply curve from *SS* to *S'S'*. The price to the consumer goes up from *OA* to *OE*. Suppliers' receipts and quantity sold remain unchanged. Tax revenue is *ABCE* and the entire burden of the tax is on the consumers.

In Figure 12.1 (c) both demand and supply are elastic and respond to a change in price. The price before tax is *OF* and the quantity sold *OU*. A tax of *BC* is imposed and *SS* shifts to *S'S'*, but neither the price to the consumer is increased nor supplier's receipts are decreased by the full amount. The tax is split between them. The price goes up from *OF* to *OE* and the supplier's receipts go down from *OF* to *OA*. The total tax revenue is *ABCE* of which the consumer contributes *FGCE* and supplier *ABGF*. In Figure 12.1 (c) the tax burden is shared equally.

The case of a perfectly elastic demand and perfectly elastic supply have not been illustrated since neither is likely to be found in the real world. Perfectly inelastic demand, however, is a more realistic concept. The price of salt, for example, may double or halve but people will not react to the change in price buying more or less as a result. The level of consumption is not likely to change. Perfectly inelastic supply exists in the case of land. Its supply cannot be increased – reclamation schemes add so little that they do not matter. All that can be done is to change the use of land from, say, agriculture to a building site for local authority houses.

Equilibrium analysis (Figure 12.1 (c)), can be used also to show the effect of a subsidy. *DD* remains as before but *S'S'* is now the original supply curve and *C* is the original equilibrium point. A subsidy can be shown by lowering of the curve to *SS*. The effect is a drop in price from

OE to *OF*, the amount bought increases from *OW* to *OU* by an amount equal to *WU*.

The true tax burden for the taxpayers will depend on how much worse off they are as a result of paying taxes and how much better off they are as a result of benefits financed out of public expenditure such as subsidies. Tax payment reduces the economic welfare of all the taxpayers and the state benefits increase the welfare of some more than of others.

INCIDENCE OF BENEFITS

Figure 12.2 shows the incidence of taxes and benefits for different households. The data has been published annually since 1976 by the government to indicate the effect of taxation and of public expenditure (social services, cash benefits and consumer subsidies) on the distribution of incomes between the different types of households. This information also indicates the true burden of taxation and on whom it falls by taking into account the incidence of benefits.

Interpretation of data on the incidence of taxation and benefits needs, however, to be treated with caution. The incidence of some indirect taxes is difficult to estimate since the burden can be shifted from suppliers to consumers. The incidence of benefits that are not directly paid to households is even more difficult to calculate. Statisticians have to ascribe to households the value of such benefits as housing and food subsidies and have to find a way of allocating to individuals benefits from collectively consumed services, such as defence or police protection. The tax burden for an individual taxpayer or household cannot, therefore, be calculated with any degree of accuracy. At best the figure remains a rough estimate.

INTERNATIONAL COMPARISON OF THE TAX BURDEN

A tax burden of a country is easier to compare over a period of time than internationally. The latter exercise can only be done for countries that operate on the basis of the same economic system. Conclusions will only be meaningful if countries use similar definitions of national income and tax revenue and have data that is of comparable accuracy. The problem of international comparisons is illustrated by the following example. The British Treasury observed, 'Many people firmly believe that Britain is

Stages of redistribution

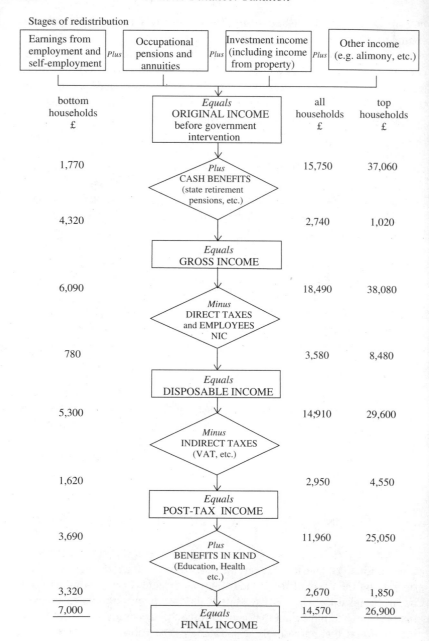

Figure 12.2   Incidence of taxes and benefits
Note: Data for 1992.
Source: *Economic Trends*, 48 (London: HMSO, 1994).

more heavily taxed than any other country and that it is more heavily taxed than it used to be. Neither of these beliefs is altogether true as it stands' (*Treasury Economic Progress Report*, September 1977). A survey carried out at that time by a consumer magazine, *Money Which*, showed that 66 per cent of the people interviewed thought that the UK was highly taxed compared with other countries, whereas the figures that the Treasury had published and those of the OECD suggested that the UK had a relatively moderate tax burden. The question therefore arises as to why British people persisted in believing the contrary. The answer is that it all depends on how the tax burden is measured. The Treasury and OECD did so by reference to the national economy, expressing the total tax revenue as a percentage of the gross national product or the gross domestic product of each country (see Table 12.2). Indication of the tax burden by reference to the taxpayers gives different results (see Table 12.3).

Direct taxes

For international comparison of individuals as taxpayers a standard tax unit, such as, for example, a married man with two children, needs to be used to take into account the various tax allowances. The table shows that during the period to which the Treasury referred: (i) The income tax threshold in the UK was lower than in France, Germany and the Netherlands. It was also lower than in the USA. This meant that British people were liable to income tax who in other countries would have been

Table 12.2   Burden of taxation: international comparison

	Taxes and social security contributions as a percentage of gross national product at factor cost			
	1971	*1978*	*1981*	*1991*
Sweden	51	60	51	50
Norway	52	56	50	48
Netherlands	47	52	45	48
Germany	40	45	41	41
France	40	44	42	44
UK	41	39	38	35
Italy	31	36	32	40
USA	32	33	30	29
Japan	22	25	27	31

Source: K.J. Newman, 'International comparison of taxes and social security contributions, 1971–78', *Economic Trends* (London: HMSO, 1980). Figures for 1981 and 1991 are abstracted from *Economic Trends* (London: HMSO, 1994).

Table 12.3   Income tax on the earned income of a married man: international comparison of rates

Country	Threshold (£)[1][2]	1975 Initial rate %	1975 Maximum rate %	1992 Initial rate %	1992 Maximum rate %
Belgium	1 290	14 (14.8)[3]	72 (75.6)[3]	25	55
France	3 120	5	53.5	0	56.8
Germany	1 800	22	56	19	53
Italy	1 320	10	72	10	50
Netherlands	2 300	20	72	38.5	60
UK	1 383	35	83 (98)[4]	25	40
Sweden	1 150	7 (30)[3]	56 (79)[3]	...	...

Notes:
[1]   Sterling equivalent on 8 March 1976.
[2]   The thresholds take account of deductions for a married man with two children, both under 11 years.
[3]   Figures in brackets show rates inclusive of local income tax or of general additional charges.
[4]   Rate of income tax if recipient has some investment income. Local authority rates are not taken into account.

Source: *Hansard* (25 March 1976) and Commission of the European Communities, *Taxes* (Brussels, 1994).

exempt. (ii) The UK had the highest initial rate of tax on lower incomes and (iii) it also had the highest maximum rate. The progression to this higher tax range was also accelerated by inflation (see 'fiscal drag' p. 161).

In addition to inflation other factors contributing to a higher overall tax burden on individuals are taxes on consumption and capital.

Indirect Taxes

Taxes on goods and services are, as we have seen, to some extent 'optional' but as the UK relied more heavily than some of the other countries on direct taxation British people had less scope to reduce their tax burden by cutting down on consumption (see Table 9.2 and 16.1). Although the VAT rate was relatively lower than some of the rates in the European Community, this advantage was eroded by higher inflationary pressure.

Inflation

As prices rise the tax burden increases. To illustrate this point let us assume a 10 per cent VAT rate. A consumer who bought a good priced £100 would have paid £10 in tax. If the price subsequently doubles as a result of inflation, tax liability increases to £20 without a change in the rate of tax. Inflation also affects the market price of capital assets and, consequently, liability to death duties and capital gain taxes. Unless indexation is allowed, illusory appreciation in the value of property is taxed. Inflation rates for Member States of the European Community, the USA and Japan differ considerably.

Capital Taxes

The burden of capital taxes on British taxpayers was also heavy in the 1970s, reaching the top rate of 75 per cent which was higher at that time than in the other countries in Europe. Also, unlike the common European practice where descendants and close relatives pay lower rates depending on the closeness of the relationship and only unrelated beneficiaries are liable for tax at the top rate, in the UK no such relief was applied, except in the case of property transfer to a spouse when the tax payment is postponed. Furthermore, the whole estate is assessed for tax whereas in the other countries in the European Community beneficiaries pay tax only on the share of the estate that they receive. The overall tax burden is therefore lower when the rates are progressive and the tax liability depends on the size of the estate received and not on the amount left by the deceased.

Social Security Benefits

For people the burden of taxation is mitigated by state benefits that they receive but, as in the UK social expenditure as a percentage of gross domestic product is below the average for the European Community, the relief to the British taxpayers is likely to be less (see Table 16.3).

Business

The burden of taxation on companies is even more difficult to compare internationally than the burden on individuals, as companies in different countries are entitled to a variety of allowances, reliefs and grants which may depend on the size or the location of the business. Nevertheless, the rate of tax on profits is indicative of the tax burden and in the UK companies were subject to a high rate of tax (see Table 8.4).

Thus, it can be demonstrated that the tax burden on British taxpayers was higher than on their counterparts abroad, and their standard of living was reduced still further by the relatively low level of incomes in the UK, as compared with those of other major developed countries. In the 1980s and 1990s, rates of income tax, corporation tax and inheritance tax were cut in the UK and the British tax burden became relatively light compared with that of other developed countries.

There is a case, therefore, for arguing that to express the total tax revenue as a percentage of the national income of a country is a misleading indicator of the tax burden and of its effect on the welfare of the people.

A *hypothetical example* (see Table 12.4) will serve to illustrate the point that people in a country which appears to be more lightly taxed, may have a heavier tax burden. Suppose there are two countries, Lilliput and Sundra. Both are small islands and on each there are only 100 people who receive incomes. Their total incomes are therefore the national income of the country. These islands have only income tax and consumption and capital transfers are untaxed. The following facts emerge from Table 12.4: (i) the island of Lilliput has a lower tax burden if it is calculated by expressing total tax revenue as a percentage of the national income; (ii) Lilliput is relatively poorer as there are fewer people with bigger incomes; (iii) People in Lilliput start paying tax on an income of £1,000 but in the island of Sundra such an income would be tax exempt. At each level of income in Lilliput they pay tax at a higher rate. The total tax revenue is, however, smaller so they can expect to receive less in State benefits than the inhabitants of Sundra. People in Lilliput will, therefore, be worse off in every way, in so far as their economic welfare is concerned, even though the tax burden of the country ostensibly appears to be smaller.

It is individual people who pay taxes, feel their burden and enjoy the benefits financed out of taxation. It is therefore perhaps more meaningful to measure the tax burden in relation to individuals than to the national economy.

A tax burden which is perceived by people to be excessive, even though it is not easily defined and quantified, will in democratic countries spur

Table 12.4   Hypothetical example of the tax burden for Lilliput and Sundra

(a) Island of Lilliput

Income level (£) (£)	Number of income recipients	Total Income	Rate of tax (%)	Tax paid
1,000	5	5,000	exempt	0
1,500	20	30,000	33	10,000
2,000	50	100,000	40	40,000
5,000	20	100,000	55	55,000
10,000	5	50,000	75	37,500
	100	285,000		142,500

Note:
Total tax revenue as a percentage of national income equals 50 per cent.

(b) Island of Sundra

1,500	5	3,000	exempt	0
2,000	8	16,000	30	4,800
5,000	60	300,000	50	150,000
10,000	30	300,000	60	180,000
	100	619,000		334,800

Note:
Total tax revenue as a percentage of national income equals 54 per cent.

taxpayers to put pressure on governments through the ballot box to bring the level of taxation down. This has happened in the 1980s and early 1990s. In Europe, rates of personal, business and capital taxes have been cut. In the UK, the transition from some of the highest rates to relatively low taxation was particularly striking (see p. 335).

THE HIDDEN COST OF TAXATION: COMPLIANCE AND AVOIDANCE COSTS

No analysis of the tax burden should ignore a major contributory factor that is not usually allowed for in official estimates and in international comparisons – the hidden cost of taxation. For taxpayers the hidden cost of taxation is the cost of compliance with the taxes that a government imposes and the cost of avoiding those taxes.

Compliance costs to the taxpayers are: (i) the fees to advisers, accountants and others in connection with making tax returns; (ii) the value of taxpayers' time that is spent in making tax returns themselves; and (iii) the costs to firms in operating PAYE, administrative costs of national insurance and of acting as the government's agent in collection of the proceeds of taxation.

Avoidance costs incurred by the taxpayers are: (i) expenses involved in devising and implementing schemes whereby, by taking advantage of any loopholes in the legislation, tax liability can be avoided; (iii) intangible costs associated with the distortions in the running of businesses in order to take advantage of tax avoidance schemes.

Compliance costs are easier to measure than the costs of tax avoidance but there is relatively little information on either. A major study of the compliance costs of direct taxation and of avoidance in England and Wales has been published by Professor C.T. Sandford, *Hidden Costs of Taxation* (London: Institute of Fiscal Studies, 1973). His research showed that approximately 8.5 per cent of personal taxpayers employed paid advisers and 3.5 per cent relied on unpaid advisers. At least 72 million hours were spent by taxpayers themselves on their tax affairs. Administrative, operating and measurable compliance costs of taxpayers amounted to between 3.8 and 5.8 per cent of the total tax revenue and the cost of work associated with taxation but not shown as such, represented an additional 4 per cent. Costs of compliance varied with taxes and were particularly high for capital gains tax. The total hidden costs of taxation would appear on the basis of Professor Sandford's work to have contributed substantially to the tax burden.

His original research was followed by surveys looking at compliance costs in relation to: (a) VAT (1977–78); (b) The Pay-As-You-Earn (PAYE) scheme for income tax and National Insurance Contribution deductions by employers (1981–82); (c) personal income tax and capital gains taxation (1983–84), and (d) VAT (1986–87). Professor Sandford's, Goodwin's and Hardwick's work (details in further reading at end of chapter) produced updated and more comprehensive estimates of the costs of compliance and administration showing them to be about 4 per cent of total revenue in 1986–87. In the 1990s, this figure is likely to be higher following the introduction, in 1993, of a new practice of Autumn budgets, the closing of some tax loopholes, changes in allowances and introduction of new taxes in 1994.

Efficiency of Tax Collecting Authorities

What the cost of compliance and the tax burden will be in the end, depends to some extent on the efficiency with which taxing authorities assess taxpayers' liability and the efficiency with which payments are collected. Comparable international data on this is difficult to find, but even in the UK, which has a relatively efficient system, both assessment and collection have been matters of some concern. Thus for example the Inland Revenue at the beginning of 1994 sent to taxpayers over one million notices of codings that were wrong. Since the codings are used to calculate tax liability it is estimated that as a result over £100 million of income tax will be overpaid and a similar amount underpaid. According to the Chairman of Inland Revenue in evidence to the House of Commons', Public Accounts Committee only 10 per cent of all the codings contained errors, but a number of major accountancy firms claim that up to 50 per cent of the their clients' codings were incorrect (*The Times,* February 16, 1994). According to the Inland Revenue it is up to the taxpayers to check their assessment.

As more people turn to accountants to sort out their tax affairs, the cost of professional advice increases compliance costs for taxpayers. For the Inland Revenue, the expense of rectifying coding errors is reflected in an increased tax burden for everybody in so far as the expenditure is recouped from additional taxation.

The hidden costs of taxation also make its equitable distribution more difficult on two counts. First, compliance costs appear to be of a regressive nature, in the sense that the cost bears little relationship either to the income of the taxpayer or to the amount of the tax payment itself. Second, the cost of professional advice may deter those with small incomes from seeking it and, through ignorance of allowances and other legitimate deductions, they may pay more in tax than they need to. As a consequence, the poor bear more than their fair share of the tax burden.

THE 'HIDDEN' ECONOMY AND THE TAX BURDEN

The greater the burden of taxation the greater the temptation to resort to the 'hidden economy', and to evade taxes. This eventually increases the burden still further for those who pay taxes. The 'hidden economy' involves: (i) concealment of earnings, (ii) understatement of income, (iii) overstatement of expenses, (iv) 'moonlighting', when income from secondary sources, such as payment for jobs done in the taxpayer's spare time, is not disclosed to the Inland Revenue.

New estimates by the Inland Revenue using recent research findings of the Institute for Fiscal Studies (London) put the figure for undeclared incomes for 1994–95 somewhere between £41 billion and £54 billion. On this basis the size of the 'hidden economy' in the UK is 6 per cent to 8 per cent of the country's gross domestic product, or roughly equivalent to half the value of British exports. Loss of tax revenue to the Treasury is likely to be in the region of £14 billion to £19 billion. Had this amount been collected it would, for instance, have been sufficient to finance about half of the government's expenditure on the health programme.

The need for revenue provides an incentive for governments to tackle the problem of tax evasion and expanding 'hidden economy'. According to the National Audit Office Report of March 1994 – *Inland Revenue: Selective Examination of Accounts* – for each £1 spent by the Inland Revenue on improving tax compliance, the investigation of individuals produces an extra £5 and investigation of companies an extra £9.

The extent to which incomes are undeclared is difficult to calculate since, as the term 'hidden economy' suggests, much of the activity is not apparent. The signs that it exists however, are there. They can be identified in various ways such as: (a) the comparison of household spending and declared incomes from self-employment (the Institute of Fiscal Studies found that actual income of the self-employed was one and a half times the income disclosed for tax purposes), (b) the change in the level of registered unemployed and the number of new jobs created (the number of registered unemployed went down by 200,000 in 1993 but there was little increase in job totals to account for this); (c) the expected improved yield from taxes as the economy recovers from recession and the *actual* receipts by the Treasury.

Awareness of the existence of the 'hidden economy' is a starting-point towards finding ways to deal with the problem. One way is to reinforce the tax inspectorate. As the Audit Office report has shown, spending more money on enforcing tax compliance can produce results. Another way is to cut taxes. There is evidence to suggest that, paradoxically, lower taxation increases revenue (see Laffer Curve, p. 134). During the Reagan administration, when taxes were cut revenue increased, though other factors were also likely to have contributed to this effect. Nevertheless, as the burden is reduced there is less incentive to evade taxes and to risk heavy penalties for small gains. Thus the 'hidden economy' is brought out into the open.

SUMMARY

1. The taxable capacity of a country is the proportion of its national income that is above the subsistence level.
2. A limit to taxable capacity of 25 per cent of national income has been suggested by Colin Clark and endorsed by Lord Keynes. Most leading industrial countries have exceeded it.
3. Incidence of taxation indicates on whom the final burden of a tax rests. It can be either formal or effective incidence.
4. Some indirect taxes can be shifted to consumers depending on the price elasticity of demand. This can be illustrated by diagrams (see Figure 12.1).
5. The tax burden can be measured by reference to the taxpayers or to the national economy.
6. International comparisons of the tax burden on the basis of tax thresholds, exemptions, allowances and rates of tax and comparisons of the percentage of national income absorbed by taxation, can lead to different conclusions as to the relative tax burden of different countries.
7. What is a high or a low tax burden is a relative concept.
8. State benefits should be taken into account in assessing the true tax burden on taxpayers.
9. The hidden costs of taxation are the costs of compliance and tax avoidance.
   They add to the tax burden but are difficult to estimate and are not usually included in its calculation.
10. The existence of the 'hidden economy' and associated tax evasion means that the tax burden is not spread on an equitable basis.

SUGGESTED FURTHER READING

Audit Office, Inland Revenue; Selective Customs and Excise Board, *Annual Reports and Accounts, 1994.*

H.J. Easson, *Taxation in the European Community* (London: Athlone Press, 1993).

Eurostat, *Social Protection and Receipts* (Brussels: Commission of the European Communities, 1994).

Inland Revenue, *Annual Reports*.

S. James and C. Nobes, *The Economics of Taxation* (London: Prentice-Hall, 1992).

J.A. Kay and M.A. King, *The British Tax System* (Oxford: Oxford University Press, 1980).

R.A. Musgrave and P.B. Musgrave, *Public Finance in Theory and Practice* (New York: McGraw-Hill, 1989).

C.T. Sandford, *Hidden Costs of Taxation* (London: Institute of Fiscal Studies, 1973).

C.T. Sandford, M. Goodwin and P. Hardwick, *Administrative and Compliance Costs of Taxation* (London: Fiscal Publications, 1989).

EXERCISES

1. Discuss the measurement of taxable capacity and the significance of the concept.
2. On what basis can the tax burden be compared internationally?
3. Why is it useful to distinguish between formal and effective incidence of taxation in economic analysis?
4. In what circumstances can the burden of an indirect tax be shifted?
5. What is meant by incidence of benefits? In what way is it relevant to a study of the tax burden of direct taxation?
6. What is the legal and economic incidence of a personal tax on income? Consider policy implications of your answer.
7. Consider the reasons for the existence of the 'hidden economy' and its consequences for the tax system and the national economy.
8. In what sense can the costs of tax compliance be regarded as the 'hidden cost' of taxation?
9. Suggest ways of reducing the cost of the administration and collection of tax revenue.
10. 'The money that society pays in taxes is returned to it through public expenditure. A tax burden cannot therefore arise.' Comment on the validity of this statement.

Part 4

Budgets and Borrowing: Finance of Central and Local Government and the European Community

13 Central Government Finance

THE BUDGET

The nature and purpose of governments' budgets has changed over time and differs from country to country. Powers, policies and obligations of federal, state and national central governments vary and so do their financial requirements.

The budget is an account of the State, showing how much the government spends and on what and how it finances the expenditure. The budget in its modern form in the UK dates back to the Pitt administration in the eighteenth century. It was originally concerned with the finance of the State and not with the management of the economy by means of public expenditure and taxation.

In the UK, the Chancellor of the Exchequer has in the past presented the budget to the House of Commons, usually in March or April when the British fiscal year ends. This practice changed when, in December 1993, the Chancellor introduced the first unified budget, giving Parliament the opportunity to consider both the expenditure proposals and the means of financing them. He may still present an emergency or a mini-budget at any time if changes in economic conditions make it necessary. Contents of a budget are a closely-guarded secret which is only revealed when the Chancellor rises from the bench to speak. This is an occasion steeped in tradition and gives an opportunity for a display either of fine oratory or somnolent delivery. William Gladstone in 1853 gave the longest speech lasting 4 hours and 45 minutes. By contrast, Benjamin Disraeli's was the shortest, a mere 45 minutes. In the last twenty years the average duration was 1 hour and 15 minutes. By custom the Chancellor may refresh himself with an alcoholic drink. No such comfort is allowed to his listeners and this privilege is unique to the Budget.

The budget speech now contains: (i) a review of finances in the preceding year; (ii) estimates of expenditure for the forthcoming year; (iii) the proposed changes in taxation and borrowing; and (iv) a statement of policy outlining the government's economic, social and political objectives to be achieved through the fiscal policy. Monetary policy measures, such as a change in interest rates, are sometimes mentioned in the budget speech, but they are not part of the budget itself.

Budget proposals are set out in the *Finance Bill*. This is presented to the House of Commons, which debates the proposals, makes alterations, votes on them, accepts the Bill and passes the necessary legislation. The House of Lords concurs – having lost the power to amend financial bills in 1911. The sovereign assents and the Finance Act becomes the law of the land.

Budgets tend to be controversial by nature. In the last twenty years or so there have been two budgets that have perhaps aroused more controversy than most. They were:

(a) *The conditional budget of the Labour Government in 1976.* This departed from the established principle and practice that it is the function of an elected government to govern and of the Chancellor of the Exchequer to make budget decisions. The conditional budget left the final decision on taxation not, as had previously been the case, with the peoples' representatives in Parliament, but with the members of the trades unions. In return for the trades unions' agreement to endorse an incomes policy and to abide by a voluntary pay limit of around 3 per cent, the Chancellor offered to give tax allowances in full. If there was no such agreement, then tax allowances were to be reduced for all taxpayers.

(b) *The free enterprise budget of the Conservative Government in 1979.* This departed from the post-war policy that a government should aim to provide for all 'from the cradle to the grave' and was based on the principle that the state should provide for those who cannot provide for themselves. Others were to be given the opportunity to decide for themselves what they wanted to spend their money on. The corollary of this was a policy to reduce public expenditure and to cut taxation.

Types of Budget

There are three types of budget:

(a) Balanced budget (where expenditure equals revenue).
(b) Deficit budget (where expenditure exceeds revenue). Government borrows.
(c) Surplus budget (where expenditure is below revenue). Government saves.

A balanced budget can be regarded as neutral. It has been called an 'orthodox' budget, reflecting the Treasury view of sound finance. A deficit budget is expansionary as more money is pumped into the economy than is withdrawn in taxation. The borrowing that this policy requires is likely to have an inflationary effect in some circumstances. During the Great Depression of the 1930s, governments sought to stimulate economic activity by means of deficit budgets (see p. 418). A surplus budget is deflationary insofar as the government takes out more than it puts into the money flow (see p. 419). Which type of budget a Chancellor of the Exchequer will present will depend on the government's assessment of the economic situation and the overall economic, social and political policy it seeks to pursue. However, within the three types of budgets there is scope to vary taxes and expenditure to achieve the desired effect (Table. 13.1).

The budget can be approached from two angles. First, the Chancellor decides on expenditure both on current account (government's consumption of goods and services, transfer payments, grants, subsidies, interest payment) and on capital expenditure (investment in physical assets, grants). He then adjusts taxes to cover expenditure entirely or partially and then borrows the rest. The second approach is on the basis of the principle of 'living within one's means'. The Chancellor assesses the total resources

Table 13.1   Types of budgets and budgetary changes

	Balanced Budget		
Revenue (£300 billion)	=	Expenditure £300 billion)	
	Deficit Budget		
	Revenue	Expenditure	
Change from balanced budget	post change tax revenue	change from balanced budget	post change expenditure	deficit
0	300	+	330	30
–	270	0	300	30
–	260	–	290	30
+	320	+	350	30
		Surplus Budget		
				surplus
0	300	–	260	40
+	340	0	300	40
+	370	+	330	40
–	290	–	250	40

(0) No change.
(–) decrease in tax revenue or expenditure.
(+) increase in tax revenue or expenditure.

available to him. He then works out how much he can 'afford' to spend on different programmes to keep his total expenditure within the limits of the available resources.

The British government, faced with a high level of public expenditure, a high level of taxation and big debt, adopted the second approach in 1968 in a White Paper – 'Public Expenditure: a New Presentation' (Cmnd. 4017, 1969).

PREPARATION OF THE BUDGET: ADMINISTRATIVE FRAMEWORK

Work on the budget goes on throughout the year. Soon after one budget is out of the way preparations on the next one begin and government departments start work on estimates of their expenditure for the forthcoming year. The revenue departments – the Inland Revenue and the Customs and Excise Board – prepare estimates of revenue on the basis of unchanged tax rates. Inter-departmental economic forecasts are made and departments continue their work on estimates and agree the figures with the Treasury, in case any adjustments are needed as a result of some changes in the economic conditions.

The Chancellor consults with the Treasury, revenue and other departments involved, and with the Bank of England. He receives advice from outside experts and representations from interested parties, such as the Confederation of British Industry (representing employers) and the Trades Union Congress (representing employees). Various pressure groups and individuals send their views to him. He then makes up his mind on the proposals and presents the budget to Parliament. Documents published in association with the budget and made available to the members of Parliament and the public are the White Paper on Public Expenditure, the Financial Statement and the Budget Report.

THE TREASURY

The Treasury is a government department headed by the Chancellor of the Exchequer who is also Master of the Royal Mint and responsible for the coinage of the realm. Chancellors, as Ministers of the Crown, are political appointees of which ever party is in power and can be replaced at any time should the Prime Minister decide to reshuffle a cabinet. Whilst in office a Chancellor is assisted by Treasury Ministers (Figure 13.1). Management

```
┌─────────────────────────────────────┐
│       Chancellor of the Exchequer    │
└─────────────────────────────────────┘
```

Chief Secretary	Financial Secretary
Responsible for: Public expenditure planning and control Value for money in the public sector	Responsible for : Parliamentary financial business Inland Revenue Privatisation European Community business

Minister of State	Economic Secretary
Responsible for: Customs and Excise Civil Service pay and management	Responsible for : Monetary policy and financial markets International issues Official statistics North Sea oil

Figure 13.1   Ministerial responsibilities within HM Treasury
Source: HM Treasury, *Economic Briefing*, no. 1 (1990).

of the Treasury is in the hands of the Permanent Secretary, who is one of the two top civil servants.

Treasury functions which reflect its importance within the administrative machinery are to:

1. Operate a central system for planning and control of expenditure,
2. Prepare proposals for allocation of resources to government departments to finance their expenditure programmes,
3. Advise departments on improvements in their management strategies and on obtaining value for money,
4. Organise spending plans and estimates for publication,
5. Co-ordinate strategy on taxation,
6. Administer economic and monetary policy and borrowing,
7. Liaise with the European Community, International Monetary Fund, the World Bank and other organisations,
8. Analyse financial developments worldwide,
9. Forecast changes in the economy and finance,

10. Make the Treasury Forecasting Model for the UK economy available to the public,
11. Publish information and statistical data for the benefit of interested parties and to assist the government and Parliament.

ROLE OF PARLIAMENT

It is the function of Parliament to impose taxes, to grant appropriate supplies, i.e. money to finance public expenditure, and to exercise control over both.

Provision of Finance

The Consolidated Fund is a government account at the Bank of England into which are paid all the proceeds of taxation and other revenues and out of which money is paid to finance public expenditure. These are classified as follows:

(a) Charges under permanent legislation. These are charged on the Consolidated Fund (e.g. interest on national debt) and are not debated in Parliament.
(b) Supplies for the current year. These are subject to debate.

Approximately 90 per cent of annual expenditure is voted annually. Supplies are not granted in a lump sum but are appropriated on the basis of individual estimates which are called votes. Navy estimates, army estimates and civil estimates are examples of group headings. There are some 170 individual votes and they are classified into fifteen classes which correspond to the various expenditure programmes.

The whole of the House of Commons used to consider the supplies. Its job was to examine the estimates and to consent to them, a task for which twenty-nine days were allocated in the parliamentary timetable. The time factor and the number of members involved made it impossible for the House of Commons to study and discuss supply figures in detail. It therefore confined itself to discussion of policy. This practice has been changed and 'supply days' have been replaced by 'Opposition days and Estimate days' for debates and votes. The job of looking at the estimates in detail is left to a *Select Committee on Estimates* that can call for expert advice and can summon representatives from the departments. A Parliamentary Select Committee on the Treasury and Civil Service had been set up, following the recommendations of a Select Committee on Procedures in 1978, whose brief is to report to Parliament on financial matters and issues of fiscal and monetary policy.

Parliament can reduce supplies but cannot increase them, since it is the responsibility of the government to initiate expenditure. The government may present supplementary estimates during the course of the year, if the authorised supplies prove inadequate to meet the expenditure for some reason – such as an acceleration in the rate of inflation. A number of funds have been set up for specific purposes, such as:

(a) *The Contingency Fund.* This has been set up to provide for emergencies in anticipation of subsequent provision by Parliament. Such funds have to be repaid.

(b) *Specific Funds.* They have been set up under permanent legislation and can dispense money without having to obtain annual authorisation from Parliament.

(c) *The National Insurance Fund.* National insurance legislation governs the rate of contributions and benefits. Parliament does not have to authorise total disbursements but the government actuary does, however, bring to its notice estimated effects of changes in the rates on the Fund.

(d) *The National Loan Fund.* An Act of Parliament specifics who can get loans and with what limit. The authorisation to provide the money does not run out at the end of the financial year.Nationalised industries and local authorities (through the Public Works Loan Board) borrow from this particular fund.

AUDIT OF PUBLIC EXPENDITURE

The audit of public expenditure dates back to the seventeenth century. Local justices and various bodies were involved in ensuring that public money was not misspent. In 1844 the District Audit Service was set up to audit the accounts of the Poor Law Unions – the predecessors of local authorities. In 1972, Parliament gave them the powers to choose and appoint auditors, who might be a firm in the private sector. This practice caused concern about the independence of the auditors and the system of auditing was changed. An independent body, the *Audit Commission*, was established under the *Local Government Finance Act (1982)* with responsibility for the District Audit Service. The former Exchequer and Audit Department was replaced by the *National Audit Office* under the *National Audit Act* of 1993. The duties of this office are to: (i) examine and certify government departments' accounts and those of other public bodies;

(ii) carry out 'value for money' investigations; (iii) examine the economy, efficiency and effectiveness of public expenditure programmes; and (iv) report to Parliament.

CONTROL AND MANAGEMENT OF PUBLIC EXPENDITURE

Management of a national economy requires management of public expenditure and this involves control. An audit is a necessary check but the correct keeping of accounts is not equivalent to control of public expenditure. To control and manage it the following steps need to be taken: (i) identification of needs; (ii) establishment of policy objectives; (iii) preparation of forecasts; and (iv) planning.

Identification of Needs

The Treasury published in 1979 the results of a first interdepartmental study on the relative needs for public expenditure in England, Wales, Scotland and Northern Ireland. The purpose of the study was to ascertain what expenditure would be required to achieve a comparable level in provision of public services throughout the UK, within the framework of the government's overall policy for the economy.

Policy Objectives

To formulate a policy, questions have to be asked and decisions made on such points as:

(a) *Aims*. What is to be achieved? These objectives may be economic, social and political.

(b) *Means*. How can the objectives best be achieved? The required goods and services may be best provided by either the private or the public sector.

(c) *Appropriations*. To whom in the public sector should funds be allocated? Some services are shared by the central government and local authorities. Division of responsibility is not just a matter of financial convenience.

(d) *Resources*. How much can the country afford to spend to achieve the objectives?

Economic Forecasts

Forecasts of both needs and means are a prerequisite for plans to implement a government's policies. Forecasts are divided into: (i) *short-term forecasts*, such as the budget forecast which is for one year ahead; (ii) *medium term-forecasts* can be variously defined, but a five-year period is usual, (iii) *long-term forecasts* can be of any length, for some purposes such as the government's energy policy they may be as much as twenty years ahead. The longer the period the more difficult and the more unreliable the forecasts are likely to be. Forecasting is not, however, merely crystal ball-gazing. Forecasts are made on the basis of the analysis, interpretation and projection of existing data and on prediction of the course of events in the light of past experience. For this purpose, a forecasting model is sometimes constructed and a number of different assumptions fed into a computer. What the forecast for public expenditure will be depends, among other things, on whether it was based on an assumed rate of unemployment of say, 5, 10 or 12 per cent. A government may decide to base its plans on the average forecast.

The Treasury, under the *Industry Act (1975)*, has to publish its economic forecasts and to make its forecasting model available to the public.

Planning

Plans are concerned with provisions to put policy objectives into practice. The planning of public expenditure is a continuous process. The greater the needs and the more limited the resources, the more important it is to plan for their most effective use. Planning, Programming and Budgeting Systems (PPBS) has been developed as an aid to planning. Its purpose is to provide, in a systematic way, information and analysis for government departments on what inputs are required, in terms of resources, to implement specific objectives and what outputs will result if a plan is fulfilled.

PPBS, is, therefore, a sort of input–output form of analysis (see p. 9) and is concerned with the following: (i) the effectiveness of particular programmes; (ii) alternative methods available to achieve objectives; (iii) probable consequences of implementing particular policies; and (iv) procedures for review of plans as conditions change. A programme budget is arranged according to objectives and related programmes. For instance, if the object is to educate children then the budget will be split into programmes dealing with nursery education, primary schools and other aspects. The programmes are related to persons who are to be educated rather than to the institutions providing the education. The Ministry of Defence has undertaken pioneering work in this field of functional costing.

Developments in control and management of public expenditure.

There have been a number of important developments leading to an improvement in the control and management of public expenditure. The following rank among them:

(a) *Implementation of the Plowden Report's proposals.* The report of the Committee on the Control of Public Expenditure (the Plowden Report, Cmnd. 1432) was published in 1961. Its recommendations were: (i) decisions on future expenditure should be made on the basis of surveys of the total expenditure over a number of years, (ii) the relative importance of different kinds of expenditure should be compared; and (iii) expenditure should be considered in relation to the available resources.

  The report was followed by the setting up of the Public Expenditure Survey Committee (PESC) and, from 1961 onwards, publication of the White Paper 'The Government Expenditure Plans', on the lines suggested by the report. The Papers show: (i) final expenditure of the public sector; (ii) functional analysis on a programme basis; and (iii) economic category analysis on the basis of current and capital expenditure. The surveys were for a five-year period. Planned expenditure was shown for four years ahead and the preceding year was given for comparison. Figures were expressed in survey prices so that changes could be seen in real terms. This created a problem insofar as prices fours years ahead may be very different from those of the survey year. The amount of revenue that would have to be raised to finance the actual expenditure might be well above the planned figure at survey prices. Consequently, a change was made and figure were expressed in cash terms.

(b) *New presentation of public expenditure.* It was a focus on the implications for resources that led to changes in the presentation of public expenditure. A White Paper, 'Public Expenditure, New Presentation' (Cmnd. 4014, 1969), introduced the practice of presenting public expenditure in relation to total revenue from taxation, trading surpluses and other revenue of the whole public sector.

(c) *Monitoring of public expenditure.* To exercise effective control, a government has to monitor public expenditure. Monitoring requires up-to-date information which is now provided by a computerised financial information system. Each department of the central government has its own information system and all departments supply the Treasury with a monthly breakdown of their voted expenditure.

Actual spending is compared with projected expenditure and then the government publishes Public Expenditure Survey Plans and end of the year outturn figures. In addition, nationalised industries submit monthly statements and local authorities provide a flow of information on their activities. All this enables the Government to take an overall view of the national economy in general, and of the public sector in particular.

Cash Limits

The various improvements in the management, control and presentation of public expenditure have not succeeded in keeping it in check. In the 1970s, it began to outstrip revenue and to exceed the percentage of national income that was considered indicative of the resources that could be made available to the public sector. Cash limits were introduced to put a brake on the growth of public expenditure. They were first announced in a White Paper 'The Attack on Inflation' (Cmnd. 6151, 1976) and first applied to expenditure for 1976–77. It was the government and not Parliament that set the cash limits, but they were regarded as a measure to supplement and not to replace Parliamentary control over public expenditure through the supply estimates.

Cash limits can be defined as an administrative ceiling on public spending. Their purpose is to impose a stricter financial control on the spending authorities, and to get the message across that increases in costs would result in cuts in public services, as expenditure has to be kept within the set limits. Cash limits applied to three categories of public expenditure.

(a) *Central government.* About 75 per cent of the expenditure voted by Parliament – both on the supply and supplementary estimates – was subjected to cash limits. The expenditure was divided into cash control blocks. A department would usually be responsible for several blocks and could juggle the expenditure so as to find the most efficient way of achieving the objectives of various programmes within the cash limits. The Department of Education for example had been given five blocks – for instance, one for schools and another for universities. Cash control blocks applied to both current and capital expenditure. Excluded from the cash limits was expenditure that is demand-determined and therefore could not be predicted accurately in advance, e.g. unemployment benefits.

(b) *Local authorities.* The central government had no direct powers to control local authorities' current expenditure and to apply cash limits to what they spent. It could exercise control indirectly by applying cash limits to general and supplementary grants made to the local authorities. Since they rely for the bulk of their finance on the central government (see p. 324) the cash limits acted as a check to their spending. On capital expenditure, cash limits applied either to the amount to be spent or to be borrowed.

(c) *Nationalised industries.* The expenditure of the nationalised industries was subject to a form of cash limits related to their financing requirements that had to be met by loans, grants and public dividend capital (see p. 372). Thus cash limits applied to the amounts of money that the nationalised industries were allowed to raise.

THE NEW SYSTEM

During the 1980s, general government expenditure (excluding proceeds from privatisation) fell as a percentage of the national income of the UK (Figure 13.2). With the onset of recession in the early 1990s, and the consequent decline in economic growth and rise in unemployment, public spending was on an upward trend again.

With the object of reducing the rising share of resources absorbed by the public sector, the government in 1992 changed the way in which public expenditure is planned and controlled. The basis for this is the *Public Expenditure Survey*. It enables the government to review its past spending and plan future expenditure.

General Government Expenditure is defined to include:

central government	local authority	nationalised industries'
spending	expenditure	financial support
plus local authorities		from central
expenditure financed		government
by central		
government		
minus grants to		
local authorities		
plus support to		
nationalised industries		

The New Control Total replaced the 'planning total'. It now excludes social security expenditure directly related to unemployment and is considered to

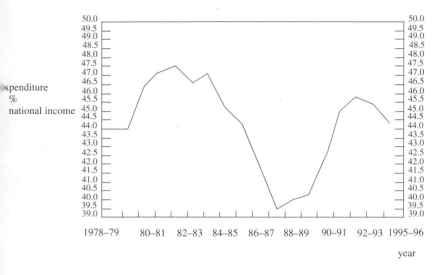

Figure 13.2   General government expenditure
Source: HM Treasury, *Economic Briefing*, no. 5 (1993).

be a better indication of the trend in government spending which is no longer distorted by cyclical fluctuations. NCT annual ceilings are stated in cash terms but are limited to a percentage growth rate in real terms.

In the past, Ministers of spending departments and the Chief Secretary to the Treasury responsible for public expenditure, negotiated and compromised on allocation of resources. In the Treasury's view: 'This bottom-up approach was liable to give too much weight to what expenditure was desirable rather than to what was affordable'.

The present system operates on the basis of 'top-down' approach, whereby NCT sets annual ceilings and money is allocated within these limits. The first Public Expenditure Survey carried out on the new basis was in 1992 and set the NCT for 1993–94. The procedure for allocation was as follows:

(a) Ministers meet to discuss their departments' spending.
(b) Chief Secretary submits his report of these meetings (bilaterals) to a Cabinet Committee.
(c) The Committee then arrives at what it considers to be the preferred distribution of resources within the set limits and recommends it to the full cabinet.
(d) The Cabinet collectively determines spending priorities.

The Business of Government

The problems of constraining public expenditure focused government's attention in the 1980s on measures to get better *value for money* in the public sector. This requires greater efficiency in delivery of outputs or outcomes. When it is achieved, standards of service can be maintained or improved and provisions extended without additional or even with reduced inputs.

Cost reduction was seen by the government as a matter of major importance that needed to be tackled in a variety of ways, exposing government departments to competition with the private sector where this was feasible and introducing business ethos into the public sector. Lord Rayner of Marks and Spencer, one of the most successful British companies, was appointed in 1980 to advise the Prime Minister and was instrumental in setting up of the *Efficiency Unit and Management Information System* for ministers. The White Paper 'Efficiency and Effectiveness in the Civil Service' (Cmnd. 8616, London: HMSO, 1981) followed. The Government's stated intention was to 'Promote in each department and organisation a system in which managers at all levels have:

(a) A clear view of their objectives, and means to assess and, wherever possible, measure outputs and performance in relation to those objectives.
(b) Well-defined responsibility for making the best use of resources, including a critical scrutiny of output and value for money.
(c) The information (particularly about costs), the training and the access to expert advice that they need to exercise their responsibilities effectively.'

The outcome of these proposals was the launch in 1982 of the *Financial Management Initiative (FMI)*. The Efficiency Unit went on the publish 'Management in Government: The Next Steps' (1988), named the Ibbs Report after Sir Robin Ibbs, who had succeeded Lord Rayner. Changes in the administrative machinery led to the creation of *Executive Agencies* that replaced some government departments and were to be run on more business-like basis (see p. 104).

The government over the years had implemented a variety of measures to keep public expenditure in check, improve efficiency in delivery of services, reform administrative machinery and the way that resources are allocated, controlled and spent by government departments and public bodies. These measures deal with:

1. Decentralisation of the work of government departments,
2. Establishment of Executive Agencies,
3. Setting up in the National Heath Service of trust hospitals and budget-holding General Practitioners, and in education the introduction of local management of schools,
4. Exposure of public sector providers to competition, both within the public sector itself and with suppliers from the private sector,
5. Contracting-out work previously done within public sector to businesses,
6. Privatisation (see p. 376),
7. Private finance initiative.

PRIVATE FINANCE INITIATIVE

This represents a major departure from the way that governments in the past had financed projects and services which have been traditionally perceived as their responsibility. Instead of using departments' own resources (money, manpower and management skills), the Government in 1992 introduced a scheme to bring in private finance and entrepreneurial experience. The object was not only to keep expenditure down but also to increase efficiency and create or protect jobs in the private sectors, particularly in the construction industry which had been badly hit by the recession of the early 1990s. Following the Chancellor of the Exchequer's announcement of the relaxation of Treasury rules on private finance in November 1992, ninety projects were completed or were in the pipeline by the beginning of 1994. Many of them are intended to improve transport facilities such as the extension of the Docklands Light Railway in London, the Manchester Metrolink, the Heathrow Express (a link between Paddington Railway Station and the airport) and the Second Severn Crossing (bridge). Tenders for the Channel Tunnel Rail Link were to be invited in 1994. The Channel Tunnel, a private sector joint venture with France which was opened in 1994, represents an earlier example.

Types of private finance projects are numerous but basically they fall into three categories:

(a) *Financially freestanding projects* that do not require any public expenditure. Costs fall on the private sector contractors and are recouped from payments by users, e.g. toll charges to cross the Severn bridge, during a period for which a concession was granted.

(b) *Jointed ventures* between public and private sectors may necessitate some public expenditure but do not represent an open-ended commitment. The contribution may, for example, be in the form of a grant or a loan on favourable terms. Private sector partners remain in control but risks may be shared. Capital outlay and operating costs are recovered from charges. An example of such a venture is the Channel Tunnel Rail Link.

(c) *Service projects* are those that are undertaken by private sector businesses to provide services to the public sector. This may be in place of its own provisions or in addition. For example, a security group may be employed to escort prisoners to courts in order to free police officers to be employed more effectively on other duties.

To be approved, private finance projects have to give value for money and to be of some general benefit to the public.

The *benefits* to the government are that:

(i) It does not need to provide capital outlay and cover operating costs of projects that are desirable but might not be affordable within controlled public expenditure ceilings.
(ii) Services may be provided to the public using less resources as businesses are likely to be more cost-conscious than government departments.
(iii) Some projects yield a financial return which can be shared between the public sector and its partners in the private sector.
(iv) New jobs may be created helping to reduce unemployment.
(v) Social gains, even though they may not be quantifiable, are expected to benefit the public in general.

There are, however, also *disadvantages* to private finance projects:

(i) Suitable partners in the private sector may be difficult to find.
(ii) The government has less control over them than over its own departments if they fail to meet their commitments satisfactorily.
(iii) A private sector contractor can go bankrupt and, if a contribution to the project had been made from public funds, it may be lost.

NATIONAL LOTTERY

This is much more than a private finance project that provides funding for public expenditure programmes. In the press it has been described as 'the biggest start-up project ever attempted in Britain', 'the UK's largest consumer industry', 'Britain's biggest business with an annual turnover of £6.5 billion', 'the world's biggest lottery' and 'television's great attraction', with over 25 million viewers switching on to watch the draw. The lottery is set to become a national institution. As with taxation, it will extract money from every household but the difference is that, in this instance, people will contribute to the Exchequer out of their own free will. According to estimates, an average household in the UK will pay £100 annually for lottery tickets. In return, the lottery will make someone into a millionaire almost every week. This prospect has fired public imagination, in a way which fiscal policies for greater equality never have.

The idea of a national lottery is not new. Many countries already have them. There have been state lotteries in the UK in the past – one such provided money for the foundation of the British Museum in 1753. In the nineteenth century lotteries fell into disrepute. Reforming politicians and preachers saw them as morally damaging, particularly in their impact on the working classes. Deprived of state lotteries gamblers turned to horse and dog racing, (London alone had 17 dog racing tracks), and from 1923 to football pools. On gambling politicians divided on party lines. Lord Wilson, a former Labour Prime Minister, had observed that in the history of the Labour party, Methodism was more important than Marxism and labelled as 'a squalid raffle' the State Lottery that the Conservative government brought back in 1956 in the form of premium bonds. Mr Harold Macmillan, the Prime Minister at the time, was portrayed as opening 'doors to decadence'. In reality, there was nothing very rakish about the premium bonds. They were designed with a key redeeming feature – unlike other forms of gambling, buyers of premium bonds did not lose their stake. The unlucky ones just did not win a modest prize. Generating little excitement for the punters, premium bonds also provided little revenue for the government.

In contrast, the new National Lottery is glamorous, but it also has a built-in redeeming feature. Some of the proceeds will go to charities and some will finance worthy public projects which are desirable, but not essential. These will be schemes which the government is under no obligation to undertake.

In some countries, the state runs national lotteries or subcontracts their running. In the UK the government invited bids for the franchise from companies in the private sector, and in May 1994 it awarded the contract to a consortium, the Camelot Group. Its members have a wide range of relevant experience: Cadbury Schweppes (retail trade), Racal Electronics (data network), De La Rue (security printers), ICL (computer terminal makers and training), and GTECH (an American company that operates 65 lotteries worldwide). The Chairman of Camelot is a former chairman of the Post Office. Lottery tickets will be sold through retail outlets and over the counter in post offices, starting with 10,000 outlets and increasing to 27,000 by 1996, linked by a computer network. Retailers selling tickets can expect to get £6,600 in commission. Instant scratch game cards are also to be introduced. Some 250,000 winners will receive prizes of varying size with the average jackpot of £4–5 million possibly rising to £15 million. Results of the draw will be announced during peak hour TV review shows and provide entertainment.

The National Lottery Distribution Fund will receive a share of Camelot's profits, between 28.3 and 32.2 per cent is to be allocated to the Arts, Sport, Heritage, Charities and the Millennium Fund. By the next century, lottery proceeds may not bring taxation down or allow governments to go on a spending spree – but public finance is likely to be more fun.

SUMMARY

1. The budget shows government revenue and expenditure. It can be a surplus, deficit or neutral budget depending on the government's policy objectives.
2. In the UK the budget is now presented annually in the Autumn but there may be emergency budgets at other times during the year.
3. The House of Commons debates the budget, proposes changes and approves (or rejects) it.
4. It is Parliament that imposes taxes, makes money available by granting of supplies and controls expenditure.
5. Parliamentary control is exercised through select committees. Expenditure in scrutinised and audited by the National Audit Office.
6. The monitoring of public expenditure requires up-to-date information and comparison of outturn with planned expenditures. Planning is done for several years ahead. Public expenditure surveys are used.
7. Cash limits had been introduced (1976–77) to check the growth in public expenditure by setting ceilings on how much the public sector could spend.
8. New system of controlling public expenditure introduced Control Totals and a 'top-down' approach to spending.

9. Government has sought to incorporate some business concepts and practices into public administration and some government departments have been remodelled into Executive Agencies.
10. Joint ventures between partners in the public and private sectors have grown in numbers and extended the scope of their activities with far-reaching consequences for finance and the provision of public services.

SUGGESTED FURTHER·READING

C.V. Brown and P.M. Jackson, *Public Sector Economics* (Oxford: Basil Blackwell, 1992).

Chancellor of the Exchequer, Budget Speeches and Financial Statements, *Hansard*, annually.

R. Common, N. Flyn and E. Mellon, *Managing Public Services* (London: Butterworth-Heinemann, 1993).

Efficiency Unit, *Management in Government: The Next Steps* (London: HMSO, 1988).

Efficiency Unit, *Making the Most of Next Steps* (London: HMSO, 1991).

HM Treasury, 'The Treasury' *Economic Briefing*, no. 1 (London: Central Office of Information, 1990).

HM Treasury, *Next Ten Years: Public Expenditure and Taxation into the 1990s*, Cmnd. 9189 (London: HMSO, 1984).

R.A. Musgrave and P.B. Musgrave, *Public Finance in Theory and Practice* (New York: McGraw-Hill, 1989).

White Paper, *Efficiency and Effectiveness in the Civil Service*, Cmnd. 8616 (London: HMSO, 1982).

EXERCISES

1. Can a 'conditional budget' be justified? Give reasons for your answer.
2. What is an 'orthodox budget'? Consider its effect on the economy.
3. Discuss the difference between forecasting and planning in relation to preparation of a budget.
4. Consider ways of controlling public expenditure that are likely to be most effective.
5. 'An audit is a necessary check, but correct keeping of accounts is not equivalent to control of public expenditure'. Comment on the validity of this statement.
6. The influence of the Treasury is all pervading throughout the British economy. Justify or refute this assertion.
7. In what way, if any, could the 'private finance initiative' be regarded as a privatisation measure?
8. Explain what is meant by the expression 'value for money' in the pubic sector, and give examples.
9. Certain infrastructure projects such as road building and maintenance have traditionally been undertaken by central and local government. What reasons, if any, are there for changing this practice?
10. Suggest whether business practices and market forces are relevant and appropriate for public administration, raising of state revenue and determining priorities in public sector spending.

14 Public Sector Borrowing

NATIONAL DEBT DEFINED

National debt is the amount of money borrowed internally or externally by the government of a country on the behalf of its citizens collectively. The money is lent in different forms and comes from a variety of sources, such as:

(a) *Internal loans,* which are made by individuals, businesses or institutions within the country.
(b) *External loans,* which are advanced by individuals, business or institutions abroad and by foreign governments.
(c) *International loans,* which are external borrowing when the money is lent by international institutions such as the International Monetary Fund (IMF).

The conditions, terms and consequences of external and of internal loans are somewhat different and therefore it is useful to distinguish between them.

It has been argued that the term 'national' can only be appropriately applied to the debt when the money has been borrowed externally and that a more meaningful description would be a 'government debt' or a 'public debt'. In the USA, the term public debt is employed. In the UK it is generally referred to as the national debt and that is its official designation in the government's publications and those of the Bank of England.

The British national debt represents money which is: (i) borrowed by the central government for its own purposes; (ii) made available to the nationalised industries; or (iii) provided to local authorities through the Public Works Loan Fund. Local authorities' direct borrowing (see p. 289) is not included in the national debt.

STRUCTURE OF THE NATIONAL DEBT

The national debt consists of different securities and advances and is divided into categories which are: (i) *Funded debt* (long-term borrowing); (ii) *Floating debt* (short-term borrowing); (iii) *Other unfunded debt* (varying maturities); (iv) *Debt payable in external currencies* (loans of varied durations) (see p. 298).

Funded debt is that part of the national debt that the government is under no obligation to repay, but on which it pays interest. Stocks in this category can be bought and sold on the Stock Exchange (e.g., Consols). *Floating debt* consists of Treasury Bills and Ways and Means Advances. This is the method by which government departments that have surpluses lend them to the Treasury. *Unfunded debt* consists of issues such as: (i) Stocks of various maturities that the government has to repay at specified dates. The stocks do not have to be held until then and can be sold on the Stock Exchange at any time before their maturity date. (ii) Savings Bonds and certificates. They are intended for small savers, e.g. 'Granny' bonds and National Savings Certificates and have to be held to maturity to get full benefit of the investment.

National debt consists of both marketable and non-marketable debt.

(a) *Marketable debt* can be traded on the Stock Exchange. A purchaser of a government stock that is marketable may decide to sell it to somebody else before the maturity date. Marketable stocks are called gilts or gilt-edged stocks, because at one time stock certificates were decorated with gold round the edges.

(b) *Non-marketable debt* comes in two forms: (i) securities which cannot be traded on the Stock Exchange and have to be redeemed by the original buyer; (ii) loans, such as those from the International Monetary Fund, for which no stocks are issued.

Innovations

Two types of bonds were issued that marked a departure from the principles on which offers had been made in the past.

(a) *Premium bonds.* The issue of premium bonds established a form of state lottery. A buyer of a bond is not entitled to an interest payment on the capital but instead participates in a draw and may win a prize. At each draw there are a number of prizes of varying sizes. The government hoped to attract people who had a few pounds to spare and who would not normally invest. The early premium bonds were offered in denominations of £1. The premium bond offers an alternative to betting on football pools, dogs, horses and other forms of gambling but with the difference that a holder of a premium bond does not lose his money if his number does not come up, he is entitled to participate in succeeding draws until such time as the bond is cashed in.

Premium bonds were controversial when introduced – they were attacked as encouraging gambling. They were defended on the grounds that people could enjoy the excitement of a draw without risking their capital. Many of those buying premium bonds would gamble anyway – judging by the popularity of gaming and betting in the UK – so it was argued they might just as well benefit the state and not the bookmaker. Premium bonds are no longer an emotional issue. They have been on offer for nearly forty years and age has conferred 'respectability' on them.

(b) *Index-linked issues* were introduced as a result of inflation. During the 1970s, as prices rose, the attractiveness of investment in government stock, particularly for small savers, declined. An investment of £100, when the same amount was repaid a few years later, might be worth only half of the original value in terms of its purchasing power, if inflation had eroded its value.

The principle of index-linked government stock is that the amount originally invested is increased on repayment in line with the rate of inflation, as measured by changes in the Retail Price Index. Instead of interest payable on an annual basis during the period that a stock is held, there is a bonus payment on redemption. Various forms of index-linked stock have been tried out in Continental Europe.

In the UK, index-linked savings bonds were first introduced in 1974. Their purchase was restricted to pensioners and to a maximum holding of £500. A second issue of index-linked bonds was launched in 1980, the age limit for men was reduced to 60 years but the purchase of the bonds remained restricted to the elderly. In 1981 there were two developments which may prove to have far-reaching consequences. (i) Index-linked National Savings Certificates were made available, up to an individual limit of £3,000, to any man, woman or child who wished to purchase them. This issue may make time deposits with such institutions as building societies appear less attractive and in time reduce the flow of money to finance, e.g. house purchase. (ii) Index-linked Treasury stock, which is marketable and matures in fifteen years, was put on offer with the novel feature that it was restricted to certain financial institutions. Pension funds, life insurance companies and friendly societies are eligible to hold this Treasury stock in respect of the UK pension business.

Implications for industry in general, of the issue of index-linked government stock, are difficult to assess at this stage. Companies in the private sector that cannot issue index-linked shares may be at a disadvantage in the competition for funds. Index-linking has the advantage that it protects investors' capital from inflation, which reduces its real worth[1]. Both private and public issues can fall in value in this way.

Fluctuations in the Price of Government Stocks

Marketable securities that are traded on the Stock Exchange have a daily quotation which indicates the price at which they can be bought and sold. It need not be the price at which they had been first issued and may be above or below the original price depending on the supply and demand for a particular stock. The price of fixed interest government stock changes in an inverse proportion to a change in interest rates. The price goes down if interest rates go up; it goes up if interest rates go down. Suppose a person bought 5 per cent stock issued at £100, giving an annual return of £5. If the rate of interest increased to 10 per cent, an investor could get a return of £10 on his £100 in some other form of investment and would not be prepared to pay £100 for a stock that yielded only £5. The market price of the original issue would therefore drop to £50 when the return on capital would be 10 per cent. So far as the national debt is concerned that stock will still be shown as an indebtedness of £100 on which 5 per cent interest is payable.

New Issues and Conversions

New issues increase the national debt. To raise additional funds the government, through the Bank of England, has to offer new stocks or bonds. It can issue them at: (i) *par*, when the face value of the stock is the same as its price, e.g. both are £100; (ii) *below par*, when the price (e.g. £95) is below the face value (e.g. £100). The interest rate, however, is still related to the face value. The purpose of below par issues is to make the stock more attractive to investors. *Conversion*, depending on the terms, need not increase the national debt. It is a method of postponing repayment of maturing stocks. A government will need to offer investors incentives to convert. Firstly, it can do so by offering to convert the old stock to a new one, that has a higher rate of interest, e.g. offer to exchange 10 per

---

[1] A person who in 1932 invested £100 in 3 per cent War Loan (which was not indexed) and sold his holding in October 1981, soon after inflation peaked in the UK, would have got £25 for it. In terms of purchasing power this is equivalent to what approximately £1.8s.0d. would have bought in 1932. Thus the fall in the real value of £100 investment is approximately £98.00.

cent stock maturing in the year 1999 for 12 per cent stock maturing in the year 2005. Secondly, it can offer to convert stock to a higher face value, so that a stock of £100 at the end of the extended period would be repaid, for example, at £120. This does not provide the government with more money and by increasing its liability adds to the national debt.

ACQUISITION OF NATIONAL DEBT HOLDINGS

Investors can acquire national debt holdings by taking up offers of new issues and buying issued stocks on the Stock Exchange. Their purchase represents a transfer of ownership from one investor to another and does not affect the size of the national debt. Only the pattern of distribution is changed (see Figure 14.1).

The reasons for acquiring government issues will to some extent differ depending on who the investors are. Individuals are the biggest single

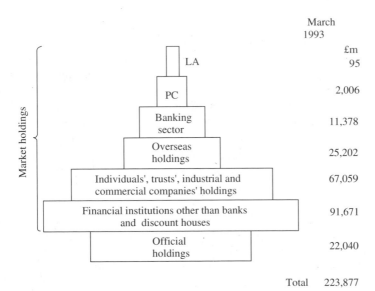

	March 1993 £m
LA	95
PC	2,006
Banking sector	11,378
Overseas holdings	25,202
Individuals', trusts', industrial and commercial companies' holdings	67,059
Financial institutions other than banks and discount houses	91,671
Official holdings	22,040
Total	223,877

Figure 14.1   Distribution of the national debt of the UK

Notes:
1. Total national debt including nationalised industries' stocks guaranteed by the government.
2. LA = Local Authorities, PC = Public Corporations.

Source: Bank of England, *Quarterly Bulletin* (December 1993).

group of holders of government stocks, bonds and certificates and may invest in them for any of the following reasons:

(a) *Income.* An annual return on capital invested is assured.
(b) *Safety.* Gilts are regarded as safe in the sense that, short of · revolution or some other disaster that puts an end to the country's political and economic system, the state does not go bankrupt. It can therefore be taken for granted that £100 invested in government stock that is held until maturity will be repaid in full. But if there is inflation it may not have retained its purchasing power.
(c) *Capital gain.* Since prices of marketable stocks fluctuate, by buying when prices are down and selling when they are up, it is possible to make a capital gain which is untaxed.
(d) *Convenience.* Government issues, such as the National Savings Certificates, provide an outlet for small savings. People with a small amount of money to invest would find the services of a broker expensive. The government provides a number of schemes for small savers and facilities to buy some issues conveniently and cheaply at a local post office.

Financial institutions, such as banks and insurance companies, finance houses or building societies invest in gilts out of choice and out of necessity.

(a) *They find gilts convenient.* Commercial banks need short-term securities such as Treasury bills to maintain their liquidity.
(b) *Investment in government stock can also be profitable.* Certain financial institutions are required by law to keep a proportion of their assets in government stock to safeguard the money that the general public has entrusted to them.

Foreign investors – who may be individuals, businesses, financial institutions or governments – may have similar reasons for investing in gilts. In addition, if the level of interest rates is higher in the UK than abroad, they may want to take advantage of this by buying British government's stocks.

NATIONAL DEBT AS AN ASSET AND AS A LIABILITY

The national debt is an *asset* for investors which yields an income, and is safe and convenient. It may also be marketable and result in a capital gain, thus providing an alternative to investment in the private sector.

The national debt is a *liability* for a government that has to pay interest on the borrowed money and repay some loans. This imposes both an internal and external burden on the country, but against it we have to offset the advantages of the national debt. It enables the government to spend now and to pay later. This may or may not be desirable and will depend on circumstances. The national debt allows the burden of loans to finance public expenditure (e.g. schools, hospitals) to be spread over the succeeding generations who will benefit from it. Servicing of the national debt and repayments of maturing loans requires a supply of funds. There are three sources for a government to tap:

(i) *Taxation.* 'Unproductive' or deadweight debt is the result of borrowing that has not created wealth which generates income. Interest on such debt has therefore to be paid out of taxation.
(ii) *Earned income.* Loans to finance investment in plant and machinery in the nationalised industries in theory should increase earnings out of which interest on productive debt can be financed. In practice, this has not always been so.
(iii) *Further borrowing.* Payment of interest on existing debt out of new loans is not generally regarded as a sound financial practice and governments have recourse to it as the last resort.

MANAGEMENT OF THE NATIONAL DEBT

The decision on how much of the public expenditure is to be financed out of taxation and how much by borrowing is made by the Chancellor in consultation with the Treasury and the Bank of England. Management of the national debt is the Bank's responsibility. The Bank is concerned with: (i) the sale of government securities; (ii) negotiation of foreign loans; and (iii) interest policy.

The monetary policy of the Bank of England on interest rates is relevant to the management of the national debt. The policy affects the cost of borrowing and the return that has to be offered on government stock to attract investors. The introduction of the new monetary system (Bank of England Paper, 'Competition of Credit Control') in 1971 and the subsequent replacement of the Bank of England *Bank Rate* by *Minimum Lending Rate* (MLR) weakened its control over the money market. Banks became free to fix their own interest rates in response to the demand for and the supply of credit, instead of following the official lead. The suspension of MLR in 1981 shifted still further the emphasis from interest rates to the open market operations. National debt is a tool of monetary policy that can be used to stimulate or to reduce the level of economic activity by means of open-market operations and changes in interest rates.

Open-market Operations

If the government wishes to follow an anti-deflationary policy then the Bank of England can expand credit creation of the financial institutions by engaging in open-market operations. In the past it was the government broker (the firm of Mullens) and now it is the Bank's official who is instructed to go to the market to buy government stocks. Commercial banks that sell them receive cash in exchange which they can then lend. The borrowed money will be spent. Some of it will be used to purchase goods and services, some on investment in plant and machinery. Demand will increase and this, in theory, will stimulate the economy – assuming that the fall in the level of economic activity had been due to insufficient demand.

If the monetary policy is aimed at restricting inflation then the Bank of England will seek to restrict credit and will go to the market to sell government securities. Commercial banks will purchase these, thereby reducing their liquid assets so they have less money to lend. People will find it more difficult to get loans. As they borrow less, they spend less, and the demand for goods and services drops. This brings down the level of economic activities and counteracts inflation.

By the use of open-market operations to control credit creation the Bank of England also exercises control over the level of deposits with the financial institutions. Such deposits are defined as part of M_3, which is the stock of money. The national debt is therefore instrumental in controlling the supply of money. In certain circumstances increase in the supply of money is inflationary.

Management of the national debt can also produce either deflationary or inflationary effects by changes in the policy on maturities of government issues. Long-term borrowing is less inflationary than short-term borrowing.

The offer of government stocks with high interest rates tends to raise the general level of interest rates. If, as a result, money is channelled into savings rather than into consumption then the effect may be deflationary. Much will depend on what happens to the savings. If the government borrows the money that had been saved, and spends it, the deflationary effect will be reduced. The effect of interest rates on the decision to save is controversial, but insofar as low rates of interest discourage savings, then they may add to inflationary pressure.

Table 14.1   The UK national debt, 1694–1993

		Size of the national debt (£ million)
1694	Creation of the Bank of England	1
1727	Accession of George II	52
1784	End of the American War of Independence	243
1815	End of wars with France	861
1918	End of the First World war	5 921
1945	End of the Second World War	27 733
1981	Peace	110 117
1993	Peace	223 877

The use of the national debt as a tool of monetary policy to manage the economy of the country is relatively recent. In the past, governments simply borrowed because they were short of money.

ORIGIN OF THE BRITISH NATIONAL DEBT

Some historians date the origin of the national debt to the time when London goldsmiths began to advance money to the Exchequer on the security of the assignment of some public revenue. The national debt, in the sense that the term is now used, came into existence in 1694 when the Bank of England was incorporated. In return for its charter, it agreed to lend over £1 million to the government. Parliament reserved the right to repay the debt at any time after 1705. Ways of doing so continued to be discussed and recommendations made as late as the report of the Colwyn Committee on National Debt and Taxation in 1927. In the meantime the debt went on accumulating.

The reasons for the growth of the national debt are complex – economic, social and political factors have contributed to it (Figure 14.2). Briefly, some of the major causes are:

(i) *Wars* which gave rise to enormous expenditure that could not be financed out of taxation.

(ii) *Public works*, that were undertaken during the great depression of the 1930s to provide employment, necessitated borrowing.

(iii) The *Welfare State*, which was established in 1948, resulted in an increasing social investment which, to a large extent, was financed out of loans.

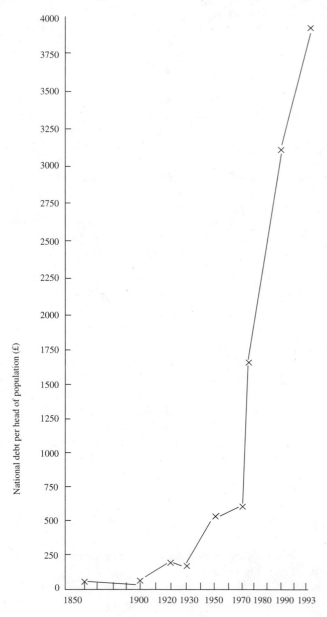

Figure 14.2   Central government borrowing
Source: Bank of England *Quarterly Bulletins* (up to December 1993).

(iv) *Nationalisation* of major industries in the 1940s and 1950s involved compensation payments to former shareholders and this was given in the form of government stock.

(v) *Budget deficits* which were either the result of a short-fall in revenue or part of the policy to manage demand, necessitated borrowing.

(vi) *Balance of payments crises* led to borrowing abroad. Inflation in the 1970s and early 1980s increased expenditure on provision of public goods and services to a level where it substantially exceeded the revenue of the public sector. Large loans had to be raised at high interest rates, thus increasing the national debt and the cost of servicing it. In the early 1990s recession adversely affected tax yields and increased public expenditure. As a result, public debt continued to rise.

ATTEMPTS TO REPAY THE NATIONAL DEBT: THE SINKING FUND

Sinking funds were set up in an attempt to repay the national debt. The intention was to set aside a proportion of government revenue from time to time and pay it into a sinking fund. The money was then to be used to reduce the national debt in stages. In 1786 William Pitt the Younger created the Permanent Sinking Fund. It was followed by a succession of sinking funds but they made little impact on the national debt. In 1828 a Select Committee of the House of Commons expressed the view that, 'the excess of revenue over expenditure is the only real sinking fund by which public debt can be discharged'. The New Permanent Fund, which was set up in 1875, aimed to provide for gradual redemption of the debt by annual provisions instead of periodic payments, as had been done in the past. Another new Sinking Fund followed in 1923. The Colwyn Committee considered a capital levy to repay the national debt, and recommended that the Fund should be increased to a required level by repayment of allied loans, which arose out of the First World War, and by an increase in government revenue. This did not happen, because within two years financial markets throughout the world crashed, the crisis spread, and the Great Depression set in. A brief period of recovery was followed by the Second World War. National debt soared to unprecedented levels and its repayment ceased to be a practical proposition.

PUBLIC SECTOR BORROWING REQUIREMENT (PSBR)

Public sector indebtedness is largely, but not wholly, represented by the national debt. Local authorities can and do borrow directly on their own account at home and abroad. Public corporations are also permitted to raise loans in foreign capital markets. To arrive at the public sector borrowing requirement the government has to take into account its own borrowing, as well as that of local authorities and public corporations. (Figure 14.3 shows the determinants and financing of the PSBR).

The term Public Sector Borrowing Requirement came into use in the mid-1960s, data on it had been compiled since then (see Table 14.2). The PSBR is an important economic indicator which shows how much the public sector taken as a whole has to borrow to finance its expenditure programme. It is a key statistic that has to be taken into account in the

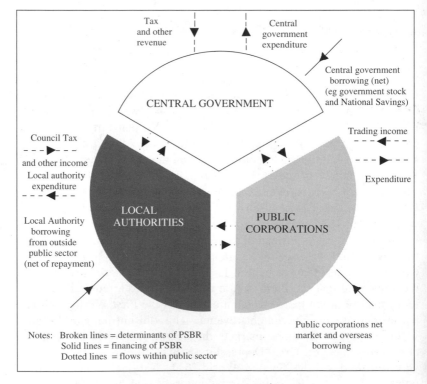

Figure 14.3 Determinants and financing of the PSBR
Source: HM Treasury, *Economic Briefing*, no. 6 (1994).

Table 14.2   Public sector borrowing requirement, 1965–98

Financial Year	1965–66	1970–71	1975–76	1979–80	1981–82
PSBR as percentage of GDP	2.8	1.5	9.6	5.1	4.8
PSBR (£billion)	1	0.8	11	10	10

Financial Year	1992–93	1993–94[1]	1994–95	1995–96	1996–97	1997–98
PSRB as percentage of GDP	5.75	8.0	6.50	5.50	4.50	3.75
PSRB (£billion)	35	50	44	39	35	30

Note:
1. Forecast and assumptions thereafter. Between 1987 and 1991 there were public sector debt repayments.

Source: *Economic Trends* (London: HMSO, 1982); and HM Treasury, *The Budget* (1993).

formulation of a government's economic policy and in the assessment of the effects of fiscal and monetary measures on the economy. PSBR is expressed by reference to the total resources available in the country and is calculated as a percentage of the gross domestic product. The higher the percentage the greater the share of the national resources that are absorbed by the public sector.

CONSEQUENCES AND BURDEN OF THE NATIONAL DEBT

The consequences of an increase in the national debt are both direct and indirect, numerous and widespread. The following generalisations can be made:

(i) Money that is available to a government for current or capital expenditure programmes increases.
(ii) Resources are transferred from the private to the public sector of the economy.
(iii) Higher taxes are necessary to repay loans and for servicing of the debt.

(iv) The balance of payments account, in the case of external borrowing, improves on receipt of foreign currency but worsens as interest payments start and when loans have to be repaid.

(v) Inflation in certain circumstances accelerates as more money is pumped into the economy.

Whether the overall effect of government borrowing will be beneficial or detrimental to a country depends on the purpose of the borrowing, the timing of loans, how the money is used, the timing of expenditure and the management of the national debt.

THE INTERNAL AND EXTERNAL BURDEN OF THE NATIONAL DEBT

The burden of a national debt is difficult to estimate. It has been argued that a discussion of the burden is only relevant in relation to external debt as internal debt merely represents a transfer of resources within the economy. Such a transfer can, however, impose a burden on individuals and on the economy.

Internal burden

Interest payment and repayment of capital has to come out of taxation, if the loans have been spent on current consumption or 'unproductive investment' and results in transfer of income from the taxpayers to investors in government stocks. If they are not one and the same person then the tax burden falls on the taxpayers. When the taxpayers are also the investors, then they effectively pay interest to themselves out of their taxes; but they are again taxed on the interest they receive. The opportunity cost of government borrowing – the foregone use of resources for productive purposes in the private sectors – can result in a burden on the whole domestic economy, if as a result economic growth declines.

External burden

The burden of an external debt is greater than that of a debt that is held internally. The reasons for this are:

(i) Foreign loans have to be repaid, whereas internal borrowing can be transformed into permanent national debt, or the repayment can be postponed by a conversion to longer dated stock.

(ii) Interest charges on external loans are determined by the lender and the government has no control over them.

(iii) A fall in the value of the borrower's currency in internal money markets increases the burden of interest payments and of repayment of capital.

(iv) Payments have to be made at a time specified by the lender and not at the convenience of the borrower.

(v) Default on either interest or capital repayment results in penalties for the defaulting country, making it difficult for it to obtain credit in the future.

(vi) Resources are lost to a country as foreign currency has to be used in payment of interest and this means that it is not available to buy imports, or for other purposes.

(vii) The balance of payments will worsen both on the capital and on the current account unless the proceeds of the loans have been used to increase exports of home industries or result in a decline of imports.

(viii) Loss of sovereignty is an indirect price of foreign loans. There are usually conditions attached to them, particularly if they are from international institutions such as the International Monetary Fund, that may require a government to follow certain economic policies.

THE INTERNATIONAL MONETARY FUND (IMF)

The International Monetary Fund and the International Bank for Reconstruction and Development, established in 1945, were the outcome of the Bretton Woods Conference held in the preceding year to discuss financial problems in the aftermath of the Second World War.

The IMF is like an international club which countries can join and, on payment of a subscription, become entitled to facilities that are available to members. Originally there were 38, by 1992 membership had risen to 168 and by the late 1990s it is expected that most countries of any size will be included. The objectives of the IMF are to: (i) promote international monetary co-operation; (ii) facilitate the expansion of international trade and the achievement of a balanced pattern of trade; (iii) establish a multilateral payments system; and (iv) lessen the duration and extent of the disequilibrium in the balance of payments of member countries.

Resources

IMF resources come from members' contributions. Each country pays a quota related to its national income and its share of the world trade.

Seventy-five per cent of the quota is in the countries' own currency and twenty-five per cent in gold and foreign currency. More recently, Special Drawing Rights were added to this (see below). The quotas are periodically revised to take into account changes in countries' relative importance. The resources of the fund are further increased by loans from member countries.

Facilities

These contributions create a pool of foreign currencies on which members countries can draw (borrow) for a period between three to five years. The right to draw is in tranches or slices, which are related to a country's quota. The first tranche, referred to as the gold tranche, is automatic and amounts to 25 per cent of the quota and can be drawn by any member that has a balance of payments problem, with no questions asked. Subsequent tranches are subject to conditions and are progressively more difficult to obtain. For the first of the conditional tranches a member country has to show that it is making efforts to deal with its balance of payments problems. For the remaining tranches the member has to show, to the IMF's satisfaction, that the government is taking appropriate monetary and fiscal measures and following acceptable trade and exchange rate policies.

Charges

A country that draws on the Fund has to pay an annual charge (interest payment). The rate tends to be below the current market rates of interest.

Developments

The IMF showed relatively little activity until the mid-1950s. Its resources were limited and the field of international finance was dominated by the USA. Then currency crises developed and, in 1961, the ten richest members of the IMF set up a supplementary pool to support each other's currencies.

The International Monetary Fund was not originally intended to be a kind of credit-creating central bank that would operate on an international basis. It did not assume the responsibility for creation of international reserves until 1967 when the Special Drawing Rights were introduced.

Special Drawing Rights (SDR) were the first deliberate attempts by the international community to create international liquidity. SDR are a book-keeping entry in the accounts of the IMF. Member countries are allocated SDR in proportion to their quotas. The rights then become a reserve and can be used to make payments when imbalances between member countries arise. The value of SDR was fixed in terms of a basket of 16 major currencies of countries which had over 1 per cent of the share of world exports. Each currency was given a weight in relation to its importance in international trade – for example the USA has a weight of 33 per cent and the UK 9 per cent out of the total of 100 per cent for all the currencies in the market.

Oil facilities at the IMF

The Middle East oil crisis in 1973 led to large increases in the price of oil and oil-based chemicals. Developing countries were particularly affected by this and the Organisation of Petroleum Exporting Countries (OPEC) was asked to contribute to a special IMF account to help those of the Third World countries that ran into balance of payments difficulties. How much a country could borrow was determined by the oil related deficit.

THE INTERNATIONAL BANK FOR RECONSTRUCTION AND DEVELOPMENT

The World Bank, as it is usually now called, concentrates on lending to developing countries. Countries with a per capita gross national product of over US$4,300 (1992 – previously US$1000) do not as a rule borrow from the bank. Its funds come from the following sources: (i) member countries' subscriptions that are related to their IMF quotas – 10 per cent of a subscription is paid up and the rest represents a guarantee; (ii) issue of bonds in the world's capital markets; and (iii) net income from the bank's operations.

The World Bank investigates, supervises and finances projects that will lead to economic growth, but over the years the priorities have changed. Loans for which approval was given were largely for schemes with emphasis on: *Phase 1, infrastructure,* such as transport, power or water supplies; *Phase 2, diversification* in agriculture and the development of productive potential; *Phase 3, socially-orientated projects* with no immediate return. The bank charges interest on its loans but since countries borrow from it to a large extent for 'productive' purposes, this helps to mitigate the burden of their national debt; *Phase 4, environment* became a major issue in the 1990s and the Bank embarked on a National Environmental Plan on a country-by-country basis. In considering individual projects it now takes environmental implications into account.

SUMMARY

1. National debt is the result of borrowing by the government. It is internal debt if the loans have been raised in the domestic money market, and external debt if the money comes from abroad.
2. In the UK the national debt consists of central government borrowing on its own account and on behalf of the nationalised industries. Direct borrowing by local authorities is not included.
3. The government issues stocks, bonds and certificates in return for the money lent to it. Those government issues that can be traded are the marketable debt.
4. To attract funds government stocks have to be offered of a type that investors want and at a price and yield that will appeal to them.
5. An important innovation has been the issue of index-linked bonds. Indexation protects the value of an investment from erosion by inflation.
6. National debt performs a useful function. It provides an outlet for small savings and an asset for investors in general and for various institutions, including banks that need to keep some of their reserves in a safe and relatively liquid form.
7. National debt is a liability for a country. Some loans do not have to be repaid; others mature on specific dates. An attempt to repay national debt by means of sinking funds has not been successful. The burden of national debt is greater when the money has been borrowed from abroad. It has to be repaid and can adversely affect the balance of payments.
8. The government can use the national debt as a tool of its monetary policy.
9. The need to exercise control over the increase in the national debt has led to the introduction of public sector borrowing requirements.
10. The International Monetary Fund is concerned with promotion of international trade and financial assistance to member countries. In the past, The UK has borrowed from the IMF.

SUGGESTED FURTHER READING

J. Alexander and S. Toland, 'Measuring the Public Sector Borrowing Requirement', *Economic Trends* (London: HMSO, August 1980).
A.S. Courakis (ed.), *Private Behaviour and Government Policy in Interdependent Economies* (Oxford: Clarendon Press, 1991).

HM Treasury, 'The Public Sector Borrowing Requirement', *Economic Briefing,* no. 6 (1994).

HM Treasury, *The Budget* (London: HM Treasury, 1993).

International Bank for Reconstruction and Development, *Annual Reports.*

International Monetary Fund, *Annual Reports.*

P.M. Jackson (ed.), *Current Issues in Public Sector Economics* (London: Macmillan, 1992).

R. Musgrave and P. Musgrave, *Public Finance in Theory and Practice* (New York: McGraw-Hill, 1989).

C.T. Sandford, *The Economics of Public Finance* (Oxford: Pergamon Press, 1992).

EXERCISES

1. 'A national debt can be an asset as well as a liability'. Consider the validity of this statement.
2. What are the advantages and disadvantages of index-linked government stock?
3. Why is the burden of external debt generally regarded as heavier than that of internal debt?
4. Explain the reasons for and consequences of the public sector borrowing requirement.
5. In what ways does borrowing from the IMF differ from loans from private lenders abroad?

15 Local Government Finance

ORGANISATION AND FUNCTIONS OF LOCAL GOVERNMENT

The UK is governed by a two-tier system of government: the central government and local government in the form of local authorities (which in turn are subdivided into county, urban and district councils). They are the only political bodies, besides Parliament, that are elected by the people and play an important part in preserving democracy. Local authorities are answerable to the electorate but they are not sovereign bodies – they derive their powers from Parliament. These powers are circumscribed by statutes.

The organisation and functions of the local authorities have evolved over the years. Local government in its modern form emerged towards the end of the nineteenth century. The Redcliffe-Maud and Wheatley Royal Commissions led to a further reorganisation of local government in England and Wales. This was carried out in 1974 under the Local Government Act 1972 in England and Wales and the 1973 Act in Scotland, but structural changes in local government were undertaken without providing for changes in the methods of finance. The financial arrangements of the local authorities came increasingly under criticism. Eventually a Committee of Enquiry into Local Government was appointed. Its report on Local Government Finance (Cmnd. 6453, 1976), known as the Layfield Report, was an important study of the problems of Local Government finance which showed a need for the construction of a coherent financial system that would reflect the roles in the public sector of the central and local government.

As these roles began to change in the 1980s and 1990s the structure of local government and its finance once again came under scrutiny. The government announced the establishment of the Local Government Commission to look at the structure (in England) and to suggest improvements, and the Secretary of State for Wales issued a consultative document in 1991. Local government structure (Table 15.1) in the UK developed over the years. The present system in England was created by the London Government Act 1963 and Local Government Acts of 1972 and 1985. In Wales the structure dates back to 1974 and in Scotland to 1975. Dissatisfaction with the organisation of local authorities has arisen because:

(i) There are problems in co-ordinating activities of the different tiers of local government that are responsible for closely-linked services, such as housing and social services. This can lead to duplication of work and waste of resources in administration and finance.

(ii) Division of the responsibilities of the local authorities is not clear. For example, when it is a district council that sends out bills for local tax and collects revenue whereas the county Council spends most of the money.

(iii) There is no clearly perceived accountability to the public.

Table 15.1   The structure of local government in the UK, 1994

	England		*Wales*
non-metropolitan counties (39)	metropolitan counties (6)	Greater London	Counties (8)
Non-metropolitan districts (296)	metropolitan districts (36)	London boroughs (32)	districts (37)
	*parishes (10,000)	City of London (1)	Community Councils (865)

	Scotland		*Northern Ireland*
Regions (9)	Island Councils		district councils
Districts (53)	single tier (for three island areas)		single tier (36)

Notes:
* some areas are not within any parish.
Counties, districts, regions and boroughs have elected councils.
Figures in brackets show the number of local authorities in each group.

The underlying assumption of the present system has been that local authorities would provide services directly to the public. This has changed. In the 1980s and 1990s local authorities instead of being providers of services have increasingly become purchasers and enablers of services provided on their behalf by private sector firms and voluntary organisations. This has meant changes in the functions of local authorities. Central government wanted them to 'concentrate more on identifying local needs, co-ordinating and targeting resources, setting standards for quality of service, and monitoring performance and cost effectiveness' (Consultative Paper, 1991).

By the end of the 1990s a new structure of local government will be in place. The objective is to establish a basis for: (i) Clearer accountability to the local electorate; (ii) Better co-ordination in the provision of local services, leading to improved quality and cost effectiveness; (iii) Greater administrative efficiency, which should lead in due course to a reduced burden on taxpayers.

FEATURES OF A FINANCIAL SYSTEM

To perform their functions local authorities need a sound financial system. Its requirements are as follows:

(a) *Accountability*. This means more than the keeping of accounts and involves the management and control of both expenditure and revenue. Local authorities have to be answerable to the local electorate.

(b) *Fairness*. The system should be equitable in provision of benefits and the distribution of the burden of local taxation among individuals and between areas. This requires a formula for redistribution of resources from richer to poorer authorities to equalise their means.

(c) *Indicativeness*. Financial arrangements should be indicative of the consequences of policy decisions on consumption and investment.

(d) *Clarity*. The system of raising revenue and of providing benefits should be comprehensible, not only to the decision-makers but also to the electorate.

(e) *Stability and Flexibility*. Financial arrangements that provide both stability and flexibility are difficult to implement in practice since they are of somewhat incompatible nature.

PROVISION OF PUBLIC GOODS AND SERVICES

Certain goods and services are provided only by central government (e.g. defence – the armed forces) and others only by local government (e.g. refuse disposal). Provision of some is a joint responsibility (e.g. education). Finance arrangements have been complicated by the reorganisations of local authorities and by the fact that they represent a three-tier system of local government. There are over 500 local authorities in Britain, varying in both size and resources. The largest authority covers some 1.5 million acres and

Table 15.2 Functions of local authorities

(a) Responsibility (X) for some major services in English local authorities

	Metropolitan		Non-metropolitan		London area			
	Joint Authorities	District Councils	County Councils	District Councils	City of London	London Boroughs	London fire and Civil Defence	Metropolitan Police
Education		X	X		X	X		
Housing		X		X	X	X		
Planning applications		X		X	X	X		
Strategic planning		X	X		X	X		
Transport planning		X	X		X	X		
Passenger transport [1]	X		X					
Highways		X	X		X	X		
Police	X		X		X			X
Fire	X		X				X	
Social services		X	X		X	X		
Libraries		X	X		X	X		

Leisure and recreation		X		X	X X X
Refuse collection		X		X	X X X
Refuse disposal ²	X	X X			X
Environmental health		X		X	X X X
Local taxation		X		X X	X X

Notes:

¹Passenger transport in London is provided by London Regional Transport which is outside the local authority sector.

²Refuse disposal for some areas of London is carried out by separate waste disposal authorities.

(b) Example for Scotland

	Regional council	District council	Islands council
Refuse collection		X	X
Fire service	X		X

Source: General Statistics Service, *Local Government Statistics* (London: HMSO, 1993–4).

the smallest 1,000 acres. In some fields, local authorities exercise considerable autonomy. Generally speaking, they are responsible for services of a local nature. What they do depends on the type of authority involved (see Table 15.2). Changes in the authorities' functions require an Act of Parliament. Over the years they have shed some old and acquired some new functions. For instance local authorities ceased to supply electricity and gas and this became the responsibility of the public corporations. The social security system shifted the bulk of the burden of providing relief to the poor and sick from the local governments to the central government (DSS) and the National Health Service. The *Local Education Reform Act (1988)* enabled schools, if they so wished, to 'opt out' of local authority control. In 1993, responsibility for sixth form colleges and further education was transferred to the Further Education Funding Council and local authorities relinquished control over polytechnics. These institutions became universities and are now financed by the Higher Education Funding Council. Local authorities acquired some new responsibilities out of choice, such as the running of lotteries. Others were imposed on them by the central government in pursuit of national policies to achieve specific objectives. One such policy is concerned with care of people in the community. The *National Health Service and Community Care Act (1990)* gave local authorities a greater role in the development of community care, and in 1993 they became responsible for implementing the new community care legislation.

Prescribed Standards

A range of public services such as health and education are in part provided by the local authorities but since the services belong to a system operating on a national basis, the authorities have to maintain comparable standards.

The *Education Reform Act (1988)* legislated for the progressive introduction of the National Curriculum in primary and secondary schools. To implement this policy, the Department of Education and Science (as it was then called) funded the National Curriculum Council and the Welsh Office set up the Curriculum Council for Wales. National attainment targets were set and provisions were made for assessment and national tests for children at the age of 7, 11 and 14 prior to public examinations such as the General Certificate of Secondary Education (GCSE). This gave rise to opposition from teachers and under pressure the Department for Education modified the curriculum and reduced the extent of testing.

In 1994 the Department sent the new Parent's Charter to every home in the country to provide information on improvements taking place in our schools and the drive to raise standards. Some services, such as housing, need to conform to required technical specifications. Prescription of standards requires co-operation between the central and local government and division of the costs.

PATTERN AND GROWTH OF LOCAL AUTHORITIES' EXPENDITURE

The pattern of local authorities' expenditure has changed as their function and powers have altered. Since the end of the last century, over a period of nearly one hundred years, the share of total expenditure devoted to administration and to provision of law and order had declined whilst the relative importance of education and housing had increased. They are now major services in terms of combined current and capital expenditure (see Table 15.3).

In the past decade, the government's education reforms and the housing policy of selling council houses to tenants has had some impact on the pattern of local government expenditure. Increased crime rates have also increased the share of local authorities budgets allocated to law and order.

In the future, changes in the way that public sector services are delivered, contracting-out and privatisation, will have far-reaching implications for allocation of resources in the public sector. Political, economic and social developments which may be outside a local government's control are nevertheless reflected in their spending and the pattern of resource allocation. In the light of the experience of the last hundred years, local government expenditure is likely to keep on rising.

Growth of Local Authorities' Expenditure

The growth of local authorities' expenditure has not been confined to any one geographical area. Total expenditure increased in: (i) absolute terms, from £50m to £33,000m, over the period 1890 to 1980; and (ii) in relative terms, from about 3 per cent to some 23 per cent of national income when both current and capital expenditure are taken into account. This growth had not, however, been continuous throughout the period. During time of wars, local authorities' spending, which was mainly of a civilian nature, was held down and became subordinate to the central government expenditure, which increased more steeply as a larger proportion of it was for military purposes. In the 1980s and 1990s

Table 15.3   Local authorities' expenditure: (a) current, (b) capital account

(a) EXPENDITURE (£m)	1982	1990	1991	1992
Final consumption:				
Current expenditure on goods and services:				
General public services	536	1 950	2 242	2 482
Civil defence	10	29	32	32
Public order and safety:				
Police	2 415	4 962	5 753	6 219
Fire services	569	1 111	1 273	1 357
Law courts	274	590	698	724
Education	11 229	18 719	20 610	21 958
Social security:				
Concessionary fares	275	399	419	433
Housing benefit administration	7	379	297	284
Personal social services	2 372	5 022	5 725	6 122
Housing and community amenity:				
Housing	140	303	363	395
Community development	380	620	699	786
Sanitary services	1 178	1 823	1 989	2 135
Street lighting	181	255	252	265
Recreational and cultural affairs	1 110	2 176	2 375	2 360
Agriculture (including land drainage and coast protection)	101	55	39	34
Mining manufacturing and construction:				
Consumer protection	61	120	137	153
Transport and communication	1 229	1 961	1 938	1 963
Other economic affairs and services	90	169	191	204
Total	22 157	40 643	45 032	47 906
Non-trading capital consumption	1 206	2 183	2 088	1 995
Total final consumption	23 363	42 826	47 120	49 901
Subsidies:				
Housing	571	129	–	–
Water supply	25	–	–	–
Passenger transport	656	263	286	315
Other economic affairs and services	173	273	299	311
Current grants to personal sector:				
Education	1021	1 453	2 250	2 794
Rent rebates and allowances	275	4 481	5 627	7 088
Debt interest:				
On loans from central government	1 747	4 628	4 648	4 476
Other	2 551	843	664	550
Total current expenditure	30 382	54 896	60 894	65 435

Table 15.3   (continued)

(b) EXPENDITURE (£m)	1982	1990	1991	1992
Gross domestic fixed capital formation:				
General public services	332	511	468	563
Civil defence	–	3	2	2
Public order and safety:				
Police	99	205	187	227
Fire service	39	73	59	68
Law courts	11	85	52	89
Education	488	1 026	901	968
Social security:				
Personal social services	87	248	194	184
Housing and community amenity:				
Housing	–297	1 310	824	863
Community development	119	73	167	167
Water supply	31	69	76	97
Sanitary services	113	229	211	204
Street lighting	20	20	15	18
Recreational and cultural affairs	259	663	601	376
Fuel and energy	–	–	–	–
Agriculture (including land drainage and coast protection)	140	25	38	25
Mining manufacturing and construction	2	–	–	–
Transport and communication	655	1 521	1 281	1 609
Other economic affairs and services	109	183	191	195
Total	2 207	6 244	5 267	5 655
Capital grants to personal sector				
Housing	428	848	1 063	1 198
Capital grants to public corporations				
Transport and communication	116	16	16	16
Total capital expenditure	2 751	7 108	6 346	6 869

Source: CSO Blue Book, *UK National Accounts*, annually (1993).

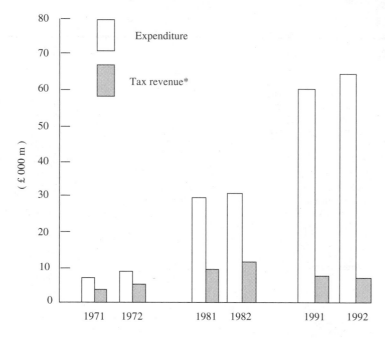

Figure 15.1   Local authorities' expenditure and tax revenue

Note:

*Tax: Rates, replaced by Community Charge. This, in turn, was later replaced by the Council Tax.

Source: CSO, Blue Book, *National Accounts for the UK* and *Local Government Statistics* (annually).

central government measures to reign back local authorities' spending have slowed down the rate of growth. It has, however, continued on its upward trend (Figure 15.1).

REASONS FOR GROWTH

The reasons for an increase in local authorities' expenditure are similar to those that account for the rise in central government spending (see p. 82). They reflect the extensions of the range of services and of the scale and provision and rising costs. Some of the following factors that affected the overall level of expenditure of the public sector have had specific implications for local authorities.

(a) *Demographic changes* have affected various areas differently. Local authorities with a high proportion of children of school age or with many elderly, retired people, have had to spend more to provide facilities for them.

(b) *The mobility of population* has created problems for influx areas resulting in an additional demand for education, housing and other services. The outflow areas have not experienced a corresponding drop in demands on them. Many village schools still have to be kept open even when the number of children attending them has dropped. Street lights cannot be turned off, though fewer people may live in a town. Facilities may not be fully utilised but they are still needed and cost money.

(c) *Depressions and recessions* recurring in the last sixty years have resulted in measures not just by the central government but also by local authorities to deal with the consequences.

(d) *Inflation* has affected both the private and the public sector, but local authorities are particularly vulnerable as they are labour intensive. Pay awards, made to bring the wages of council employees more in line with earnings of industrial workers, have increased the local authorities' wages bill considerably.

(e) *High interest rates*, which were part of the government's policy to counteract inflation, have increased the cost of local authorities' borrowing. They have to pay more for their loans than does central government.

(f) *Public expectation* of improvements in the quality, range and level of provision of services made it difficult for governments facing re-elections to cut down the growth in public expenditure.

SOURCES OF FINANCE

Local authorities obtain money to finance their expenditure from the following sources: (i) a local tax; (ii) charges for some services provided; (iii) government grants; and (iv) loans. The first two sources are largely under their own control.

RATES

Rates, levied until 1990, were the oldest major source of local authorities' revenue, dating back to 1601 and for a long time they were the most important one. They were imposed on occupiers of non-agricultural land, domestic dwellings and on industrial and commercial properties. Rates can therefore be regarded either as a tax on capital, or real estate, or as a tax on the use of land and buildings and consequently as a tax on consumption. Liability to rates was determined by reference to: (i) the rateable value and (ii) the rate poundage of the property. Rateable value was taken in most cases to be the net annual value, being the amount for which the property could be let. Valuation on this basis was a somewhat theoretical exercise in the case of domestic dwellings, since approximately 50 per cent of households lived in owner-occupier houses and most of the rest in local authority houses. An open market in rented property had virtually disappeared as a result of rent controls and legislation to provide security of tenure. There was no satisfactory way in such circumstances of determining what a 'going' rent would be.

The basis of rating remained substantially unchanged from 1840 until the *Local Government Act (1948)* when the valuation of domestic property in England and Wales, but not in Scotland, was transferred to the Inland Revenue. In their evidence to the Layfield Committee, the Inland Revenue emphasised the increasing difficulty of valuing domestic property in the absence of information on the open market rents that was: (i) adequate; (ii) continuing; (iii) covering the whole country; and (iv) relating to all types of property. The Inland Revenue had undertaken revaluation of properties, but this had not been done either regularly or frequently. Valuations consequently did not fully reflect changes in the price level of property.

The right of appeal was therefore an important safeguard. A ratepayer could appeal against a valuation, first to the valuation officer then to the Local Valuation Court and lastly to the Lands Tribunal, the decision of which was final except on a point of law.

Rate poundage can be regarded as a rate of tax which is expressed as so many pence per £1 and, when applied to rateable value of properties, determines the liability of ratepayers and the size of local authorities' revenue. *Penny product* showed the yield of rate of one penny in the pound of rateable value after a deduction of the costs of collecting the revenue.

Arguments in Favour of and Against Rates

Rates as a form of taxation that was available to local government had a number of advantages. The arguments in their favour rested on the following grounds:

(i) Rates have been levied for over three hundred years. Once tax-payers get used to a tax system they tend to resent old established taxes less than new ones. There was therefore a case on this ground for leaving rates well alone.

(ii) The tax base for rates was wide and they provided a substantial yield (see p. 314) without imposing a heavy tax burden on individual households. The Layfield Committee estimated that payment of net rates, after a deduction for rebates, represented 1.9 per cent of their incomes for all households.

(iii) The cost of collection of rates was relatively low compared with that of other taxes.

(iv) There was no scope for evasion of rates as they were levied on visible and immovable property.

(v) The property tax was located within the area of the taxing authority, and the tax base could not be shifted to take advantage of lower rates that some other local authorities might levy.

(vi) The tax base was certain, in the sense that local authorities knew what revenue a rate poundage applied to the rateable property would produce. Rateable values did not fluctuate during a year, although the number of properties that were assessed might change as old buildings were demolished or new ones built.

(vii) The yield was also predictable in a way that revenue from other taxes was not. Proceeds of indirect taxation depended on consumption that could change substantially during a period. Yields of direct taxes were difficult to predict if during the year changes in the level of employment were expected. A local authority treasurer could estimate more accurately revenue from domestic rates, since if the unemployed persons were not able to pay them, the Department of Health and Social Security (as it was then designated) paid on their behalf. The yield from business rates, however, was more difficult to forecast. Some firms might go out of business unexpectedly and close the factories. Other firms might move into the local authority's areas and become liable to rate payment.

(viii) The taxing authority was also the spending authority in the area and was accountable to local electorate.

(ix) Taxpayers, in theory, knew in advance what their tax liability in a forthcoming year would be and could make payments in instalments, though later supplementary rate demands had undermined the validity of this argument.

There were also several arguments against rates which can be briefly stated as follows:

(i) Rates were not related to the ability to pay and tended to impose a relatively greater burden on people with smaller incomes. The assumption that people who live in bigger houses have bigger incomes and a greater ability to pay more in rates was not necessarily true.

(ii) The amount paid in rates was not related to the benefits received by the ratepayer as a result of local authority expenditure, so that there was no 'compensation' to mitigate the burden of rates. An old age pensioner's household with a small income could have paid more in rates than a large family with higher earnings who also benefited from the local authority expenditure, e.g. on education.

(iii) Rates had to be paid out of disposable income in relatively large lump sums, even when payment was on an instalment basis.

(iv) Rates lacked buoyancy. Revenue did not rise with inflation as did the yield of income tax or the proceeds of *ad valorem* taxes when prices went up.

Modification of the Rate System

An attempt has been made to reduce the regressiveness of rates as a form of taxation. As a result of the findings of the Committee of Inquiry into the Impact of Rates on Households (the Allen Committee Report, 1965), the central government introduced a rent rebate scheme whereby it bore some 90 per cent of the cost of rent rebates. People on social security could have had their rates paid for them entirely. Other could have had the rate burden reduced by a rebate which was related to the means of the ratepayer. It had been estimated that over 50 per cent of households received some rate rebate. In this way rates were to some extent related to the ability to pay but the regressiveness of this form of taxation has not been altogether eliminated. The burden of rates on small incomes was greatly increased in 1980–81 as a result of supplementary rate demands by local authorities that expanded their expenditure programmes.

THE COMMUNITY CHARGE

The Community Charge, or as it was generally known, the 'Poll Tax', replaced rates in 1990 as the local tax. In spite of modifications, rates remained unpopular with the general public and the main political parties. The Labour Government had, for some years, been examining ways of making rates more acceptable or of replacing them. The Conservative Party when still in opposition in 1974 committed itself to the abolition of rates and eventually, after much consultation, did so.

The new tax was short-lived. Whereas rates had been levied for over three hundred years, the Community Charge lasted for only 3 years. It took the form of a flat rate of tax payable by all adults with few exceptions, hence the reason why it became known as the Poll (or 'head') Tax. It was levied on the principle of the benefit theory of taxation (see p. 115) which postulates that all who benefit from the state should contribute to its finance. The problem was that some people had low incomes. In their case their tax liability was reduced to 20 per cent and the rest was, as if it were, paid by the state on their behalf. Nevertheless they still had to pay the 20 per cent and many claimed they could not do so. The amount of the Community Charge was determined by the charging local authority and differed between local authority areas.

The non-domestic rate, that is the tax on businesses, was collected by the charging authorities – district councils, Council of the Isles, and in London the borough councils – within whose area the business property was located. The proceeds were then paid into a central national non-domestic rating pool (NNDR) and distributed to the various local authorities on a capitation basis – that is on the basis of adult resident population.

Arguments *in favour* of the tax were:

(a) It was a 'visible' tax since everybody had to contribute something. The public would have an incentive to put pressure on local authorities to keep their expenditure down. Under the rate system there was no such incentive as some two-thirds of the citizens did not pay them.

(b) It was a fairer tax in the sense the burden of financing provision of public goods and services would be more evenly distributed as the tax base was wider than under the rate system.

(c) The charge had no disincentive effect since it was unrelated to income (apart from the 20 per cent liability) and would not discourage unemployed people from seeking jobs.

(d) As the charge was not based on property it did not add to the cost of housing and affect inflation.

Such arguments however failed to convince people of the merits of the Community Charge.

For local authorities it was: (i) expensive to collect and (ii) lacked buoyancy and increases in poundage were necessary if revenue were to be increased; this made councils unpopular and did not help politicians get re-elected; (iii) the charge bore little relationship to the use of services made by the taxpayers.

They considered it unfair because it was not related to the ability to pay and it was regressive, imposing a heavier burden on people with lower incomes.

Community Charge demands were not paid, and court actions and custodial sentences followed. There were widespread protests and a spectacular riot in London in March 1990 which started with a march of some 200,000 people objecting to the introduction of the poll tax. This gave a foretaste of the civil disobedience that ensued on a scale unprecedented in the UK.

COUNCIL TAX

The government capitulated and in April 1993 scrapped the Community Charge replacing it with a Council Tax. It is a tax on property reminiscent of the rates, but featuring some improvements to make it more fair.

The Council Tax is paid by residents to a local authority, based on the market value of their dwellings, that is the price the property would have fetched if it had been sold 1st April 1991. The amount of tax payable depends on the valuation band. Owners or tenants of dwellings in the lowest band A will pay less in Council Tax than those in band H (Table 15.4). This, to some extent, takes ability to pay into account on the assumption that a person in a house worth more than £320,000 can afford to pay more in Council Tax than somebody living in a £40,000 house.

Use of local authorities' services is also taken into account in that the full Council Tax bill is calculated on the assumption that there are two adults living in a dwelling that is their main home. If there is only one resident the bill is reduced by 25 per cent.

Exemptions

Certain groups of people are exempt from Council Tax. They include: students, monks and nuns, people in prison, except for those who are there

Table 15.4 Council Tax valuation bands for dwellings

Valuation Band	Range of Values*
A	up to and including £40,000
B	£40,001 to £52,000
C	£52,001 to £68,000
D	£68,001 to £88,000
E	£88,001 to £120,000
F	£12,001 to £160,000
G	£160,001 to £320,000
H	More than £320,000

Note: *Each dwelling has been allocated to one of eight bands according to its open market capital value at 1 April 1991. Each band of property pays a different relative amount of Council Tax.

for non-payment of Council Tax.

Council Tax Benefit up to the maximum of 100 per cent is granted to people on low incomes to help them to pay their Council Tax. Entitlement depends on the level of a person's income, capital (savings) and family circumstances.

Business Rates

Businesses are taxed under the provisions of the *National Non-domestic Rates Act (1993)*. Introduction of a uniform national business rate has the advantage that it does not distort the location of industrial, commercial and financial undertakings. In the past, local authorities in greatest need of the influx of new businesses to relieve local unemployment, had a small tax base and little choice but to charge high rates which discouraged immigration of firms.

NEW SOURCES OF REVENUE

To preserve local authorities' independence, various new sources of revenue have been suggested either as additions or as alternatives to the existing ones. The new revenue could be under the authorities' own control or represent a proportion of national taxation assigned to them.

Different local taxes that were considered were: (i) local income tax, (ii) local sales tax, (iii) local motor vehicle tax, (iv) local payroll tax. Alternatively, it was suggested that the central government could assign to the local authorities a certain proportion of one of the national taxes – income tax, corporation tax, VAT or motor vehicle licence revenue.

The Layfield Committee found in favour of a local income tax as an additional revenue to rates. A local income tax has the advantages and disadvantages of a national income tax but there are additional problems arising out of the imposition of two separate taxes on income. Administrative and collection costs are likely to rise, whether the two taxes were imposed independently or jointly by the central government and the local authorities. At the local level the system would become more complex as the new tax was added to the rates. Neither the Labour Government nor the succeeding (1979) Conservative Government found the idea of a local income tax attractive and they took no steps to introduce it. Local authorities still have only one tax of their own – the Council Tax.

CHARGES AND FEES

It is Parliament that decides which services local authorities have to finance out of taxation and for which they may make a charge. The power to levy charges is subject to statutory provisions. The level of charges is, to a large extent, at the discretion of the local authorities, though under the *Housing Finance Act (1972)* rents for housing have to represent eventually a fair rent.

The services to which charges apply are those that: (i) benefit the consumers personally and directly; (ii) give them the choice whether to avail themselves of particular goods and services; and (iii) allow for individual or household consumption to be measured. Public transport provides an example of such a service. A person going on a bus benefits personally from public transport. They do not have to travel by bus, but if they do, the length of the journey can be determined and they can be charged accordingly. Of the services for which local authorities make charges the most important has been housing, in terms of capital expenditure, subsidies required and revenue receipts. The importance of housing in local authorities' budgets has, however, declined as the government pursued a policy of selling dwellings to tenants.

THE MARKET MECHANISM IN THE PUBLIC SECTOR

A system of fees and charges for local authority services has the merit that it is indicative of the demand for different services and of the value that consumers put on them. This helps to allocate resources in relation to public preference, to avoid waste and over-supply. Would-be consumers who lack the means to purchase the necessary services can be helped by such measures as: (i) rent rebates in the case of housing, (ii) reduced fares on public transport for children and pensioners, (iii) total exemption from charges for some services on the basis of a means test (e.g. provision of a place in a home for the elderly).

PRICING POLICIES OF LOCAL AUTHORITIES

Local authorities can impose charges for some social services and for trading services. Their pricing policies are based on various principles. The price that a consumer pays may be one of the following:

(a) *Cost price.* Charges for such social services as children's homes and homes for the elderly are intended to cover the cost of provision of the facilities.

(b) *Subsidised price.* A price may be reduced by a subsidy and goods or services are then made available at the subsidised price to everybody or to some people only, on the basis of a qualification. For some years now, the government policy has been to do away with subsidies.

(c) *Economic price.* Charges for trading services are more likely than those for social services to be based on the principle of an economic price that allows not only for costs to be covered but for profit to be made. It can be argued that there is no reason why local authorities should provide some entertainment or recreational services, e.g. golf courses at prices below that which the market will bear. They can then use the profits generated to finance other services or to reduce Council Tax.

(d) *Deterrent prices.* Charges based on the deterrent principle are not intended primarily to provide revenue but to achieve a specific objective, such as a reduction in city traffic congestion by heavy parking charges to motorists bringing cars into a city centre.

Competition in Provision of Certain Services

To improve provision of goods and services and to achieve better value for money, local authorities are now required by the government to be competitive. Services such as refuse collection, or maintenance of public parks, can be undertaken by local authorities themselves through *Direct Labour Organisations* (DLOs) or by firms in the private sector, depending on the outcome of *competitive tendering*. Direct Labour Organisations legislation has resulted in a considerable amount of work being contracted out to outside contractors by local authorities, which have become purchasers of services instead of being direct providers. Exposing them to competition and market forces was seen as a way of improving cost-effectiveness. The process was met with considerable opposition.

Opponents of contracting-out argued that:

(i) Such competition would make long-term strategy for delivery of services more difficult.

(ii) Labour relations would suffer.

(iii) Employment opportunities in local government would be adversely affected.

(iv) Earnings would drop as private contractors were likely to pay lower wages.

(v) Lower costs of providing services would be reflected in lower standards of service.

(vi) Setting targets and ensuring that standards of commercially-run services were maintained would create problems.

The question arises not only as to what standards of provision of public services can the public reasonably expect, but also what would be ideally desirable and what is an acceptable and affordable standard.

THE FINANCIAL SYSTEM OF LOCAL AUTHORITIES

The present system reflects a number of changes that the government has introduced since 1990. Proceeds of the local tax (now the Council Tax), income from charges, grants, and other receipts are paid into local authorities' General Funds (Figure 15.2) and used to finance their expenditure programmes. What the government considers to be the appropriate provision is indicated by the *Total Standard Spending* (TSS). Support for this is provided through *Aggregate External Finance*. This includes non-domestic rates (business tax) and a variety of grants.

Inadequate revenue from local tax and charges to finance the increased expenditure of local authorities has meant a greater reliance by town halls on grants from the central government, which transfers some of the proceeds from national taxation to the local authorities by means of grants. Grants include the following:

(a) *Revenue Support Grant* is the most important of the grants. It has replaced the Rate Support Grant which was considered to be unsatisfactory as it enabled high spending authorities to get bigger grants on the basis of their past expenditure. The new Revenue Support Grant does not vary with the spending of an individual local authority.

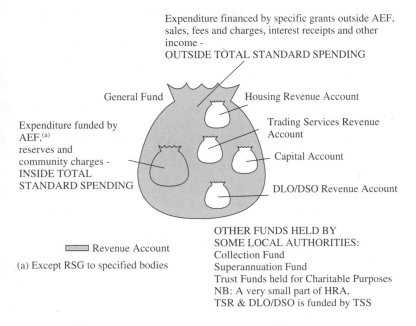

Expenditure financed by specific grants outside AEF,
sales, fees and charges, interest receipts and other
income -
OUTSIDE TOTAL STANDARD SPENDING

General Fund

Housing Revenue Account

Expenditure funded by
AEF,[a]
reserves and
community charges -
INSIDE TOTAL
STANDARD SPENDING

Trading Services Revenue
Account

Capital Account

DLO/DSO Revenue Account

▭ Revenue Account

(a) Except RSG to specified bodies

OTHER FUNDS HELD BY
SOME LOCAL AUTHORITIES:
Collection Fund
Superannuation Fund
Trust Funds held for Charitable Purposes
NB: A very small part of HRA,
TSR & DLO/DSO is funded by TSS

Figure 15.2   The structure of local authority general funds

Notes:
AEF: Aggregate External Finance; DLO/DSO: Direct Labour Organisation and
Direct Services Organisation; RSG: Rate Support Grant (replaced by Revenue
Support Grant; HRA: Housing Revenue Account; TSR: Trading Services
Revenue; TSS: Total Standard Spending; GREA: Grant Related Expenditure
Assessment by Standard Spending Assessment (SSA).

Source: General Statistics Service, *Local Government Statistics* (London: HMSO,
1993–94).

(b) *Specific grants* have to be used by the local authorities for the
   purpose for which they have been allocated.
(c) *Supplementary grants* are given to finance for example national
   parks that are the authority's responsibility.
(d) *Transitional grants* are paid to local authorities to help cover
   certain costs arising, for example, from changes in local government finance e.g. Council Tax Preparation Grant (1992–93) or some
   short term obligation, e.g. Yugoslav Displaced Persons Grant.

Specific grants are usually fixed as a percentage of the expenditure on
particular projects and the size of supplementary grants is at the discretion
of the Secretary of State for the Environment.

The purpose of a system comprising a variety of grants is to achieve a range of objectives, such as to: (i) enable local authorities to provide services at a required level and of comparable standard by equalising their resources; (ii) encourage them to undertake specific projects; and (iii) influence the pattern of local government expenditure and to exercise some control over the total amount spent.

Grants from the European Community for regional development are available to local authorities in the UK. The *European Regional Development Fund* (ERDF) helps to finance local authorities' expenditure on certain investment projects that have an impact on the structure of the regional economy.

The disadvantage of the grant system is that it reduces local authorities' independence – the central government pays the piper and calls the tune. Critics of the system have also argued that it encourages excessive spending by local authorities. Increases in expenditure add little to the local tax burden since the cost of providing benefits falls largely on the central governments. Local taxpayers, therefore, stand to gain more than they lose and the local electorate does not have an incentive to check increases in spending.

CHANGES IN LOCAL AUTHORITIES' CAPITAL FINANCE AND BORROWING

A new system of capital finance of local government projects came into operation in April 1990. Instead of imposing annual limits on expenditure as in the past, the government now applies control to the sources from which local authorities can obtain finance. These are:

1. Borrowing and credit arrangements, within the levels of credit approvals issued by the government each year.
2. Capital grants from central government.
3. Usable receipts, that is those which are not required to be set aside as the authority's provision for credit liabilities. Generally, authorities are required to set aside 75 per cent of receipts from the sale of council houses and 50 per cent of most other receipts.
4. Revenue (current revenue or accumulated revenue balances). Traditionally, local authorities have been able to borrow from: (i) central government through the Public Works Loan Board; (ii) the domestic money market – banks, insurance companies, other financial institutions and from individuals and business; (iii) foreign lenders. Borrowing from abroad requires Treasury approval.

BUDGET AND POLICIES

An increasing number of local authorities have adopted a corporate management system. The budget preparatory work is done by the authority's Policy and Resources Committee and the Corporate Management team. Preparation of a budget requires forecasts of the following variables:

(i) *Local authorities' resources.* The anticipated revenue will depend on the authority's own ability to raise revenue from its tax and charges and on the central government's support. Estimates of the yield from its tax will be made assuming different levels of tax that would be required to finance different levels of expenditure.

(ii) *Local authorities' needs.* The level of expenditure will be determined by statutory obligations to provide certain services and by the authorities' own policies and those of the central government, and by factors outside the control of either of them, such as demographic changes.

(iii) *Borrowing requirement.* The need to borrow will depend on the cost of capital projects approved, less any resources available to finance them. The ability to borrow will, among other factors, depend on the central government's policy on the public sector borrowing requirement.

Finally a budget is agreed on.

Capping

Local authorities are given the opportunity by the government to constrain their budgets voluntarily in the light of the capping criteria that it announces ahead of the time when their budgets are set. An authority that produces a budget that the Secretary of State considers to be excessive or way above the previous year's level is then 'capped'. The following figures illustrate the extent of capping:

Year	1990–91	1991–92	1992–93
Number of authorities capped	21	14	10

Political considerations

At any one time some local authorities' councils may be Conservative, Labour or Liberal Democrat and therefore not all will be of the same political persuasion as the central government. Their political philosophies as well as social and economic considerations are likely to be reflected in their budgets.

Policy

The freedom of local authorities to pursue their own policies is, however, restricted to some extent by the following factors: (i) statutory obligations imposed on them, such as Care in the Community; (ii) shortage of their own resources to finance expenditure requirements and increased reliance for finance on central government with a consequent loss of some independence.

Local authorities have no responsibility to manage their area's economy so as to stimulate or to restrict the total level of demand and of economic activity by means of a budgetary policy. Their actions do, however, have social, political and economic consequences that reinforce or weaken national policies of the central government. It has therefore become increasingly concerned to develop strategies for the whole of the public sector. Over recent years, there has been a gradual shift of economic and social power from local authorities to the central government. 'While the governing bodies of the cities, the municipal councils, lost one after another almost all their rights of self-government and were reduced to the position of unpaid agents of the state ... the staff of state officials, alike in the capital and in the provinces, grew in numbers and importance'. This observation does not come from some twentieth century Royal Commission but was made by a historian of the Roman empire. England and Wales ceased to be part of the Roman Empire in the first century AD. In Europe towards the end of the twentieth century similar changes were taking place and these will be discussed in Chapter 16.

SUMMARY

1. Local authorities are the second tier of government. They are elected bodies with statutory obligations to provide certain services.
2. Some functions are shared with the central government; others are the responsibility of local authorities alone.
3. The pattern of expenditure by public authorities has changed and there had been a sharp increase in their level of spending.
4. Local authorities finance their expenditure out of a local tax, charges, grants and borrowing.

5. Rates were a form of tax on property levied on domestic dwellings, industrial building and non-agricultural land. They were replaced by the Community Charge which was a capitation tax and became known as the 'Poll Tax'. It was highly unpopular and was in turn replaced by the Council Tax, based on the market value of dwellings. Businesses are now taxed at a uniform national rate.

6. Charges are made for certain services – the most important in terms of revenue are rents for council housing. Consumers pay a price for trading services provided by local authorities. It may be a market price, a subsidised price or a deterrent price.

7. Grants from the central government are the Revenue Support Grant and Specific grants. There are also grants available from the European Community. The grant system has been criticised in that it reduces the independence of local authorities.

8. The Layfield Committee considered alternative sources of revenue for local authorities and recommended a local income tax.

9. Local authorities can borrow but their ability to obtain capital is curtailed by the public sector borrowing requirement.

10. The budget of a local authority is formulated by reference to its obligations to provide services, local needs and resources. Local authorities are not required to manage an areas's economy by budgetary means.

SUGGESTED FURTHER READING

Alternative to Domestic Rates, Cmnd. 8449 (London: HMSO, 1981).

General Statistics Service, *Local Government Statistics, 1993–94* (London: HMSO, 1993).

S. James and C. Nobes, *The Economics of Taxation* (London: Prentice-Hall, 1992).

D. King (ed.), *Local Government Economics in Theory and Practice* (London: Routledge, 1992).

Layfield Report, *Local Government Finance,* Cmnd. 6453 (London: HMSO, 1976).

S. Leach, J. Stewart and K. Walsh, *The Changing Organisation and Management of Local Government* (London: Macmillan, 1993).

Local Authorities: County Councils and District Councils, Community Charge and Council Tax demand notes and explanatory leaflets, 1990–4.

W.J. Meadows, *The Response of Local Authorities to Central Government Incitement to Reduce Expenditure* (London: Public Finance Foundation, 1987).

Note: The Chartered Institute of Public Finance and Accountancy provides useful information and statistics. The Institute also publishes a periodical entitled *Public Money*.

EXERCISES

1. What are the social, political and economic consequences of the growth of local authorities' expenditure?
2. Discuss the significance of the changes in the pattern of local authorities' expenditure.
3. Discuss alternative systems of financing local authorities to that which presently operates.
4. Suggest which services local authorities could offer to consumers on the basis of an economic price and consider arguments for such a policy.
5. Discuss the ways in which a local authority budget differs from that of a central government.
6. To what extent should local authorities be free to decide how much to borrow, on what basis and where?
7. In what sense if any is the Council Tax an improvement on the Community Charge?
8. Is compulsory tendering by local authorities to provide services in competition with firms from the private sector likely to improve efficiency? Give reasons for your answer.
9. Over the years the autonomy of local authorities has been reduced. Suggest reasons for this and consider arguments for and against increased control by the central government.
10. Rising level of local government expenditure has created problems among members of the European Union. Why has this become an international phenomenon?

16 Towards the European Union: Objectives, Policies and Finance of the European Community

ORIGINS AND TRANSFORMATION

What began as the European Common Market and was designated as the European Economic Community (EEC) under the Treaty of Rome subsequently evolved into the European Community (EC) and was transformed into the European Union after the Maastricht Agreement on the provisions of the Treaty on European Union and Economic and Monetary Union.

Politicians envisage its future variously as: the United States of Europe, a federation or a looser form of association. Governments disagree on the direction and the speed that the Union should take. People in the member-states are divided on some of the major issues involved. In their first referendum, the Danes rejected the Treaty on European Union. Similarly, nearly 50 per cent of the French voted against it. In the UK there was no referendum and so people could not make their views known through the ballot box – nevertheless many voiced their opposition. The British and Danish governments succeeded in negotiating opt-out clauses from some of the requirements of the Treaty.

An opinion poll (*Eurobarometer*, March–April 1993) showed that in the European Community only some 40 per cent of the people were in favour of the Maastricht Agreement. In the UK the figure was approximately 30 per cent. Sixty per cent of Germans did not want to enter the European Monetary Union and give up the Deutschmark. Nevertheless the Treaty on European Union was ratified. Peoples' approval and action by their elected representatives in this case did not quite coincide. However, over 50 per cent of the people polled in the European Community said that membership of the Community was 'a good thing', though only approximately 45 per cent believed that their country had benefited from it. But then public opinion can be fickle, with polls showing greater support for membership at times of prosperity and lower support in recessions. During its lifetime the European Community has experienced both.

Over time, as the nature of the Community has changed, so have its objectives, policies and financial needs, to implement an ever-increasing range of measures that have been required following the expansion of the Community, the passing of the Single European Act and the Maastricht Agreement. In comparison the original provisions were modest.

The *European Economic Community* came into being in 1958 under the Treaty of Rome. Its signatories in 1957 were: Belgium, West Germany, France, Italy, Luxembourg and the Netherlands. So there were six in the initial Common Market. In 1972, the UK, Denmark and Ireland signed the Treaty of Accession and in 1973 the enlarged Community came into existence. Greece joined in 1981, Spain and Portugal followed in 1986, and the unification of Germany resulted in the incorporation of the East German economy into West Germany. The original objectives of the European Economic Community were set out in article two of the Treaty of Rome. These were '... establishing a Common Market and progressively approximating the economic policies of the Member States to promote throughout the Community a harmonious development of economic activities, a continuous and balanced expansion, an increased stability, an accelerated raising of the standard of living and closer relations between its Member States'.

In 1978 the European Parliament resolved to omit the word 'economic' from the European Economic Community, so that it became simply designated as the *European Community*. This reflects the developments that have taken place within it, with greater emphasis being put on political and social issues. It also hints at its more ambitious overall aims. Austria, Finland and Sweden joined on 1 January 1995.

THE EUROPEAN COMMUNITY AND INSTITUTIONS

Institutions charged with the formulation, implementation and enforcement of the policies and associated measures are:

The Council of Ministers consisting of representatives of the Member States. This is the main decision-making body of the Community (Figure 16.1).

The European Commission drafts directives, introduces policies and implements measures.

The European Court of Justice deals with Community law and its application in Member States.

The European Parliament provides a forum for debate for elected representatives from Member States. Its previously limited powers have been extended by the Treaty on European Union which gave to the

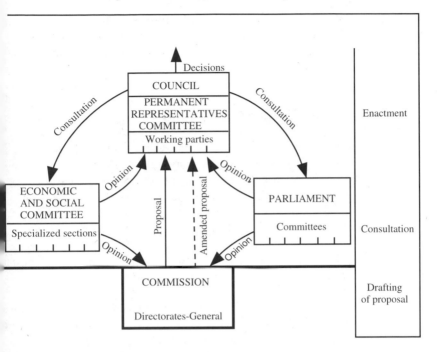

Figure 16.1 The European Community's decision-making process
Source: P. Fontaine, *A Citizen's Europe* (Luxembourg: Commission of the European Communities, 1991).

Parliament increased decision-making powers and right of enquiry.
 Powers of the European Parliament relate to:

(i) *Joint decision-making.* Parliament had been given new powers to make in certain areas, joint-decisions with the Council of Ministers. If the two bodies fail to reach an agreement in the Joint Conciliation Committees on a proposal then the Parliament can reject it by an overall majority.

(ii) *Control of administrative machinery.* The Parliament will have powers to require from the Commission information on its spending and financial control. The Commission will then act on the Parliament's decision in these matters.

(iii) *Financial control.* 'The European Parliament will be able to ask the Commission to give evidence on spending and financial control and the Commission will be obliged to act on the Parliament's decisions and observations'.

(iv) *Representation*. Parliament has the powers to draw up proposals for uniform election procedures. An increase in the size of the European Parliament has become necessary as a result of the enlargement of the European Community.

MOVE TOWARDS THE EUROPEAN UNION

The organisation into which the European Community is being transformed is still in the early stages of development and the process is not expected to be completed until the end of the century at the earliest. At present, the European Community, or Union, as it is increasingly described in the press, has a population of some 340 million living in twelve Member States. Some of these are among the wealthiest countries in the world (Table 2.6). There are, however, considerable disparities in the Community both at the national and regional level. The richest member-state is Denmark with a GDP per head of some US$26,900 (1993–94) and the poorest is Greece with a GDP of US$7,700. There are also differences in the standard of living *within* individual countries: for example, in Italy between the relatively poor South and the affluent North; in Germany between what was East and West Germany and, as in the UK and France, between the areas where the old heavy industries were located and the new centres of economic activity.

The extent and pattern of industrialisation and the importance of agriculture to the Member States' national economies also varies and this has a bearing on fiscal policies of the Member States and on those of the Community where agricultural support is a major issue.

Governments' ability and willingness to redress the imbalances depends on their available resources to finance expenditure programmes, preferences, priorities and the requirements of the European Commissions' directives, such as the harmonisation of taxation and welfare benefits.

THE LEVEL AND PATTERN OF TAXATION IN THE COMMUNITY

It can be shown that the level and pattern of taxation within the Community varies (Tables 16.1 and 16.2). The Danish government in 1992 took 48.9 per cent of the country's GDP in taxation and in social contributions which is the highest figure for the Community (the lowest was for the UK at 35.8 per cent). The British Exchequer relies more heavily on corporate taxation than the other Member States (see p. 188), whereas Greece favours indirect taxation as Table 16.1 shows. Under pres-

Table 16.1 Some differences in the pattern of taxation in the European Community

Taxes as a percentage of total tax revenue and social security contributions

	Taxes on profits		Taxes on Consumption		Taxes on Capital	
Highest	UK	8.9	Greece	51.9	France	1.5
Lowest	Germany	4.1	Netherlands	26.7	Italy	0.1

Source: see pp. 188, 210, 216.

Table 16.2 Level of taxation in the European Community

Total receipts from taxes and social security contributions as a percentage of Gross Domestic Product at market prices

	1991	1992		1991	1992
Sweden	50.5	50.4	Germany	36.6	40.0
Denmark	48.2	48.9	Ireland	37.9	38.0
Netherlands	47.2	46.7	Finland	37.9	37.7
Belgium	42.0	45.4	Spain	34.6	35.9
France	43.9	42.4	UK	36.2	35.8
Italy	40.5	42.4	Portugal	...	...

Source: *Economic Trends*, 483 (London: HMSO, 1994).

sure from the electorates, governments in the European Community have been cutting taxes. Some countries have done so partly for ideological reasons. The British Government's view has been that by reducing the tax burden so as to leave people with higher disposable incomes after tax, they will be better able to provide for themselves, which will reduce their dependence on state support.

SOCIAL PROTECTION EXPENDITURE AND HARMONISATION OF MEASURES

Social protection expenditure in the Community has risen steeply but unevenly in the last twenty years (Table 16.3), reflecting not only disparities in means and needs but also in social and political preferences.

Comparison of the scales of protection in the Member States might suggest that a citizen of the Community, who is now able to move freely from one country to another, would do best to have a large family in France, be unemployed in Luxembourg, fall sick (with a short-term illness) in Germany, become disabled (long-term) in Belgium and grow

Table 16.3   Current social protection expenditure a percentage of GDP

	Belgium	Denmark	Germany	Greece	Spain	France	Ireland	Italy	Luxembourg	Holland	Portugal	United Kingdom	Europe
1970	18.7	19.6	21.5	na	na	19.2	13.2	17.4	15.9	20.8	na	15.9	na
1975	24.2	25.8	29.7	na	na	22.9	19.7	22.6	22.4	26.7	na	20.1	na
1980	28.0	28.7	28.7	12.2	18.1	25.4	21.6	19.4	26.5	30.8	14.7	21.5	24.4
1983	30.8	30.1	28.2	17.2	19.5	28.3	24.1	22.9	27.2	33.2	16.1	23.9	25.3
1986	29.4	26.7	28.1	19.4	19.5	28.5	24.1	22.4	24.8	30.9	16.3	24.3	26.0
1989	26.7	29.8	27.5	20.7	20.1	27.6	20.2	23.1	25.2	31.0	16.6	21.9	25.2
1991	26.7	29.8	26.6	na	21.4	28.7	21.3	24.4	27.5	32.4	19.4	24.7	26.0

Source: Eurostat, Social Protection and Receipts (Luxembourg, 1993) and Commision of the European Communities (Brussels, 1994).

Table 16.4   Differences in social security benefits in EC countries

Benefits as percentage of net average earnings

	benefit				
Type of benefit	*highest (per cent)*		*lowest (per cent)*		*EC average (per cent)*
Retirement	Portugal	94	Ireland	42	75
Sickness/invalidity	Belgium	100	UK	28	69
short term	Germany	100			
	Greece	100			
Sickness/disability	Belgium	97	Portugal	30	50
long term					
Unemployment					
1st period*	Luxembourg	85	UK	23	61
2nd period	Spain	70	Italy	0	42
Family allowance					
children 1	Luxembourg	20	France	1	6
2	Luxembourg	28	Spain	3	12
3	France	50	Spain	5	20
Benefit to single					
parent with no record					
of contributions	Netherlands	63	Portugal	0	40

Note: * Duration varies from Italy (6 months) to Denmark (30 months). The EC average is 14 months.

Source: Commission of European Communities, *Social Protection* (Brussels, 1994).

old in Portugal or Greece. As Table 16.4 indicates, social security benefits as a percentage of net earnings vary enormously, but before rushing to emigrate, it is worth remembering that, as the level of earnings also differs, a lower percentage of a bigger pay packet may not mean that a person is worse off.

Increasingly governments are becoming concerned with notions of welfare mentality and the first signs in Europe of the *'underclass' phenomenon*. It was observed in the USA in the 1970s and the term 'underclass' came into use to describe a category of people who are unable or unwilling to break out of deprived urban ghettos. These are perceived as areas where drug addicts hang around, criminals run protection rackets,

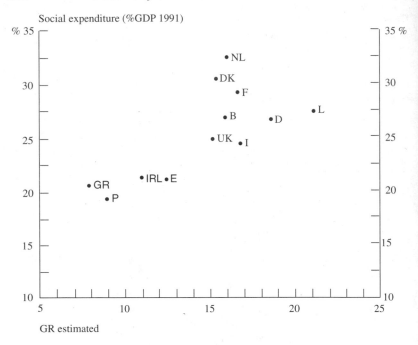

Social expenditure (%GDP 1991)

Figure 16.2   Social protection expenditure and GDP per head, 1991

Source: Eurostat, *Social Protection and Receipts* (Luxembourg, 1993) and the Commission of the European Communities (1994).

children carry guns to school and people live with little prospect of employment and a better way of life.

In Europe it had been believed that the Welfare State would provide a safety net for those in need, support them during periods of illness and unemployment and, through retraining and other programmes would enable people to support themselves at a reasonable level when they resumed employment. But now the Welfare State is in crisis – the increasing costs of provision of social protection, rising public expectations and an ageing population that absorbs a greater proportion of available resources have forced governments to review their policies. Some governments have begun to shift from the concept of the Welfare State to that of Welfare Society as a basis for the provision of welfare services (see p. 103).

This brief overview of disparities in the European Community is intended to highlight the scale of the task of achieving social cohesion. It is the avowed objective of the Community to achieve equality in the provision of social benefits by raising the levels in states lagging behind to those at the top.

THE SINGLE EUROPEAN ACT (1987)

Article 130 of the Act: (a) defined 'the objectives of economic and social cohesion; harmonious development of the Community and a reduction in disparities between the various regions and the backwardness of the least favoured regions' (b) specified the means of achieving these objectives: co-ordination of Member States' economic policies, common policies and the internal market, structural instruments; (c) set out tasks: helping to redress the principal regional imbalances through participating in the developments of regions whose development is lagging behind and in the conversion of declining industrial regions; (d) called for reform of structural funds.

THE MAASTRICHT AGREEMENT AND THE TREATY ON EUROPEAN UNION AND ECONOMIC AND MONETARY UNION

The agreement at Maastricht on 11 December 1991 on the Treaty on European Union and Economic and Monetary Union marks a landmark in the process of European integration. The Treaty extended and added to provisions of previous EC legislation relating to:

Union citizenship

Citizens of the Member States of the European Community become, under the Treaty, citizens of the Union and as such they have the right to: (i) diplomatic and consular protection by any Member State in a non-EC country; (ii) the right to vote and stand as a candidate in local elections outside their own country and in the elections to the European Parliament; (iii) petition the Parliament; and (iv) apply to an Ombudsman appointed by the parliament.

Parliament

Its size and powers had been extended (see p. 332).

Political cohesion

The Treaty provides for 'the implementation of a common foreign and security policy which shall include the eventual framing of a common defence policy'.

Economic and Monetary Union

This is to be achieved in three stages. The Community is to move 'irrevo-cably' towards EMU and the decision on currency union is described in the protocol to the Treaty as 'irreversible'. Its new monetary institution, policies and measures are discussed later on.

Concessions

British objections to the draft Treaty on provisions on social policy resulted in an opt-out clause for the UK. The other eleven Member States have gone ahead to adopt the *Social Charter*. A qualified majority vote will be required on decisions relating to: health and safety; working conditions; information and consultation of workers; equality of work between men and women; and integration of persons excluded from the labour market.

A unanimous vote will be required for decisions relating to: social security and social protection of workers; protection of redundant workers; representation; collective defence of workers and employers; conditions of employment for third country nationals; and financial contributions for promoting jobs.

The British Government's view is that the Charter will impose an additional burden on businesses, make them less competitive and thereby endanger jobs.

Subsidiarity

This concept is dealt with by Article 3b of the Treaty. In matters that are not within the Community's jurisdiction it will take action 'only if and in so far as the objectives of the proposed action cannot be sufficiently achieved by the Member States'. This reinforces the Community's earlier stance that 'Community instruments should play, alongside national and regional policies and in harmony with them, an important role in promoting the convergence of economies'. An EC communication 'Making a success of the Single Act – a new frontier for Europe' (1987) points out that 'experience also demonstrates the importance of regional and local initiatives, since no centralised or systematic organisation of development action can take full account of diversity of local situations'.

POLICIES OF THE EUROPEAN COMMUNITY

A wide range of policies can be grouped under the following main headings:

The Common Agricultural Policy (CAP) absorbs the biggest share (over 60 per cent) of the EC budget and has come under a great deal of criticism. It was held to be responsible for high prices, over-production, butter mountains, beef mountains, wine lakes and generally squandering resources. A much-cited example is the set-aside scheme for land under which farmers are paid for *not* producing food.

The object of the CAP is to provide support for farmers by setting floor prices for their produce. When prices drop below the set level, EC authorities step in and buy the produce that the farmers offer to them. This will then be stored, sold or destroyed if no buyers can be found. The scheme is somewhat similar to a commodity cartel. If buyers are found abroad then the exporters are entitled to a refund of the difference between the world prices which tend to be lower than the EC prices which tend to be higher. This encourages over-production. Under the Structural Funds reforms of 1988, measures were introduced to achieve a better balance between market capacity and production by such methods as: (a) the 'set-aside' scheme; (b) afforestation; (c) stopping production of some produce; and (d) price cuts.

Regional Policy is the second most important EC policy in terms of expenditure. The objectives are to 'strengthen the economic potential of the regions, support structural adjustment and growth and create permanent jobs' and 'redress principal regional imbalances in the Community' (No. 4254 new regulation). For further discussion of the regional policy see p. 445.

A new policy innovation has been the setting-up of the *Committee of the Regions* which consists of 189 representatives of regional and local authorities of the Member States to make representation to the Council or the Commission and in turn to be consulted on matters pertaining to the regions.

Social Policy and Education Policy overlap to some extent. *Social policy* is concerned not only with issues covered by the Social Charter but also with vocational training and, in particular, with training in advanced technologies to improve employment prospects of people who have difficulties in finding jobs: women, migrant workers and handicapped persons. *Education policy* is concerned with education at different levels, exchanges of students and staff from different Member States such as the ERASMUS (European Community Action Support for Mobility of University Students) scheme.

Industrial and Commercial Policies arise out of the Commission's obligations to act as a regulator, promoter and facilitator. It may investigate and regulate monopoly practices. It may encourage competition within the Community. The scope of the industrial and commercial policies is however very wide and they relate to many aspects of economic activity including international trade.

Monetary Policy is reflected in the provisions for European Monetary Union and is discussed later on (see p. 345).

The Research and Investment Policy of the Community is to encourage and facilitate research and investment in joint research projects such as those on the peaceful uses of atomic energy. These policies are, however, constrained by limited resources. Research and investment programme accounts for around 3 per cent of the EC budget expenditure, as compared with some 60 per cent that goes on price support of agricultural produce.

Foreign Aid Policy reflects, to some extent, Member States' national foreign policies, and in recent years has seen a shift in emphasis to assist countries of Central and European Europe in their transition from Communist to market economies. One of the earliest schemes was PHARE (Poland and Hungary Action for Reconstruction of the Economies, 1989). In 1990 PHARE was extended to other countries to facilitate education and training. Policy for channelling investment funds into Central and Eastern Europe is being implemented by a bank set up by the Community for the purpose.

Environmental Policy is linked to a variety of policies. Protection and preservation of environment is financed out of the European Agricultural Guidance and Guarantee Fund (EAGGF).

Economic Policy is difficult to define by reference to the issues that it covers as many of them are also relevant to other policies. Thus, for example economic, regional, social and education policies may all have as their objective a reduction in unemployment, though this may be by different means. An economic policy can encompass some and reinforce others. It is consequently likened to an umbrella that covers a number of policies including fiscal policy.

FINANCE AND BUDGET OF THE EUROPEAN COMMUNITY

Finance of the institutions of the Community, their activities and the cost of implementation of policies are apportioned to a number of expenditure programmes. The European Community has the powers to spend money in its own right and to raise revenue but its resources are limited.

The *European Community budget* amounts to approximately 1 per cent of the combined GDP of the Member States, and to some 3 per cent of their public expenditure but, unlike national budgets, the Community budget has to be balanced and cannot be used as an instrument of fiscal policy to manage aggregate demand by means of budget deficits and surpluses.

Under the Treaty of Rome and subsequent legislation, rules and regulations had been laid down governing both the revenue side and the expenditure side of the Community budget. A distinction was also drawn between expenditure programmes:

(a) *Compulsory expenditure*, as the terms implies, was made obligatory under the EC legislation and, although the Council of Ministers was given powers to determine the level of compulsory expenditure, it had to be within set limits. Included in this category was agricultural price support and foreign aid.

(b) *Non-compulsory expenditure* is in a sense optional. The European Parliament has a say on how much money is spent and to what programmes it is allocated, thereby influencing the level and pattern of expenditure.

Structural Funds through which money is channelled are:

The European Agricultural Guidance and Guarantee Fund (EAGGF)
The European Regional Development Fund
The European Social Fund

The budget also covers Research and Investment (Euratom), foreign aid, administration and miscellaneous expenditure.

Revenue side of the Budget

To finance its expenditure the European Community raises revenue, labelled as 'own resources', from a number of prescribed sources. These are:

(a) *Customs duties* and other levies on goods imported from outside the Community.

(b) *Equalising* levies on imported agricultural produce amounting to the difference between. lower world prices and the higher Community prices.

(c) *Tax equivalent*, 'the amount which would be raised if Value Added Tax (VAT) up to a maximum specified rate (1.4 per cent) were levied on the same basket of spending on goods and services in each Member State'.

(d) *Payments by Member States* related to each country's GNP. Richer countries with higher a GNP are expected to contribute more reflecting the 'ability to pay' principle of taxation. The total amount payable depends on the yield of the Community's own resources [revenue (a) to (c)] and its expenditure.

Financial Reforms

Increasing Community expenditure, concern over the waste of money, the share of EC budget absorbed by the Common Agricultural Policy (CAP) and the enactment of the Single European Act, led to calls for reforms of the finances of the Community. They were initiated in 1988 by the European Council to make better use of resources. Measures were implemented to: (a) limit by law growth in expenditure on agricultural guarantees; (b) introduce 'stabilisers' for agricultural production, making use of quotas and price cuts when these were exceeded; (c) planning and controlling of expenditure with the so-called 'financial perspective' – five-year framework.

A key feature was the reform of the Structural Funds, not only to put the Community's finances on a more sound footing but also to further more effectively the objectives of economic and social cohesion under the Single European Act. The European Commission set out the broad principles underlying the reform of the Funds: (i) concentration of assistance on priority areas; (ii) partnership with Member States, required to bring their economic policies closer together; (iii) consistency of Community policy, particularly with Member States' economic policies; (iv) improvement in the administration of Funds; (v) simplification, monitoring and flexibility.

The Commission is now required to give assurances when submitting proposals for new measures that the costs can be covered from the Community's resources.

Greater control over the expenditure side was extended to the revenue side of the budget and a legally-binding ceiling was placed on the total 'own resources'. From 1992 onwards this is to be set at 1.2 per cent of the Community GNP.

The overall budgetary control over EC finances was tightened by raising the profile of the *Court of Auditors*.

Fontainebleau Abatement

Contributions by individual Member States to the finance of the Community had been, for a long time, a source of contention. The burden on some countries was greater than on others. For example, although the UK was poorer in terms of GDP per capita than Denmark or the Netherlands, the latter two countries received a net benefit while the UK did not. It has been estimated that British contributions to the total of the Community revenue ('own resources') is around 20 per cent whereas the UK share of the Community's GNP is some 16 per cent. The relatively high British payments into the EC Budget and relatively small receipts from it in benefits are partly explained by the fact that the UK imports agricultural produce from abroad which is subject to EC levies and her small (in terms of employment) and efficient agricultural sector receives less in subsidies under CAP.

Eventually an abatement agreement was reached. The Fontainebleau Abatement (1984) provides for British contributions to be scaled down.

PROGRESS TOWARDS THE EUROPEAN MONETARY UNION
AND MONETARY POLICY

To appreciate the implications of the European Monetary Union and the implementation of its monetary policy, it may perhaps be helpful to examine first, the creation of the European Monetary System and some of the developments within it that had taken place.

European Monetary System, the Exchange Rate Mechanism

The setting-up of the EMS was an important step towards the economic and monetary union of the Member States of the European Community. Their governments approved the basic structure of the EMS in 1978 and arrangements came into operation in 1979.

The *purpose* of the EMS is to maintain the stability of currencies, control inflation and promote economic growth through co-operation. The cost of the EMS membership for governments is the loss of their independence in pursuit of national monetary policies. The cost for the Member States is the consequence of compliance with the requirements imposed by the Exchange Rate Mechanism.

The European Monetary System comprises:

The European Currency Unit (ECU)
The Very Short-Term Financing facility (VSTF)
The European Monetary Co-operation Fund (EMCF)
The Exchange Rate Mechanism (ERM)

All countries within the System are entitled to join the ERM but entry into the ERM is not a prerequisite for membership of the EMS. Thus, although the UK has participated in its arrangements from the beginning, sterling did not go into the ERM until October 1990 and subsequently left in September 1992.

The Exchange Rate Mechanism has been defined as 'a semi-fixed system of rates of exchange which allows currencies to go up and down between agreed limits.' On entry into the ERM or on realignment, a central rate for a currency is determined in relation to the ECU, and this is used to fix its central rate against each of the other currencies in the mechanism. Thus, for example, sterlings central rate against the Deutschmark was £1 = DM 2.95. Against the French franc it was £1 = 9.89389. Currencies were allowed to diverge from their central rates within specified margins of about 2.25 per cent (the narrow band) or, in the case of sterling and the peseta, 6 per cent (the wide band). Central banks of countries in the ERM were obliged to keep their currencies within the agreed limits. If for example, sterling (a weak currency) reached its limits against the Deutschmark (a strong currency), then the Bank of England and the Bundesbank would be obliged to support the weak currency. Thus, both would go into the market using Deutschmarks to buy sterling. At the Bank of England Deutschmark reserves would go down and, at the Bundesbank, sterling reserve would go up. In addition to their own foreign reserves, credit facilities are available to member countries.

The Very Short-term Financing scheme enables the central banks of countries within the ERM to provide their own currencies to each other for the purpose of intervention to keep a currency under pressure within the prescribed margins. This credit facility is automatic, but drawings have to be repaid within a short time.

The European Monetary Co-operation Fund operates a swap system. In exchange for 20 per cent of their gold and dollar reserves, central banks can obtain ECUs from the EMCF which they can then use in settlement of transactions arising from participation of the Exchange Rate Mechanism.

Realignment of currencies may, however, become unavoidable if intervention, interest rates policy and fiscal measures fail to achieve stability and contain fluctuations within the agreed limits. Such realignment of currencies amount to either an *upward revision* in value or *devaluation*, and requires the consent of all the ERM members. When a currency is realigned, new margins are fixed and the central bank is required to maintain its value within those limits. During the early phase of the ERM, realignments were fairly frequent. There were seven. In the second phase (1983–1992) they became less common as converging economic and monetary policies of governments committed to the mechanism had a stabilising effect on currencies. Then, in 1992, the relative calm in the foreign exchange markets was shattered by the turmoil as one currency after another came under pressure: sterling, lira, peseta, punt. The French franc was also in difficulties. Central banks moved in to support their currencies. There was a massive intervention by the Bank of England but help from the other members of the ERM, particularly the Bundesbank, was not forthcoming on a sufficient scale to stabilise sterling. Matters were made worse by German reluctance to reduce interest rates. They were kept at a high level by the Bundesbank for domestic reasons after the unification of East Germany and West Germany. However, within the ERM these high interest rates were 'exported' to other countries, and aggravated their problems.

Suspension of sterling from the ERM was announced by the British Chancellor of the Exchequer on September 16, 1992, as he told the Parliament 'We are floating and we will set monetary policy in this country to meet our objectives.' Important among these objectives was the reduction in interest rates to help get the UK out of a recession. The immediate effect of the changeover to a floating rate of exchange was what amounted to a devaluation of some 11 per cent. The day after the announcement the FTSE-100 Index of leading shares soared in anticipation by the financial markets of cuts in interest rates.

The reaction of industrialists, as extensively reported in the press, was generally favourable. Devaluation made British exports more competitive in international markets and stimulated an export-led recovery from the recession. Lower interest rates were seen as necessary to sustain economic growth. Some economists however predicted that the departure from the ERM would lead to dire consequences – resulting in higher inflation and higher unemployment. They were proved wrong in the medium term. Two years after the suspension of sterling the unemployment rate in the UK of 9.3 per cent was down on the previous year. Comparable rates for 1994 in

Europe were: for Spain 24.3 per cent; Belgium 14.6 per cent; France 12.6 per cent; Denmark 12.5 per cent; Italy 11.6 per cent and all were up compared with 1993 (September or August). Over the same period, the percentage change in consumer prices at annual rate was 1.9 for the UK; 4.8 Spain; 3.6 Italy; 2.9 Germany; 2.6 the Netherlands and 2.5 Belgium. Furthermore whereas by the first quarter of 1994 growth in Germany's GDP was 0.5 per cent, the industrial output of the UK increased over a period of 12 month by 5.6 per cent and was the highest growth rate for five years. As Table 2.1 shows, UK emerged from the world recession faster than the other countries in the European Community.

The British government has not announced a date for sterling's return to the ERM. It must be noted that, in the long term, pursuit of an independent monetary and exchange rate policy is not compatible with the membership of the European Union to which the UK is pledged.

Under the Maastricht Agreement, Member States of the European Community have committed themselves to an economic and monetary union that is to be achieved in three stages. A clause in the Treaty on European Union provides for an opt-out so that the UK does not have to enter Stage III without a separate decision by British government and parliament (*The British Protocol*).

Stage I   A start was made in 1990 under the then existing EC powers, and emphasis was placed on policies leading to economic and social cohesion, acceptance of the principle that national economic policies are of common concern to all Member States, the need to observe budgetary discipline and to achieve greater harmonisation in public finance necessary for the next stage.

Stage II Establishment of the European Monetary Institute is the essential feature of the second stage begining in 1994. The EMI role is to: (a) strengthen co-operation between the national central banks and co-ordinate monetary policies; (b) facilitate the use of the ECU, and oversee its development as a currency and supervise the ECU clearing system; (c) monitor the European Monetary System.

By mid-1998 at the latest, the European System of Central Banks, including the European Central Bank, is to replace the EMI. Functions of the new institution will be to: (i) define and implement Community monetary policy; (ii) conduct foreign exchange operations; (iii) hold and manage official foreign reserves of Member States; and (iv) promote the smooth operation of the payments system.

Stage III   It is to begin in 1999, if not before, depending on when the Member States have met the four convergence criteria on price stability, exchange rates, interest rates and the size of government deficits.

The Economic and Monetary Union will then be in place.

Implications and Consequences of the Measures

The Single European Act and the Treaty on European Union will transform the European Community, but their impact will, in the long term, depend on the extent of integration that the Member States achieve. If they succeed in meeting the objectives of economic, social and political cohesion – as envisaged by the signatories to the Maastricht Agreement – the role of national governments and parliaments will become subordinate to that of the Union's institutions. Member States will no longer have the powers to manage their economies and to use fiscal and monetary policies in order to achieve their own aims, which may not necessarily coincide with those of the Union on some matters, as for example on redistribution of income and wealth. In the European Parliament, after the 1994 elections, Socialists are the biggest group but they are a minority in parliaments of some of the Member States which have Conservative governments. Their views and those of the socialist parties are likely to differ not only on the desirable level of equality but also on such issues as state intervention in industry, the relative size of the public and private sectors, regulation of businesses and on the role of market forces.

The political composition of the European Parliament and that of national parliaments of the Member States differs now and may differ in the future. As the Community expands, a consensus of opinion may increasingly be difficult to reach.

RELATIONSHIP BETWEEN NATIONAL CENTRAL GOVERNMENTS AND LOWER-TIER AUTHORITIES OF THE UNION

The implication of the Treaty on European Union for lower tiers of government in the Member States are even more difficult to predict.

The European Community has recognised the importance of the lower-tier authorities in the Member States. The Committee of the

Regions had been set up to give regional and local bodies better access to the Community's institutions. In achieving economic and social cohesion at the national level envisaged in the Maastricht Agreement, the problem of diversity of local governments in Member States – government structures, powers and policies – will have to be tackled. The basis of central – local financial relationships differs from country to country. In the 1980s, as local government spending increased sharply, in some cases to a crisis level, central governments sought in different ways to exercise greater influence and control over local authorities. Their constitutional and legal rights, powers and degree of autonomy vary, as do the prevailing official views on the size of the public sector. In the Federal Republic of Germany, for example, the political autonomy of local government is guaranteed by the constitution and the Länder are obliged to provide finance to enable local authorities to carry out functions for which they are responsible under central legislation, otherwise they are free to pursue expenditure policies and raise revenue without direct intervention by the Länder. In Luxembourg the Ministry of the Interior has to approve local authority budgets and will normally do so only if the budgets are balanced, whereas in Portugal, central government has no powers to approve local authority budgets.

The restructuring of local governments' finances in the 1980s has changed the relationship with the central governments for the 1990s, but it has not provided a basis for common policies.

Persistent budget deficits and the problems of rising public expenditure lead to diverse measures, as the following examples illustrate:

Limited Measures

In Denmark the government's preferred option was to increase local authorities' powers to make their own decisions on the assumption that central government intervention and compliance with its requirement increases local expenditure.

Extensive Measures

Belgium, Italy, Luxembourg, Portugal and Spain introduced short-term measures to avert fiscal crises and long-term measures to restructure local finance. In Belgium, restraints on public expenditure were introduced and local authorities were allowed to determine their own rate of local income tax. In Italy, maximum rates of growth in public expenditure by local authorities were set centrally. In Luxembourg, government used indirect means of control, making awards of grants conditional on good house-

keeping. In Spain, regulations were drawn on preparation of local authorities' budgets and control over grants was tightened.

Countries where the central government has considerable powers to
influence local government spending are Ireland, Netherlands and the
UK. In Ireland, abolition of local tax on dwellings by local authorities
increased their dependence on the central government. In Netherlands,
the government had taken steps to apply the principle of user–payer in
the finance of public services. Decentralisation, deregulation and
privatisation measures were incorporated into public expenditure-cutting
policies and this was linked to grant reduction for local authorities'
programmes.

British local finance was discussed in Chapter 15.

No Measures

Unlike some of the other Member States of the European Community,
such as the UK, which are commited to the reduction in the size of the
public sector in favour of market economics, the governments of France
and Greece had been elected on manifestos pledging to protect and
strengthen the public sector. Thus making it difficult for them to pursue
policies to restrain local authorities' spending in the 1980s and to lay new
foundations for policies in the 1990s for fiscal retrenchment.

This brief overview highlights how diverse is the public sector at the
local government level in the Member States and how far off it still is
from the ideal of the European Union based on social, economic and political conformity. Restruturing on such a scale will need time.

THE SHAPE OF THE NEW EUROPE BY THE TWENTY-FIRST CENTURY

The coming together of nations to create the European Community began
in the second half of the twentieth century when two organisations were
set up, the European Common Market (EEC 1957) and the European Free
Trade Association (EFTA 1960). The latter group preferred a looser form
of association concerned primarily with removal of barriers to trade.
Members included: Austria, Denmark, Ireland, Liechtenstein, Norway,
Portugal and the UK. In 1972 the UK and Denmark left, and as other
countries begin transferring to the EC, the future of EFTA has become
uncertain and amalgamation in the future is likely. In January 1993 the
two organisations set up the European Economic Area which is the largest
integrated market in the world.

The European Economic Area stretches from the Artic Circle to the shores of the Mediterranean Sea. Austria, Sweden, Finland, Norway, Iceland, Switzerland and Liechtenstein became entitled to benefit from the Community's 'four fundamental freedoms': free movement of people, goods, services and capital. The first three of these countries have recently applied for a full membership of the EC and joined in 1995.

Then there are the countries of the former Soviet Block–Poland, Hungary and the Czech Republic. They have already acquired an associated status and are waiting to join. The Baltic Republics wish to follow them.

By the start of the twenty-first century European Union with such diverse membership will be very different from the European Community that committed itself in 1991 to the Maastricht agreement. Objectives and policies endorsed then may well have to be redrafted to serve the enlarged Community.

SUMMARY

1. The European Common Market was established under the Treaty of Rome. Over a period of nearly forty years, the EEC developed into the European Community and, following the Single European Act and the Maastricht Agreement, became the European Union.

2. Its objectives are to achieve the social and economic cohesion of the Member States.

3. This cohesion will have far-reaching implications for national fiscal and monetary policies, as harmonisation of social security benefits and taxation is required, and a European Central Bank is to be set up.

4. At present, the level and range of social security provisions in the Member States varies considerably as does the percentage of individual countries' GDP that is absorbed in financing their welfare policies.

5. The tax burden and the extent of reliance on direct and indirect taxation in the Member States also differs. So far more progress has been made in harmonisation of taxes on consumption in the European Community than of other forms of taxation.

6. The European Community has its own budget to finance its activities. It has revenue from its 'own resources' and can spend money on specified programmes. Unlike national budgets, that of the Community must balance.

7. The largest share of the budget goes on agriculture and agricultural produce price support, particurlarly through the operation of the CAP. This has created problems and led to over-production.

8. The European Community, concerned about rising expenditure, introduced stricter controls on spending and limits on Member States' contributions. Reform of the Structural Funds was also initiated and a shift from a Welfare State to a Welfare Society is being considered.

9. The Community's institutions responsible for formulation and implementation of policies, regulation and enforcement of EC law are: the European Commission; the Council of Ministers; the European Parliament; the European Court of Justice; and, once the monetary union is acheived, the European Central Bank.

10. As the integration of the Member States proceeds, it will change the role of national central governments and their relationship with their respective local national authorities. At present there is a considerable diversity between local government structures, functions and responsibilities in the individual Member States.

SUGGESTED FURTHER READING

R.J. Barro and V. Grilli, *European Macroeconomics* (London: Macmillan, 1994).

A.W. Cafruny and G.G. Rosenthal, *The State of the European Community: Maastricht and Beyond* (Harlow: Longmans, 1993).

Commission of the European Communities, *European Social Protection* (Brussels, 1993).

Commission of the European Communities, P. Fontaine, *A Citizens' Europe* (Luxembourg, 1991).

Commission of the European Communities, *Report of the Committee of Independent Experts on Company Taxation* (Brussels, 1992).

Commission of the European Communities, *Guide to the Reform of the Community's Structural Funds* (Brussels, 1992).

Commission of the European Communities, *The European Union* (Brussels, 1992).

Various pieces of European Community Legislation: Treaty of Rome.

The Single European Act.

Treaty on European Union.

EXERCISES

1. What were the benefits that governments sought to gain by establishing the European Common Market? To what extent have they been realised?
2. Suggest main reasons for the creation of the European Union and consider its consequences for the Member States.
3. In view of different traditions, culture and resources of the Member States of the European Community, harmonisation of social security protection throughout the European Community is an ideal rather than a practical proposition. Comment on the validity of this statement.
4. Suggest reasons why harmonisation of indirect taxation in the European Community has been easier to achieve than bringing into line taxes on incomes, profits and capital.
5. The EC requirement to balance the Community's budget means that fiscal policy cannot be used to counteract unemployment and inflation. Give your reason for agreeing or disagreeing with this statement.
6. What is the justification, if any, for allocating a major share of the Community's budget to agricultural produce price support? For what alternative purposes could the funds be used to achieve greater overall benefits?
7. Consider the implications of the enlargement of the European Community and the likely effects on the policies to achieve social and economic cohesion in the Union.
8. What are likely to be the consequences of the establishment of the European Central Bank and introduction of a single currency on Member States governments' ability to pursue their own monetary policy to manage national economies?
9. As more powers are transferred from national central governments to the European Union institutions, what future is there for local authorities as providers of social services and taxing authorities?
10. In the European Union citizens will have little say, through the ballot box and direct representation, on how much they pay in taxes and on what their money should be spent. Comment on the validity of this assertion.

Part 5

The Public Sector of Industry and Public Investment

17 Nationalised Industries and Public Sector Enterprises: An Historical Review

The public sector of industry has had a major impact on national economies of many countries throughout the world and on public finance for some forty years, since the post-Second World War period when governments embarked on nationalisation. The extent and speed with which enterprises and whole industries were transferred from the private to the public sectors varied. In the former Union of Soviet Socialist Republics it was sudden, in the aftermath of the Bolshevik Revolution of 1917. The private sector was outlawed and the state became the producer and distributor of goods and services. This role came to an abrupt end with the collapse of the USSR in 1990.

In many countries, nationalisation and the subsequent dismantling of the public sector of industry was not extreme, but was rather a selective and gradual process that gathered momentum in the 1980s. Nationalisation, however, is not just a matter of historical interest. Some nationalised industries and undertakings continue to operate. A study of the subject – the reasons for nationalisation, the growth of the public sector and its consequences – can provide an insight into the international phenomenon of privatisation in the 1980s and 1990s. Before looking at how this privatisation came about it may be helpful to examine nationalisation policies, problems and ways of dealing with them in the light of the British experience.

COMPOSITION OF THE PUBLIC SECTOR OF INDUSTRY

Public enterprise in the UK is a hybrid – neither a government department nor a commercial undertaking but with discernable features of each. Some public enterprises resembled one aspect of the hybrid more than the other. For instance, the Post Office was a government department and British Leyland was a company in the private sector of industry before they became public enterprises.

Table 17.1 The public sector of industry before privatisation

Type of industry:	heavy manufacturing service	shipbuilding automobile (British Leyland) transport (National Bus Company)
Extent of state ownership:	nationalised industry state shareholding	coal mining British Petroleum (BP) Ltd.
Market condition:	monopoly imperfect competition	Post Office British National Oil Corporation (BNOC)
Market supplied:	home international	British Gas British Airways
Basis of operation:	commercial social service	British Steel Corporation British Railways
Use of resources:	capital intensive labour intensive	Electricity Generating Board Post Office (mail)

The public sector of industry consisted of a variety of public enterprises belonging to different industries and differing in functions, size and importance to the economy. At one extreme there were public corporations responsible for a whole nationalised industry, at the other there were enterprises in which the state had acquired a majority holding but which operated in the private sector alongside similar businesses.

The diversity of the public sector can be indicated by the classification of some of the enterprises in Table 17.1. Frequently, enterprises qualify under more than one heading. This classification is also relevant to the study of their pricing and investment policies that they had followed.

The degree of monopoly within the public sector varied, and so also did the justification of its existence. The Bank of England is a state bank but it is also a central bank. Since no country can have more than one central bank it is necessary for the the Bank of England to have monopoly powers in order to carry out its functions. Legislation that forbade businesses to compete with the Post Office in provision of postal and telecommunication services established it as a monopoly – the nearest example of a pure monopoly in Britain at that time. This changed, however, in 1981 when British Telecom was set up as a separate public corporation and, although the Post Office retained a monopoly in postal services, the telecommunication services were exposed to competition. Similarly, The National Coal Board, British Gas and the Electricity Council were all monopolies so far as their own industry was concerned – yet all three, together with the oil industry, were in competition with each other as sources of energy. British Shipbuilders Corporation

Table 17.2 The size of nationalised industries in the UK at the start of the privatisation programme

Industries and State holding in companies 1981–82	Turnover (£ million)	Capital employed (£ million)	Employees
Electricity Council and Boards	6,094	7,179	158,780
Post Office	5,193	7,923	422,902
British National Oil Corporation	4,323	979	1,651
National Coal Board	3,740	2,376	297,000
British Gas Corporation	3,503	2,584	104,100
British Steel Corporation	3,105	2,341	181,000
British Leyland	2,877	1,268	157,460
British Railways Board	2,645	1,209	239,680
British Airways	1,920	967	56,866
Rolls-Royce	1,258	744	58,800
British Shipbuilders	870	112	72,700
South of Scotland Electricity Board	625	844	13,624
National Bus Company	582	212	5,879
British Broadcasting Corporation	488	138	27,973
London Transport Executive	466	1,116	59,879
National Freight Corporation	439	128	32,861
Cable and Wireless Ltd.	255	259	11,599
North of Scotland Hydro-Electric Board	243	658	4,115
British Airports Authority	191	364	7,655
Scottish Transport Group	142	133	12,333
British Transport Docks Board	137	179	11,272
National Enterprise Board	124	1,523	4,160
Independent Broadcasting Authority	27	47	1,300
	36,608	30,875	1,869,472

Source: *Annual Report and Accounts* and *The Times* 1000, London, 1982.

had a virtual monopoly in shipbuilding at home but had to compete for orders in domestic and international markets with foreign shipbuilders.

The public sector's relative importance to the national economy can be measured and compared in terms of: (i) sales; (ii) investment; and (iii) employment. This is shown in Table 17.2 up to the time when the privatisation process began.

The sales figures (turnover) are arrived at by multiplying output by the price. The government policies to control price increases to counteract inflation and to subsidise production in order to achieve social objectives had resulted in some prices being below the cost of production. Consequently, the size of the public sector on the basis of sales data was underestimated. The employment figures, on the other hand, overstated the importance of the public sector. The government policy for some years had been to counteract unemployment. Overmanning – e.g. in British Steel Corporation – was therefore allowed to continue for a time, to keep unemployment from rising still further in areas where there was little alternative work. For the same reason, some coal mines that were no longer profitable remained open and the contraction of the industry was more gradual than would have been expected under stricter market conditions.

The *investment figures* as an indicator of the size of the public sector of industry and its absorption of resources (capital) can be downright misleading. This is because when a public corporation accumulated a large deficit as a result of recurrent losses on its trading activities, a capital reconstruction followed. Losses were written off, the value of assets was reduced and the capital employed in the business appeared, in the accounts, to be less than the use of resources (investment funds) that it represented. The figures in Table 17.2 however, indicated that public corporations invested heavily. They had to rely on external financing as their savings were insufficient to provide the capital they needed.

The exact size of the public sector and its rate of growth can, therefore, be questioned, but there is no doubt that it was large and dominated the national economy, containing as it did the basic industries: energy, transport, communication, steel.

THE GROWTH OF THE PUBLIC SECTOR OF INDUSTRY

Growth occurred in different ways such as:

(a) *Nationalisation* of all companies in a particular industry, thereby bringing it wholly into public ownership, e.g. the railways.
(b) *Transformation* of a government department into a public corporation, e.g. the Post Office.
(c) *Take-over* of a failing company but leaving other companies in that industry in private ownership, e.g. British Leyland.
(d) *Acquisition of a shareholding* in a profitable company, e.g. British Petroleum.
(e) *Setting up of a new public enterprise* where no private enterprise of the kind operated before, e.g. the BBC.

Phases of Growth

There were distinct phases in the growth of the public sector which can be identified as follows:

(i) *Pre-First World War.* The Port of London Authority was set up in 1908.

(ii) *Interwar period, 1918–39.* Several public undertakings of a very different kind were formed: BBC, 1926; Central Electricity Board, 1926; London Passenger Transport Board, 1933; British European Airways and British Overseas Airways, 1939. During this phase the public undertakings were largely concerned with the control of public utilities run by the municipalities and using regulatory measures.

(iii) *Post-Second World War period, 1940s.* This was the major phase of nationalisation. Public corporations were set up one after another to take responsibility for a whole industry: coal (1947), railways (1947), gas (1948), and iron and steel, (1949).

(iv) *1950s and 1960s.* During this time additions to the public sector of industry were individual concerns of the 'lame duck' variety that were in danger of collapse (e.g. British Leyland).

(v) *1970s phase.* There was a widespread acquisition of shareholdings in a variety of companies in the private sector through the National Enterprise Board. In addition two entire industries, shipbuilding and aerospace, were nationalised.

REASONS FOR NATIONALISATION

Entire industries and individual concerns were nationalised for a variety of reasons, some on the grounds of political theories and others as a matter of economic expediency.

The election of the Labour Party to office led to the two major nationalisation phases of the 1940s and 1970s. The Labour Party was committed to the public ownership of industry by its constitution of 1918 (Clause Four) which remained unchanged until 1995 when it was amended. Clause Four as it stood required the Party 'to secure for the workers by hand or by brain, the full fruits of their industry and the most equitable distribution thereof that may be possible upon the basis of common ownership of the means of production and the best obtainable system of popular administration and control of each industry and service'.

Successive Labour governments have not, however, been in favour of complete nationalisation. Political thinkers, such as Beatrice and Sidney Webb, who had considerable influence on the British Labour movement, favoured a gradual transfer of industry from private to public ownership, since they believed that in Britain there would be little support for a sudden change.

The reasons for nationalisation, put forward over the years by its supporters, were diverse, as is shown by those listed below:

(a) Industries essential for the country should be under state control which can best be achieved under public ownership (e.g., the railways).

(b) Industries can be run more efficiently under one management. Their activities can then be co-ordinated, wasteful competition can be avoided and the size of industry allows for economies of scale that arise from producing in large quantities (e.g., the steel industry).

(c) Some industries could not survive without large injections of capital. The necessary investment could only come from the state, since the industries were unprofitable and would be of little interest to private investors (e.g., the shipbuilding industry).

(d) Labour relations would improve since people working for the state would be effectively working for themselves and would therefore be less likely to strike.

(e) Stability of employment would be maintained since public corporations could take a long-term policy and rely on financial help from the state to tide them over temporary difficulties.

(f) Consumers would benefit from lower prices that would be possible as a result of greater efficiency and the obligation on nationalised industries to operate in the public interest rather than to maximise profits.

(g) Salvage operations are needed to rescue individual companies, when their bankruptcy would create serious unemployment problems or reduce competition in an industry that is already dominated by a few multinationals. The Labour government, for instance, took British Leyland into the public sector and the Conservatives added Rolls Royce.

The controversial issue in the UK was not the principle of a mixed economy but the size of the public sector of industry. The nationalisation of some concerns raised little opposition, while that of others was strongly contested. Nationalisation of the Bank of England in 1946 was generally regarded as unavoidable. It had been acting as a central bank and the government's bank and was, to all intents and purposes, a public institution before nationalisation. The supply of gas and electricity was largely provided by undertakings run by municipalities. Nationalisation of the two industries was therefore a transfer of ownership and responsibilities within the public sector which met with little opposition. Nationalisation of iron and steel, road transport and the ship-building industry, however, was controversial and contested. Some road transport was transferred back to the private sector. Steel was denationalised and renationalised in 1967 and then privatised again.

PERFORMANCE OF THE NATIONALISED INDUSTRIES

The expectations of good industrial relations, of stable and high levels of employment and of lower prices were largely not fulfilled by the nationalised industries. There had been strikes with far-reaching consequences in the coal industry, in the steel, shipbuilding and electricity industries and on the railways. British Leyland had been recurrently paralysed by official and unofficial strikes. Nationalised industries proved no more immune to inflation and recession than the rest of the economy. Their unemployment problem had been, in fact, worse, since the public sector of industry was dominated by heavy industries that were in decline even before the recession of the 1970s. The efficiency of the public sector of industry taken as a whole, and measured in terms of output her head, was lower than that of the private sector.

The question of the relative efficiency of public and private enterprise is not new. When a Commission of Inquiry (1802) of the Board of Admiralty toured the dockyards, the commissioners found that, in private shipyards 300 men could build 7 ships a year, whilst in naval yards 3,000 men could barely manage to repair 7 ships a year.

Although there were exceptions, the overall performance of the public sector of industry compared unfavourably with that of the private sector, according to the National Economic Development Office's 'Study of UK Nationalised Industries' Report, HMSO,1976.

The public sector of industry had been a matter of concern for some years. In 1973 the Select Committee on Nationalised Industries recommended an inquiry into 'the role of the nationalised industries in the economy and the way in which they are to be controlled in the future'. In 1975, the Labour Government asked the National Economic Development Office to undertake an enquiry. Their report was critical of the state of affairs in the public sector of industry.

ORGANISATION AND CONTROL OF NATIONALISED INDUSTRIES

The setting-up of public corporations to run industries in the public sector was the result of a compromise on nationalisation and of the influence of Herbert Morrison on the trade unions. He advocated the concept of a public corporation and won their support for a public enterprise operating on a commercial basis but with the responsibilities of a social service, a kind of half-way house between a government body and a company.

A public corporation was established for each nationalised industry and undertaking. By 1995 a number of them still operate. Like a company, a public corporation has a board of directors. Its members come from different areas of the economy and there was a cross-section of managers from the private sector, trade unionists, academics and others with relevant experience. The British National Oil Corporation (BNOC), founded in 1975, was the first public corporation to have the statutory requirement that some civil servants should be appointed to its board. Chairmen and directors of public corporations are not elected, as in the private sector, but were appointed by a minister of the government's sponsoring department. Duties of the boards were not clearly defined in the nationalisation statutes for the different industries, and a distinction was not drawn between executive and non-executive functions. As a result of this, the practice of the different boards varied. Some industries were given regional boards as well as a national board.

Duties of the public corporations were set out in the statutes in general terms. They referred to the obligation to ensure supply of goods and services, to be efficient and to undertake research and development. These obligations were subject to interpretation and the various public corporations interpreted them differently, with reference to their specific circumstances: (i) enterprises had been nationalised for different reasons; (ii) they varied in economic and social importance to the economy; (iii) the corporations operated under different market conditions; (iv) and the industries were of a different nature: manufacturing, mineral, extractive, and service industries. The boards did not conceive their duties to be identical.

The various statutes had imposed certain duties on some corporations without specifically requiring them of others. Thus, the British Steel Corporation (BSC) was to promote exports and British Gas to advance the skills of its employees. The Post Office had the duty, 'to exercise its powers to meet social, industrial and commercial needs of the British Islands'. The Electricity Boards had one of the few specific non-commercial duties, to provide for 'extension to rural areas and cheapening of supplies of electricity'. All the corporations had in common the obligation to break-even while carrying out their other duties.

'At Arm's Length' Philosophy

The corporations were intended to operate 'at arm's length' from the government and were therefore given considerable independence in managing their affairs within the framework of their prescribed duties, with the government however having a say in general policy matters. In later years the government's intervention in the running of the industries had increased and in some cases the relationship between the corporations and successive governments had become strained.

PARLIAMENTARY CONTROLS

Public corporations are not directly answerable to Parliament. They submit their annual reports and accounts to the minister of the sponsoring government department, who then presents them to Parliament.

Parliamentary Questions

Members of Parliament may ask questions relating to a nationalised industry. Guidelines for Parliamentary questions were introduced in 1948. Generally speaking, questions on the day-to-day running of the corporations are disallowed, but a minister can be called upon to answer questions on the industry itself and on policy matters.

Parliamentary Debates

The House of Commons has the opportunity to debate issues concerning public corporations when statutory instruments, for example those dealing with subsidies or the borrowing requirement, are presented. The first full debate on a nationalised industry was in 1949 when the annual report and accounts of the National Coal Board (NCB) were considered. Since the House of Commons can devote only a limited amount of time to such debates, it established in 1952 a Select Committee on Nationalised Industries, backed by a full-time staff to study and report on individual nationalised industries. This provided for Parliamentary scrutiny but preserved the 'at arm's length' control of the nationalised industries. In 1980 the system was changed. Fourteen department-based Select Committees were set up to examine the expenditure, administration and policy of the respective departments and associated bodies. The

Committees dealing with individual nationalised industries could form a sub-committee to consider matters common to all of them.

The government exercised control over the nationalised industries in the following ways: (i) establishment of a financial framework within which the nationalised industries were expected to operate; (ii) target for industries' profits; (iii) guidelines on pricing policy; (iv) principles for investment appraisal; and (v) limits to borrowing.

PLANNING

Public corporations had to plan to meet the demand for their output, to function efficiently and to achieve the required returns. This needed co-operation between the government's sponsoring departments and the nationalised industries.

Public corporations required information from the government on its economic and social policies, its long-term objectives and the prospects for the economy. In return, the government required the corporations to provide information on their output, production capacity, employment, markets and other data relating to their operations. Sir Henry Benson was called upon in 1970 to advise on improvement in the information flow. This led to the development of formalised information systems and resulted in the Benson Brochures. The procedures ('bensonary') for transfer of information were implemented by a number of the nationalised industries.

Public corporations had to prepare plans which included: (i) short-term plans and annual investment reviews; (ii) medium-term plans – 5-year development plans that were integrated into the government's public expenditure programmes in the Public Expenditure surveys; and (iii) long-term plans.

The length of the period for which plans were drawn was to some extent dictated by the nature of the industry's assets. A power station may have a lifespan of some forty years and it may take ten years from approval date to reach the operational stage. The electricity industry, therefore, had to plan replacements and new projects a long time ahead. Conversely, the National Bus Corporation (NBC) could adjust its new investment programme within a period of some two years.

The planning assumptions that public corporations had to make differed from industry to industry. Those that sold in international markets, such as BSC, needed to make assumptions about the future trends in world trade in manufacturing. The electricity industry, National Coal Board and

British Gas – catering for the home market – had only to anticipate UK energy consumption and the government's strategy. British Rail, since it provided transport for coal, had to take the Coal Board's plans into account.

The relative importance of the various assumptions for the individual corporations differed but the two assumptions concerning trends in gross domestic product and retail prices were universally important.

The problem with planning is that the best-laid plans can be invalidated by: (i) international events, such as wars or oil crises over which neither the corporations nor British government could have control; and (ii) changes in the government's own economic and social policies. A government in the UK has to seek re-election at least every five years. On average they change every four years and government ministers hold office, within a particular department, on average for about two years. Political parties have different priorities and different views on economic and social policies in general, and on the obligations of the nationalised industries in particular.

FINANCIAL AND ECONOMIC OBLIGATIONS OF THE NATIONALISED INDUSTRIES

There is one point on which successive governments had agreed, namely, that the public corporation had an overall duty to earn a return on invested capital. The Labour government went as far as to state that 'an adequate level of nationalised industry profits is essential to the continuing well-being of the industries and their customers, and of the economy' (Cmnd. 7131, 1978). The nationalised industries had, however, been given little specific guidance in the past, by any government, on how to meet their financial and economic obligations. Eventually three White Papers were published to aid them:

(a) 1961 White Paper, 'The Financial and Economic Obligations of the Nationalised Industries' (Cmnd. 1337).
(b) 1967 White Paper, 'Nationalised Industries: A Review of Economic and Financial Obligations' (Cmnd. 3437).
(c) 1978 White Paper, 'The Nationalised Industries' (Cmnd. 7131).

Return on capital was an obligation that all the papers emphasised. The first White Paper did not set specific required returns on the invested capital but made it clear that public corporations were expected to earn a commercial rate of return. Their revenue from commercial activities was not intended to finance the social service obligations of the corporation, but how these obligations were to be paid for was not explained. The money eventually came from the government.

The 1967 White Paper introduced *financial targets* and recommended the use of a *test discount rate* to help public corporations to achieve similar rates of return to that of low-risk companies in the private sector. The rate was originally fixed at 8 per cent and was later raised to 10 per cent.

The 1978 White Paper gave further guidance on financial matters. The government came to the conclusion that, because of the differences in the nature of the nationalised industries, a uniform financial target was not practical. Consequently, the White Paper introduced different targets for different public corporations, taking into account the specific circumstances of their industries.

(a) Profitable industries had their targets determined by reference to the capital that had been invested in a particular industry, that is on the basis of 'average' net assets employed by the industry. The expected profit was expressed as a percentage of the assets.

(b) Some industries had their targets expressed as a percentage return on their turnover/sales. This method is more appropriate for labour intensive rather than for capital-intensive industries.

(c) Deficit industries – that did not cover their costs and depended on government grants to finance their operations – had their targets fixed by reference to the size of the deficit or grant, e.g. surface transport industries.

The level of targets for the different industries was influenced by a variety of factors such as the sectoral and social objectives of an industry, its market prospects, the level of existing investment and the scope for increased productivity. However, all industries were required to take into account opportunity cost, which the 1978 White Paper introduced into public sector finance.

The *opportunity cost* of the use of resources in the public sector of industry is their foregone use in the private sector. Thus, if the nationalised industries ran at a loss and did not cover their costs, this could means a diversion of resources from a more efficient to a less efficient use. The government therefore issued an instruction that nationalised industries 'should take into account the cost to the nation of the investment of the resources that they used, i.e. the opportunity cost of capital'. Resources invested in nationalised industries were to earn a return to the nation comparable to that which they would have achieved elsewhere. The measure of opportunity cost that the nationalised industries were to use was the *required rate of return (RRR)*. It was fixed at 5 per cent in real terms before tax on new investment over its working life. This figure was considered to be comparable with the rate that companies in the private sector earned or were likely to achieve.

INVESTMENT POLICIES

Nationalised industries needed new investment to: (i) meet new or increased demand for their output; (ii) become more competitive in home and overseas markets; and (iii) take advantage of new technology. But they also needed new capital to replace old assets as they wore out, because in a time of inflation depreciation funds were proving insufficient.

The 1967 White Paper emphasised the importance of investment and the point that investment decisions must be made on the basis of the appropriate criteria, but did not make it explicit what they were. The general guidelines on investment were: (i) new projects should earn a satisfactory commercial return; (ii) the rate of return could be modified to take into account social costs and benefits; (iii) a distinction should be drawn between new capital and overall return on net assets; and (iv) discounted cash flow technique and a test rate of discount should be used to appraise new investment projects (see p. 403).

Experience showed the test rate of discount to be inadequate in relating the cost of capital projects to the nationalised industries' financial objectives. Only a small percentage of projects had been subjected to this form of appraisal. There were several reasons for this. A large proportion of investment in the public sector of industry was not optional for the following reasons:

(a) *Replacement of assets* had to be undertaken if a service or a level of output was to be maintained. For example, approximately 80 per cent of investment by British Rail went on replacements.

(b) *Investment in technology* had to be undertaken if the required standard of service was to be met. Some 90 per cent of investment by the Post Office telecommunications section (later British Telecom) fell in this category.

(c) *Strategic investment* may be essential to the safety of a country and be part of an overall government policy – for example, the development of the supply of North Sea gas. In the case of British Gas, expenditure for the strategic purpose was estimated to account for 75 per cent of its investment.

The test discount rate was replaced in 1978 by opportunity cost as the criterion for undertaking new investment projects and the new required rate of return was intended to apply to investment of a nationalised industry as a whole, and to determine: (i) the setting of financial targets for industries; (ii) decisions on the scale of investment; and (iii) the pricing policies of industries where prices were market determined.

PRICING POLICIES

Public corporations had been given guidelines on their pricing policies but had found it difficult to reconcile the recommendations in practice. Their instructions were:

(i) To balance their accounts, taking one year with another over a period of five years, after providing for interest and depreciation at historic cost (1961 White Paper).
(ii) To adopt pricing policies so that 'revenues should normally cover their accounting costs in full' and take into account both short-run and long-run marginal costs, i.e. costs of producing an additional unit of output (1967 White Paper)
(iii) To take the opportunity cost of capital into account in pricing their output (1978 White Paper).

The framework provided for the pricing policies of the public corporations had to be flexible because of the difference in the nature of the industries. Some nationalised industries had their prices largely determined by the market forces, having to compete at home and abroad. Others, as has been seen, were monopolies. The extent to which the corporations had to provide social services varied. Each of these factors had a bearing on the prices they charged.

The pricing policies of the nationalised industries had in practice, been based on the following general principles:

(a) Consumers should pay the *true cost* of the provision of goods and services where it can be identified.

(b) *Cross-subsidisation* between profitable and unprofitable services within the industry might be permitted in some circumstances. For example, British Rail could use a surplus earned by commuter services to subsidise loss-making rural services.

(c) *Below-cost prices* could be charged when there was a surplus capacity and a reduction in price would stimulate demand.

(d) *Differential prices* might be charged when demand fluctuated and was heavier at certain times, so that prices were higher at peak times and lower at the off-peak time (e.g. charges for a telephone call of the same duration and over the same distance were lower after business hours).

(e) *Multi-tariffs* could be introduced, listing charges that were related to the volume of goods transported or purchased and customers could be offered reduced charges.

The corporations had found implementation of *marginal cost pricing policies* difficult. British Rail could not price some of its services on the basis of marginal costs. The Post Office estimated that marginal cost pricing would have added to its costs as it would have required the establishment and operation of computer models, and the results would not have been substantially different from those of a pricing policy based on average costs.

In theory, public corporations were free to follow their own pricing policies within the guidelines. In practice, they had increasingly come under the government's scrutiny and control. Nationalised industries had an enormous impact on the economy, on account of their size and because they provided many basic goods and services that directly or indirectly entered into the costs of production of all other industries. If the corporations' pricing policies were such that their output was provided at a price below the cost of supply, excess demand would have been created. Higher prices, that provided for a return regarded by the corporation as satisfactory, would add to the cost of living and might prove inflationary.

Government intervention had affected the nationalised industries' pricing policies and their ability to cover costs in the following ways:

(i) Under the different versions of prices and incomes policy that successive governments have followed, the freedom of the corporations to increase their prices had been restricted.

(ii) Price rises, if allowed by the government, had at times been delayed.

(iii) Government had influenced the corporations' decisions on inputs. This had affected their costs and the prices they needed to charge, e.g. the electricity industry's choice of fuel for new power stations had to be considered in relation to the government's policy to maintain demand for coal.

(iv) Government had restricted the corporations' scope to buy cheaper inputs abroad.

BORROWING

Inadequate revenue, lack of internal resources and the high cost of investment projects had forced public corporations to borrow on a large scale. Up to 1965 they were able to raise medium- and long-term finance on the London money market. Since then, their capital needs had been met by the government from the Consolidated Fund and, from 1968 onwards, from the National Loan Fund. The corporations were also able to borrow on their own account abroad. The Bank of England advised them on foreign capital markets and the Treasury acted as guarantor.

The advantages of foreign borrowing were that: (i) it enabled the corporations to raise the loans more cheaply if rates of interest were lower abroad; and (ii) the capital was obtained from outside the UK and did not result in an internal transfer from the private to the public sector. Foreign loans did, however, add to the external burden of the national debt and, as we have seen (p. 298), interest payments and subsequent capital repayments may have adversely affected the balance of payments.

PUBLIC DIVIDEND CAPITAL (PDC)

A different way of financing the corporations' investment projects is by means of public dividend capital provided by the government. To qualify for this type of capital, a corporation had to show that it was, or potentially could be, commercially viable and that its revenue was subject to cyclical fluctuations. The corporations that were deemed to qualify and be entitled to PDC were British Aerospace, British Airways, National Post Office Giro, British Shipbuilders and British Steel.

Public dividend capital corresponded to risk capital in the private sector, where investors in equities acquired an entitlement to a share in the profits of a company. This was paid in the form of dividends. The shareholders are regarded as the owners of a company and not lenders. The state was the owner of a nationalised industry and was thus entitled to the public dividend. The advantage of PDC to corporations was that, whereas interest on loans is payable whether profits are earned or not, dividends are only paid if a surplus has been earned. This gave them greater flexibility in their financial management.

END OF AN ERA

Guidance, intervention and changes in methods of finance by successive governments over nearly forty years did not ensure the benefits that the public came to expect from nationalisation. The public sector of industry was criticised for: not delivering the level and quality of output that would enable it to meet its financial obligations; not demonstrating efficient use of resources; not meeting such competition as there was; and not satisfying customers. Dissatisfaction with the performance of the nationalised industries and undertakings mounted. In the 1980s the process of privatisation by governments began in the UK and in other countries throughout the world.

Governments transferred nationalised enterprises in increasing numbers back to the private sector and the era when they dominated national economies came to an end.

SUMMARY

1. The public sector of industry in the UK comprised nationalised industries and individual public enterprises in manufacturing and service industries in the private sector. Some of these are still in operation.
2. The size, growth and importance of the nationalised industries to the national economy can be measured in terms of sales, employment and investment.
3. Reasons for nationalisation were political, social and economic. Both Conservative and Labour governments nationalised some public enterprises, but the main nationalisation phase was during the post-war Labour administration of 1945 to 1951.
4. Public corporations have been set up to manage nationalised industries. They were a compromise between a government department and

a company. The duties were set out in statutes only in general terms
and were subject to individual interpretation.

5. Three White Papers had been published – in 1961, 1967 and 1978 – to
give more specific guidance to the corporations on their financial and
economic obligations.

6. Relations between the corporations and Parliament were based on the
'at arm's length' philosophy, but Members of Parliament could raise
Parliamentary questions and debate policy matters, though not, as a
rule, the day-to-day running of the corporations. Governments' intervention in the management of the nationalised industries had
increased as a result of a policy to exercise greater control over public
spending and borrowing by means of imposing cash limits and
restricting the public sector borrowing requirement.

7. Nationalised industries were expected to earn the required rate of
return (RRR), taking into account the opportunity cost of investment
projects.

8. The pricing policies of the corporations were aimed at covering costs
but the social service element was financed out of grants. Over the
years, governments have sought to reduce subsidies to the nationalised industries.

9. Public corporations obtained their capital from the government but they
could also borrow on their own behalf abroad. One particular innovation in finance was the introduction of public dividend capital (PDC).

10. A major role of the nationalised industries in provision of goods and
services came to an end by the 1990s. The public sector of industry
was greatly reduced in size and in importance in the UK and in many
other countries throughout the world.

SUGGESTED FURTHER READING

National Economic Development Office, *A Study of UK Nationalised Industries*
(London: HMSO, 1976).
Nationalised Industries, Cmnd. 7131 (London: HMSO, 1978).
Open University, *Nationalised Industries*, Course D203, IV (Milton Keynes: Open
University Press, 1976).
R. Pryke, *Nationalised Industries, Polices and Performance* (Oxford: Martin
Robertson, 1980).
J. Redwood, *Public Enterprise in Crisis* (Oxford: Basil Blackwell, 1980).
L. Tivey, *Nationalisation in British Industry* (London: Jonathan Cape, 1973).
M.G. Webb, *The Economics of Nationalised Industries* (London: Nelson, 1973).

Note:

There has been a dearth of books on nationalised industries since the early 1980s.

EXERCISES

1. With hindsight, which arguments for nationalisation of the basic industries do you consider to be still valid?
2. Consider the consequences of monopoly powers of some of the public corporations.
3. Is it realistic to expect public corporations to operate on a commercial basis?
4. Discuss the problems in assessing the size and importance to the economy of the public sector of industry.
5. Consider the practicality of having one set of pricing policy guidelines for the whole public sector of industry.
6. Examine arguments for and against subsidising a public enterprise that operates in the private sector of industry.
7. What factors are relevant to formulation of investment plans by a nationalised industry.
8. Define 'public dividend capital'. Explain its advantages from the point of view of a public corporation.
9. It has been suggested that the organisation and finance of the public sector of industry was in need of re-organisation. Give your views on this.
10. Suggest possible reasons why the nationalised industries did not succeed in meeting public expectations to which nationalisation gave rise.

18 Privatisation

The word *privatisation*, according to economic folklore, first appeared on a printed page in *The Economist* in the early 1960s. 'It was suggested by somebody now dead who may have subconsciously pinched it from something published earlier somewhere else' (*The Economist*, January 3 1992). Attribution may perhaps be eventually resolved when 'privatisation' finds its way into the *Oxford English Dictionary*. Currently the word is taken to mean: (a) transfer of ownership of state assets from the public to the private sector; or (b) transfer of provision of services from public bodies to private enterprise. 'Privatisation' is synonymous with denationalisation. The years of the 1940s, 1950s, 1960s and 1970s were the period of nationalisation when Socialist ideology was being put into practice throughout the world. The means of production, distribution, finance and communication were taken over by the state to a varying extent in different countries. The 1980s saw a return to a modified version of the *laissez-faire* philosophy and to market economics. The UK pioneered privatisation in 1979. It became, and continues to be, an international phenomenon in the 1990s.

The *aims* of the privatisation programmes are political and economic. The relative importance of the reasons for privatisation differs from country to country but basically they are:

    (i) Disenchantment with Communism and Socialism as the poor performance of command economies became apparent.
    (ii) Failure of nationalised industries in general to meet consumers' needs effectively.
    (iii) The wish to reduce the power of the state and its role in the economy.
    (iv) Belief that an enterprise-based economy would allow for greater flexibility and a better response to consumers' demands.
    (v) Determination to create capital-owning democracies.

Thus governments privatise to:

    (i) Reduce the size of the public sector of industry.
    (ii) Increase competition in the markets.
    (iii) Improve efficiency among suppliers of goods and services.

(iv) Extend share ownership in companies by investors with small amounts of savings.

(v) Ease the pressure on central governments' budgets.

The expectation is that, as state monopolies are broken up and a competitive environment established, privatised firms will have to improve their efficiency, cut costs, and reduce prices or keep them below the level up to which they would have otherwise risen. Firms that are not competitive will, unlike state enterprises, go out of business. Privatised companies that are profitable or have profit potential will attract investors and enable shareholders with small amounts of capital and employees to acquire shareholdings. Private funding of industry reduces claims on public finance. The help to the government comes on both sides of the budget. On the *expenditure* side, the state no longer has to support loss-making nationalised industries and provide them with capital, thereby increasing the public sector borrowing requirement. On the *revenue* side, proceeds from the sale of state assets increase governments' resources enabling them to increase public spending or cut taxation, or both.

Opponents of privatisation argue that: privatisation of 'natural monopolies' merely substitutes private for state monopoly; that the social service elements in provision of services by profit-driven companies will disappear and measures to cut costs will lead to unemployment. These arguments did not win the day. Conservative, Liberal and Socialist governments went ahead with privatisation programmes throughout the world. They privatised by selling state assets to the private sector; contracting-out services by central government, local authorities and other public bodies, exposing public sector providers to market forces by legal requirement to tender for contracts in competition with private firms (see p. 323).

MECHANISM OF PRIVATISATION

How state-owned enterprises are privatised depends on a variety of factors, such as whether: the country is developed, developing or emerging from a centrally-planned economic system; the relative size of the public sector of industry; the sophistication of the national capital market and the financial framework. The state of international capital markets is also important. It may reach a saturation level if a large number of privatisation share offers are made concurrently and national governments restrict the extent of foreign investment that may be allowed. Timing and local legislation are therefore important factors. What is also relevant to a decision on the choice of privatisation method is the nature and size of privatisation. On offer may be: (a) a *minority* share-holding in a company – for example the French government announced its decision to keep a majority holding in Renault (51 per cent); (b) a *controlling* stake in a company e.g. in Instituto Mobiliare Italiano; (c) a state-owned company already operating in competitive international markets, e.g. British Airways; (d) a whole nationalised industry, e.g. the electricity industry in the UK; or (e) potentially the whole of the economy e.g. in Russia, if privatisation proceeds.

Depending on the circumstances the transfer from state to private ownership may be by means of:

A public flotation

Shares are offered to the general public and can be traded subsequently on the stock exchange. This method is only appropriate for privatisation of large enterprises. The British Telecom flotation (1984) was the biggest-ever offer of ordinary shares in the world.

Placing

Brokers acting on behalf of a government arrange for the purchase of shares by placing them with a group of investors or one large investor who may wish to hold or gradually sell off the stock.

Trade sale

A state enterprise is sold to a private sector company or consortium, e.g. ENSA (a truck maker) was sold to Fiat. A trade sale is likely to be on the basis of a tender and financial markets are bypassed.

Management/workers' buy-out

A state-owned undertaking may be sold to employees because it is loss-making or faces closure and companies in the private sector are not interested in buying it. There may, however, be a possibility of turning it round to run on a profitable basis. Management/worker buy-outs can save jobs. It may be an attractive proposition to a government for reasons other than financial. For instance, in the UK the buy-out of National Freight created a highly successful business.

Auction

In cases of smaller properties owned by the state, sale by auction may be a relatively simple way to privatise but the practicality of this depends on there being a sufficient number of bidders with adequate funds to purchase. In Russia a local authority in Nizhny Novgorod, with help from the World Bank, successfully auctioned state-owned shops.

Grant of statutory right to purchase .

People may be granted by law the right to purchase specified state property, provided they meet certain requirements. Thus for example, in the UK, tenants living in local authority houses are entitled to purchase them on favourable terms. As a result a high proportion of public housing stock has been transferred to private ownership.

Generally, it is easier to privatise single companies and small units than whole industries, but much depends on the profitability, past or potential, of the enterprise. Thus, in France, of the two state-owned firms, privatisation of the profitable insurer AGF is likely to be easier than that of the loss-making computer firm, Groupe Bull. The British government sold off two profitable nationalised industries, gas and electricity, ahead of the loss-making coal industry. Sale of the remaining pits was completed in December 1994. British Rail is still to be privatised.

The ease and success of privatisation also depends on the absence of conditions to the sale that may deter potential investors. During the first phase of privatisation in Portugal, government restriction on foreign ownership of privatised companies to 25 per cent was thought to be responsible for the lack of interest in the sales abroad.

PRICING OF STATE ASSETS TO BE PRIVATISED

In putting a price on state assets to be sold, governments face a dilemma. To maximise proceeds from the sale they would, in the interests of the taxpayers, need to fix prices at a high level, but to ensure the privatisation is a success the price needs to be low enough to be attractive. The judging of a high or low valuation is relative. It is difficult to determine when there is no basis for comparison, as in the case of privatisation of a whole industry which is a 'natural monopoly'. When there is a market valuation

380 Public Sector Industries and Investment

Table 18.1 Privatisation: capital gains

Privatised company	First day dealings in previous government share offers price per share in pence* on:		
	Offer	First Deals	First day closing
British Telecom (1984)	50	90	93
Enterprise Oil (1984)	100	98	100
British Gas (1986)	50	62	64
BAA (1987)	100	145	147
British Airways (1987)	65	107	110
Rolls-Royce (1987)	85	141	141
British Steel (1989)	60	62	$61\frac{1}{2}$
Water Companies (1989)	100	135–156	132–156

*1st instalment
Source: *The Times* (London) (12 December, 1990).

in the sense that there are counterparts to the state undertakings in the private sector then putting a value on the state assets is easier. The tendency is for governments to underprice shares in privatised companies offered to the public. So far none of the issues in the European Community have flopped. Some have been heavily oversubscribed. The sale of Banque National de Paris was oversubscribed five times by individual and institutional investors. In the UK investors in the government share offers have seen their initial stake increase in value appreciably (Tables 18.1 and 18.2).

Under the European Union law, governments of Member States are obliged to give equal opportunity to invest to all the citizens of the Union. However, some governments have appeared disinclined to see foreign nationals benefit from their privatisation sales. The British government, however, adopted an international outlook. Offer for sale of British Telecommunications plc clearly stated that some of the company's share capital was to be offered abroad in the USA, Canada and Japan and an intensive marketing campaign on an international basis followed.

The eventual price of shares or houses will be determined by the market forces of demand and supply. Demand will be influenced by attractiveness of the offer as compared with other investment opportunities. Inducements such as bonus shares, low price/asset value ratio, spread of payments over a period of time and arrangements to facilitate purchase will push prices up. Prices may be depressed by government restrictions on share ownership by foreign nationals or a risk of re-nationalisation, e.g. the British Telecommunications plc prospectus warned that 'The Labour Party has

Table 18.2   Return on investment in privatised companies

Company	Start date month/year	Issue price pence	Price 8/9/94 pence	Total return* %
British Telecom	11/84	130	394½	504.4
British Gas	12/86	135	298	354.6
British Airways	02/87	125	410	522.2
BAA	07/87	122.5	495**	426.6
BP	11/87	330	420	240.0
Rolls-Royce	10/87	170	186	166.3
British Steel	12/88	125	152½	188.9
Anglian Water	12/89	240	572 x	351.1
North West Water	"	"	572 x	346.8
Nthumb Water	"	"	698 x	416.9
Severn Trent	"	"	564½ x	344.9
South West Water	"	"	542 x	349.7
Southern Water	"	"	595 x	364.9
Thames Water	"	"	518 x	315.1
Welsh Water	"	"	694 x	420.9
Wessex Water	"	"	694 x	383.9
Yorks Water	"	"	567 x	340.3
East Mid Electry	12/90	240	750 x	414.7
Eastern Electry	"	"	782½ x	428.4
London Electry	"	"	714 x	380.1
Manweb	"	"	866 x	454.9
Midland Electry	"	"	818 x	431.5
Northern Electry	"	"	822½ x	452.3
Norweb	"	"	814 x	431.8
Seeboard	"	"	444 x	477.4
S Wales Electry	"	"	824 x	441.6
S Western Electry	"	"	793 x	436.0
Southern Electry	"	"	773 x	413
Yorks Electry	"	"	776 x	412.5
National Power	03/91	175	493	360.0
PowerGen	03/91	175	576	408.9
Scot Hydro	06/91	240	391	194.1
Scottish Power	06/91	240	393	194.7
Nthn Ire Electry	06/93	220	386	186.3

Notes:

* Total Returns, including dividends, as percentage of initial investment.
** After share split. x If sold at present, seller retains right to forthcoming dividend.

Source: *The Times* (London) (10 September 1994).

called for re-nationalisation of British Telecom with compensation to be paid on the basis of no speculative gain'. Demand is also likely to be weaker at a time of recession or when capital markets are flooded with new issues. A government cannot fix the demand at any particular level. It can, however, control the supply of share in privatised companies.

It can stagger flotations. Supply of shares will depend on the scale and speed of the privatisation programmes and the capacity of the capital markets to absorb them. When demand outstrips supply investors can make appreciable capital gains as traded prices exceed issue prices (Tables 18.1 and 18.2). Government policy to expand share ownership and to attract small and new investors carries a risk for the inexperienced and those unfamiliar with the ways of capital markets. In the UK, the prospectus for the privatisation of the Regional Electricity Companies carried the usual warning for the would-be purchasers of shares – 'their value can go down as well as up'.

The UK began the privatisation drive. The British experience in transferring state-owned undertakings to the private sector gave rise to the development of expertise by professionals in areas such as finance, banking, law and accountancy. This 'Know How' became a valuable British export as countries throughout the world began to privatise.

When the Conservative government came into office after the general elections in 1979 they were pledged to privatise. In the same year, they started disposing of state holdings in British Petroleum. Throughout the 1980s privatisation after privatisation followed (see Table 18.3). By the end of its second term of office about two-thirds of the nationalised sector of industry had been privatised. Different methods were used, which ranged from management/workers buy-out for relatively small concerns such as National Freight, to the flotation of millions of shares in international capital markets when British Telecommunications plc was put up for sale. In the UK a 'public company' is the term used for a private sector joint stock company with a limited liability (plc) owned by shareholders, whereas a public corporation (see p. 363) is a statutory body set up by the government to run a state owned undertaking or a nationalised industry.

Privatisation of the so-called '*natural monopolies*' presents a wide range of problems and is a particularly controversial issue. The following examples illustrate the difference in approaches and outcomes.

Gas, water and electricity were all state-owned industries and regarded as 'natural monopolies'. Inclusion of telecommunications in this category was more controversial. Privatisation changed the structure of the industries and as private sector companies they became:

British Telecom	–	duopolist (initially)
British Gas	–	monopolist
Water and Sewerage Companies	–	local monopolists, subject to 'yardstick' competition
Regional Electricity Companies	–	competitors
Electricity Generating Companies	–	oligopolists

Table 18.3   Privatisation, major sales since 1979

British Petroleum*	1979, 1983 and 1987
British Aerospace	1981, 1985
Cable and Wireless	1981
Amersham International	1982
National Freight Consortium	1982
Britoil	1982, 1985
Associated British Ports	1983, 1984
Enterprise Oil	1984
Jaguar	1984
British Telecom	1984, 1991
British Gas	1986
British Airways	1987
Royal Ordnance	1987
Rolls-Royce	1987
BAA	1987
Rover Group*	1988
British Steel	1988
Water & Sewerage Companies	1989
Regional Electricity Companies (England and Wales)	1990
Generating Companies (National Power & PowerGen)	1991
Scottish Electricity Companies	1991
Northern Ireland Electricity Distribution	1993
British Coal	1994

Work in progress on privatisation of:

British Rail	1993 onwards

Note: *private sector companies.
Source: HM Treasury, *Economic Briefing*, no. 5 (1993).

Telecommunications

The *British Telecommunications plc* flotation in 1984 was not only the biggest ever offer of sale of equity capital in the world, but was also the first privatisation of a whole industry and 'natural monopoly' in the UK. The company was granted a licence to run its public networks within a framework of regulations for telecommunications. BT is obliged to provide nationwide services and to continue some of its community services. However, it is no longer a monopoly supplier. The government also granted a licence to Mercury, creating a duopoly with the intention to encourage further competition from other companies. Nevertheless, BT still operates one of the largest telephone networks in the world. It provides local, national and international telephone services, telex, radio-phone, radio-paging, data communications and information services, and supplies telephone apparatus for rent or purchase.

The sale of BT shares was handled by a merchant bank, Kleinwort Benson. Apart from a percentage of the issue reserved for certain UK institutional investors, the rest was offered to any member of the general public who had a minimum of £260 to invest. As the government's intention was to encourage investors with small amounts in savings, the purchase price was payable in instalments. Ordinary shares were offered at 130 pence each, with the first payment of 50p due in 1984, 40p in 1985 and 40p in 1986. In all 3,012,000,000 shares were issued and these were heavily oversubscribed. Shares at the opening price of 50p by the end of the first day of trading were being sold at 93p. There were various reasons why the flotation was so popular. BT was a profitable state enterprise before it was privatised. Its prospects as a private company were good. Not only was the price attractive but inducements were also offered of premium shares and concessions on telephone bills. Many people as users of BT services were familiar with the name and had a good idea of the nature of its business. Nevertheless, steps were taken to make information on the company easily accessible. Not only were prospectuses published in national papers, but copies of the prospectuses were made widely available at post offices, branches of high street banks as well as at the premises of stockbrokers. Investors did not, however, need to use their services – thus saving themselves purchase costs. There were no dealing costs for people who bought the shares on offer. The government retained a proportion of the issue with the intention of disposing of it later. The '*golden share*' gives the government limited powers over the 'future ownership, control or conduct of a privatised company', but the BT prospectus made it clear that the government 'did not propose to exercise its right as an ordinary shareholder and become involved in management decisions'.

Telecommunications Regulations

Some restrictions were, however, placed on BT pricing policies. Prices for line rental and most inland telephone calls were limited for the initial five years to 3 per cent below the general level of inflation (RPI – 3). Other services representing some 45 per cent of the turnover were not subjected to regulation.

The Office of Telecommunications (Oftel) – a non-ministerial government department – exercises overall supervision over telecommunications and holders of licences who provide services; protects interests of consumers; and deals with complaints and anti-competitive practices. Thus, though the state is no longer responsible for the running of the industry, the government has introduced measures to protect the interests of the general public.

Electricity Industry

Electricity industry privatisation was perhaps the most complex of them all. It required restructuring of the industry and breaking it up into units. These were sold off as separate companies in the private sector. The 'natural monopoly' of the state-owned industry was brought to an end, but Nuclear Electric was left in the public sector. In peoples' minds, nuclear energy generation is associated with risk and, after disasters such as Chernobyl, there is widespread concern over safety. Privatisation was further complicated as electricity companies in England and Wales were privatised ahead of Scotland and Northern Ireland (Table 18.3).

The size of the task of restructuring of the industry is to some extent illustrated by the range of its activities. These are:

'Generation: the production of electricity at power stations.
Transmission: the bulk transfer of electricity from the national grid and its delivery, across local distribution systems, to consumers.
Supply: the purchase of electricity from generators... and its sale to customers'.

Whilst electricity was a nationalised industry, the Central Electricity Generating Board (CEGB) generated electricity in England and Wales, operated the National Grid and inter-connections with Scotland and sold electricity to twelve Area Boards that were also state owned. They then supplied customers in their area. After the restructuring in 1990, two companies, National Power plc and PowerGen plc acquired fossil fuelled power stations from CEGB. Nuclear Electric plc took over nuclear power stations. Regional Electricity Companies (REC) replaced the Area Boards and shares in the privatised companies were offered to investors in 1990. 80 per cent of ordinary share capital in each company was offered in the UK and 20 per cent abroad.

Electricity flotation

The share offer price of 240p was the same for each of the Regional Electricity Companies and payable in instalments of 100p in 1990, 70p in 1991 and 70p in 1992. Again the aim was to attract people with small amounts of savings, and to encourage them to continue as investors by offering bonus shares to those who held on to their shares until 1993.

Special concessions were made to existing customers. They were offered either bonus shares or electricity vouchers. In all over 1000 million shares were issued and they were heavily oversubscribed (Table 18.2 and Figure 18.1).

Whereas in Regional Electricity companies the entire equity capital went on offer, when National Power plc and PowerGen plc were privatised, government retained 40 per cent holding in each.

In Scotland Scottish Power plc and Scottish Hydro-Electricity plc were floated on the stock market in 1991. Scottish Nuclear Ltd is responsible for nuclear energy and has not gone on sale.

Electricity industry regulation

Having transferred most of the industry to the private sector the government nevertheless retained some regulatory powers. It established the Office of Electricity Regulation (OFFER) headed by the Director-General of Electricity Supplies (DGES) who is responsible for economic regulations and supervision in general, and for setting performance standards. The DGES and the Secretary of State for Energy are also required to promote efficiency in generation and supply of electricity, and in its use, taking into account environmental factors. They also have a duty to protect the interests of consumers.

Furthermore, regulatory provision was extended to pricing. *Supply prices* for all customers are controlled by an overall RPI $- X_S + Y$ formula. The Y term allows the costs incurred in the purchase and delivery of electricity to be passed through to customers. The RPI $- X_S$ component covers profit and supply own costs not passed directly into prices through the Y term. The initial value of X has been set at zero. The formula is subject to

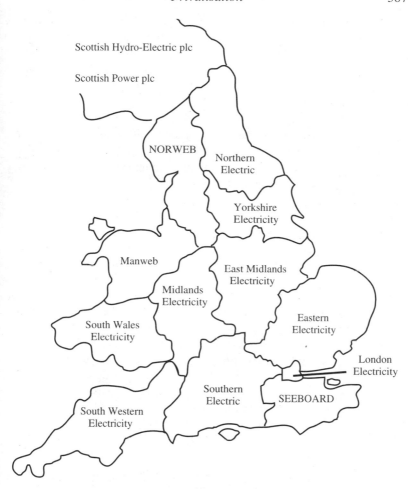

Figure 18.1   Regional Electricity Companies' authorised areas
Source: The Regional Electricity Companies Share Offers, Prospectuses (1990).

review. Thus, although electricity is now privatised the electricity companies still remain subject to some degree of government control.

Gas Industry

In comparison with the electricity industry, privatisation of gas was relatively simple. It was transferred as a monopoly from the public to the private sector. British Gas Corporation became British Gas plc and the regional gas boards became gas regions managing business at the local level.

Regulation of the industry is now the responsibility of the Office of Gas Supply (OFGAS). Its head, the Director-General of Gas Supply is, however, independent of Ministerial control. OFGAS functions are to: (i) supervise the industry, (ii) fix charges for reselling gas and charges for access to pipelines; and (iii) deal with complaints.

Issue of shares in British Gas plc was extensively publicised. They too were attractively packaged and heavily oversubscribed. So far as customers were concerned, the change in ownership did not in practice have a noticeable effect. Peoples' meters were read, bills sent out, and payments made, very much as before. New regulations applicable to the industry continued to protect customers interests.

Water Industry

Water privatisation was, perhaps, the most unpopular of them all. The original proposals had to be revised and the government embarked on a campaign to reassure people. Many issues gave rise for concern. Water is essential for people and animals to live. Industry needs water. Sewerage and industrial effluent pollute rivers and beaches and are damaging to: health, water leisure activities and the environment generally. The European Commission had criticised standards of water and the extent of water pollution in the UK. To comply with the requirements of EC regulations would require massive investment – purification of water, pipelines, sewage treatment and disposal is needed. Fears were expressed that private sector water companies would have to recoup their costs and raise charges and, since there is no substitute for water, consumers would suffer as a result of the transfer of the state monopoly to the private sector.

Until the time of privatisation there had been nine regional water authorities in England and one in Wales. Under the *1989 Water Act* provisions were made for water to become a private sector industry under public regulation and ten companies were formed as follows:

Anglian Water Services Ltd.	Southern Water Services Ltd.
North West Water Ltd.	Thames Water Utilities Ltd.
Northumbrian Water Ltd.	Welsh Water plc
Severn Trent Water Ltd.	Wessex Water Services plc
South West Water Services Ltd.	Yorkshire Water Services Ltd.

Shares in all the companies were offered to the general public. The government was anxious that the issue be taken up and wished to 'clear the decks' as a very large flotation of the Regional Electricity Companies was coming on to the market shortly afterwards. In the event, water shares were oversubscribed and their price during the first day's trading rose sharply (Table 18.1).

Each company had a local monopoly but the government claimed that there was a 'yardstick competition' in that their performance profits and charges could be compared against each other.

Water charges created problems. When local authorities levied rates (see p. 315) on domestic property, water and sewerage charges were assessed on the basis of its value. Since the rates had been abolished, water companies were given, under the Water Act 1989, the opportunity to devise a new system of charges by the end of the century. The alternatives were: (i) a flat rate; (ii) a charge related to property banding; or (iii) charges based on metered consumption as is the case with industrial and commercial property.

The companies are subject to a system of price control and the Director-General of Water Services who heads the Office of Water Services is responsible for protecting the interests of consumers and supervising the industry. In addition there is the Drinking Water Inspectorate. Its duty is to assess the quality of water supplies.

The National Rivers Authority, set up at the time of privatisation, is concerned with pollution control and the management of water resources. However, in Scotland and Northern Ireland responsibility for the water industry was left with their respective Secretaries of State and public sector authorities.

This brief review indicates to some extent how privatisation methods of the 'natural monopolies' were adapted to the specific circumstances of the particular industries. This policy was also followed when other state undertakings were transferred to the public sector.

THE RANGE OF PRIVATISATION INITIATIVES

The diverse nature of the undertakings that were privatised is highlighted in Table 18.3. In the case of British Steel, matters were complicated by the fact that it had been nationalised, denationalised, re-nationalised and privatised. This reflected the political views of successive governments.

From 1979, the Conservative Government employed a variety of privatisation methods ranging from huge stock exchange flotations with appeal to international investors, to management/worker buy-outs on a small scale.

Privatisation was not confined to the transfer of the ownership of industry from the public to the private sector. Contracting-out of services provision by the central government, local authorities, the National Health Service (see p. 105) and other public bodies to private sector suppliers had far-reaching repercussions introducing some market economy practices into the public sector.

CONSEQUENCES OF PRIVATISATION IN THE UK

Some consequences are easier to identify and assess than others.

1. The size of the public sector and the power of the government was reduced.
2. A greater degree of competition has been achieved, though some monopolies continue to operate.
3. Sale of state assets brought a considerable amount of money into the Treasury, thereby helping to finance government expenditure programmes and to allow for tax cuts. The success of the share flotations and the subsequent capital gains by investors was seen by critics to be a result of underpricing of the issues and failure to maximise proceeds of the sale.
4. Management of privatised companies are now accountable to the shareholders and exposed to the discipline of the market. They can prosper or go bankrupt.

To what extent the government's long-term objectives of increasing efficiency and more widespread share ownership have been achieved is more difficult to assess. It can be argued that the performance of companies is reflected in the market price of their shares. Their value has risen considerably since privatisation. It is interesting to note that, when we look at capital appreciation in comparable companies in the electricity and water industries, some have done better than others. It can thus be presumed that some have improved their performance to a greater extent. Rising share prices indicate demand for them, and therefore the willingness of investors to hold stocks. But whether in the long run small investors will not cash in on their capital gains remains to be seen.

Nevertheless, the experience of privatisation in the UK has encouraged other countries to follow and to seek British expertise to assist them along that road.

PRIVATISATION IN EUROPE AND ELSEWHERE

Although governments of many countries throughout the world have committed themselves to privatisation, the degree of commitment, scale and speed of privatisation differs. Much of the scope for privatisation depends on the nature and size of the public sector of industry within a country. Neither the USA. nor Japan had gone in for nationalisation programmes in the first place – opportunities for privatisation of industry are therefore somewhat limited. In Japan however, as a result of the deregulation of the domestic telecommunications sector, the state-owned Nippon Telegraph Telephone (NTT) became a joint stock corporation and, as a result of other transfers, the proceeds from privatisation were substantial. In Europe, neither in Denmark nor in Switzerland, is the state involved in the management of industries to any appreciable extent. When there is virtually no public sector of industry scope for privatisation will lie in the contracting-out of services in public administration at the central and local government level.

Table 18.4 Privatisation programmes in selected countries

Country	Privatisation Period	Accumulated privatisation proceeds Absolute (£ equivalent) Billion		As % of average annual GDP over the privatisation period
Austria	1987–90	Sch 12.7	(£0.6)	0.9
Canada	1984–90	C$ 3.1	(£1.6)	0.6
France	1983–91	FF 82.4	(£8.2)	1.5
Germany*	1984–90	DM 9.7	(£3.3)	0.5
Italy	1983–91	L 13,500	(£6.3)	1.4
Japan	1986–88	Y 11,000	(£47.8)	3.1
Netherlands	1987–91	FL 4.9	(£1.5)	1.0
New Zealand	1987–91	NZ$ 9.0	(£3.0)	14.1
Portugal	1989–91	Esc. 364	(£1.5)	4.3
Spain	1986–90	Ptas. 207	(£1.2)	0.5
Sweden	1987–90	SKr. 14	(£1.3)	1.2
Turkey	1988–91	TL 3,500	(£0.3)	1.6
UK	1979–91	£ 44.5		11.9

Note:
*Area of Federal Republic of Germany before unification.
Calculation by Barrie Stevens.

Source: Barrie Stevens, 'Prospects for Privatisation in OECD countries', *National Westminister Bank Quarterly Review* (August 1992).

Among the privatising countries, besides the UK, New Zealand has also launched a widespread privatisation drive (Table 18.4). The government sold off state interests in such diverse ventures as Air New Zealand, New Zealand Steel and Post Office Bank. Similarly, although compared with the British privatisation programme the French one is more modest, it has ranked high among the government's priorities. The importance attached to privatisation is perhaps, to some extent, reflected in the title of a senior minister who is designed as 'the Minister for Finance, the Economy and Privatisation'. The French government came to office pledged to privatise within five years: banks, finance houses, insurance companies and five major industrial groups that had been nationalised in 1982. Candidates for privatisation in 1986 were:

Industrial group:	Banks:	Assurance companies:
Thomson-Brandt	Banque Nationale de Paris	UAP
Saint-Gobain	Crédit Lyonnais	AGF
Péchiney	Societé Générale	GAN
CGE		
Rhône-Poulnec		*Financial holding companies:*
		Paribas
		Suez

On a further 'short list' was Elf-Aquitaine (energy/oil) and a number of others. By 1994 some of them have yet to be floated on the stock market.

In Spain and Portugal, the limitations of their capital markets have made the sale of state enterprises to the private sector more difficult. Nevertheless, governments are pursuing privatisation policies bypassing financial markets and relying on tenders. In Spain, Instituto National de Industria (a state-owned holding company) is implementing the privatisation programme. Some businesses have been sold – for example, hotels and fishing companies. In others, state holdings have been disposed of, as in the case of Seat (the Spanish vehicle manufacturer) when a majority stake was purchased by Germany's Volkswagen. Privatisation issues scheduled to come to the market in 1994 included Ence (forest products), ENDESA (utilities), Repsol (Energy) and Telefonica.

In Italy, privatisation has been somewhat piecemeal. Instituto per la Riconstruzione Industriale (IRI) and Ente Nazionale Indrocarburi (ENI) began to divest themselves of enterprises in the early 1980s. The privatisation programme was two-fold: (i) Government holdings in a number of larger companies were sold. These included Banca Commerciale Italiana, Banco Centro Suid, Sitiri and SIP (telecommunications). (ii) Various small companies were offered for sale. By 1994 further transfers of financial institutions to the private sector by means of share flotations were in the pipeline.

In the Netherlands in 1985 a committee scrutinised the state holdings in companies. The government reduced both its minority (Hoogovens–Steel) and majority (ECM–Airline) interests and sold shares in KLM (the national airline). However, the extent of privatisation scheduled was comparatively limited.

West Germany began to privatise in the 1980s and the government sold its holding in Veba which was, at the time, the largest industrial group in the country. However, privatisation was on a relatively small scale and progress was slow. This changed following the unification of Germany in the 1990s. Onto the thriving West German market economy, a collapsed East Germany had to be grafted. As a member of the Soviet Bloc it had operated on Marxist principles of state ownership of the means of production and distribution. Thus, the German government had to face the task of privatising just about the whole of the economy of East Germany. Action followed quickly. Treuhand, the privatisation agency, transferred some 15,000 small businesses from the public to the private sector within nine months. Privatisation of bigger enterprises was more difficult, particularly as some had many lines of production that did not fit into a structure of a single organisation. Many relied on antiquated machinery to produce output for which the market was no longer there. The Treuhand classified them into: (a) 'hopeless cases'; (b) 'unprofitable but salvageable'; and (c) 'profitable and sellable'. In privatising East Germany, the government had the great advantage of availability of financial resources, access to capital markets and supply of manpower with the 'Know-How' from its West German neighbours. Nevertheless there was still a price to pay. It has been seen that the restructuring of industry in East Germany reduced overmanning, but in the process the labour force was cut by 75 per cent. With a prosperous West German economy to support them, the unemployed could be retired, retrained and reabsorbed into the labour market. The cost to the West German taxpayers was, however, high. East German privatisation does not provide a blueprint for other countries that were members of the Soviet Bloc. These other countries would not have such a back-up available to them.

PRIVATISATION IN FORMER CENTRALLY-PLANNED ECONOMIES

Mass privatisation in Central and Eastern Europe is quite different from the experience of privatising in Western countries. To all intents and purposes, the former members of the Soviet Bloc had to undertake the privatisation of their entire economies. To start off they had no private sector to which state enterprises could be transferred. There was no legal, administrative, financial and economic framework for a market economy. Private property and company laws had to be enacted. Financial institutions, capital markets and stock exchanges had to be established. Manpower needed training to work in a very different political and economic environment and the management role had to be redefined. Under the Communist system, the government decided what was to be produced, who supplied inputs, who manufactured the final product, who delivered it, to whom, for whose consumption and at what price. The level and direction of investment was centrally planned. Managers carried out instructions and reported back to the Ministries. As this system came to an end, new management structures and techniques appropriate to a market economy had to be developed.

To privatise, governments had to restructure their countries' industries, break up large state organisations into saleable units and to set up Privatisation Ministries or Agencies to attract buyers and to dispose of state assets. The newly privatised businesses have no financial history and uncertain futures. Thus, for potential investors they are risky ventures. Small businesses, such as shops and restaurants, that require relatively little capital, are easier to value and are more marketable.

The scope for privatisation in Central and Eastern Europe differs. In Russia, according to the Privatisation Minister, 97 per cent of the economy is state-owned. Much of it is probably unsaleable. According to him transfer of the enterprises on such a scale to the workers is 'socially unfair, economically ineffective and politically dangerous'.

In contrast, in Poland, even before the country's transformation to a market economy, there was, by Soviet Bloc standards, a considerable degree of private enterprise (Table 18.5). Collectivism in agriculture had not been enforced on the USSR scale and Polish farmers had been allowed to own land and sell some of their produce on the market.

Thus, the scope for privatisation is partly determined by the extent of state ownership of assets and by their nature, but much also depends on the determination of the governments to press ahead with the privatisation policies and on foreign help to implement them. Britain, for example, has

Table 18.5   Share of private enterprise in GDP in Central and Eastern Europe

Centrally planned economies before privatisation programmes	Percentage
Poland ·	14.7
Hungary	14.6
Czechoslovakia	3.1
Bulgaria	8.9
Romania	2.5
Market economies percentage OECD average 1988	70–80

Source: Commission of the European Communities, *European Documentation 1990* (Luxembourg, 1990).

provided help through the 'Know-How' Fund. Other members of the European Union have also pledged support. IMF help is conditional on appropriate measures being taken to achieve the transfer to market economies. There is something of a 'chicken and egg' situation, because the measures are difficult to achieve without funding, yet the funding is not guaranteed until measures are undertaken. Choice of the ways to privatise depends on the means and particular circumstances of the formerly centrally-planned countries. 'Hence the need for ingenious and unconventional mass privatisation programmes designed to help create capitalism without capital. Poland was a pioneer in this' (*Financial Times* commentator). A variety of programmes have been initiated.

Restitution of confiscated properties to their former owners is one form of privatisation. It is far from simple. Properties have to be identified and ownership rights established many years after the state had taken over industrial, commercial and financial businesses in pursuit of the Communist ideology of a society without private property. Owners of dwellings had also been expropriated. In returning private residences to them or their heirs, governments have to resolve the problem of sitting tenants who had been allocated accommodation in them by the State. In Germany, expropriations under Soviet occupation between 1945–49 have been declared, under the new constitution, to be irreversible. Small State enterprises on the whole are relatively easier to privatise but even their sales can present problems when potential buyers do not have sufficient funds so that, as in some cases in Russia, the assets are handed over to the workers at nominal prices.

Trade sales can be arranged for larger concerns that are more marketable and likely to attract foreign buyers. For example, in Poland a detergent manufacturer (Pollena Bydgoszcz) was sold to Unilever and Amino, in the dehydrated food industry, to the makers of Knorr products.

In Hungary a refrigerator maker (Lekel) was bought by Electrolux. The problem with trade sales in Central and Eastern Europe are that foreign buyers are unlikely to be interested unless the businesses on offer have modern plant and machinery, appear profitable and there are no restrictions on repatriation of profits. In a buyers' market, even such firms can be bought at rock bottom prices. Where these are perceived locally to be well below the true worth there is likely to be resentment. However, to achieve mass privatisation, foreign investors are needed and central and Eastern European countries vie for them.

Flotations of shares in privatised companies have been handicapped by lack of experience in share dealing and a lack of investors with sufficient funds to take up the issues. Under the Communist system, ownership of capital was not allowed so the savings now needed for investment could not have been accumulated. Several different ways to get round this problem had been devised, as the following examples illustrate:

(i) The Polish President proposed a scheme under which all citizens would be entitled to an interest-free ten year loan, in the form of coupons that could be exchanged for assets under the privatisation programme. The amount of the loan, equivalent to US$10,000, would be repayable in cash in twenty years.

(ii) In the former Czechoslovakia people were offered books of vouchers at a price corresponding to one week's average wage. They could use these vouchers to invest in state-owned enterprises.

(iii) In Romania, citizens are to be given 30 per cent of the capital of commercial enterprises to be held on their behalf in Mutual and Private Ownership Funds. The remaining 70 per cent of the capital is to be offered to foreign and other investors.

Progress in privatisation in Central and Eastern Europe has been uneven. Poland is in the forefront of the privatisation drive. As *The Economist* has pointed out 'No other ex-Communist country has done so much so quickly to escape its past .... In 1990 the Poles were the boldest of reformers'. By 1993 some 80 per cent of shops and restaurants had been privatised. According to estimates, the private sector accounted for some 45 per cent of the country's domestic product and employed more than 60 per cent of the labour force, compared with 45 per cent in 1990.

After the initial phase, progress in privatisation in Central and Eastern Europe has slowed down. This may be explained by the fact that those enterprises that were easier to dispose of were put up for sale first. The restructuring of others will take time. Foreign buyers willing to pay what would be regarded as satisfactory rather than bargain prices are not easy to find.

Short-term consequences of privatisation created problems. As companies reduced overmanning and inefficiency, jobs were lost. Wages went down from what was already a very low level by Western standards and prices rose. Privatised businesses, unlike state-owned enterprises, could not go on producing without covering costs and showing a return on invested capital.

Long-term benefits of privatisation will take time to be reflected in more competitive economies, faster growth rates and higher standards of living. Both in Western and in Central and Eastern Europe, privatisation has provided new opportunities for people to invest across national borders. This internationalisation of businesses and shared interests is a major step towards the greater economic and social cohesion in Europe.

SUMMARY

1. Privatisation has become an international phenomenon in the 1980s and governments of different political persuasions are continuing, in the 1990s, to transfer state owned undertakings and industries to the private sector.

2. Reasons for privatisation are political and economic: disillusionment with socialism, the failure of centrally-planned economies; and the poor performance of nationalised industries, with their heavy claims on public funds, both on the current and capital accounts.

3. Governments throughout the world have embarked on privatisation programmes with the aim to: raise money from the sale of state assets to reduce budget deficits, foster competition, promote efficiency and encourage share ownership among people with small amounts of savings, thereby creating capital-owning democracies.

4. Various methods of privatisation have been used and are being tried out by governments: flotations of shares on capital markets, share placings, trade sales, management/worker buy-outs, auctions, and grants to people of a statutory right to purchase of assets such as local authority houses. What is the appropriate method of privatisation will depend on the type of the assets to be disposed of and on the nature of the country's economy.

5. Contracting-out services provision to the private sector by the central government, local authorities and various public bodies has come to be regarded as a form of privatisation.

6. The UK has pioneered privatisation. The Conservative government elected to office in the 1979 general election was pledged to the reduction of the role of the state in the economy. A wide range of privatisation programmes was launched. Services were contracted out, state holdings in enterprise were transferred to the private sector and whole industries were privatised. Experience gained in the process has become a valuable British export of 'Know-How' to other countries.

7. Privatisation of 'natural monopolies' is particularly difficult and the British experience of privatising electricity, gas, water and telecommunications industries shows how this can be achieved and a regulatory system set up to protect the interests of consumers.

8. Under the European Union law all citizens of the Union must be given equal opportunities to invest in privatised companies. There has been a tendency for governments to under-price state assets offered for sale and, consequently, investors have been able to make considerable capital gains.

9. The scope and speed of privatisation in different countries has varied, reflecting their specific circumstances. In Europe, after the UK, the French government has launched the second most ambitious privatisation programme. In Germany unification has required the restructuring of industry on a vast scale to incorporate a centrally-planned East Germany into a market economy.

10. Privatisation in countries of the former Soviet Bloc requires, in the first place, the setting up of a legal, administrative and economic framework of a market economy, and the creation of a functioning private sector to which state-owned means of production and distribution can be transferred. It takes time before the results of privatisation become apparent. Any assessment of long-term benefits (and costs) of privatisation must therefore lie in the future.

SUGGESTED FURTHER READING

P. Cook and C. Kirkpatrick (eds), *Privatisation Policy and Performance* (Hemel Hempstead: Harvester Wheatsheaf, 1993).

Z. Dobosiewicz, *Privatisation in Eastern Europe* (London: Routledge, 1993).

House of Commons Library Research Division, *Water Privatisation and Water Bill*, no. 425 (London, 1988).

A. Kumar, *State Holding Companies and Public Enterprise in Transition* (London: Macmillan, 1993).

A.F. Ott and K. Hartley, *Privatisation and Economic Efficiency* (Cheltenham: Edward Elgar, 1991).

Prospectuses of privatised companies and Share Offers, published in newspapers.

White Paper, *Privatising Electricity*, Cmd. 322 (London: HMSO, 1988).

Note: News items in *The Times*, *The Financial Times* (London) and *The Economist* provide useful information on flotations of privatised companies worldwide and on share prices.

EXERCISES

1. Suggest reasons why privatisation became an international phenomenon in the 1990s and consider some of the major consequences.
2. When governments continue to regulate 'natural monopolies' after they had been transferred from the public to the private sector, what was the point of privatising them?
3. Suggest what are the main problems in valuing of state assets that a government may wish to offer for sale.
4. What are the prerequisites for a successful flotation of shares in a privatised company?
5. One of the objectives of the British privatisation programme was to increase share ownership by people with small amounts of savings and to create a share-owning democracy. What benefits, if any, are likely to result from this policy?
6. Consider the validity of the proposition that privatisation leads to greater efficiency in industry.
7. Privatisation methods need to be tailored to fit individual undertakings that are to be transferred from the public to the private sector. Furthermore what is appropriate in one country may not be practical in another. Comment on this statement and give examples.
8. In what sense, if any, can contracting out of services by central and local government be regarded as privatisation?
9. Use of proceeds from privatisation has helped governments to finance their increased expenditure programmes and to cut taxes without creating or adding to budget deficits. Is this a sound fiscal policy? Give reasons for your answer.
10. Governments have tended to underprice shares offered to the public in privatised companies, and as a result did not maximise proceeds from the sales. Suggest reasons for this and the consequences.

19 Investment Appraisal

THE PURPOSE OF INVESTMENT APPRAISAL

Investment appraisal is an aid to decision-making in the allocation of scarce resources to competing uses in the private and public sector. Such appraisal helps to maximise profits or minimise losses in the provision of social services where commercial considerations are not of overriding importance.

PROCEDURE IN THE DECISION-MAKING PROCESS

To reach a decision on investment it is necessary to take the following steps:

(a) Formulate objectives that the investment is intended to achieve, e.g. to improve transport.
(b) Establish the existing demand and future demand for a service.
(c) Determine whether the demand can be met with the existing productive capacity or whether new investment is required to increase supply.
(d) Consider alternative projects that would enable the objective to be achieved.
(e) Appraise the investment projects.

Private Sector Investment

If the appraisal indicates that the service can be provided profitably, then the investment project that shows the biggest return on the invested capital is chosen.

Public Sector Investment

The same consideration will apply to investment by public enterprises that are intended to operate on a commercial basis. However, some nationalised industries and other sections of the public sector have to provide social services, which, because of their nature, cannot be profitable. The criteria in selecting such projects is one of maximising social benefit and of minimising financial losses. These factors will influence a decision on the desirability of an investment project. The ability to invest depends on the availability of resources, such as land and capital, and on the government's economic policy. A ceiling on public sector borrowing would make it impossible to raise more capital for an investment project irrespective of whether it would be commercially viable or socially desirable.

PAY-BACK METHOD OF INVESTMENT APPRAISAL

There are several methods that can be used to appraise investment of which the *pay-back method* is one of the simplest. Projects are assessed on the basis of the period that it would take to generate sufficient net income to repay the original outlay. The shorter the period, the more advantageous the project is judged to be. If it is decided to use a cut-off date of, say, ten years hence, then only projects that can be paid off in that period will be considered. Suppose there are a number of projects that could provide a required service, such as transport from an airport to a city centre, but only two projects qualify on the 'cut-off date' basis. Project *X* requires the purchase of five coaches and project *Y* of ten minibuses. The capital investment is the same for both projects but project *X* would generate net profits that would repay the original outlay in eight years. Repayments would take nine years for project *Y*. On the basis of the pay-back method of assessment, project *X* would be chosen.

The *advantage* of the pay-back method is that it takes into account a preference for an early return of the capital invested. The capital is then available for other uses. The *disadvantage* of the method is that it fails to allow for returns/cash flow after the end of the pay-back period. Over the whole lifetime of the two projects, earnings of project *Y* might well have been the higher.

AVERAGE RATE OF RETURN METHOD

Investment in different projects can also be appraised on the basis of the ratio of the net profit after tax to the capital employed. Returns for each year are added and averaged by dividing them by the number of years of the project. Suppose £10,000 is to be invested and the expected return is:

Year	1	2	3	4
£	400	600	800	200

This would give a total return of £2,000 – an *average return* for the four years of £500 and an *average rate of return* on the invested capital of 5 per cent, assuming that the capital does not depreciate. If the capital had to be borrowed at 10 per cent per year, the project would not be worthwhile, considered on a purely commercial basis.

DISCOUNTED CASH FLOW (DCF) TECHNIQUE

The discounted cash flow technique is more sophisticated than either of the two previous methods. It recognises that it is preferable to have money now, rather than the same amount at a later time. The future is uncertain and in the meantime capital can be earning a return. DCF allows for the effects of taxation and for investment allowances.

Projects are appraised on the basis of the *net present value (NPV)*. first the net cash flow expected from a project is calculated by estimating all cash receipts and deducting from them all the expenditure arising out of the project. The net cash flow is then discounted to give its present value. The rate used to discount the cash flow is the required rate of return which may differ for the private and public sector of industry. The test discount rate (TDR), which was set for the nationalised industries, took into account the fact that the government can borrow more cheaply than other borrowers because lending to the state is relatively free of risk.

The sum of the present value of cash flows over the life of the project gives the present value, which can be calculated as follows:

$$P = \frac{S}{(1+r)^n}$$

where P is the amount of money invested, r is the rate of interest, S is the sum of money to be received in the future after a number of years (n).

OUTLINE OF COST–BENEFIT ANALYSIS

Cost–benefit analysis is a method of investment appraisal and an aid to decision-making which is of special relevance to projects in the public sector for which there is no market valuation. Appraisal on a cost–benefit basis aids decisions about whether a project is worth undertaking and indicates priority-ranking when a number of schemes are under considera-tion. As a method of determining the desirability of a project, it goes further than the other methods that have been outlined by taking into account *private and external* costs and benefits.

Private costs are those that are incurred by the producer of goods and services and are a result of a decision by the management of a business, e.g. to employ labour or to buy raw materials. *External costs* are not paid for by the producer but fall on those affected by his actions. An example of an external cost is that industrial production gives rise to pollution; a factory chimney may spoil the beauty of the countryside, but the producer is not responsible for such *externalities*. The cost in this case falls on those who live in the vicinity. It may be a measurable cost, such as the need to redecorate houses more often because of the smoke, or a cost which cannot be readily expressed in monetary terms, such as the effect of increased noise on the people in the area.

Private benefits are gains accruing to a producer. They may take the form of additional profits that result from a decision to invest in new plant or machinery. *Social benefits* are the indirect gains to the society for which it made no payment. New machinery may be less noisy, so that there is less disturbance to people in the neighbourhood.

Cost–benefit analysis is used to express both private and external costs and benefits in monetary terms and to offset one against the other. If total benefits outweigh the costs then a proposed investment is shown to be desirable.

DEVELOPMENT OF COST–BENEFIT ANALYSIS

Early studies relevant to the development of cost–benefit analysis date back to the turn of this century when Professor Vilfredo Pareto formulated his concept of 'improvement' now known as *Pareto improvement* (see p. 60). Pareto was concerned with the study of economic actions that make members of a society better off without anyone being made worse off. Pareto improvement provided the basis for cost–benefit analysis. Some years later, Professor A.C. Pigou drew a distinction between private and social costs and benefits, but for many years cost–benefit analysis remained confined to the theoretical study of welfare economics.

Pioneering work on the practical application of cost–benefit analysis was done in the 1950s in USA in connection with the river development projects (J.V. Krutilla and O. Eckstein, *Multiple Purpose River Development* (Johns Hopkins Press, 1958)). In the UK the early studies in the 1960s were in the field of transport. The cost–benefit analysis of the construction of the Victoria underground railway line, by Professor

M.E. Beesley and C.D. Foster ('Victoria Line', in D. Munby (ed.), *Transport* (London: Penguin Books, 1968)), demonstrated the desirability of the project. It was approved and is now in operation. There was also a study of investment in the London–Birmingham motorway and cost–benefit analysis of the alternative sites for the third London airport (Roskill Report, 1971). This method of investment appraisal has also been applied to such diverse fields as education and health services.

Growth of Interest in Cost–Benefit Analysis

The growth of public expenditure in major industrial countries and the increasing share of resources absorbed by the public sector have focused attention on cost–benefit analysis as a basis for the allocation of resources between the private and public sectors and to projects within them. In the UK, the emphasis of the Plowden Report (1961) on the need to control and appraise expenditure (see p. 274) gave impetus to cost–benefit analysis.

Application of Cost–Benefit Analysis

Applying cost–benefit analysis to projects requires a step-by-step approach. The analysis needs to: (i) define the project; (ii) evaluate the need for it; (iii) calculate current costs of operation including external costs; (iv) calculate current benefits, including social benefits; (v) express both total costs and total benefits in monetary values; (vi) compare them; (vii) decide whether to proceed with the project – where costs exceed benefits the project would be discarded; and (viii) relate annual benefits (returns) less costs to the capital outlay using DCF or another method of calculating the 'profitability' of the project.

AIRPORT–CITY CENTRE LINK

The application of cost–benefit analysis can be illustrated with a hypothetical example. Suppose the object is to provide a quick means of transport between an airport and a city centre. A government may consider leaving the provision of the service to private enterprise and investing only to improve an access road. This would result in road construction costs but there would be no direct return to the government on the capital outlay. Motor vehicle licences paid by the operators of the service in the private sector would, however, contribute to the tax revenue.

Alternatively, the government might consider investment projects to provide public transport, and apply cost–benefit analysis to the different schemes, e.g.

Scheme *A*   –   to improve existing public bus services;
Scheme *B*   –   to provide a road link service to the nearest railway station;
Scheme *C*   –   to construct a new underground railway line and link it to the city network.

The schemes would require different capital outlays. Cost–benefit analysis can help to decide which one would provide the greatest benefit.

Costs

Schemes *A* and *B* would add to traffic congestion; scheme *C* would not, but it would require a bigger investment of capital. All three schemes would have operating costs: labour, administration, materials, fuel, etc. There would also be external costs such as increased noise and pollution. Social costs might result from traffic accidents that led to death or injury. There could be adverse effects on other sectors of the economy.

Benefits

The schemes would result in some direct and indirect gains and only a few of them can be mentioned. The three projects would all produce some revenue from sales of tickets. In so far as travelling was speeded up, there would be a saving of time. If scheme *C* reduced the number of road accidents, there would be a gain from fewer deaths and injuries.

In real life the government decided to improve the link between Heathrow Airport and the centre of London by extending the Piccadilly underground line in the 1980s.

PROBLEMS IN VALUATION OF EXTERNAL COSTS AND BENEFITS

It is difficult to express some costs and benefits in terms of money but monetary value has to be put on intangibles such as time, pain and death. What any saving in time would be worth in money terms would depend on whose time was taken into account. The value of the time of a chairman of a multinational company travelling on business would not be the same as that of a child going to visit its grandparents. The cost of injury or death involves loss of expected earnings for dependents, emotional deprivation of the bereaved and loss to society in general. Courts and insurance companies, in assessing damages, have to put a price on death and pain but they do so only after the background of the deceased or injured is known. For cost–benefit analysis, such calculations have to be made before the events occur. *Shadow pricing*, therefore, has to be used for valuation of costs and benefits that are not readily quantifiable.

LIMITATIONS OF COST–BENEFIT ANALYSIS

It would not be practical to apply cost–benefit analysis to all investment projects. The method has its limitations which stem from the following points:

(i) *Present state of knowledge.* Calculations have to be made on the basis of the present state of knowledge relating to resources, technology or medical treatment. Major investment projects such as roads or new underground lines may take fifteen years or even longer from the drawing-board to completion and then can have a lifespan of thirty-five years. It is difficult to predict what will happen in fifty years time. For example, fifty years ago North Sea oil platforms had not been heard of.

(ii) *Unavailable data.* Cost–benefit analysis is less applicable to the private than to the public sector. Individual firms are not in a position to take a global view of external costs and benefits and do not have access to relevant information that may be available to the government.

(iii) *Difficulty of quantification.* Concepts of time gained or beauty lost when a road is cut through the countryside cannot be objectively measured.

(iv) *The opportunity cost* of a factory site may be the foregone use of land to build a school or a hospital. A firm would not take either of these social investment projects into account in estimating how much capital it will need to buy the land on which to build a factory.

(v) *Expense.* Cost–benefit analysis is an expensive way of appraising investment that requires highly-trained manpower and cannot be undertaken in some cases without the use of computer facilities.

The government, concerned about the way that investment projects were assessed in the public sector, appointed an Advisory Committee on Trunk

Road Assessment (the Leitch Committee) to examine the methods used for appraising new road projects. The Report (1977) was critical of the cost–benefit analysis as applied by the Department of Transport on the grounds that it was dominated by factors that could be readily valued in terms of money while ignoring, to a large extent, environmental factors that were not easily quantifiable. The committee came to the conclusion that personal judgement is preferable to predetermined values for taking environmental factors into account when each new project is considered on its own merits. This did not mean that cost–benefit analysis was of no value. The Report recommended that when there were competing schemes, for example one involving rail and the other road transport, then both new investment projects should be appraised on the basis of cost–benefit analysis.

USEFULNESS OF COST–BENEFIT ANALYSIS

For all its shortcomings, cost–benefit analysis performs a useful function in appraising investment projects: (i) it allows for externalities to be taken into account; (ii) it can be applied when there are no market-determined indicators of the desirability of competing projects; (iii) it provides a basis for more rational and better informed decision-making. Of course, final investment decisions may have to be made for political or economic reasons in the light of what is feasible in particular circumstances – rather than on the basis of which is the most desirable project.

THE CHANNEL TUNNEL – A CASE STUDY

Perhaps the most outstanding case for study of cost–benefit analysis is the Channel Tunnel, the longest stretch (31.03 miles) of tunnel in the world – linking Britain to the continent of Europe and providing transport facilities for passengers and freight carriers.

The project involved political decisions by governments of the UK and France, economic, environmental and social issues and a European dimension.

Political Decisions

In 1981 the Prime Minister of the UK, Margaret Thatcher, and the President of France, revived the idea of the Tunnel. The Emperor of France, Napoleon Bonaparte considered it in 1802 but abandoned it three years later after the collapse of the Peace of Amiens. In 1880 work on the

Tunnel had actually started but then it was stopped by the British Prime Minister, William Gladstone, who feared invasion. As late as 1957 Field-Marshal Lord Montgomery argued against a land link on the grounds that it would weaken British defences, but this argument was not sustainable. Mrs. Thatcher and President Mitterrand signed the Treaty of Canterbury in 1986 which provided for legislative procedures to be initiated and in 1989 the Franco-British Fixed Link Treaty was ratified.

Private Finance Decisions

A study of a privately-financed link had been authorised some years earlier by the British and French Ministers of Transport. The decision that the two governments had to make was how the project was to be financed without state funding. Eventually the money was raised by borrowing and share issue.

(a) *Loans.* The European Investment Bank agreed in 1987 to lend £1 billion, and two banks, one British and one French, set up a joint office to act as an agent for 233 banks that were to be associated with the project. This created the largest private-sector banking syndicate in the world.

(b) *Share issue.* The first offer of shares in the Eurotunnel was offered to the public in 1987 and £770 million was subscribed. A rights issue in 1990 provided another £566 million.

Choice of Promoters

The two governments invited proposals for a fixed cross-channel link from prospective promoters who submitted four schemes in 1985. In the following year the concession was awarded. Five British and five French construction companies formed Transmanche-Link and Eurotunnel plc and Eurotunnel SA were incorporated.

The first test shafts were sunk in 1986, and in 1990 the undersea service tunnels from England and France met. The Queen and President Mitterrand opened the Channel Tunnel in May 1994 and celebrations began to mark one of the great technological achievements of linking Folkestone and Calais.

Operation of the Tunnel

Trains going through the Tunnel will provide transport for passengers and freight. 'Tourist' wagons will provide accommodation for cars, motor cycles and other light traffic. Coaches will travel on single deck wagons and lorries on freight wagons. Le Shuttle will run at frequent intervals and the Eurostar will provide high speed travel.

Economic Issues

Economic gains envisaged are: a reliable and convenient service without, as in the case of ferries and airlines, delays and cancellations due to bad weather, rough seas or fog-bound airports. As competition between carriers intensifies, the prices of tickets are likely to come down, thereby reducing transport costs to individuals and industries.

There are also indirect gains, both short term and long term. Construction of the Tunnel has created jobs in the building industry in both countries. It also created demand for the output of supply industries, e.g. steel and for rolling stock. As the Tunnel becomes fully operational, there will be employment associated with the running of the services and maintenance.

There are, however, economic costs such as the opportunity cost of capital, land and labour absorbed by the Tunnel project. Companies operating ferry services and airlines may see diminution of their traffic and loss of revenue resulting in job losses.

Environmental Issues

Provision of access to the Tunnel both in Britain and in France will require additional roads, rail trucks and terminals. These demands for land are likely to have unfavourable effects on the countryside and create more pollution, reducing the attractiveness of adjoining areas and depressing the housing market. Whether the environmental costs will prove to be greater than would have been incurred by alternative ways of dealing with increasing demands for transport remains to be seen.

Social Issues

The road and rail network will have effects on areas far beyond the vicinity of the Tunnel, changing patterns of location of industry and, population and, in the long run, may lead to greater social cohesion in the European Community.

Symbolic Achievement

The Tunnel is more than an engineering feat and a commercial undertaking with a great potential. It is also symbolic of Britain's place in

Europe. For the first time since the Ice Age, some 12,000 years ago, Britain is physically linked with the continent.

SUMMARY

1. Investment appraisal is needed in both the private and public sectors of industry to allocate resources to the best advantage.
2. Appraisal aids decision on the choice of competing projects, to maximise profits or to minimise losses when the proposed investment is of a social nature.
3. Methods used to appraise investment are: the pay-back method; the average rate of return method; the discounted cash flow technique; and cost–benefit analysis.
4. Cost–benefit analysis takes into account both the social and economic costs and benefits of investment projects.
5. It enables externalities to be expressed in monetary terms and to be included in the calculation of the returns on investment.
6. A major problem in cost–benefit analysis is to quantify and put a price on such concepts as time or happiness.
7. Appraisal of some investment projects on the basis of cost–benefit analysis requires forecasts of developments that cannot be foreseen, with any degree of accuracy, on the basis of present knowledge.
8. Early work on cost–benefit analysis has been done in the USA in connection with river development projects. The analysis has been applied in the UK in diverse fields: education, the health service, but mainly in public transport.
9. The limitations of cost–benefit analysis make it less suitable for the private sector, since businesses do not have the data or the need to calculate social costs and gains and opportunity cost of the investment projects.
10. Cost–benefit analysis in the public sector has been criticised but its value in appraising alternative projects is broadly accepted.

SUGGESTED FURTHER READING

N. Hanley and C.L. Spash, *Cost–Benefit Analysis* (Cheltenham: Edward Elgar, 1993).

P.-O. Johansson, *Cost–Benefit of Environmental Change* (Cambridge: Cambridge University Press, 1993).

C.D. Foster and M.E. Beesley, 'The Victoria Line', in D. Munby (ed.), *Transport* (London: Penguin Books, 1968).

R.H. Parker, *Macmillan Dictionary of Accountancy* (London: Macmillan, 1992).

G. Walshe and P. Daffren, *Managing Cost–Benefit Analysis* (London: Macmillan, 1990).

A. Williams and E. Giardina, *Efficiency in the Public Sector: The Theory and Practice of Cost–Benefit Analysis* (Cheltenham: Edward Elgar, 1993).

EXERCISES

1. Discuss the different factors that have to be taken into account in deciding whether to invest in the public or in the private sector. Give an example.
2. Consider how external costs can be paid for.
3. 'To appraised investment projects with a pay back period of twenty years, an accountant has to exercise the skills of a fortune-teller.' Comment on this statement.
4. Discuss the problems in 'quantifying the unquantifiable' for the purpose of cost–benefit analysis.
5. 'When an investment project such as the Channel Tunnel is of political and social importance for both the UK and France, calculation of a commercial rate of return is not a meaningful exercise.' Give your reasons for agreeing or disagreeing with this assertion.

Part 6

Management of the Economy

20 Fiscal Policy to Stabilise the Economy

BACKGROUND TO FISCAL POLICY

Fiscal measures to counteract fluctuations in the level of economic activity associated with the trade cycles (see p. 50) have been in use for over fifty years. Governments in the 1930s accepted that they not only could, but should, adopt a fiscal policy to stabilise national economies so as to prevent the evils of unemployment and inflation from developing.

In the nineteenth century, there was little discussion of the need for a government to maintain employment. The doctrine of *laissez-faire* prevailed and Say's law of markets, which postulated that unemployment could not occur, was widely accepted. Jean Baptist Say's theory, which he published in 1803, has been summed up by the famous phrase, 'Supply creates its own demands'. As various producers supply goods and services to the markets where these goods and services are sold or exchanged for one another, the aggregate demand will correspond to supply. If the supply of goods and services is doubled, the aggregate demand will double. On the basis of this line of argument, there will be no overproduction, no deficiency of aggregate demand and no unemployment. Thus supply will create the means that enables the aggregate demand to absorb output. Say's view was shared by other eminent writers of the time. For instance, David Ricardo (1772–1823) wrote, in reference to a nation, 'supply can never exceed demand'.

These arguments were so convincing that, as late as 1909, the Royal Commission on the Poor Law and Relief of Distress was able to dismiss the idea that the demand for labour might fail to keep pace with its supply. By the 1920s the possibility of unemployment could no longer be dismissed. It palpably existed, and by the 1930s it was an international phenomenon.

KEYNESIAN PRESCRIPTION

It is impossible to discuss fully in a few pages such an important and difficult subject as the management of an economy and the Keynesian point of view. We will therefore consider it in broad outline.

417

In 1936 Lord Keynes published *The General Theory of Employment, Interest and Money*, which influenced fiscal policy for several generations to come and has its supporters to this day. Lord Keynes argued that aggregate demand *need not* equal supply and that by managing aggregate demand a government could maintain an equilibrium. If people did not spend enough then the government should spend on their behalf.

Economy is in equilibrium when	AD	$=$	S
Unemployment develops when	AD	$<$	S (less than)
Inflation develops when	AD	$>$	S (greater than)

AD = Aggregate Demand, S = Supply

Management of Aggregate Demand

Fiscal measures can be used to follow policies for: (i) *expansion*, if the aggregate demand is insufficient to absorb available resources so that there is unemployment; or (ii) *contraction*, when demand is excessive and the price level rises.

Expansionary policy

This is achieved by a government budget deficit, so that more money is pumped into the economy by means of public expenditure than is taken out in taxation.

Budget measures are therefore likely to be as follows:

Budget (Deficit)

Revenue side	*Expenditure side*
Decrease	Increase
(i) direct taxation	(i) current government expenditure on goods and services
(ii) indirect taxation	(ii) transfer payments
	(iii) capital expenditure (investment)

A government will have to borrow to cover the deficit.

Capital taxes are of little use in the management of aggregate demand because: (i) their total yield is small (see p. 147); (ii) the revenue generated is not regular, liability to a capital transfer tax arises only when a capital transfer is made; (iii) at a time of recession and falling prices capital gains on the disposal of assets are unlikely. Thus there will not be a tax base for a capital gains tax. A government will therefore rely on taxes on consumption and income.

A reduction in direct taxation can be achieved by a cut in:

(a) *Income tax.* A government may reduce tax rates, increase allowances or raise the level of tax thresholds.
(b) *Corporation tax.* Similar changes to those to income tax can be made.
(c) *National Insurance Contributions.* They can in theory be reduced but this is unlikely since they finance benefits and at a time of a recession or slump claims for unemployment benefits increase.

The effect of any cuts in direct taxation is to increase the disposable income of the taxpayers, so that individuals and companies are left with more money to spend and to save. How the economy will be affected will depend on the taxpayers' choice. If they save the full amount by which taxes have been reduced, the measure will have little expansionary effect. The size of the expansion will depend on the proportion of the additional income that they spend. A reduction in indirect taxation will encourage expenditure, as its effect is to reduce prices to consumers. However, if they do not spend enough, then the government can increase its own expenditure. By raising transfer payments it can transfer resources by means of benefits to lower income groups that have a higher propensity to consume than the taxpayers with higher incomes. The increased public expenditure will set the 'Multiplier' effect in motion and help to stimulate the economy (see p. 48).

Contractionary policy

This is applied to check inflation, which has been defined by Hugh Dalton (a Labour Chancellor of the Exchequer) in the now famous phrase as 'Too much money chasing too few goods'. Fiscal and monetary measures need, therefore, to reduce the amount of money in circulation or to increase the supply of goods to restore the equilibrium. To this end a government will budget for a surplus that will require the following measures:

Budget (Surplus)

Revenue side	*Expenditure side*
increase	decrease
(i) direct taxation	(i) current government expenditure on goods and services
(ii) indirect taxation	(ii) transfer payments
	(iii) National Insurance Contribution
	(iv) capital expenditure investment

At the same time, measures are needed to encourage industry to increase the supply of goods and services by means of grants and tax allowances that would result in investment, leading to greater competitiveness and productive capacity. The problem is that grants increase public expenditure, and allowances reduce tax revenue. Higher personal tax may produce a disincentive to work (see p. 152). Higher tax on profits reduces the incentive to increase the supply of goods and services and the ability to finance new investment out of a company's own resources.

Both expansionary and contractionary fiscal policy may also have to be reinforced by monetary measures.

MONETARY POLICY: FRIEDMAN'S MONETARIST PRESCRIPTION

In recent years, governments of the leading industrial countries have shifted the emphasis in the management of their economies from fiscal to monetary policy. The chief exponent of monetarism has been Professor Milton Friedman. A government implements its monetary policy through the central bank. The Friedman prescription for control of the economy is to control the money supply. The money supply is affected by interest rates and the liquidity of the money market.

Interest Rates

Changes in interest rates can be used to expand or to contract an economy:

(a) A cut in the official interest rate is generally followed by a reduction in interest charges by financial institutions such as banks, finance houses and building societies. Credit becomes cheaper and this provides an inducement to individuals and businesses to borrow, to spend and to invest. If, as a result of this, the aggregate demand rises and total expenditure is increased, the supply of money goes up and there is an expansionary effect.

(b) An increase in interest rates makes borrowing more expensive. There is therefore likely to be less demand for credit and less expenditure. The supply of money is consequently reduced.

Liquidity

The central bank can increase or decrease the liquidity of the financial institutions by their ability to create credit by repayment of special deposits and by open market operations see (p. 292). They can be used to provide the financial institutions with liquid funds (money) which are then made available for loans. The financial institutions' ability to lend is therefore increased.

The expansionary effect of a monetary policy depends on peoples' willingness to borrow and on the financial institutions' ability to lend. It will not occur, however low interest rates and plentiful funds are, if people are unwilling to borrow. Individuals may not be prepared to enter into debt if they are unemployed or expect to lose their jobs. Businesses may not be prepared to borrow to finance new investment if they do not expect it to be profitable. The contractionary effect is achieved by a reversal of the measures.

In the late 1970s and early 1980s, neither high interest rates nor changes in liquidity succeeded in reducing the supply of money to the required levels. The criticisms of monetary policy as a means of stabilising an economy have increased and the call has been made in the 1990s to revert to a greater reliance on fiscal measures.

The debate on the relative merits of monetary and fiscal policies continues. In 1981, 364 economists signed a statement to *The Times* asserting that 'There is no basis in economic theory or supporting evidence for the Government's belief that by deflating demand they will bring inflation permanently under control and thereby induce an automatic recovery in output and employment'.

Other economists did not agree. Professor Tim Congdon, writing in *The Times* (July 14, 1983), argued that 'Contrary to the claim of the 364 economists, there is a mass of "supporting evidence" on the issue'. Whatever the underlying theories of the government's policies, by 1994 inflation and unemployment came down and the UK has emerged from a world recession ahead of the other major industrial countries in Europe (Table 2.1). Nevertheless, inflation and unemployment continue to be matters of worldwide concern.

INFLATION AND STAGFLATION

To deal with inflation it is necessary first to define it (p. 419) and then to measure the size of the problem. What will be the appropriate measures to control inflation will differ when the rate runs at 2 per cent, 10 per cent or 20,000 per cent plus as it did in Argentina in 1990 (see Figure 20.1).

There are different ways in which inflation can be measured and, depending on the method used, the result may differ. In any comparison of

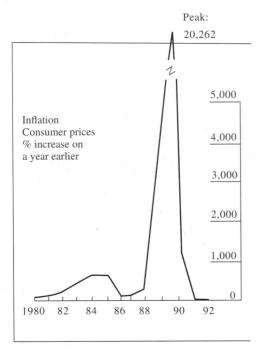

Figure 20.1   Inflation in South America: Argentina
Source: *The Economist* (London) (18 April 1992).

the rates of inflation, particularly at the international level, it is necessary to ensure that the statistics that are to be compared have been calculated on a comparable basis.

The consumer price index is the most commonly used indicator of inflation. In the UK this is the *Retail Price Index (RPI)*. It shows changes in the cost of a basket of goods and services by households, excluding the poorest and the richest groups. In all some six hundred items are covered and the index is adjusted from time to time to include new goods and leave out others for which demand has declined. As the patterns and levels of consumption change the importance of particular goods and services in households' budgets alters. Consequently, the weights attached to them are revised.

The rate of inflation may be indicated by changes in the index numbers and seasonally adjusted percentages. Figures for inflation can be shown as: (a) annual averages; (b) quarterly figures; or (c) monthly figures, calculated by reference to prices on a particular day.

Statistics on the *underlying rate of inflation* exclude mortgage interest payments (as these can give rise to short-term fluctuations) and thus conform more closely with the common practice of calculating inflation in other industrial countries.

The *Tax and Prices Index (TPI)* in the UK is similar to the Retail Price Index and both are published at the same time. In addition to indirect taxes that are levied on goods and services and included in the RPI, the TPI takes into account changes in employees' National Insurance Contributions and direct taxes (Income Tax) that affect peoples' disposable incomes. Thus TPI indicates by how much taxpayers' gross incomes would have to change if they were to be able to maintain the same standard of living in real terms. What an income will buy also depends on what producers charge for their output.

The Index of Producers' Output Prices shows changes in prices of manufactured goods as they leave the factory gate. In time these changes will be reflected in the consumer price index.

There are also two wider indicators of inflation.

(a) *Consumer Expenditure Deflator* covers expenditure at home and abroad by consumers and differs from RPI in that it is not confined to households or to spending within the country.

(b) *Gross Domestic Product Deflator* measures changes in costs and prices (excluding imports) for the whole of the economy and thus shows domestically generated inflation.

The ways of measuring inflation that have been outlined here can give different results. The question therefore arises as to which method is the best and gives the 'true' rate of inflation. The answer is that there is no one single rate and the choice of the method depends on the purpose for which the information is required. This makes assessment of the effectiveness of governments' anti-inflationary policies and international comparisons more difficult. Symptoms of inflation are, however, easily recognisable. The level of prices rises and the value of money falls both internally and in terms of other currencies.

In economic jargon, *'stagflation'* refers to a situation when stagnation and inflation exist at the same time – as occurred in the 1970s and early 1980s. It is characterised by unemployment and rising prices occurring simultaneously. Expansionary policies that help to reduce unemployment increase inflation. Contractionary policies that reduce inflation increase unemployment. Governments, therefore, seek a compromise package of measures: reduction in public expenditure, particularly in certain areas deemed as 'unproductive', reduction in direct taxation providing incentives to increase supply of goods and services, and an increase in indirect taxation to discourage consumption. But paradoxically this anti-inflationary measure can add to inflation.

There are two principal types of inflation; *demand-pull inflation*, when prices rise as a result of excessive demand and *cost-push inflation*, when prices rise because costs of production go up. An increase in taxes on consumption tends to reduce the demand for goods and services but this results in a fall in the standard of living. To compensate for this the labour force seeks pay increases. If employers raise wages and salaries, the costs of production go up. It is a matter of debate which is the cause and which is the effect. The consequence is the same. The purchasing power of money falls and a spiral of cost-push and demand-pull inflation develops (see Figure 20.2).

The spiral may start for a number of reasons: (i) employers may give a pay rise when there is no increase in productivity; (ii) producers abroad increase their prices and the cost of imports increases; and (iii) the government prints more and more money and currency in circulation exceeds supply of goods and services. Figure 20.2 illustrates the process: (1) A pay rise is given and/or the price of imports goes up. (2) Cost of

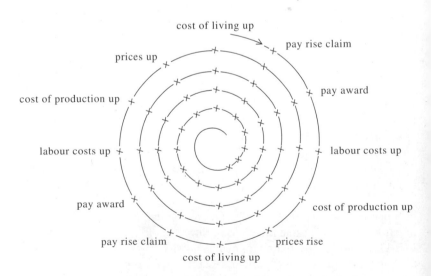

Figure 20.2   Inflationary spiral

production increases (cost-push inflation). (3) Manufacturers may absorb the higher cost but they are more likely in time to pass them to consumers in a price rise. (4) Cost of living goes up. (5) Employees will put in a pay claim to enable them to maintain their standard of living and to cover anticipated further inflationary price rises. (6) Employers agree to the pay rise rather than risk industrial unrest. Employees now have more money to spend (demand-pull inflation). (7) Higher wages increase the cost of production. (8) Prices rise again and so the process resumes.

The German and Hungarian experience (see Tables 20.1 and 20.2) provides a cautionary tale of what may happen when inflation gets out of hand. The whole economic system collapses, social and political reactions are set in motion and undermine the fabric of society. Some governments, however, were slow to learn. In the 1980s hyperinflation spread in South America – in Bolivia, Argentina and Brazil. In the 1990s hyperinflation reappeared in Europe. Following the break-up of Yugoslavia, in 1993 the economy of Serbia collapsed. 'Shops are bare, inflation is believed to be 10 or 20 per cent per day, but nobody is sure; year on year it could be 10 billion per cent. ... Untold thousands of billions of dinars were printed ... As ever more fresh and worthless dinars pour off the printing presses the

Table 20.1   Hyperinflation in Germany

(a)	Internal Price Index (1913) = 100)	(b)	External Value of the mark (marks to a US dollar*)
31 July 1923	161,000	July 1914	4
28 Aug 1923	1,666,000	Jan 1919	8
25 Sept 1923	34,600,000	July 1919	14
30 Oct 1923	17,700,000,000	Jan 1920	65
27 Nov 1923	1,382,000,000,000	July 1920	39
27 Dec 1923	1,125,000,000,000	Jan 1921	65
		July 1921	77
		Jan 1922	192
		July 1922	493
		Jan 1923	18,000
		July 1923	353,000
		Nov 1923	4,200,000 billion

Notes:
* To the nearest mark.
Source: (a) By courtesy of Peter Wilsher.
         (b) M.Gibbs, Phillips and Drew, *Market Review* (January 1975).

Table 20.2 Hyperinflation in Hungary

Internal price index	
mid-1938	100
1941	139
1943	217
15 July 1945	9,200
30 September 1945	38,900
31 January 1946	7,089,000
31 July 1946	12,572,000,000,000,000

Source: P. Falush, 'The Hungarian Hyper-inflation', *National Westminster Quarterly Review* (August 1976).

value of the currency has gone into a freefall' (*The Times* July 23, 1993). At the beginning of July 1993, the one-million dinar note went into circulation. Some three weeks later the government issued fifty-million dinar notes. The purchasing power of these notes was approximately £2.50.

In 1994 as fighting in what had been Yugoslavia raged on, money became more and more a piece of worthless paper. Similarly, in some of the former republics of the USSR, hyperinflation also occured, adding to political and economic chaos. In the Ukraine in July 1993 inflation was running at 40 per cent, in September the figure rose to 50 per cent and unemployment which in the previous year had been around 14,400 was expected to reach 1.5 million in December (*Rzeczpospolita*, September 2, 1993).

In some cases, the onset of hyperinflation was sudden and brought about by external forces. In other countries, hyperinflation resulted from the mismanagement of national economies over a long period of time, and the inability or reluctance of the governments to act, making the task of bringing inflation under control that much more difficult.

PRICES AND INCOMES POLICIES

In the 1960s and 1970s, governments in various countries, faced with the problem of rising prices and growing unemployment, which fiscal and monetary policies had failed to counteract, turned to prices and incomes policies. The purpose of the new measures was to manage the economy and to reinforce the old measures. Thus a higher tax on consumption, or a higher rate of interest that increased the cost of credit, could be made more effective measures in restricting spending. Those people affected could be prevented by an incomes policy from securing pay increases that would enable them to maintain or even to increase their standard of living. The UK, the USA and France all, at one time or another, had some kind of a prices and incomes policy. None were popular and the policies were abandoned or reformed the 1980s.

An incomes policy can take different forms and appear under various names (see Table 20.3). It may be a statutory policy which is legally enforceable or a voluntary policy depending on the goodwill of the parties concerned: the government, the trade unions and employers. As this tends

Table 20.3   Different forms of incomes policy in the UK

Government	Period of policy	Form of income policy	Period of pay award	Average earning increase during pay round (%)	Retail Price inflation at the start of the round (%)
Con.	1961–62	Pay pause, then guide lines of 2–2½% increases related to productivity			
Lab.	1965	Guidelines of 3–3½%	1964–65	6.6	4.5
Lab.	1966	Freeze-statutory stand still on pay increases	1965–66	6.8	4.8
Lab.	1967	Period of 'severe restraint'	1966–67	3.8	3.7
Lab.	1968	3½% ceiling. Delaying powers up to 12 months	1967–68	7.7	1.5
Lab.	1969	Breakdown of incomes policy	1968–69	7.8	7.7
Lab./Con.	1970	Voluntary policy, 2½% to 4½% increases	1969–70	12.9	5.1
Lab./Con.	1970	June–Oct. 1972 government exhortations but no statutory policies	1970–71	11.2	6.8
Con.	1972	Stage One, statutory pay freeze	1971–72	12.0	10.1

Table 20.3   *continued*

Government	Period of policy	Form of income policy	Period of pay award	Average earning increase during pay round (%)	Retail Price inflation at the start of the round (%)
Con.	1973	Stage Two, statutory increases of £1 + 4% with a limit of £250 per annum	1972–73	14.5	6.5
Con./Lab.	1974	Stage Three, statutory pay increase of £2.25 or 7% whichever greater	1973–74	19.8	9.2
Lab.	1974	Social contract, increases to maintain income in real terms	1974–75	26.4	16.9
Lab.	1975	Voluntary policy £6 limit on earnings but no increase for those earnings more than £8,500 per year	1975–76	13.4	26.5
Lab.	1976	Voluntary policy guide lines, 5% limit within range of £2.50–£4	1976–77	7.9	13.7
Lab.	1977	Government intention 10% increase	1978–79	15.8	7.9
Con.	1980	Limit for public sector employees increases of up to 6%	1979–80	20.0	16.6
Con.	1983–	Public sector pay restraint, different rates	1983– onwards		

Source: By permission of Phillips and Drew.

to be lacking, voluntary versions are in danger of quickly being watered down to become 'guidelines' to pay settlements or a social contract. It is not really a contract between the government and the trade unions, but rather something in the nature of a statement of hope that the latter will take note of the former's intent to keep wage settlements in check. Whether the policy is statutory or voluntary, its provisions may be similar in many respects. It may seek to introduce a pay freeze for a specified period, or stipulate wage increases expressed as either a fixed sum or a percentage. There may or may not be a limit to such increases. Although not officially designated as a pay policy, a limit to pay increases for employees in the public sector does have considerable impact on settlements in the private sector.

In theory it should be easier for a government to regulate incomes within a country than to regulate prices, as the latter are affected by factors abroad over which the government may have no control. An increase in world prices for oil or commodities will raise the internal price level of the country that imports them. If a home producer, whose costs have gone up, is not allowed to increase the prices of these products, profits will fall or turn into losses, in which case the firm may go out of business. This does not, however, mean that a prices policy is not possible in a country that relies heavily on imports.

A government's prices policy may be aimed at: (i) limiting the extent to which prices are allowed to increase to take into account higher costs; (ii) controlling profit margins of businesses; or (iii) encouraging competition to bring down the price level.

THE BRITISH EXPERIENCE

Successive British governments used a wide range of policies to stabilise the economy. The following summary shows the fiscal and monetary measures that were taken during the two main periods of recession in twentieth-century Britain.

	Great Depression *1930s*	*Stagflation* *1970–83*	*Recession* *1990–93*
Fiscal Policy:			
Public expenditure	cut	cut*	up
Direct taxation	up	cut	cut
Indirect taxation	up	up	up

	Great Depression 1930s	Stagflation 1970–83	Recession 1990–93
Monetary Policy:			
Interest rates	cheap money	dear money	falling rates
Bank Rate or			
Minimum	2 (1932–51)	17	
Lending Rate		(discontinued	
(%)		in 1981)	
Prices (%)	down	up[**]	up
Unemployment peak (%)	22	13	9.9

[*]from 1975, expenditure as percentage of GDP down.
[**](highest rate of inflation – over 25% was in 1975).

The Great Depression started with the Wall Street Crash of 1929 and spread throughout the world, reaching its worst stage in the UK in 1932. The turning-point came in 1936 with the beginning of the rearmament programme which was probably more instrumental in stimulating the British economy than the fiscal and monetary measures that had been followed by the coalition government.

Since the Great Depression, whenever a threat of recession has emerged, calls have been made urging the government of the day to pump more money into the economy. Lord Callaghan, a Chancellor of the Exchequer in a Labour government and later Prime Minister, wrote in his memoirs: 'We used to think that you could spend your way out of a recession and increase employment by cutting taxes and boosting government spending. ... I tell you in all candour that the option no longer exists, and that in so far as it ever did exist, it only worked on each occasion since the war by injecting a bigger dose of inflation into the economy, followed by a higher level of unemployment as the next step' (James Callaghan, *Time and Change* (London: Collins/Fontana, 1988)).

In the period between 1970 and 1980 both the Conservative and Labour parties were in power. Where they differed was in the emphasis and on the extent of changes, rather than on the principles of fiscal and monetary policies. Measures taken by both the Conservative and Labour Governments to deal with stagflation were: (i) to cut public expenditure and apply cash limits; (ii) to cut direct taxation; (iii) to follow a high interest rates policy; (iv) to attempt to reduce public sector borrowing requirements; (v) to attempt to reduce money supply; and (vi) to rely on prices and incomes policies to reinforce fiscal and money policies. Different forms of incomes policy were tried and, *one after another*, each was replaced with a new version. Both the political parties, when in office, had statutory and voluntary policies. Successive governments differed less on the need for and the principle of a prices and incomes policy than on the regulatory machinery, comprising the National Board for Prices and Incomes and the Price Commission. The Conservative government decided to do without them. From 1979 to the 1990s its policy has been to exercise a moderating influence through pay settlements in the public sector. The cumulative effect of the policies was that the rate of inflation dropped to around 2 per cent but, although unemployment declined, it continued to be a problem. No government on its own, whatever its policies, can pull a country out of a world recession, isolate it from inflationary forces and stabilise its economy. The fiscal, monetary and incomes and prices policies of each country have international repercussions.

SUMMARY

1. Fiscal policy to stabilise a national economy is concerned with measures to counteract fluctuations in the level of economic activity.
2. These fluctuations reflect phases of trade cycles that are characterised by periods of boom, recession, slump and recovery.
3. To control an economy, a government needs to manage the aggregate demand which requires adjustments of taxes and benefits.
4. Deficit budgets are intended to create an expansionary effect and surplus budgets to create a contractionary effect.
5. Fiscal measures on their own are not likely to be effective.
6. Governments have tried to reinforce fiscal measures by monetary policy, which involves changes in the supply of money, rates of interest and the availability of credit.
7. In recent years, views of the monetarist school of thought have gained widespread support and governments have shifted emphasis from fiscal to monetary measures.
8. In the UK in the 1970s and 1980s neither fiscal nor monetary policy has proved effective in counteracting inflation and successive governments have tried out different versions of a prices and incomes policy – both statutory and voluntary. The 1990s witnessed low levels of inflation.
9. There are two types of inflation: demand-pull and cost-push.

10. Stagflation presents a particularly serious economic problem since it is a condition in which stagnation and inflation exist at the same time. Measures to counteract one will tend to make the other worse.

SUGGESTED FURTHER READING

P. Beckerman, *The Economics of High Inflation* (London: Macmillan, 1991).

D. Begg, S. Fisher and R. Dornbush, *Economics* (London: McGraw-Hill, 1994).

C.V. Brown and P.M. Jackson, *Public Sector Economics* (Oxford: Basil Blackwell, 1992).

G.C. Hockley, *Fiscal Policy* (London: Routledge, 1992).

F.S. Mishkin, *Money, Interest Rates and Inflation* (Cheltenham: Edward Elgar, 1993).

R.A. Musgrave and P.B. Musgrave, *Public Finance in Theory and Practice* (New York: McGraw-Hill, 1989) .

M. Parkin and D. King, *Economics* (Wokingham: Addison-Wesley, 1992).

P.A. Samuelson and W. Morhaus, *Economics* (London: McGraw-Hill, 1992).

C.T. Sandford, *The Economics of Public Finance* (Oxford: Pergamon Press, 1992).

EXERCISES

1. Consider why there is a need for a fiscal policy to stabilise an economy.
2. Suggest why fiscal measures may fail to stimulate economic activity.
3. Explain how income tax has a built-in stabiliser.
4. Outline a fiscal policy to achieve an expansionary effect and the problems involved.
5. Suggest how a prices and incomes policy can be used to reinforce fiscal policy to create a contractionary effect.
6. Distinguish between the two types of inflation and suggest appropriate fiscal measures to deal with each one.
7. Why does stagflation present such a serious problem for the Chancellor of the Exchequer?
8. Outline a policy for controlling the aggregate demand at a time of economic boom.
9. Why are capital taxes of little use in the controlling of an economy.
10. 'Monetary policy and fiscal policy are not alternative but complementary policies'. Comment on this statement.

21 Fiscal Policy in Relation to Employment

FULL EMPLOYMENT

Fiscal policy to maintain full employment is equivalent to a policy to prevent unemployment. Since unemployment is exportable, the leading industrial countries in the world agreed in the late 1940s to take preventative measures if the number of unemployed rose above 3 per cent of a country's labour force. In the UK the commitment to full employment goes back to the famous White Paper on Employment published by the Coalition government in 1944. In consequence, all the major political parties were pledged to maintain full employment. When, in later years, the Conservative and Labour government came to differ, it was not over the desirability of full employment, but over the best ways of achieving it.

Definition of Full Employment

Full employment is a concept that is difficult to express precisely. It can be defined in different ways. In official documents the term is used as being synonymous with a high level of employment. Some economists define full employment as 'the level at which a marginal addition to demand will not cause unemployment to fall further'. More simply, full employment can be defined as a situation that exists in a labour market when demand for labour equals the supply of labour. Alternatively, full employment can be said to exist when the number of vacancies exceeds the number of people looking for jobs. This definition can be extended to postulate that the type of jobs, location of employment and wages offered have to be such that a person can reasonably be expected to apply for the job and be accepted for it. Full employment does not, however, mean that every person able and willing to work has to be employed at any given time for this is an impossibility.

In a dynamic society, incomes, the level of expenditure and the pattern of consumption change; new technology is developed; old industries die and new ones are born. During the period of adjustment demand for labour will be affected. Some skills will become obsolete, while others will have to be acquired. In a democratic society, people are free to

434

Table 21.1 Unemployment in the UK, 1900–94

Percentage of unemployment in the UK

Year	per cent	Year	per cent	Year	per cent	Year	per cent	Year	per cent	Year	per cent
1900	2.5	1929	10.4	1947	3.1	1959	2.3	1971	3.4	1983*	10.5
1905	5.0	1930	16.0	1948	1.8	1960	1.7	1972	3.8	1984	10.7
1910	4.7	1931	21.3	1949	1.6	1961	1.6	1973	2.7	1985	10.9
1919	2.1	1932	22.1	1950	1.5	1962	2.1	1974	2.4	1986	11.1
1921	12.9	1933	19.9	1951	1.2	1963	2.6	1975	4.1	1987	10.0
1922	14.3	1934	16.7	1952	2.1	1964	1.7	1976	5.7	1988	8.1
1923	11.7	1935	15.5	1953	1.8	1965	1.5	1977	6.2	1989	6.3
1924	10.3	1936	13.1	1954	1.5	1966	1.6	1978	6.1	1990	5.8
1925	11.3	1937	10.8	1955	1.2	1967	2.3	1979	5.8	1991	8.1
1926	12.5	1938	13.5	1956	1.3	1968	2.5	1980	7.4	1992	9.7
1927	9.7	1945	1.2	1957	1.6	1969	2.5	1981	11.3	1993	9.8
1928	10.8	1946	2.5	1958	2.2	1970	2.7	1982	12.2	1994	9.3

* 1983 – *Regional Trends*, no. 28, 1993 (Definition of unemployment was changed in 1982).

Source: D.I. Trotman-Dickenson, *Economic Workbook and Data* (Oxford: Pergamon Press, 1969); *Annual Abstract of Statistics*, *Monthly Digest of Statistics (1994)*.

change jobs. Some unemployment at any one time is, therefore, unavoidable and is not incompatible with what may be regarded as a state of full employment. Thus the questions are: what level of unemployment is acceptable and when does it become a problem? An international agreement in 1948 set the limit at 3 per cent. In the UK in the 1940s and 1950s the rate of unemployment averaged 1½ per cent (see Table 21.1). A figure of 3 per cent therefore appeared high. By the standard of the 1970s and early 1980s when the rate went over 8 per cent, a figure of 3 per cent appeared low. What is high and what is low unemployment percentage is therefore a relative figure. This applies to analysis of national trends and to international comparison.

MEASUREMENT OF UNEMPLOYMENT

Countries measure their unemployment figures differently and for international comparison adjustment of national figures may be necessary (see Tables 21.1 and 21.2). This task is made more difficult when the way in which a government defines unemployment is changed from time to time, as had happened for example in the UK. Apart from minor adjustments, there had been eight major changes relating to: (a) benefit entitlement (four); (b) procedures (two); and (c) the measurement system itself (two). A fall or rise in the unemployment figures may, therefore, reflect changes in the methods of calculation rather than in the state of the labour market.

Table 21.2 Unemployment: international comparison, 1980–93

Year	UK	Germany	France	Italy	EC	USA	Japan
1980	6.4	2.9	6.3	7.5	6.4	7.0	2.0
1985	11.2	7.1	10.2	9.6	10.8	7.1	2.6
1986	11.2	6.4	10.4	10.5	10.5	6.9	2.8
1987	10.3	6.2	10.5	10.9	10.6	6.1	2.8
1988	8.6	6.2	10.0	11.0	9.9	5.4	2.5
1989	7.2	5.6	9.4	10.9	9.0	5.2	2.3
1990	6.8	4.9	8.9	10.3	8.4	5.4	2.1
1991	8.7	4.4	9.4	9.9	8.7	6.6	2.1
1992	9.9	4.8	10.3	10.5	9.5	7.3	2.2
1993*	10.6	5.5	11.0	9.1	10.2	6.9	2.3

Note:
*1st. quarter.
Source: *Economic Trends*, 477 (London: HMSO, 1993).

There is no one right measure of unemployment that is appropriate for all countries at all times. Thus, governments have used different bases for counting the unemployment such as:

(a) *Registered unemployment basis.* In the UK unemployment was measured by expressing the number of people who registered for work as a percentage of the total insured working population. Thus only the registered unemployed were counted. Government unemployment statistics date back to the introduction of a limited National Insurance Scheme in 1911. Subsequently, the general application of the scheme provided a detailed record of unemployment for each region and industry.

(b) *Benefit claimants basis.* In 1982, the method of calculating unemployment data was changed. Instead of being the number of people who registered as out of work, it is now the number of people who claim unemployment benefit – expressed as a percentage of the total workforce. This change of definition of unemployment had the effect of reducing the figure of 3.3 million unemployed by some 7 per cent, as not all of them were entitled to, and therefore registered for, the unemployment benefit.

(c) *Samples basis.* In the USA and several other countries labour force sample surveys have been used as the source of unemployment statistics. Persons covered by the surveys were asked whether they were employed, seeking work, unable or unwilling to work. The sample method covers the unregistered unemployed who, in the UK, are left out of the official statistics. It is therefore more indicative of the real size of the unemployment problem and gives more information on the unemployed.

Appreciating this, the British government decided to supplement the existing unemployment statistics by new data from the *Labour Force Survey (LFS)* which covers some 60,000 households and defines the unemployed as people who said that they were available for work, did not have a paid job and have sought employment in the past four weeks. As this definition corresponds to that of the *International Labour Office (ILO)* which is internationally accepted now, it should facilitate comparison of unemployment levels between Britain and other countries.

For some time, many countries have been seeking ways of measuring unemployment more accurately. There is a need to count vacancies and jobs created as well as people out of work and to compare the figures over a period, and internationally, for a clearer picture of the unemployment problem and the state of the labour market.

BASIS FOR A POLICY

For policy purposes it is not enough to establish that unemployment exists. It is also necessary to construct a detailed picture of the situation by taking the following steps:

(a) Determination of the size of unemployment and its geographic distribution.

(b) The drawing-up of a profile of the unemployed showing their characteristics, such as age, sex, academic attainments and skills. The incidence of unemployment is not evenly distributed amongst the population. It tends to be higher for school leavers, elderly workers, some ethnic minorities and the unskilled.

(c) Analysis of the causes of unemployment and identification of the types of unemployment that are affecting the economy. The types of unemployment are: frictional; structural; cyclical; seasonal; regional; and voluntary.

In the formulation of a policy, the choice of measures will be determined by the scale and type of unemployment and will be influenced by the ideological and political preference of a government. There is no one policy or measure for use in all circumstances.

FRICTIONAL UNEMPLOYMENT

Frictional unemployment is temporary and is not incompatible with full employment as it has been defined – it may even be regarded as desirable if an economy is to be flexible. Frictional unemployment arises out of the mobility of labour. People may wish or need to change jobs, their employers or location. They may have just left school, college or university. While they are looking for employment and waiting to start a new job they may be out of work for a short time, that is frictionally unemployed. The underlying assumption is that this unemployment is not due to lack of demand for labour but rather to disorganisation in the labour market.

The government policy to deal with frictional unemployment aims to reduce the transitional period between jobs by bringing job-seekers and potential employers into contact. This has been done by setting up a sort of labour agency run by the Department of Employment and financed out of public funds. The first Labour Exchange in the UK was set up under the *Labour Exchange Act (1911)*. They continue to operate to this day under the name of Employment Offices or Jobcentres. Employers notify the offices of vacancies that they have and job seekers go there to find out what is on offer. If the period of looking for jobs extends beyond a few weeks, then this is likely to be an indication that another form of unemployment has developed.

SEASONAL UNEMPLOYMENT

As its name suggests, seasonal unemployment arises out of seasonal fluctuations in the level of economic activity of certain industries. In the UK those parts of the economy particularly affected by the changes in demand for labour are:

(a) *Agriculture*. Employment is higher at harvest time and falls in winter. Rural areas throughout the country are affected by seasonal unemployment.

(b) *Construction industry*. Building nationwide contracts in winter when the weather is bad, and expands as the weather improves in spring, provided there are no other factors to depress building starts – such as cuts in local authority expenditure on housing, or high mortgage rates that reduce demand for new houses in the public or the private sector.

(c) *Tourist industry*. Seaside areas are subject to localised seasonal unemployment. People tend to take their holidays in the summer and there is relatively little demand for accommodation and recreational activities in the off-peak periods.

Seasonal unemployment is self-correcting, but it still is a problem imposing a hardship on the industry's labour force during the periods when the level of activity is relatively low.

To deal with seasonal unemployment a government has a choice of measures:

(i) It can accept the fact that, in some industries, periods of unemployment are a way of life and use state benefits to relieve the plight of those temporarily unemployed.
(ii) It can offer inducements to firms to move to certain rural and holiday areas to provide alternative employment to agriculture and tourism. This has been tried but presents problems. Any incoming employer is likely to require a labour force all the year round and, in the case of the tourist industry, factories may reduce the appeal of holiday resorts.
(iii) Public funds can be made available, or tax concessions granted, to encourage technological developments in the construction industry that would make it possible, as in Scandinavian countries, to carry on construction work in adverse climatic conditions.
(iv) Fiscal policy can be aimed at increasing mechanisation by means of grants and investment allowances. This would reduce the demand for labour but would enable the industries to keep a small labour force permanently employed. Such a solution to the seasonal unemployment problem would, however, lead to structural unemployment.

STRUCTURAL UNEMPLOYMENT

Structural unemployment results from a permanent decline in demand for labour by certain industries, the main causes of this condition are:

(a) *Developments in technology.* Improved methods of production enable firms to produce greater output with fewer workers.
(b) *Permanent loss of markets.* This results from intensified international competition from countries that had not been previously industrialised and were able to apply new technology and produce at lower cost than the long-established industries of their competitors.
(c) *The nature of the industry itself.* Extractive industries must eventually suffer from structural unemployment. Mineral resources are finite. There will be no demand for miners when there is no more coal, or for oilmen when oil runs out.

In the UK the major industries to be in structural decline were coalmining, steelmaking and shipbuilding. They are located in close proximity to each other in three main areas – South-West Scotland, North-East England and

South Wales. The permanent contraction in the demand for labour by the heavy industries has thus created a regional unemployment problem as well. The fiscal measures that can be used to counteract structural and regional unemployment are the same, but the two forms of unemployment are not synonymous.

REGIONAL UNEMPLOYMENT

Regional unemployment may arise because of: (i) an area's economic dependence on one, or a small number of, industries that are in decline; or (ii) the lack of industrial development on an appreciable scale and a growing population. To counteract structural and regional unemployment the British government has tried both policies to 'take workers to work' and to take 'work to the workers'.

Transfer Policy

The first policy to be tried was to encourage the unemployed workers, who were surplus to the industry's requirements, to move to areas where jobs were available. For this purpose the Industrial Transference Board was set up in 1928. The government made funds available for resettlement and even for passages to Australia. This policy, however, met with little success. There were strong family and community links in the areas of unemployment that made people unwilling to leave. Within a year came the financial crash and the Great Depression of the 1930s. There were few jobs anywhere to move to. The transfer policy was widely condemned on social and on economic grounds. Even if it had been successful in reducing structural unemployment, it would have resulted in the depopulation of some areas and the congestion of others. There would have been a waste of under-used social capital in areas of emigration and a need for more public spending to provide houses, schools and various public services for the incoming population in immigration areas.

Distribution of Industry Policy

Governments opted, therefore, for the alternative policy of encouraging firms to move to the areas of high unemployment. This, it was hoped, would have a twofold effect of providing jobs where they were needed and of reducing concentration of the industrial population in the industrial areas of the country.

Special Area legislation

The depressed areas were designed as Special Areas in need of special assistance. The *Special Areas (Development and Improvement) Act (1934)* and the Amendment Act 1937 provided powers and finance to: (i) improve social and economic amenities of the Special Areas; and (ii) attract new industries to them. The main inducement was the provision by the government of purpose-built factories on industrial estates available on lease and at subsidised rents. These estates had little time to make any impact on structural unemployment. The first estate was built in 1936 and the Second World War broke out just three years later.

Development Areas Legislation

After the war the unemployment rate dropped to 1.2 per cent for the UK and the highest figure in the next 25 years was in 1970 when unemployment reached 2.7 per cent. In the Special Areas, renamed Development Areas, there were pockets of higher unemployment but these hardly constituted an unemployment problem. The government therefore concentrated on a policy to safeguard against future structural unemployment by seeking to secure a balanced distribution and development of industry.

The first step towards planning of the distribution of industry on a national basis was the implementation of some of the proposals of the Royal Commission on the Distribution of Industrial Population (Barlow Report, 1940) and through the *Distribution of Industry Act (1945)*. It scheduled certain areas as Development Areas to which firms wishing to set up in business or to expand were to be steered, largely by fiscal measures involving public expenditure and tax concessions. The policy adopted was one of inducement and not of coercion. Firms were not directed to a particular Development Area, but in the early stages of the policy the government had the powers to prevent them from building or extending factories elsewhere. In the 1970s structural unemployment again became a problem. The range of inducements offered was extended and, under the *Industry Act (1972),* the government differentiated benefits according to local needs. The areas were split into Special Development Areas, Assisted Areas and Intermediate Areas.

Benefits offered to firms were:

(a) Government-built factories available for lease or purchase.
(b) Assistance with transfer costs to the new location.

(c) Assistance with running costs, such as rent subsidy.
(d) Assistance with capital costs – loans on favourable terms, grants for new machinery and plant, interest relief.
(e) Payment related to labour – financial aid to key personnel moving to a new location, help with the training costs of workers and, later, grants for jobs created.
(f) Tax concessions.

As conditions in the regions changed the government revised its regional policy. The *Industrial Development Act (1982)* required the Ministers 'to have regard to all the circumstances actual and expected, including the state of employment and unemployment, population changes, migration and the objectives of regional policies'.

The Assisted Areas map of 1984 became out of date and was redrawn. A new map (Figure 21.1) came into effect in 1993 showing revised designated areas: the Development Areas (DAs) and Intermediate Areas (IAs). They respectively cover 16 per cent and 18 per cent of the working population of Great Britain. Inclusion of a locality in an assisted area depends on a number of factors, including: (a) current rates of unemployment; (b) the persistence of unemployment rates above the national average over recent years and the proportion of long-term unemployed in the local workforce; (c) the likely future demand for jobs in the area (taking account of the growth or decline in local industries and demographic changes); and (d) other measures of economic performance: activity rates, inner city and urban problems, peripherality (distance from markets), and major closures or rundown known to be in prospect (DTI, *Regional Policy*, 1994).

The increased cost of implementing the regional policy forced the Government to focus aid on particular businesses and projects. The *Regional Development Grant* scheme had been substantially revised as the major tool of regional policy, and new criteria for payment of grants were introduced. Projects from outside the manufacturing sector were included and the scheme was extended to certain service activities such as computer services, management consultancy, market research, research and development, mail order, freight services and administrative service at headquarters of companies. The amount of the grant depended on the eligibility of a project on the grounds of either job creation (job grant) or of expenditure (capital grant).

Cost-effectiveness of the scheme came to be questioned, as assistance was automatic and given to businesses that might have to come to the Development Areas without aid. To get better value for money the

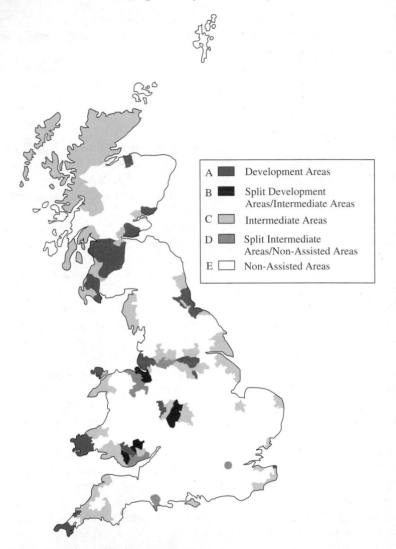

Figure 21.1   UK Assisted Areas
Note: As defined by the Department of Trade and Industry at 1 August 1993.
Source: Department of Trade and Industry, Welsh Office, *Regional Policy, Review of Assisted Areas of Great Britain* (HMSO, 1993).

government not only introduced a new map of assisted areas but also switched to *Regional Selective Assistance (RSA)* in the designated areas. Each tier of the DAs and IAs had to be negotiated with the European

Commission and the Regional Selective Assistance had to fit into the Commission's state aid regime.

EUROPEAN COMMUNITY REGIONAL POLICY

The Community's regional policy has been formulated in response to developments within the Member States and in the Community as a whole. The major events in recent years were:

(a) Enlargement of the Community from 10 Member States to 12 by the inclusion of Spain and Portugal, which further increased regional disparities and resulted in doubling of the population of the least favoured regions, defined as those with per capita GDP of less than 50 per cent of the Community average; (b) Enactment of the Single European Act. Its key requirement is promotion of economic and social cohesion of the Community. The objectives of this policy are summarised as follows: (i) Promoting the development and adjustment of regions whose development is lagging behind (i.e. where per capita GDP is less, or close to 75 per cent of the Community average). (ii) Converting regions or part of regions ... seriously affected by industrial decline. (iii) Combating long-term unemployment (above age of 25, unemployed for more than 12 months). (iv) Facilitating the occupational integration of young people (job-seekers below the age of 25). (v) Promoting development of rural areas.

The means of achieving these objectives are the structural instruments. These are three structural funds that award grants and four organisations that give loans. Grants are made available mainly from: the European Regional Development Fund (ERDF), the European Social Fund (ESF) and the European Agricultural Guidance and Guarantee Fund (EAGGF). Loans may be obtained from: the European Investment Bank, the New Community Instrument, the European Coal and Steel Community and the European Atomic Energy Community.

The amount of financial assistance has been considerable and provision was made to double the appropriation in real terms to the Structural Funds between 1987 and 1993. To improve their performance and provide greater flexibility the Funds were reformed. A feature of the reform was a shift from project-based to programme-based assistance.

The effectiveness of the Community's regional policy and measures to deal with the problem of structural unemployment depends to some extent on the level of economic activity within the member-states. The economic recession of the 1980s and early 1990s in Europe, which gave rise to cyclical unemployment and affected the restructuring programme at the national level also affected the Community's regional policy.

Costs of Regional Policy

The direct costs of the policies to reduce and then to safeguard against structural unemployment are: (i) public expenditure on capital account; (ii) payments on current account made to firms moving to the Special Areas and then the Development Areas; and (iii) loss of tax revenue as a result of tax allowances.

Indirect costs are more difficult to assess. If the firm's move to new locations away from the centre of their industry reduces their efficiency and competitiveness, then there is a loss to the country. Similarly, payment of inducements by the government diverted resources from other uses which might have been more beneficial.

Gains From the Policy

There is a the short-term gain from the reduction of pockets of unemployment in the early stages. The long-term objective of safeguarding against the return of structural unemployment has not been achieved as the unemployment figures for the 1970s and early 1980s show. However, without the industrial diversification and more balanced industrial structure of the regions, the rate of unemployment might have risen higher than it was by 1983, when the recession had spread and 10 per cent of the labour force was out of work. Similarly, during the 1990s recession, levels of unemployment might have been higher.

CYCLICAL UNEMPLOYMENT

Cyclical unemployment makes it more difficult for a government to deal with frictional, seasonal and structural unemployment. A downswing in the level of economic activity reduces employment throughout the country. The period of frictional unemployment lengthens and it becomes more difficult for those who are unemployed for seasonal or structural reasons to find other jobs. Policies to stabilise the economy are the policies to counteract cyclical unemployment (see Chapter 20).

VOLUNTARY UNEMPLOYMENT

Voluntary unemployment arises when people opt to remain unemployed when jobs are available. This may happen when: (i) the level of social security benefits is high; (ii) wages are relatively low; (iii) tax thresholds are low and the standard rate of tax and employees' National Insurance Contributions are high. As a result a family with low earnings may be financially as well off, or better off, on unemployment benefit and receiving a full range of social security benefits and rebates.

Research by Professor A.B. Atkinson and J.S. Fleming suggests that a relatively small percentage of people are in fact better off unemployed. The financial aspect is not the only consideration that influences a person's wish to work, but for many people it is an important one. Voluntary unemployment can therefore be considered to be, to some extent, of the government's own making. A solution to it would require a reformulation of the pay structure, social security system and of taxation.

COST OF UNEMPLOYMENT

This can be either personal cost, cost to the taxpayers or to the country. Personal cost to individuals who are unemployed cannot be easily quantified including as it does such factors as: feelings of uselessness, loss of social standing, depression and ill-health. On this however medical opinion is divided. There is evidence to suggest that the incidence of illness is higher among the unemployed but the question arises whether it is unemployment that brings on sickness or whether it is people who are in poor health that are more likely to be unemployed. Financial cost – the difference between lost earnings and state income support to individuals who are unemployed – can be estimated with greater accuracy.

Cost to Taxpayers

For taxpayers, the cost of unemployment is not just the taxes that they have to pay to cover government's expenditure on unemployment benefit. To calculate the full cost this figure needs to be augmented to include: (a) allowance for lost Income Tax and National Insurance Contributions, which the unemployed do not pay; and (b) indirect taxes that they would have paid had they been in work. Some of the losses are hypothetical.

Nevertheless, the Employment Unit has estimated that every unemployed person costs the taxpayer £8,000 per year – the total bill of course depends on the number of people out of work. In 1993 the amount was reckoned to be around £24 billion (*The Times* (London), February 18, 1993). The Treasury does not estimate the full cost of unemployment. fiscal policies to counteract existing unemployment and to safeguard against it in the future are likely to be based on figures that underestimate the size of the problem.

Cost to the Country

To arrive at the overall cost of unemployment to the national economy the waste of human capital has to be added to the aggregates of personal and taxpayers' costs. The level of unemployment is determined by the demand for and the supply of labour as a factor of production. Governments, through their economic, fiscal and monetary policies, may seek to influence both, but no government on its own can effectively deal with the unemployment problem.

THE 'JOB SUMMIT'

Unemployment is contagious and spreads from country to country. Thus, concerted action at international level is needed to counteract it. With this in view the first world 'Job Summit' was convened in Detroit (USA) in March 1994. Politicians readily agreed that measures should be taken to create jobs but they disagreed on what these measures should be.

In the USA and the UK governments cut interest rates to stimulate economic growth and unemployment fell. Policy-makers in other countries in Europe do not appear to accept that there is a link between joblessness and inadequate growth and attribute structural unemployment to 'Eurosclerosis' (a term introduced into the economic jargon in the 1980s and suggesting in this instance a hardening of economic arteries; thereby making a flexible response to stimulants more difficult). They are therefore not convinced by the 'American Experience', which as reports of the Summit suggest that by '... limiting employment protection, cutting payroll taxes, curbing unions and introducing tough means-tests for social security recipients, can reduce the number of workers permanently jobless once the economy returns to rapid growth'. Politicians within the European Community tend to favour legislation to limit working hours, measures to promote work-sharing and subsidies to public projects 'to create jobs'.

FUTURE UNEMPLOYMENT PROBLEMS

Future unemployment is likely to be very different from what has been experienced so far. Professor Tom Stonier's estimate submitted to the government's Central Policy Review Office, suggests that, by the beginning of the next century, some 10 per cent, possibly even 5 per cent, of Britain's labour force will be able to supply all her material needs (*The Times*, 13 November, 1978). When the microchip takes over from the workers there will still be a demand for skilled labour but those without the necessary skills are likely to become unemployed and unemployable.

Fear of technology replacing manpower is not new and we do not have to go back to the Industrial Revolution to find examples of it. In the 1960s and 1970s, as deliveries of computers for office work increased (10 in 1959, 34 in 1960, 1,030 in 1973), concern was expressed that they would displace office workers and create unemployment among them. Initially, this did not happen. Government estimated that staff requirement in automatic data-processing occupations increased from 6,775 in 1964 to 71,000 in 1974 and the new jobs more than compensated for those that had disappeared (Ministry of Labour, *Manpower Studies*, No. 4 'Computers in Offices', HMSO, 1965). However, the fact remains that not all redundant workers can be retrained for new types of employment and, in many industries, developments in technology are more likely to reduce than to increase the number of jobs available.

The prospect of unemployment need not be as bleak, however, as some of the predictions suggest, but to avoid mass unemployment we may have to change our attitude to work and leisure. We also will have to distinguish between work, which is something that we have to do, and activity, which is something that we wish to do. A government can cut the duration of the former and give us more time for the latter. A longer period of education, a shorter working week and early retirement are some of the ways of reducing unemployment and at the same time possibly improving the quality of life. As people have more time to engage in leisure activities, new jobs in industries that cater for them will be created, shifting the labour force from manufacturing to services. In the future, both the period and the pattern of employment may have to change, if unemployment is not to become a way of life for a large proportion of the adult population.

SUMMARY

1. All governments claim to have the objective of maintaining full employment.
2. The term full employment can be defined in different ways. For practical purposes governments take it to mean a high level of employment.
3. Departure from full employment is measured by the unemployment figures. These can be calculated on the basis of the insured population that is out of work and registered as unemployed, or on the basis of a sample survey.
4. To formulate an economic policy to maintain employment and to apply the appropriate measure, it is first necessary to identify the type of unemployment: frictional, seasonal, structural, regional, cyclical and voluntary.
6. Measures to counteract structural unemployment are the same, to a large extent, as those required to deal with regional unemployment. They are either the transfer of structurally-unemployed workers out of a region or bringing new firms and industries into it. These two policies of taking 'workers to the work' and 'work to the workers' have been pursued simultaneously in the UK.
7. Fiscal policy to deal with the problem of cyclical unemployment requires similar measures to that for stabilizing the economy.
8. Voluntary unemployment may arise when the level of pay is relatively low, taxation is heavy and the level of benefits is high.
9. There is no one single policy to counteract unemployment. Different fiscal measures are needed to deal with each particular type of unemployment and international co-operation is required not only within the European Community but also on a worldwide basis.

SUGGESTED FURTHER READING

H. Armstrong and J. Taylor, *Regional Economics and Policy* (Hemel Hempstead: Harvester Wheatsheaf, 1993).

D. Begg, S. Fischer and R. Dornbusch, *Economics* (London: McGraw-Hill, 1994).

A. Beharrell, *Unemployment and Job Creation* (London: Macmillan, 1992).

Commission of the European Communities, *Guide to the Reform of the Community's Structural Funds* (Luxembourg, 1989).

Department of Trade and Industry, The Scottish Office and the Welsh Office, *Regional Policy* (London: 1994).

S. James and C. Nobes, *The Economics of Taxation* (London: Prentice-Hall, 1992).

M. Parkin and D. King, *Economics* (Wokingham: Addison-Wesley, 1992).

P. Samuelson and W. Nordhaus, *Economics* (London: McGraw-Hill, 1992).

EXERCISES

1. 'Full employment is neither feasible nor desirable.' Comment on this statement.
2. Which type of unemployment do you regard as presenting the most serious problem for a government? Give reasons for your answer.
3. Discuss reasons for the development of structural unemployment and measures to counteract it.
4. 'Voluntary unemployment is of the government's own making.' Comment on the validly of this statement.
5. Explain why before a government can formulate a policy to counteract unemployment it first needs to identify the type of unemployment that has developed.
6. Suggest fiscal measures to deal with cyclical unemployment and consider whether there is a real need for them.
7. Consider the relative merits of a policy of taking work to the workers as compared with a policy of taking workers to the work.
8. Consider the argument put forward by some monetarists that to cure unemployment it is first necessary to suppress inflation. Suggest how this could be done.
9. Explain why there is no one single effective policy that could maintain a high level of employment.
10. Suggest how a monetary policy can be used to reinforce fiscal policy to counteract unemployment.

22 Fiscal Policy in Relation to Economic Growth and the Standard of Living

MEASURE OF ECONOMIC GROWTH

Economic growth is a widely accepted goal of governments. It facilitates policies to maintain a high level of employment and is the only way by means of which the standard of living of everybody in the country can be increased in the long run and economic policies can begin to eliminate poverty.

Economic growth can be defined as an increase in total output of goods and services over a period of time. It can therefore be expressed as a percentage change in the gross national product or national income of a country (see p. 18). It can either be measured at current prices or in real terms (see Appendix 3).

INTERNATIONAL COMPARISON

When the rate of economic growth is compared internationally it will show whether a country's performance is relatively high or low (see p. 19). Analysis of the economies with high growth rates may disclose features that they have in common and which may be indicative of factors that contribute to economic growth. Fiscal policies can then be used to foster those growth-influencing factors.

FACTORS INFLUENCING GROWTH

There are many factors that influence growth and we can only mention some of the more important ones.

(a) *Investment*. This is a major factor in growth. Countries that invest a high proportion of their GNP tend to have relatively high rates of growth. Investment takes different forms. Those projects that are particularly relevant to growth are: (i) investment in land to improve its fertility, e.g. irrigation schemes; (ii) fixed capital formation, i.e. investment in plant and machinery; and (iii) investment in human resources, i.e. expenditure on education to increase academic abilities and the skills of the people.

(b) *Population increase.* This may stimulate or hinder economic growth. It will all depend on circumstances. In the early stages of economic development, when capital is scarce but land and other resources are plentiful, a bigger labour force may be necessary to utilise them more fully. However, in later stages of economic development, if population outstrips resources, its increase will be detrimental to economic growth.

(c) *Research and development.* The contribution of R&D to economic growth is more controversial. In the past, innovating countries achieved economic growth but more recently the more succesful economies have been those that have applied foreign discoveries and technology and have prospered (e.g. Hong Kong).

(d) *Level of demand and profit expectations.* Firms will have little incentive to invest and carry out research and development unless there is the demand for goods and services and the expectation of making a profit.

Fiscal policy to encourage economic growth involves both tax and expenditure measures, and, in some circumstances, borrowing.

(i) Reduction in personal taxation, leaving taxpayers with larger disposable incomes enables them to spend more and encourages demand for goods and services; so do transfer payments but they have to be financed by taxes paid by others. The overall effect on expenditure will depend on the *propensity to consume* (see p. 46).

(ii) Investment allowances and reduction in taxation of profits encourage investment by firms and expansion of production.

(iii) Increase in public expenditure on education, research and development can partly be financed out of current government revenue but the policy to finance large capital projects requires borrowing.

Monetary policy to reinforce fiscal policy aimed at growth requires low rates of interest and an increase in credit creation while, at the same time, pursuing policies to avoid inflation.

LIMITS TO ECONOMIC GROWTH

Growth cannot go on unchecked. The limits to growth are: (a) *Physical restraints*. Growth depends on the availability of resources some of which, such as land or minerals, are respectively in fixed and finite supply. (b) *Financial restraints*. The ability of a country to increase its output and the rate of growth is influenced by the availability of investment funds. (c) *Public opinion*. Governments may be forced to respond to pressure groups that, for example, put greater emphasis on the preservation of the environment than on further increases in the standard of living.

ECONOMIC WELFARE AND THE STANDARD OF LIVING

The economic welfare of individuals can be regarded as synonymous with their standard of living and is a measure of the extent to which the material needs of a society or an individual are met. In discussion of the standard of living, our concern is not with the quality of life but rather with the material goods and services that consumers can acquire with their incomes. The assumption is made that it is preferable to have a high income rather than a low one.

International comparison of the standard of living on the basis of national income per head of population can, however, be misleading (see p. 35). The fact that some countries have a per capita income twice as high as that of the UK does not mean that their standard of living is correspondingly higher. People's standard of living depends, as has been seen in Chapter 2, on a great many contributory factors, but basically it is determined by how much money they have and how much they need to spend to satisfy their needs. Therefore the following points have to be taken into account: (i) personal income, (ii) the level and pattern of taxation – income tax reduces incomes and indirect taxes increase prices, (iii) state benefits – such as transfer payments that increase a person's income, (iv) public goods and services provided by the state 'free of charge', (v) availability of market goods and services, and (vi) the price level.

ELIMINATION OF POVERTY

A corollary of a policy to achieve economic growth is a policy to eliminate poverty. This requires an increase to some acceptable level in the standard of living of those persons said to be living in poverty, and raises the problem of *defining* poverty. There is no stated norm of poverty as such. Poverty can be *absolute* or *relative*. Of the two, absolute poverty is easier to measure. A person who has no permanent roof over their head, wears rags and is starving, is absolutely poor. Some people in developing countries live in such absolute poverty. Economic growth would provide the means whereby absolute poverty can first be relieved and eventually eliminated, as has been done to a large extent in the developed countries.

Relative poverty is, to some extent, the consequence of economic growth and a high average standard of living. In a country where many households have three cars and three colour television sets, a household that has only two is relatively poor. Between our two extremes there is a whole range of relatively 'poor' in the sense that there are groups of people who have a higher standard of living than their own. The relatively poor will always be with us.

Who is regarded as poor by others does, however, depend on where and when they live. Thus, for example, the 1991 *Breadline Britain Survey* showed that two-thirds of the people questioned regarded the following as *necessities*: fridge, washing machine, lawnmower, vacuum cleaner, TV set, video hire, cassette player and basic camera.

In findings published by the Joseph Rowntree Foundation (*Social Policy Research Findings*, No. 31, November 1992) these items were included in low-cost household budgets of people receiving state income support and therefore officially classified by the government as poor. In many other countries, anyone who owned all these goods would be considered as very rich indeed.

Assessment of deprivation and affluence of individuals reflects the overall standard of living in a community, and changes over a period of time. Some of the 'necessities' listed above had not been invented a hundred years ago. Poverty was therefore judged on different criteria.

The concept of poverty can have different meanings, as may be illustrated by passages written by two sons whose lives overlapped. The first extract is from a letter written by Sir Winston Churchill to his mother in 1898: '...it seems just as suicidal to me when you spend £200 on a ball dress, as it does to you when I purchase a new polo pony for £100 and I feel you ought to have the dress and I the polo pony. The pinch of the matter is that we are so damned poor' (A. Leslie, *Jennie: the Life of Lady Randolph Churchill*, Hutchinson, 1971). At the time the average wage of an adult man in manufacturing was about £70 a year.

The other extract is written by Emlyn Williams, the actor and writer, who in his autobiography, *George*, says of his mother, 'I knew her unspoken dread of her children going barefoot – to her the mark of destitution'.

FISCAL POLICY TO INCREASE THE STANDARD OF LIVING

Fiscal policy may aim to increase the standard of living of all the citizens of a country. The objective may be stated in general terms, mentioning some specific improvements, or as a planned percentage increase in the national income. This is a long-term policy and requires measures that will lead to economic growth. Alternatively, a government may opt for a short-term policy to increase the standard of some groups in the society and reduce that of others by fiscal measures to redistribute income and wealth; levying taxes on some to provide state benefits for others.

SUMMARY

1. Economic growth is widely held to be a desirable goal of government policy and, to this end, fiscal and monetary measures are applied.
2. Changes in the level of the Gross National Product are a measure of economic growth.
3. Economic growth is influenced by various factors: changes in the size and structure of population; investment; research and development; aggregate demand; and profit expectation.
4. Fiscal policy to stimulate economic growth consists of tax and expenditure measures and management of the national debt.
5. Monetary policy is used to reinforce the expansionary effect so as to expand demand and facilitate production by making credit available more easily and reducing the cost of borrowing by lowering the rate of interest.
6. There are limits to economic growth since all resources are scarce and some resources are finite.
7. The economic welfare of individuals depends on their standard of living.
8. The standard of living is measured by the extent to which individuals' or society's needs are met.
9. In the long-run, an overall improvement in the standard of living depends on economic growth.
10. In the short-run, the standard of living of some people may be improved by a redistribution of income and wealth, but this simultaneously reduces the economic welfare of others.

SUGGESTED FURTHER READING

A. Sen, *Inequality Re-examined* (Oxford: Clarendon Press, 1992).

G. Silverber and L. Soete, *The Economics of Growth and Technical Change* (Cheltenham: Edward Elgar, 1994).

R.M. Sundrum, *Economic Growth in Theory and Practice* (London: Macmillan, 1990).

W. Beckerman, *In Defence of Economic Growth* (London: Jonathan Cape, 1976).

D. Begg, S. Fischer and R. Dornbush, *Economics* (London: McGraw-Hill, 1994).

J. Creedy, *Taxation, Poverty and Income Distribution* (Cheltenham: Edward Elgar, 1994).

S. Gomulka, *The Theory of Technological Change and Economic Growth* (London: Routledge, 1990).

N.M. Healey, *Growth and Structural Change* (London: Macmillan, 1994).

M. Parkin and D. Kind, *Economics* (Wokingham: Addison-Wesley, 1992).

W.W. Rostow, *Theorists of Economic Growth from David Hume to the Present* (Oxford: Oxford University Press, 1993).

P. Samuelson and W. Nordhaus, *Economics* (London: McGraw-Hill, 1992).

EXERCISES

1. What are the problems involved in measuring economic growth?
2. Make a case for or against a government policy to foster further economic growth.
3. Of the factors that influence economic growth, which do you regard as the most important? Suggest how a government can encourage them by fiscal measures.
4. Consider the way that fiscal policy can be used to increase the standard of living in a country.
5. 'Incomes of individuals may go up, but their standard of living may go down.' Explain this paradox.

23 Fiscal Policy in Relation to Distribution of Income and Wealth

OBJECTIVE OF EQUALITY

The objective of a fiscal policy to redistribute income and wealth is to increase the standard of living of the poorer and their holding of wealth, and to reduce that of the richer so as to achieve greater equality. Much depends on the public's rating of equality and their endorsement of a government's policy for redistribution of income and wealth. A survey by Gallup International Institute (*The Economist*, September 5, 1992) showed considerable differences in attitude towards equality of people in a number of countries. Asked whether it was the government's responsibility to reduce income differences, 63 per cent of respondents in Britain said yes, 81 per cent in Italy, 64 per cent in Holland, 56 per cent in West Germany and only 28 per cent in the United States. Nevertheless, when it came to electing a government, people tend to vote for political parties that promised lower taxes, even though such a policy could not be expected to have a redistributive effect.

The problem with equality is that it means different things to different people and some would say that it does not and cannot exist. George Orwell put this in a nutshell when he wrote 'All animals are equal, but some are more equal than others' (*Animal Farm*). For practical purposes governments define their objective of achieving equality as one of reducing inequality, without specifying by how much. This leaves unanswered the questions of the degree of inequality that is permissible in an equitable society and of the best way of achieving the desired condition.

CAUSES OF INEQUALITY

To look for an answer to the questions posed above, it is first necessary to consider why inequality arises. It may be due to a variety of factors:

(a) *Genetic factors.* Some people are born healthier, brighter, more enterprising and energetic or better looking: they can take

459

advantage of such attributes to increase their earning potential. A survey of households in the United States and Canada suggested that good looks enhance earnings. After adjustment for educational attainments, men and women considered to be 'very attractive' earned about 5 per cent more per hour than people with average looks and 'plain women and plain men' earned respectively 5 per cent and 10 per cent less (D. Hammersmith and J. Biddle, Beauty and the Labour Market (*NBER Working Paper*, no. 4518). The findings of this research are likely to be controversial.

(b) *Environmental factors.* Depending on the environment into which they are born or in which they live, people may make better use of their gifts, but the most suitable environment will not enable a tone deaf person to become an opera singer. The more gifted a person the more likely they are to break out of an unfavourable environment, earn more money and accumulate more wealth.

(c) *Inheritance of wealth.* People who have wealth are likely to pass on to their children at least some of the property that remains after the state had taken its share in taxation. Any gifts or bequests will contribute to perpetuating inequality in the distribution of wealth for subsequent generations.

MEASURE OF INEQUALITY

To measure inequality the distribution of income and wealth in the country has to be looked at. The following method can be used. People are divided into groups, the top 1 per cent, 5 per cent, 10 per cent until 100 per cent is reached. If the people in the top 10 per cent group own 90 per cent of the total wealth of the country, or receive 90 per cent of the total income, then there is a very high degree of inequality. On the other hand if the top 10 per cent of the population have 10 per cent of total income or wealth of the country then distribution is equal.

If the population is divided into four groups, each with the same number of people and the groups are arranged in a descending order of income or wealth, then these are labelled quartiles. If people are arranged into ten groups then the population is shown in deciles until percentiles are reached with 100 groups.

The following figures from the Royal Commission on the Distribution of Income and Wealth showed that, to be in the top ten per cent of income recipients in the UK in 1972, a person had to have earnings of at least £2,565 after tax.

Quantile group		Personal income after tax in UK
top 1 per cent	4.0 per cent	£5,003 (income range lower limit)
2–5 per cent	8.9 per cent	£3,070
6–10 per cent	8.5 per cent	£2,565

Median income at this time was £1,470 (for a comparison with the 1990s, see Table 23.1). The Commission's findings, based on a comprehensive study, were published between 1975 and 1979. No comparable enquiry on such a scale has been carried out since, but the government has for some years now published statistics regularly on the distribution of income and wealth which are indicative of the extent of inequality that exists (Table 23.2).

LORENZ CURVE

Inequality of income or wealth can also be shown graphically by means of the Lorenz Curve (Figure 23.1). The cumulative percentage of the population of a country is plotted against cumulative income or wealth. A line

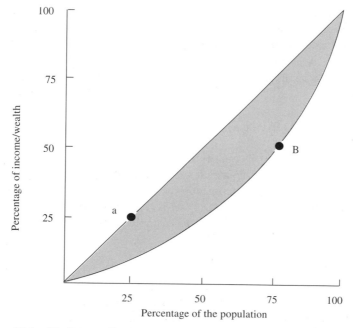

Figure 23.1   The Lorenz Curve

Table 23.1   Redistribution of wealth

Personal wealth: *distribution of marketable wealth among adult population in*
          the UK

		1966	1976	1979	1980	1989	1990	1991
Concentration of wealth percentage of wealth owned by:								
most wealthy	1%	33	21	20	19	18	18(11)	18
	5%	56	38	37	36	38	37(26)	37
	10%	69	50	50	50	53	51(37)	50

Note: 1990 figure in brackets: marketable wealth plus occupational and state pension rights.

Source: Inland Revenue Board, *Inland Revenue Statistics* (annually, 1982, 1992, 1993) and *Social Trends* (1994).

drawn through the point of origin at 45 degrees is the line of complete equality, e.g. at point *A*, 25 per cent of the population own 25 per cent of total personal income or wealth.

The Lorenz Curve shows the deviation from equality. The inequality in the distribution of income or wealth is shown by the shaded area. At point *B*, 75 per cent of the population have 50 per cent of total income or wealth. The closer the Lorenz Curve is to the line of complete equality the more equal is the distribution.

FORMULATION OF POLICY

Accepting the view that inequality is undesirable, a government in formulating its fiscal policy to redistribute income and wealth has to: (i) establish a need for the policy by determining the extent of inequality that exists; (ii) decide on the degree of equality that it considers desirable and feasible to achieve; and (iii) select measures to be applied.

PROBLEMS OF INADEQUATE DATA

First of all the government needs statistical information, but lack of data has been and still is a problem. The Royal Commission on the Distribution of Income and Wealth (Cmnd. 6161, 1975) found that statistics on both income

Table 23.2   Changes in the distribution of incomes: different measurements

(a) Before Tax

	Per cent of Total Income						
	1929	1933	1949	1959	1967	1969–70[1]	1992–93[2]
	National Income estimates						
Group of Incomes %	Clark	Lydall	Nicholson		Atkinson	Inland Revenue	Inland Revenue
Top 1	20.0	10.2	11.2	8.4	7.4	6.1	7.8
Top 5	34.1	29.0	23.8	19.9	18.4	16.2	20.4
Top 10	42.8	38.0	33.2	29.4	28.0	25.2	30.4
Bottom 90	57.2	62.0	66.8	70.6	72.0	74.8	69.6

(b) After Tax

	Per cent of Total Income					
	1938	1949	1959	1967	1969–70[1]	1992–93[2]
	National Income estimates					
Group of Incomes %	Lydall	Nicholson		Atkinson	Inland Revenue	Inland Revenue
Top 1	11.9	6.4	5.2	4.9	5.4	5.2
Top 5	24.1	17.7	15.8	14.8	14.1	14.3
Top 10	33.6	27.1	25.2	24.3	23.2	22.0
Bottom 90	66.4	72.9	74.8	75.7	76.8	78.0

Notes :
1. The distribution for 1969–70 is on a more limited basis, and is not strictly
   comparable with earlier years.

Sources:
1929:   Estimated from Colin Clark, *National Income and Outlay* (London:
            Macmillan, 1937).
1938:   H.F. Lydall, 'The Long-Term Trend in the Size Distribution of Income',
            Journal of the Royal Statistical Society, Part I (1959).
1949–59:   R.J. Nicholson, 'The Distribution of Personal Income', *Lloyds Bank Review*
            (January 1967).
1967:   A.B. Atkinson (ed.), *Wealth, Income and Inequality* (Harmondsworth:
            Penguin, 1973).
1969–70:   Estimated from *Inland Revenue Statistics*; G. Polanyi and J.B. Wood, *How
            Much Inequality?* (IEA, 1974).
2. 1992–93 figures are author's estimates using data from *Inland Revenue Statistics, 1994*.

and wealth were inadequate and recommended that studies should be undertaken to fill in the gaps and provide additional information (Table 23.2)

In the UK statistics on wealth distribution that the Inland Revenue has been publishing since 1960 are a by-product of its revenue-gathering activities. For a comprehensive early study of national wealth one has to go back to the work of Professor J. Revell. Writers on inequality, such as Professor A.B. Atkinson on one hand and George Polanyi and John Wood on the other, have disagreed on the accuracy of the various available statistics and the extent of redistribution that has already taken place (A.B. Atkinson, *The Economics of Inequality* (Oxford: Oxford University Press, 1977); G. Polanyi and J.B. Wood, How Much Inequality? (London: IEA, 1974)). Official statistics can be criticised on various grounds:

(i) The Inland Revenue is not concerned with estimates below the exemption limit for inheritance tax – therefore it has no incentive to collect reliable data for small estates. Some people appear not to possess wealth when in fact they do own assets.

(ii) The available statistics can be misleading because they are largely collected when estates are transferred on death. A larger proportion of those who die in any one year will be older people, and they are more likely than the young to have paid off a mortgage and accumulated some wealth. The statistics therefore tend to overstate the concentration of wealth.

(iii) Data on the distribution of wealth is also likely to be distorted by the way that wealth is held. Suppose parents and two children live in a house that is worth £80,000. If the house had been bought in the name of the husband, then the statistics would show that all the property was held by one person and three people (75 per cent) had no assets. On the other hand, if the house was bought in the joint names of the couple then 50 per cent of the household members would have wealth of £40,000 each and 50 per cent have no assets. In reality, of course, the whole family benefits from the house. As the value of this property is below the exemption limit for Inheritance Tax (£150,000 in 1994–95) it would be of no interest to the Inland Revenue.

(iv) State pension rights are a form of wealth. Since most people in the country are entitled to them they cannot be said to have no wealth. But Inland Revenue estimates show that several million people entitled to a state pension did not have any wealth. Distribution of wealth will look considerably different depending on whether pension rights are included or not.

MEASURES TO REDISTRIBUTE INCOME AND WEALTH

It is difficult for any government without the knowledge of the exact distribution of income and wealth to apply corrective measures and set specific objectives for the reduction of inequality. Different measures can be used and were adopted piecemeal by successive governments in the UK.

Incomes were redistributed by:	*Wealth was redistributed by:*
1. Progressive income tax.	1. Progressive capital transfer tax/inheritance tax.
2. Higher rates of tax on investment income.	2. Higher rate of tax on transfers on death than in life time.
3. State benefits to lower income groups given on a decreasing scale as income rose and a cut-off point for benefits.	3. No tax concessions to direct descendants.
4. Public expenditure to provide for equal opportunity.	4. Wealth tax in some countries In the UK capital gains tax, though not intended as such, became in fact a wealth tax until provision for indexation of gains was introduced.
5. Incomes policy that stopped any pay increases to people with incomes above a certain level.	5. Progressive tax on incomes that has reduced the ability of taxpayers to accumulate wealth out of income.

As there was no single, coherent policy for planned distribution of income and wealth, and no clearly defined objectives were set, the effectiveness of the assorted measures cannot therefore be accurately assessed in the UK. There has been, however, considerable unplanned and unintended redistribution of incomes and wealth as a result of inflation. Values of assets have changed at different rates and at times in opposite directions. House prices generally increased, reaching a peak in 1988–89. In the UK over 60 per cent of households now live in owner-occupied houses and for people with relatively small holdings of wealth, a house is their most valuable asset. Over this period, they witnessed a great increase in its value, whereas inflation led to a drop in the value of many stocks and shares as interest rates rose and companies got into financial difficulties. To the extent that the wealthier sections of society were more likely to hold portfolios in stocks and shares, inflation to some extent may have narrowed the gap between the richer and the poorer over this period. Thus, some of the increase in equality may be achieved in an arbitrary manner – not motivated by moral considerations but by the falling value of money.

Although the redistribution of income and wealth cannot be attributed to any one specific action or policy, some statistics suggest that the overall trend has been toward greater equality (Table 23.1). Nevertheless, the widespread belief that the poor are getting poorer and the rich are getting richer persists. This may perhaps be explained by focusing on particular groups of people who had been affected by certain demographic, social and economic factors:

(i)   An ageing population in the UK and in some of the other countries in the European Community has resulted in an increased number of retired people living on pensions which are below average earnings.

(ii)   Higher divorce rates have increased the number of single parent families leading to the existence of two households where previously there had only been one – with income and assets divided. This may leave one or possibly both households dependent on social security.

(iii)   Changes in the labour markets have reduced employment opportunities for people without skills who are increasingly becoming unemployable and living on welfare benefits.

(iv)   Internationalisation of earnings at the top level has meant that British pop idols, film stars, sports personalities and corporate executives have been able to earn more in a year than it would take a person on an average wage to earn in a working life. The golfer Nick Faldo was reported to have earnings averaging £10 million a year. Similarly, the actor Sean Connery and Phil Collins, the rock star, according to recent estimates are said to be in the same league.

In the 1980s and 1990s, a new class of self-made multi-millionaires has also emerged as fortunes have been made in trade, industry and finance. From its survey of 'Britain's Richest 500', the *Sunday Times* concluded that, not only are the rich in the UK becoming richer, but their number is also increasing (*Sunday Times* Survey, 'Britain's Richest 500', London: The Times Newspapers Limited, 1994).

To be included in the Top 500, one needed to possess wealth of £20 million. The combined estimated wealth of the group in 1994 amounted to £65 billion. Although this is a sizeable amount it amounted to between 2 to 3 per cent of the personal sector's wealth (Table 23.3).

As with poverty, so with wealth, there are the absolutely rich and relatively rich. Some people will always be better off than others. Thus, for example, if many ordinary people pay high prices to see on the field or on the screen others whose abilities are considered to be out of the ordinary then those individuals will be richer than the rest.

Very high rates of marginal tax in the UK in the 1970s (98 per cent on incomes and 75 per cent on wealth: see pp. 145, 223) had done little to close the inequality gap and no political party is now proposing a return to these levels of taxation. Redistribution of income and wealth is a slow process and one that involves practical and ideological considerations. Reducing absolute poverty rather than relative affluence at the top is likely to be a more attainable objective of governments' fiscal policies.

Table 23.3   Composition of the net wealth in the personal sector, UK, 1971–92

| | | Percentage | | |
Net wealth	*1971*	*1981*	*1991*	*1992*
Dwellings (net of mortgage debt)	26	36	37	33
Other fixed assets		10	10	65
Non-marketable tenancy rights	12	12	8	8
Shares and deposits with building societies	7	8	8	8
National Savings, notes and coin and bank deposits	13	10	10	10
Stocks, shares and unit trusts	23	8	8	9
Life assurance and pension funds	15	16	27	31
Other financial assets net of liabilities	–6	0	–4	–4
Total (£ billion)	172	740	2,270	2,300

Note:
Data has been revised from 1976 onwards to include certain public sector pensions.

Source: *Social Trends* (1994).

INEQUALITY AT THE REGIONAL AND INTERNATIONAL LEVEL

People with relatively high incomes and large holdings of wealth tend to be concentrated in certain areas of a country, as for example in the South East in and around London in the UK and in Italy in the North. This gives rise to disparities between regions not only within the Member States but within the European Community as a whole. National, regional and fiscal policies and the Community's economic and social measures have been implemented to redress the balance (see p. 445). Their aim is to encourage developments in the less prosperous areas and to provide better business and employment opportunities. A wide range of training and educational programmes is intended to help people to qualify for the jobs that are being created and to improve their earning potential.

Such regional inequalities as exist within the European Community are, however, relatively small when compared with the differences in the levels of incomes and wealth holdings of the developed and developing countries. In some of the latter there are great extremes between a few very rich individuals and a large proportion of people living at or below subsistence level. International figures on the distribution of income and wealth are difficult to come by, but comparison of national income or GDP per head of population is, to some extent, indicative of the inequality that exists (see p. 35).

Action at international level by governments and various organisations has done little to close the gap. Foreign aid to some of the poorest countries has not been reaching the people most in need. Civil wars in Africa and elsewhere continue to destroy such wealth as had been accumulated, and governments of some of the most impoverished nations divert a high proportion of such resources as they have to defence. For example, defence spending by Vietnam was estimated to be 11 per cent of GDP in 1992. This compares with 1 per cent by Japan (World Bank and International Institute of Strategic Studies).

For any assistance to improve the standard of living of the people of a country the prerequisite is peace and political stability. It is only then that long-term economic development can begin that will bring greater equality in the distribution of income and wealth at a global level.

SUMMARY

1. Fiscal policy to redistribute income and wealth is intended to achieve a greater degree of equality within a society.

2. Inequality is caused by genetic factors, environmental differences and inherited wealth.
3. The existing degree of equality or of inequality can be measured by dividing people into groups and arranging them in order of income or wealth-holding.
4. The Lorenz Curve is used to show the degree of equality graphically.
5. Governments do not publish targets for the degree of equality that they seek to achieve. They formulate their policies to reduce inequality by unspecified amounts.
6. There is a lack of relevant data, particularly on the distribution of wealth over a period of time.
7. It is therefore difficult to assess the extent to which fiscal policies have succeeded in redistributing income and wealth without reliable information.
8. Some redistribution of income and wealth has been achieved by progressive income tax, means-tested benefits and capital transfer taxes.
9. Greater equality has been achieved by public expenditure to provide for equal opportunities, e.g. free education.
10. Inflation has resulted in an unplanned and unintended redistribution of income and wealth that is contrary to principles of equity.

SUGGESTED FURTHER READING

A.B. Atkinson, *Poverty and Social Security* (Hemel Hempstead: Harvester Wheatsheaf, 1989).

J. Creedy (ed.), *Taxation, Poverty and Income Distribution* (Cheltenham: Edward Elgar, 1994).

J. Le Grand, C. Propper and R. Robinson, *The Economics of Social Problems* (London: Macmillan, 1992).

D. Piachaud, 'The Definition of Measurement of Poverty and Inequality', in N. Barr (ed.), *Current Issues in the Economics of Welfare* (London: Macmillan, 1993).

Royal Commission on the Distribution of Income and Wealth, First Report, Cmnd. 6171 (London: HMSO), 1975; Seventh Report, Cmnd. 7595 (London: HMSO, 1979).

A. Sen, *Inequality Re-examined* (Oxford: Clarendon Press, 1992).

A. Sen, *On Economic Inequality* (Oxford: Oxford University Press, 1992).

T. Smeeding, M. O'Higgins and L. Rainwater, *Poverty, Inequality and Income Distribution in a Comparative Perspective* (Hemel Hempstead: Harvester Wheatsheaf, 1990).

EXERCISES

1. Is equality of individuals a feasible goal of fiscal policy? Give reasons for your answer.
2. Discuss the extent of inequality in the distribution of income and wealth that you would regard as acceptable.
3. Outline a policy for redistribution of income. What are the problems involved?
4. Outline a policy for redistribution of wealth. What are the problems involved?
5. Suggest a way of measuring the effectiveness of a fiscal policy to redistribute income and wealth.

APPENDIX 1   CALCULATION OF INDEX NUMBERS

Presentation of statistical data in the form of index numbers facilitates economic analysis. A trend can be seen at a glance by looking at them. Index numbers may also be easier to plot on a graph to give a visual presentation. We will illustrate this with figures for government revenue in the UK. The *National Accounts Blue Books* show revenue rounded off to the nearest million. A greater degree of accuracy is not required to indicate a trend, but even so a large number of figures has to be handled. In Table A1 we have added fictitious figures to show how a column might look if the data were to be given in full and how the information appears when shown by index numbers.

Table A1   Government Revenue*

Year	Revenue (£)	Index number
1970	20,515,123,456	49
1975	42,107,654,321	100
1980	91,726,123,456	218
1990	189,263,123,456	449
1995†	252,400,000,000	599

*Base year 1975 = 100
†estimate.
Source: Financial statement and Budget Report 1994–95 (London: HMSO).

To calculate index numbers it is first necessary to choose a base year. The base year should be as normal as possible, that is, one during which there were no exceptional occurrences such as political, social or economic crises. For example, 1973 would not be suitable for a base year because of the oil crisis in the Middle East, which affected the British economy and countries throughout the world. An old base year for a Government Revenue Index, or any other index, may be changed if, for example, there has subsequently been a major restructuring of the tax system, severe inflation or a major disruption. A break in the series has then to be indicated.

Suppose we chose 1975 as the base year, we then say 1975 = 100 and call a previous year, 1970 year 1, 1980 year 2 and so on until we reach the last year (1995). We can then calculate index numbers with the help of the formula:

$$£m$$

$$\frac{\text{Year 1}}{\text{base year}} \times 100 = \frac{(1970 \text{ revenue})}{(1975 \text{ revenue})} \frac{20{,}515}{42{,}107} \times 100 = 49$$

$$\frac{\text{Year 2}}{\text{base year}} \times 100 = \frac{(1980 \text{ revenue})}{(1975 \text{ revenue})} \frac{91{,}726}{42{,}107} \times 100 = 218$$

$$\frac{\text{Year 3}}{\text{base year}} \times 100 = \frac{(1995 \text{ revenue})}{(1975 \text{ revenue})} \frac{252{,}400}{42{,}107} \times 100 = 599$$

If an index number is less than 100, then this shows revenue in that year to be lower than in the base year. If the index number is above 100, then the revenue is higher. We can also show the data graphically. In Figure A1 we measure revenue on the vertical axis and a period of time on the horizontal axis. Let us start with 1970. Different levels of revenue are shown on the left hand side, and we look up until we reach 49 which is the index number for the year. We then measure along a ruler to the right until we reach a point directly above 1970 indicated on the horizontal axis, and mark this point with a cross. We do the same for 1980, 1990 and so on until we reach 1995. We then join all the points and the line shows us the trend in government revenue.

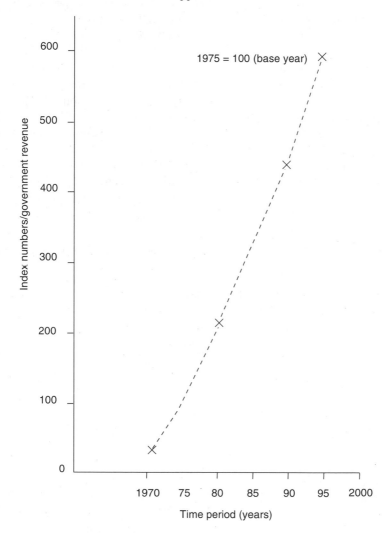

1975 = 100 (base year)

Figure A1   Index numbers

APPENDIX 2   CALCULATION OF CHANGES IN THE
PURCHASING POWER OF MONEY

The change in the internal purchasing power of a country's currency is calculated with the help of the consumer price index. In the UK it is the retail price index (RPI) that is used. The figures are published in the *Annual Abstract of Statistics* and the most recent data can be obtained from the *Monthly Digest of Statistics*. At a time of inflation the value of a currency falls in terms of goods and services as their price rises.

To calculate what £1 in 1988 was worth in 1993 we have to look up the RPI for the two years concerned. It stood at 107 and 141 respectively. Thus the purchasing power of £1 in 1988 was 100 pence and 75.9 pence in 1993. We have calculated the value of 100 pence in 1993 is follows:

$$\frac{\text{Retail Price Index (1988)}}{\text{Retail Price Index (1993)}} \times 100 \text{ pence} \quad \frac{107}{141} \times 100 \text{ pence} = 75.9 \text{ pence}$$

The value of £1 therefore fell by 24.1 pence, that is from 100 pence in 1988 to 75.9 pence in 1993.

APPENDIX 3 CALCULATION OF PUBLIC REVENUE, PUBLIC
EXPENDITURE AND NATIONAL INCOME IN REAL
TERMS

The same method can be used to calculate changes in public revenue, public expenditure and national income in real terms over a period of time, e.g. Year *A*, Year *B*. The calculation shows whether the amount received or spent is worth more or less in terms of goods and services.

$$\left.\frac{\text{Revenue or expenditure or national income}}{\text{retail price index year } A}\right\rbrace \text{year } A \quad \times \text{ retail price index year } B = \text{amount in real terms}$$

Public Revenue increased from £183,471 million in 1988 to £225,738 million in 1993 at current prices, but this increase of 23 per cent did not mean that the government could buy that much more goods and services. The purchasing power of the increased revenue is dependent upon the price level. To show a change in revenue in real terms or at constant prices we have to use the retail price index which indicates by how much prices have gone up or down or whether they have remained unchanged.

Year	RPI	Public revenue (£m) current prices	real terms (constant prices)
1988	107	183,471	183,471
1993	141	225,738	171,255
		+ 42,263 (23 per cent)	− 2,216 (−7 per cent)

The figure of £171,255m was calculated on the basis of the formula:

$$\frac{\text{Revenue 1993}}{\text{RPI (1993)}} \times \text{RPI (1988)} = \frac{£225,738\text{m}}{141} \times 107 = £171,255\text{m}$$

Thus, although the government had at its disposal a sum of money that was 23 per cent more than the amount in 1988 it could only buy a quantity of goods and services that was 7 per cent *less* than at the start of this five-year period.

Public expenditure also increased between 1988 and 1993. To calculate what the change was in real terms we again have to refer to the retail price index.

		Public expenditure (£m)	
Year	RPI	current prices	real terms (constant prices)
1988	107	173,274	173,274
1993	141	257,390	195,324
		+ 84,116 (49 per cent)	− 21,050 (12 per cent)

Using the information given above we can now apply the formula:

$$\frac{\text{expenditure (1993)}}{\text{RPI (1993)}} \times \text{RPI (1988)} = \frac{£257,390\text{m}}{141} \times 107 = £195,324\text{m}$$

We can see that the increase in public expenditure at current prices is 49 per cent but in real terms this represents a rise of only 12 per cent.

Changes in national income in real terms are calculated in a similar manner.

		National income (£m)	
Year	RPI	current prices	real terms (constant prices)
1988	107	410,828	410,828
1993	141	414,350	314,435
		+ 3,522 (0.9 per cent)	−96,393 (−23 per cent)

$$\frac{\text{national income (1993)}}{\text{RPI (1993)}} \times \text{RPI (1988)} = \frac{£414,350\text{m}}{141} \times 107 = £314,435\text{m}$$

The above figures show that in real terms national income actually fell and there was no real growth.

Index